D1084156

THE
ELUSIVE
QUARRY

THE
ELUSIVE
QUARRY

A SCIENTIFIC APPRAISAL OF
PSYCHICAL RESEARCH

RAY
HYMAN

PROMETHEUS BOOKS
BUFFALO ■ NEW YORK 14215

133
H99

Library of Congress Cataloging-in-Publication Data

Hyman, Ray.
    The elusive quarry : a scientific appraisal of psychical research
/ Ray Hyman.
        p.   cm.
    ISBN 0-87975-504-0
    1. Psychical research—Controversial literature. 2. Psychical
research—Book reviews. I. Title.
BF1042.H96   1989
133—dc20   89-3918
                                                                CIP

Contents

165392

Introduction: An Interview with Ray Hyman*

Jeffrey Mishlove

In August 1979 Ray Hyman attended, for the first time, a convention of the Parapsychological Association. He was interviewed at the convention by Jeffrey Mishlove, who holds a Ph.D. in parapsychology from the University of California-Berkeley.

Mishlove: For a long time you have been associated with a point of view that is skeptical of the claims of parapsychology. I'm very interested in getting your overall impressions of the Parapsychological Association convention and of the field of parapsychology as a whole—bearing in mind the fact that 1979 represents the tenth anniversary of the membership of the Parapsychological Association in the American Association for the Advancement of Science (AAAS).

Hyman: Coming here as a skeptic, I would say that my overwhelming impression is the high quality of the research I have heard reported and the impressive insights and awareness of problems demonstrated by the people I have met. I expected a lot of this, because I have done some reading in the field recently—but still I am pleasantly surprised that I am constantly being challenged by things that are not easy to explain away or dismiss on ordinary or superficial grounds that critics use. There are a few in attendance here who fit the stereotype of what critics believe to be the worst of parapsychology. They are people who are almost anti-

Skeptical Inquirer 5 (1) (Fall 1980), 63–67.

science. They make many statements and claims. But I see they are an embarrassment to the other people here who are trying to establish a legitimate scientific field, and there don't seem to be any more of these people here than at any other convention of scientists I might attend. It's unfortunate that it's easy to characterize the whole field by a few people like this. Generally speaking, I am very much impressed with most of the people I have met and their high quality of thought. Another big surprise to me is that I find myself in almost 100 percent agreement with most of the people with whom I have talked. They are skeptical. No one here is an out-and-out believer, or else they wouldn't be doing science.

Mishlove: What's your image of the future of parapsychology?

Hyman: I've discussed this with a lot of people here. It's an interesting topic. One scenario is that, in fact, if it does succeed in achieving some of its goals, it will put itself out of business. If it does attain the repeatable experiment, if it does find conditions under which anyone, skeptic or believer, can achieve positive results, then one possibility is that we would no longer be talking about paranormal phenomena. Parapsychology would be absorbed into various branches of physics and psychology and what have you. Another scenario, the one Martin Johnson has in mind, is that, at the moment, the field is in the same state that alchemy was. Alchemy was never a science, but it led to a new science—chemistry. He sees that parapsychology may be on the verge of doing this. The hope is that a whole new science will come out of its success—rather than its being absorbed into science as it now is.

Mishlove: Would you say that as a result of this convention you expect parapsychologists to be working more closely with members of the so-called loyal opposition—critics from outside the field?

Hyman: Unfortunately, I don't think that will be the case. My own criticisms, as a responsible critic, are of things that parapsychologists don't have control over. The way I see it, parapsychologists are doing their darnedest to do the best kind of science, in the best tradition of science. The problem is that they don't have a good phenomenon by the hand. If they do have one, it is a very elusive thing. It is very weak. It is very sporadic. They don't have a handle on it. Until they have repeatable phenomena that can be seen by most people, regardless of their belief, they really aren't going to have any chance at all of being accepted by science. It's not clear that, even if they had that, they would be accepted by science. At the moment, they are being rejected by most scientists on grounds that have nothing to do with what they are doing now. Most scientists don't even know what is going on in parapsychology. I had to come here and read the literature, to actually go out of my way, to be up on just some of what is going on. So one possibility is that, even if parapsychology met the overt criticisms of critics who are trying to be responsible, that would not overcome the hidden reasons for objecting to it. There are strong emotional factors involved in why people don't even want to accept the implications of what might come out of this.

Mishlove: You don't regard the membership of the Parapsychological Association in the AAAS as really being an acceptance of the field by science. You think that scientists are still, by and large, hostile?

Hyman: No question about it. It's hard to say which scientists. A recent survey shows that a majority of academics, regardless of field, except for psychology, are willing to say that parapsychology should be given a chance and that there may be a good chance that something will come out of it. This is quite the reverse of what people expect. But it is pretty clear that the power structure of science, which controls the journals and the funding, is still mostly hostile toward parapsychology. I would say that seems to be the case. Their hostility and their rejection of parapsychology probably have very little to do with rational grounds or with knowing what is going on.

Mishlove: Do you think that, if some of these hostile individuals had been having the kind of experience that you have been having at this convention, that might change their attitude?

Hyman: I would like to believe so. I think it would. If the people who are hostile allowed themselves to be exposed to a convention like this, I think they would have to change their grounds for objection rather dramatically. They would have to come up with some new reasons.

Mishlove: Also, you mentioned the fact that parapsychology has not come up with a repeatable experiment. At this convention it was argued that what they have attained is something they call "statistical" or "probabilistic" repeatability, where maybe one experiment in three does attain significant results. You're not impressed by that argument?

Hyman: I don't believe it is true. I disagree very respectfully with John Palmer on this, and some others—and many parapsychologists here agree with me. We don't even have that statistical repeatability. What would be statistical repeatability would be to specify a subset of conditions where, given these conditions, we can say that even 60 percent, 50 percent, or 20 percent of the time we will get results. We don't have even that. I think that most people here believe that there are conditions under which you would never get results, such as, with certain kinds of experimenters, perhaps. They don't know what these conditions are, but they believe that there are conditions that are conducive to results and other conditions that are not.

Mishlove: I think that about does it; unless you have another point that you would like to make?

Hyman: Some very interesting thoughts have occurred to me that I have discussed with different people here. Another point that may be worth making is that I, as a critic, a responsible critic, am mostly interested in learning ways in which the mind works, and the way in which science works, so that we can better learn from our mistakes and not repeat mistakes we have made in the past, and better guard against self-deception, which I am very much interested in. And I would say that this is a goal that almost every responsible parapsychologist here has. I find that I have the same goals that they have. I think we all have the common goal of wanting to make sure that, whatever we are doing, we are doing the best science we can, that we are protecting ourselves in the best way we can from known ways of fooling ourselves, and that we can learn other ways in which we might be fooling ourselves. I think that is a goal shared by everyone here. And I think that, in the best of worlds, critical organizations like the one that I belong to would be lining up to work with the Parapsychological Association on these common goals. I know that parapsychologists are just as much embarrassed by false claims for the paranormal and by people who hang on and try to exploit the Parapsychological Association. I would hope that in the best of worlds we can get together and share these common goals.

Postscript by Ray Hyman (1979)

My remarks, as set down in the interview, were made with no preparation and were completely spontaneous. Naturally, if I had had time to think about the questions, I would have phrased my answers differently and taken greater care to avoid any misinterpretation of my position. But I am willing to let my remarks stand as they are, because they are, in fact, what I did say at the time.

I think it is well known that I do not believe that extrasensory perception or psychokinesis exists or has been scientifically established. On the other hand, I find it dismaying that most of the criticism of current parapsychological research is uninformed and misrepresents what is actually taking place. Such misplaced criticism is bad both for the development of parapsychology and for the attainment of a sound evaluation by the skeptic. If those who take it upon themselves to attack parapsychological claims would also look fairly and carefully at what it is they are attacking, we might be much further along today in understanding how it is that so many highly qualified investigators can be putting forth claims that we skeptics find hard to believe.

I believe that, if many of my fellow critics had been with me at the Parapsychological Association meetings and listened to the many papers, they would have to agree with me that the quality of the design and the sophistication of the statistics were generally quite high. The discussions and criticisms of each other's papers by the parapsychologists were of high quality and quite penetrating. And the parapsychologists seem to take as much interest as we skeptics do in finding loopholes, and possible alternative explanations, in each other's work.

I am not making a case for less criticism of parapsychology. On the contrary, I believe that parapsychology needs *more* criticism. But I also think the criticism needs to be relevant and deal with the evidence at its best.

Part One

Parapsychology

Introduction

Evidence for paranormal claims comes in many guises. The overwhelming bulk of the evidence comes from personal experience, anecdotes, and folklore. Although psychologists and other scientists realize that such evidence is unreliable, almost every believer has become convinced because of such evidence.

Personal experience and testimony, as psychologists have demonstrated, can be completely fallacious, yet carry the aura of absolute certainty. I am currently a member of the National Research Council's Committee on Techniques for the Enhancement of Human Performance. The committee examines exotic and controversial claims for enhancing human performance by means of techniques such as meditation, accelerated learning, sleep learning, and the exploitation of paranormal phenomena. Although psychical researchers and parapsychologists try to accumulate scientific evidence to support their claims, the committee was dismayed to discover that important military and government leaders were proponents of techniques based on paranormal claims, not because of any scientific data but because of personal experience and anecdotal evidence.

In the second half of the last century, a group of academics and scientists decided to try to buttress their belief in paranormal phenomena with scientific evidence. In 1882 they created the Society for Psychical Research in London. This was followed in 1885 by the founding of the American Society for Psychical Research. These societies helped to create the field of *parapsychology,* which attempts to investigate scientifically paranormal claims.

The early psychical researchers carried out systematic surveys of spontaneous occurrences, such as premonitory dreams, poltergeist phenomena, and hauntings. They also attended seances to witness alleged spiritualistic phenomena, and they conducted *ad hoc* tests of allegedly psychically gifted individuals.

Beginning around 1930, J. B. Rhine and his wife, Louisa, rechristened the field of psychical research with the name *parapsychology* and tried to turn it into a laboratory science. Rhine's major tool during the first twenty years or so to test extrasensory perception (ESP) was the "ESP deck" of cards consisting of five designs, each repeated five times. In a typical experiment, a subject would guess the design occupying each position in a shuffled deck of twenty-five cards. If the subject was truly guessing randomly, then she had one chance in five of getting any one card correct. In a typical run through a deck of twenty-five cards, she could be expected to get five calls correct by chance. If a subject could consistently get more than five correct under conditions where sensory cues were eliminated, this was taken as supporting the hypothesis that some form of "nonsensory" or "extrasensory" communication had occurred.

Although much has changed in laboratory research in parapsychology since Rhine's initial experiments, the basic idea remains the same. Subjects attempt to divine or influence randomly generated targets under conditions in which all forms of normal contact or communication between target and subject have supposedly been eliminated. If the experimenter can find a nonchance correlation between the targets and the subject's behavior, then she concludes that something called *psi* has been demonstrated.

I believe that the critic of paranormal claims should treat claims that are based on laboratory evidence differently from those based on surveys and anecdotes. Most experimental parapsychologists have academic degrees, usually Ph.D.s, in physics, biology, psychology, or another scientific field. They have been trained to use the same sorts of experimental controls and statistical techniques that typify regular scientific investigations.

A fair criticism has to deal with such claims in the same way that other scientific claims are evaluated. We have to examine closely the methodology and the statistical procedures. This process can become rather technical; it also involves much time and effort. The papers in Part I of this book reflect my attempts over the past thirty years to evaluate critically the strongest and most scientifically oriented claims for the paranormal.

The most technical paper is the first one, my lengthy and detailed critique of the ganzfeld experiments. Some readers might want to skip or skim this paper. A much shorter and more readable critique is my response to D. Scott Rogo's "The Case for Parapsychology." For a historical overview of the field of parapsychology along with a skeptic's reasons for still not accepting parapsychological claims, I recommend "Parapsychological Research: A Tutorial Review and Critical Appraisal." For more details on why I find the best contemporary psi research inadequate, read

"Psi Experiments: Do the Best Parapsychological Experiments Justify the Claims for Psi?"

"The Ganzfeld Psi Experiment: A Critical Appraisal" originally appeared in *The Journal of Parapsychology,* in March 1985. The same issue contained a lengthy rebuttal by Charles Honorton, and the December 1986 issue of the same journal contained further commentaries on this debate. The reader who wants to dig deeper might want to consult these commentaries.

Some elements of the rebuttal by Honorton represented legitimate differences of opinion. However, I felt that some of his counterarguments badly misrepresented my position or were outrageously mistaken. In addition, Honorton's rebuttal included an appendix by David Saunders criticizing my use of factor analysis in the analysis of the ganzfeld data. Saunders had a few good points to make, but he also badly misrepresented what I had done and made a serious error in reconstructing how I had done it.

So I prepared a lengthy and detailed rejoinder and sent it to *The Journal of Parapsychology.* The journal was awaiting Honorton's reaction to my rejoinder when Honorton and I met at the Parapsychological Association meetings at Sonoma State College in California. As we explain in our "Joint Communiqué," we agreed that most of our differences dealt with technicalities that most readers would find hard to understand or of little interest. We decided we could do the most good at that point in the debate by publishing a paper on those points about which we were in agreement.

The paper represents a landmark of a sort: a parapsychologist and a critic collaborating in an attempt to create a common approach to the problems of deciding what would constitute an acceptable argument for psi. We went through several drafts and lengthy telephone calls before we finally settled on a document that both of us could accept.

Yet, despite this effort, readers vary widely in their perceptions about what our joint paper does or does not say. I now suspect that much of the confusion can be traced to one sentence in the abstract, which read: "We agree that there is an overall significant effect in this data base that cannot reasonably be explained by selective reporting or multiple analysis."

The sentence, as it stands, is correct with qualifications. Statisticians distinguish between *hypothesiswise* and *experimentwise* tests of significance. Assume that I conduct an ESP experiment with five different subjects. Further assume that I test the hypothesis that the results were due to chance for each subject separately. I will be making, then, five separate tests of significance in this experiment. If I test the results of each subject at the standard 5 percent level of significance, then the *hypothesiswise* level of significance is .05. This means that I have, for each subject, a probability of 5 in 100 (or 1 in 20) of mistakenly concluding that the results were significant when they were due to chance. The *experimentwise* level of significance, however, will be greater than .05 because I have made five separate tests at this same level of significance. If the tests are independent, as they probably would be in this example, then the probability of obtaining at least one "significant" outcome just by chance is approximately .25 or 1 in 4. This, then, would be the *experimentwise* level of significance.

Much of my critique of the ganzfeld experiments focused on the fact that, though Honorton was treating each separate experiment as if the experimenter had carried out one significance test—making the *experimentwise* significance level the same as the *hypothesiswise* level—in fact the typical experimenter had conducted multiple tests. I estimated that the *experimentwise* level of significance per experiment in the ganzfeld data base might be .25 or higher.

Although this estimate is still probably correct, my subsequent meta-analysis, as well as Honorton's, suggests that this could not be the only factor producing the level of the reported successes. In addition, by applying a technique devised by Harvard psychologist Robert Rosenthal, one can show that it would be unrealistic to attempt to account for the reported results entirely in terms of selective reporting of the results.

Two important points should be emphasized. First, the elimination of multiple testing and selective reporting as the *sole* cause of the observed results does not, of course, make psi the likely cause. This is because the experiments suffer from a number of other defects that might have contributed to the outcomes. Second, multiple testing and selective reporting have not been completely vindicated. The determination of the possible effect of both multiple testing and selective reporting assumes that the *hypothesiswise* tests of significance yielded the correct probabilities. Such significance levels can be considered accurate only if experimenters have taken steps to assure that the assumptions of the underlying statistical models are correct. Such steps include, among other things, the use of adequate randomization procedures. We know, however, that randomization can be considered adequate for only a small minority of the ganzfeld psi experiments.

In truth, the ganzfeld data base is too small and suffers from too many limitations for it to be possible to draw any important conclusions. That is why I agreed with Honorton that this data base, by itself, cannot be used to form any conclusions about the source of the reported results. The data do not allow us to conclude that the observed methodological defects caused the results. Nor do they allow us to conclude that psi caused the results. The data, in fact, do not allow us to conclude anything. That is why the most important conclusion from our paper is contained in the sentence that follows the one already quoted:

> We continue to differ over the degree to which the effect constitutes evidence for psi, but we agree *that the final verdict awaits the outcome of future experiments conducted by a broader range of investigators and according to more stringent standards* [emphasis added].

In other words, if Honorton and his fellow parapsychologists are correct, then they should be able to obtain the same level of success with experiments that are free from the types of flaws that Akers and I have independently documented. Rather than continue unnecessarily the often acrimonious debates, the parapsychologists—as I argue in some of the following papers—ought to clean up their act before trying to gain the attention of the rest of the scientific community.

Part I contains papers that deal with parapsychology as a laboratory science. The papers in this book were written over a span of thirty years for differing audiences and for various purposes. Consequently, each paper does not always fit neatly under a given topic. Some of the papers in other parts of this book are also relevant to the issues discussed in Part I. These include "Psychics and Scientists," "Further Comments on Schmidt's PK Experiments," and my review of *Mind-Reach,* in Part II, "A Remote Viewing Experiment Conducted by a Skeptic and a Believer," and my review of *The Mind Race* in Part III.

The Ganzfeld Psi Experiment: A Critical Appraisal*

ABSTRACT: The paper describes a critical evaluation of 42 ganzfeld psi studies reported from 1974 through 1981. Allegedly, 55% of these studies achieved significance on the primary index of psi. The first part of the critique challenges this claimed rate of successful replication. Taking into account ambiguities and inconsistencies in what is counted as an independent ganzfeld study, and citing evidence suggestive of a bias in reporting the studies, it is argued that the actual rate of success was at most 30%. The second part points out that, because of multiple testing, the true significance level was much higher than the assumed .05 level, perhaps .25 or higher. The third part tallies a number of procedural flaws involving inadequate randomization, potentials for sensory leakage, statistical errors, and the like, and strongly suggests that most of the studies in this data base were originally intended to be exploratory investigations rather than well-planned, confirmatory experiments. The final part is a meta-analysis based on indices of significance and effect size as they relate to the various categories of flaws. The flaws of inadequate security, possible sensory leakage, and multiple testing did not correlate with significance and effect size. But the flaws involving inadequate randomization and insufficient documentation did correlate with these indices. Both effect size and Z scores become approximately zero when regression equations are used to predict their values for the case in which these latter types of flaws are zero. It is concluded that

Journal of Parapsychology 49 (March 1985), 3–49. Reprinted by permission. An earlier version of this paper was presented at the joint meetings of the Society for Psychical Research and the Parapsychological Association in Cambridge, England, August 1982. Part of the preparation of the paper was done during the academic year 1982–83 while I occupied the Thomas Welton Stanford Chair for Psychical Research at Stanford University. The present manuscript benefited from the comments made on earlier versions by Susan Blackmore, Irvin Child, Robyn Dawes, Persi Diaconis, Piet Hein Hoebens, Charles Honorton, J. E. Kennedy, Adrian Parker, and Christopher Scott.

> this data base is too weak to support any assertions about the existence of psi.

In the latter half of 1981, I found myself with two assignments to provide a critical assessment of the field of parapsychology. In both cases, I had initially refused because the task seemed beyond my available resources. But I was urged to reconsider on the grounds that no other qualified critics were available. The option of trying to review the entire research literature was impractical, even if I restricted myself only to papers that had been published in refereed journals, such as the *Journal of Parapsychology, Journal of the American Society for Psychical Research,* and *European Journal of Parapsychology.* I also rejected the more feasible alternative of evaluating a random sample of this literature. Such a sample could supply a picture of the adequacy of the average research report in parapsychology, but I felt it would be fairer to try to assess the case for parapsychology at its best. I suspect that the typical contribution to any research enterprise is mediocre and that the viability of a research program is best judged by its strongest representatives. Nevertheless, I did not want to follow Hansel's (1980) approach of focusing on only a handful of the "best" individual experiments.

My compromise was to look for a research program in parapsychology that consisted of a series of studies by a variety of investigators and was considered by parapsychologists as especially promising. As a result both of reading some of the parapsychological literature and of talking with some parapsychologists, I chose the ganzfeld psi paradigm as the most appropriate. This paradigm consists of a systematic body of research that covers a span of 10 years, involves a number of highly respected investigators, and has allegedly produced significant psi scores in over half of the experiments. In addition, I was intrigued by some of the claims made about the high level of research sophistication and rigor that had been achieved in these experiments. In presenting his case for parapsychology, Rogo (1977), for example, chose the Honorton and Harper ganzfeld psi experiment (1974) as an example of a good ESP experiment. "To me," Rogo wrote, "a good experiment is one that is designed to safeguard against fraud and experimental error and uses a clear-cut method of analysis to see whether or not ESP actually occurred during the tests" (p. 41).

On August 18, 1981, I wrote to Charles Honorton to request his help in obtaining access to the ganzfeld psi data base. Honorton phoned to tell me that it would take some time but that he would gladly undertake the mission of getting me copies of every relevant study. He felt it was important to get an outside critic such as myself to assess this body of literature. He hoped that it might lead to cooperative ventures in which critic and parapsychologist could attempt careful replications. In January 1982, I received from Honorton a copy of every ganzfeld study known to him, along with his detailed analysis of the various characteristics of this sample. Honorton also included a number of papers that criticized aspects of the ganzfeld research or commented on it (e.g., Blackmore, 1980; Honorton, 1978, 1979, 1981; Kennedy, 1979a, 1979b). All told, the entire package consisted of 600 pages of reports.

The Data Base

The data base was extracted from 34 separate reports written or published from 1974 through 1981. By Honorton's count, these 34 reports described 42 separate studies. Of these, he classified 23 as having achieved overall significance on the primary measure of psi at the .05 level. This successful replication rate of 55% is consistent with earlier estimates of 54% (Honorton, 1978), 58% (Sargent, cited in Blackmore, 1980), and 50% (Blackmore, 1980). If we treat each study as a unit, then we find that 15 (36%) appeared in refereed publications (11 in the *Journal of the American Society for Psychical Research,* 3 in the *European Journal of Parapsychology,* and 1 in the *Journal of the Society for Psychical Research);* 5 (12%) appeared in a published monograph; 20 (48%) appeared only in the form of abstracts or papers delivered at meetings of the Parapsychological Association; and 2 (5%) were part of an undergraduate honors thesis in biology. The studies were authored by 47 different investigators. Carl Sargent's 9 studies and Charles Honorton's 5 account for one third of the total. Other major contributors were John Palmer with 4, Scott Rogo with 4, W. G. Braud with 3, and Rex Stanford with 3. These six parapsychologists account for two thirds of the data base. (See Appendix)[1]

Procedure

Prior to the evaluation that I made for the present paper, I had made two analyses of the same data base. The first analysis was done for a paper that I presented at the combined meetings of the Society for Psychical Research and the Parapsychological Association in August 1982. As a result of comments on that paper made by Honorton and others, I reanalyzed the data base in November 1982. For the purpose of the present critique, I began a new and more systematic analysis of this data base in July 1983 and finally finished the task in January 1984.

In the present evaluation, I tried to take into account the comments and disagreements generated by my previous two evaluations. Honorton, for example, disagreed with many of my assignments of flaws to the studies. I hope to reduce some of this disagreement by using more specific and refined categories for encoding the flaws. For example, in the previous critiques, I assigned a flaw in the category "multiple testing" to any study that was guilty of this flaw, regardless of the specific way this was manifested. The current analysis now uses six different and narrower categories to cover the same problem. I also refined and made more operational the categories for procedural flaws. In all, I used 12 systematic categories for assigning flaws to studies. These categories and their assignment to each study in the data base are listed in the Appendix.

I also noted a variety of other defects, which I did not formally assign because of a variety of reasons. Some depended on my subjective impression; others were flaws only under some circumstances; some were unique to a given context; and so on. Many of these will be discussed in appropriate places in the manuscript.

General Guidelines

A reviewer can try to use the ganzfeld psi data base to answer a variety of questions. Many of the individual studies, for example, examined the relationship between psi scores and personality variables such as extraversion. Although most investigators talk about the ganzfeld procedure as "psi conducive," only a few have actually tried to test this hypothesis by including nonganzfeld control conditions. Following Honorton's lead, I ignored questions about ganzfeld psi and personality correlates (although I could not help being startled by investigators' routinely doing factor analyses on sample sizes of 30 or less). My review focuses on two questions: (1) Does this data base, taken as a whole, supply evidence for the existence of psi? (This is the question of major concern to the outsider.) (2) Does the ganzfeld psi study yield evidence for psi that is replicable? (This is the question of major concern to Honorton and other parapsychologists.)

The basic index for both these questions is some measure of hitting or target matching compared with a chance baseline. This creates special problems when compared with more conventional measures of effect that depend on empirical comparisons between two or more groups. In particular, assumptions about probability distributions take on a greater burden in the decision about whether a given discrepancy between the observed and the theoretical value is significant.

The prototype or basic pattern against which to judge a replication is the Honorton and Harper study (Study 8). Not only was this the first published ganzfeld psi study, but also it served as the model for subsequent studies. In addition, it is relatively uncomplicated in that it consists of a single uniform condition for all subjects. No comparison or control conditions exist, and the only meaningful way to evaluate the observed number of hits is against some theoretical expectation.

In evaluating the adequacy of each study, I have tried to use criteria that I believe every competent parapsychologist, including most of the authors of papers in the present data base, would endorse. I have been guided by parapsychologists such as Palmer (1983), who has written:

> How do parapsychologists define psi? . . . One [definition] which I think most of us would accept is the following: psi is a statistically significant departure of results from those expected by chance under circumstances that mimic exchanges of information between living organisms and their environment, *provided that* (a) proper statistical models and methods are used to evaluate the significance, and (b) reasonable precautions have been taken to eliminate sensory cues and other experimental artifacts. (p. 54)

Palmer's definition also provides reasonable standards against which to judge the adequacy of a psi study. To his two general criteria of appropriate statistics and adequate controls, I would add two more. One is related to the statistical criterion. It would require that treatments and targets be assigned in such a way as to guarantee the major assumptions on which the statistical tests are based (such as independence of trials, appropriate distributions, and so forth). The other involves the inclusion of sufficient documentation to enable the reader to judge if certain departures from the model experiment do or do not make a difference (such as having some trials using friends of the percipient as agent and others using strangers).

Using these general guidelines, my critique involved the following phases:

1. *Rechecking the vote count.* The replication rate of 55% in this data base depends critically on what qualifies as an independent study. Should the sampling unit be the study, the cells of the study, the report, the laboratory, or the investigator? What counts as an acceptable ganzfeld study? To what extent could the apparent success rate be biased by unreported studies?

2. *Assessing the actual as opposed to the assumed level of significance.* Honorton accepts as "successful" those studies that achieve overall psi-hitting at the .05 level, one-tailed, as well as studies that achieve overall psi-missing at the .05 level (two-tailed). In addition, a replication is considered successful if it achieves significance on at least one of a number of different possible indices. Many of the studies exhibit other statistical practices that increase the probability of achieving significance well above the reported .05 criterion.

3. *Assigning procedural flaws to studies.* The preceding phase assesses the ways in which experiments unwittingly inflate the true significance level by multiple testing. Another threat to the validity of the statistical inferences

is the failure to ensure that randomization of targets is adequately carried out or that the statistical tests are correctly used (proper degrees of freedom, correct calculation of the p's, and so on). Other procedural flaws involve failure to secure against witting and unwitting sensory leakage and failing to adequately document information that could potentially affect the interpretation of the results. To the extent that such procedural flaws characterize the data base, the suspicion is justified that the studies were not carefully planned and executed.

4. *Making a meta-analysis of the relationships among the flaws, effect size, and significance.* For each study in the data base, the Appendix lists, in addition to the flaws, Honorton's original and revised classification of each study as significant or not. Also, for the 36 studies for which the appropriate data were available, I have supplied a common effect size as well as the Z score.

Perhaps this is the place to point out that the several statistical evaluations involving effect size, significance, and flaws were all carried out in the spirit of a meta-analysis (Glass, McGaw, & Smith, 1981; Hedges & Olkin, 1982). Because the studies in the data base are not independent (several coming from the same investigators) and are sampled from an unknown population, drawing valid statistical inferences is an uncertain procedure. In addition, the many tests, although converging and consistent among themselves, can provide only suggestive hypotheses about possible relationships. For these tests, I have used the conventional significance levels only as a convenient yardstick for suggesting possible relationships that may be worth further exploration.

The Vote-Counting Problem

As already mentioned, Honorton identifies 42 separate studies in this data base, 55% of which he classifies as successful in terms of achieving overall significance on the primary measure of psi. Light and Smith (1971), as well as subsequent writers, have indicated that this method of "vote counting" raises many problems. Nevertheless, if the count is correct, and if the rate of success expected by chance is truly .05, then such a replication rate is impressive. In the next section of the paper, I shall discuss whether the actual level of significance in these studies is higher than the advertised .05 level. In this section, I deal with the question of whether the replication rate should be considered much lower than the claimed 55%.

For the sake of the present discussion, I shall ignore the vexing and potentially important question of what the appropriate sampling unit should be for aggregating the findings across this data base. Within the separate papers, the investigators seem to treat the single trial as the independent sampling unit regardless of whether the total set of trials comes from the same or different subjects. In addition to indiscriminately pooling within- and between-subject contributions, both Honorton and the individual experimenters sometimes also pool across separate experimental conditions without trying to deal with the problem of interdependencies among the sampling units. This issue of interdependencies may also matter in deciding what the sampling unit should be for counting successes in the data base— the individual study, cells of the study, the investigator, the laboratory, or the report. A discussion of some of these issues and the problems they raise can be found in Glass *et al.* (1981) and in Hedges and Olkin (1982).

Honorton has opted for the study as the unit of replication. For much of the data base, this creates little ambiguity. Even when a report contains more than one study, these usually are easy to identify. But Honorton is not consistent. In the experiment by Braud and Wood (Study 3), which contains several different ganzfeld conditions, Honorton pools the data over trials within and between subjects as well as across conditions to come up with one successful replication. This seems to be his typical response to studies with multiple conditions. However, Honorton treats Raburn's study differently by partitioning it into its separate cells, discarding two of the cells as being too atypical, and counting one cell (Study 16) as a significant experiment and the other as an insignificant experiment (Study 17). No reason is proffered for treating the cell as the unit in this case and the total study as the unit in the other cases.

By itself, this particular inconsistency in the vote counting would not alter the results very much. But it does begin to suggest some of the problems involved in post hoc attempts to define and assess a body of research literature. Honorton and I are both concerned with the probability of successfully replicating the ganzfeld psi study. Using the Honorton and Harper study (Study 8) as the prototype, one could argue that each experimental condition of a psi study in which all subjects are treated uniformly and produce their mentations under ganzfeld conditions can be taken as a replication. This amounts to treating each separate cell of a study in which the subjects are run under the ganzfeld conditions as the replication unit. In this framework, Honorton is correct in treating the individual cells of Raburn's study as separate replications. He is incorrect, in my opinion, in discarding two of the cells on the grounds that no other ganzfeld psi studies have run subjects under conditions in which they did not realize their guesses were being scored for psi. One could just as easily argue, remembering that all of these decisions are post hoc, that many of the other replications should be discarded because they, too, contain conditions that do not appear in any of the other ganzfeld studies. Which decision one makes in the case of Raburn's report makes a difference between scoring it as contributing one successful and one unsuccessful replication or as contributing one successful and three unsuccessful replications.

In addition to Braud and Wood (Study 3), 10 other studies in the data base contain multiple conditions that could be considered as separate replications (Studies 6, 9, 10, 13, 29, 32, 33, 35, 37, 41). The issue raised by all of them can be illustrated by discussing the Braud and Wood experiment (Study 3). These investigators divided their sample of 30 subjects into two groups of 15. Each subject served in six experimental sessions. The first session for each group was essentially a replication of the Honorton and Harper experiment (Study 8). In both groups, the results on the primary measure of psi were insignificant. It would seem reasonable to argue that here we have two clear-cut failures to replicate. Each subject returned for four practice sessions. Each of these sessions differed from the original sessions in that two practice targets were "sent" in addition to a regular target. In the feedback group, the practice responses were accompanied by immediate feedback via the intercom system. In the control groups, no such feedback was given during the practice responses. Following the two practice periods, each session ended with the subjects responding to a target just as in the original ganzfeld session. Again, it can be argued that each of these eight separate practice sessions constitutes a separate replication. The same can be said of the two postpractice sessions, one of which gave significant results. All told, this one study, which is counted as a single successful replication by Honorton, could be viewed—with equal justification, and consistent with his treatment of Raburn—as contributing one successful and 11 unsuccessful replications to the total. Following this logic with the other 10 studies with multiple cells, I achieve a count of 25 "successes" out of 80 replications, for a success rate of 31%.

One could argue, of course, that treating the cells as the unit has drawbacks. It raises, again, the question of independence of units, especially when the same subjects appear in different cells. But this problem of independence of units plagues Honorton's procedures, and other vote-counting procedures as well. As I have already indicated, this problem runs rampant through this data base in a variety of ways. At this point, it is unclear just how it affects the various analyses. One could further argue that the use of the cell rather than the total study as the unit lowers the sample size per unit, thereby lowering power. Ordinarily this would be a reasonable objection; but, as we will see shortly, a peculiarity of this data base is that significance is uncorrelated with sample size.

The File-Drawer Problem

Even if we accept the present data base as complete, an argument can be made for asserting that the successful replication rate is more like 31% than 55%. But it is likely that the data base is incomplete. Parker and Wiklund (1982) included in their survey 11 ganzfeld psi studies that are not in the present data base. Honorton has subsequently added some of these to his data base (personal communication, October 2, 1982). And Blackmore's survey (1980) uncovered 19 other unpublished studies. If we add these to Honorton's initial count, we come up with a total of 53 studies, with an apparent success rate of 43%. If we add these, instead, to my adjusted count, we come up with a total of 110 studies, with a success rate of 30%. This latter estimate is an upper bound because I have not seen these 31 additional studies and do not know how many of them contain multiple conditions that have been pooled together.

The fact that the success rate decreases as we find and add previously unknown studies to the data base is consistent with both the general belief and the empirical finding (Glass *et al.,* 1981) that unreported studies tend to be those with lower effect sizes. To the extent that this is so, we would expect the success rate to be even lower if we could find and include all the currently unknown ganzfeld psi studies. Rosenthal (1978, 1979) has suggested ways to estimate the seriousness, for any data base, of this "file-drawer problem." Honorton (1979), at a time when the ganzfeld data base included 28 studies, used Rosenthal's procedure to estimate that it would require 275 unreported and nonsignificant studies "to reduce the overall significance of the reported psi ganzfeld work to $p < .05$, two-tailed." He adds:

> Considering that the average ganzfeld experiment involves 40 trials with a per-trial time investment on the order of one hour, it would take 12 laboratories nearly six months each to accumulate this number of unreported failures (assuming eight-hour days, no coffee breaks or vacations). Considering the small number of active researchers in parapsychology, and the meager resources that are available to them, we can confidently reject the hypothesis that the ganzfeld success rate is due to selective reporting of significant studies. (p. 388)

Honorton's argument seems to gain even more force when we apply Rosenthal's technique to the current data base. Using either Honorton's count or my adjusted count, I come up with estimates of between 440 and 580 unknown and nonsignificant ganzfeld psi studies needed to reduce the current data base to one selected from a distribution centering around chance expectancy. But the critic can find a number of reasons to question this argument. One of the reasons will be the subject of the next section. It deals with the assumption that studies in this data base are operating at the .05 level. If this is not so, the application of the procedure for estimating the maximum number of fugitive studies has to be either appropriately adjusted or abandoned.

Evidence for Biased Reporting

Much of the force of the argument against the seriousness of the file-drawer problem depends on the assumption that the ganzfeld study is time consuming and requires special resources to conduct. There is some merit to this argument, but it is not quite so strong as Honorton asserts. For one thing, his calculations of effort involved assume that the typical study contains 40 trials. In fact, for this data base, over half of the studies have 30 or fewer trials. But more important is the possibility that many of the unreported studies were aborted before many trials were completed. So far as I can tell, every ganzfeld psi study in this data base was conducted in such a way that the experimenters were aware of the cumulative number of successes and failures as each new subject was added to the data base. Indeed, such awareness is reflected in the reports. Palmer *et al.* (Study 11), as a result of noting that the accumulating hits were at a chance rate, made drastic changes midway in the study to try to increase the hit rate. Perhaps it is unlikely that a large number of completed ganzfeld studies remain unreported. But it is easier to imagine that a large number of experimenters, after reading about the ganzfeld, might have begun conducting some trials and then abandoned the study when the first few trials turned out to be unpromising. On the other hand, a few of these exploratory ventures might have started with initially successful trials, encouraging the experimenter either to continue or to stop and write up the result as a successful replication.

Is there any basis for such a suggestion? In fact, this suggestion occurred to me as a result of examining the relation between sample size and significance in this data base. One of the problems of the vote-counting method, of course, is that it ignores sample size. In the current data base, the studies vary in size all the way from 6 to 180 trials. (Because both Honorton and the experimenters seem to treat trials as the sampling unit regardless of whether they are within or between subjects, I shall also ignore this distinction for purposes of the present discussion.) We would normally expect to find the probability of obtaining a significant result, all other things being equal, to increase with the square root of the sample size. We can calculate theoretically expected proportions of significant studies (power) for each sample size if we know the true effect size. For this purpose, I used the data reported from all the studies in the data base that reported direct hits based on chance outcome of $P = \frac{1}{4}$. This involved 22 of the studies and eight different investigators. All told, there were 746 trials (48% of all the trials in the data base). For this situation, the estimated number of hits is 38%. Fortunately, this estimate is the same regardless of whether we compute the weighted or unweighted average of hit rates for each individual investigator. Using 38% as the theoretical true hit rate and 25% as the chance rate, we can calculate the power for various sample sizes.

To evaluate how the actual proportion of significant studies departed from the theoretically expected proportion, I grouped the 42 studies into four classes of sample size. For each class, I obtained the observed and theoretical proportion of significant studies (using Honorton's original classification, given as SIG-1 or NSIG-1 in the Appendix). For the class with 5 to 19 trials (median = 10), 5 of the 7 studies were significant as compared with a theoretical expectation of 0.91 significant studies. For the class with 20 to 29 trials (median = 20), 6 of the 12 studies were significant as compared with a theoretical expectation of 3.96 significant studies. For the class with 30 to 34 trials (median = 35), 7 of the 14 studies were significant as compared with a theoretical expectation of 6.58. And for the class with 45 to 184 trials (median = 72), 5 of the studies were significant as compared with a theoretical expectation of 6.75. This tendency for the studies with the fewer trials to have a higher proportion of significant outcomes than predicted is highly significant ($\chi^2[4\ df] = 31.42$) with most of the contribution coming from the class with a median of 10 trials.

The most obvious conclusion is that such a strange relationship is due to a selective bias. It suggests a tendency to report studies with a small sample only if they have significant results. This is understandable in that a significant outcome is likely to be accepted for publication even if the sample size is small, but a nonsignificant study with only 5 to 19 trials is easy to dismiss as having inadequate power. Another consequence of such a selective bias would be that effect size should be greater in this data base for the experiments with the smallest number of trials. As we will see later, this is indeed the case.

The "Retrospective" Study

This proposed bias toward reporting small studies only if they succeed is related to what I refer to as the "retrospective study." This is the tendency to decide to treat a pilot or exploratory series of trials as a study if it turns out that the outcome happens to be significant or noteworthy. Such a tendency, if it exists, operates to inflate the apparent success rate in a way different from the file-drawer problem. In the latter case, the observed data base has an inflated rate of success because many studies that did not achieve significant outcomes are not reported. The retrospective study inflates the success rate by adding to the data base studies that were not originally intended to be studies.

I have not formally scored the retrospective study as a flaw because of the difficulty of clearly drawing a line between it and a planned study. Two studies in the data base are clearly retrospective. Honorton (Study 7) constructed a retrospective study out of seven psi ganzfeld trials, each of which had originally been conducted as demonstrations for television film crews over a period of 1 1/3 years. The justification for doing so was that "these sessions involved the same procedure as [the] formal experimentation and included the same precautions against sensory leakage" (p. 185). But it does not matter how rigorously these demonstrations were carried out. The critic can justly point out that if the demonstrations had not resulted in significant psi-hitting, we probably never would have heard of them. After all, they were simply demonstrations. Nor is it clear at what point one stops collecting demonstrations and decides a sufficient number have accumulated to call the collection a "study."

The Child and Levi study (Study 4) also clearly qualifies as a retrospective study. These authors make it clear that this was not intended to be a formal replication:

> The instance of apparent psi-missing we report here is one that occurred with the ganzfeld procedure. The data did not emerge from systematic research, but from use of the ganzfeld procedure to demonstrate methods and perhaps outcomes of psi research in a college course. We have no way of immediately testing the replicability of the findings; indeed, anybody's attempt to do so will probably differ at least in involving a research setting rather than a completely educational one. But the outcome seems sufficiently striking to justify reporting it for its possible value in stimulating more definitive research. (pp. 279–80)

It is clear from what the authors write that they are reporting this classroom demonstration just because the results seem "sufficiently striking." And it is just as clear that if these results had not been significant they would not have been reported and would not thereby have become a member of this data base.

Strong circumstantial evidence exists to suggest that four other of the "significant" studies were also retrospective: Studies 2, 33, 34, 37. Study 2 was published almost 3 years after it was conducted. In marked contrast with the prototypical ganzfeld study, a single individual served as the experimenter and agent. In the other three, the authors referred to their studies as "preliminary," "exploratory," or "pilot." This again suggests that the only reason we are reading about them is because they gave significant results. In a few studies (*e.g.,* Study 22), the author referred vaguely to a pilot study that presumably gave negative results and thus was not worth reporting. And the only explanation I can find to account for why so many of these studies exhibit the glaring flaws that will be discussed later on is that originally they were not planned as formal experiments.

Summary

Many different reasons strongly suggest that the actual rate of successful replication is much less than the 55% reported by Honorton. By counting as the unit the experimental conditions that replicate most closely the original ganzfeld study, I find an apparent replication rate of 31% for this data base. By taking into account the evidence for a selective bias to report only significant outcomes, the reasonable argument can be made that this success rate would be much lower if we could include the currently unknown ganzfeld psi studies. In addition, it is clear that at least some, and perhaps even many, of the studies included in the current data base were not planned as formal experiments and have been given this status retrospectively just because they yielded significant results.

These considerations make it highly likely that the apparent rate of successful replications must be well below 30%. But even a success rate approaching 30% might be encouraging *if* the rate of success on the chance hypothesis is the advertised 5% level. The next section examines the possibility that the actual chance level might be much higher.

The Effective Error Rate

The task of the reviewer or investigator who is searching for the pattern or aggregate story in a body of literature would be fairly straightforward (a) if there were not the problem of which studies to include and exclude from the data base; (b) if each study used the same or overlapping independent variables; (c) if each used the same dependent variable; and (d) if each used the same planned test of significance. Under these circumstances, what Glass *et al.* (1981) refer to as the "primary analysis," "the secondary analysis," and the "meta-analysis" would be consistent with one another.

But when the studies in the same data base vary widely in independent and dependent variables and in the questions being asked by the original experimenters as opposed to those of the secondary analyst, then many confusing questions arise about what probability levels to assign to the various tests of significance. Such confusion is rampant in the attempt to find a coherent picture in the ganzfeld psi data base.

From the statistical inference viewpoint, the original Honorton and Harper study (Study 8) is appealing in its directness and simplicity. A total of 30 trials were carried out, each one on a separate subject and under identical conditions. If we can assume that the randomization of target and foils at the time of judging was properly carried out (unfortunately, there is some question about this), then the subjects' correct choices of the target, on the null hypothesis, would yield a binomial distribution with an expected value of 7.5 hits. Honorton's subjects achieved 13 direct hits. The probability of obtaining this many or more hits just by chance is .0216, which is considered to be significant. (If the subjects had obtained one less hit, then the probability would have been .0507, or just barely not significant.)

Braud, Wood, and Braud (Study 2) published the first replication of the Honorton and Harper study. Both Braud *et al.* and the parapsychologists who have published vote counts consider the Braud study to be a successful replication of the Honorton and Harper ganzfeld psi study. Yet, in their ganzfeld condition, Braud *et al.* obtained only 3 direct hits out of 10 trials. Because the probability of obtaining 3 or more direct hits just by chance in 10 trials is .22, this outcome can by no stretch of the imagination be designated a successful replication.

So, how does it happen that Honorton and other parapsychologists treat this as a "success"? The answer is that Braud *et al.* used an alternative criterion for scoring "hits." They used binary (or partial) hits. At the end of the ganzfeld session, the subject was presented with the target picture and five foils to rank in terms of how well each picture matched the mentations during the ganzfeld period. A direct hit was scored if the target was ranked first. A binary hit was scored if the target was ranked in the top half (here in the top 3) of the set. Obviously, direct hits and binary hits have to be correlated because every direct hit is also a binary hit. But such a correlation is not perfect, and the two measures can give different results, as was the case in this study. In terms of binary hits, all 10 subjects succeeded, and this is highly significant ($p = .002$).

Honorton (personal communication, October 15, 1982) has defended counting the Braud *et al.* study as a successful replication on the grounds that "the Brauds have always used 'binary hits' as their ESP index." But this is not the issue. The point is that if the Braud *et al.* study is to be counted as a separate replication, it logically implies that the parapsychologists who accept this are guided by the following rule: A successful ganzfeld psi study is one that obtains results significant at the .05 level on *either* the number of direct hits *or* the number of binary hits.

Notice that such a rule implies that the actual significance level for achieving success must be greater than .05. If the two indices were independent, the effective significance level would be approximately .10. Because they are correlated, the actual level is somewhere between .05 and .10.

But this definition must be generalized because Honorton and the other vote counters also accept as successful replications studies that achieve significance at the .05 level on at least one of the following alternative indices: direct hits, binary hits, sum of ranks, rating score, or binary coding.

This criterion obviously implies an effective error rate or chance level in excess of the advertised .05 level. Before considering just how much in excess, we need to consider the use of one-tailed versus two-tailed tests of significance in this data base. The hypothesis in most of these studies, sometimes explicit but mostly implicit, is that psi-hitting will be obtained under ganzfeld conditions. When the deviations from chance are positive, the investigators seem to uniformly use one-tailed tests at the .05 level. When the deviations are negative, the experimenters do not hesitate to test for psi-missing. However, as far as I can tell, whenever the experimenter tests for psi-missing, a two-tailed test at the .05 level of significance is used (psi-missing is considered as a possibility in 24% of the studies in the data base). This implies that within this data base the following rule applies: If the number of observed hits exceeds the chance baseline, then test for psi-hitting with one-tailed test at the .05 level of significance; but if the number is less than the chance level, then test for psi-missing with a two-tailed test at the .05 level.

Note that this rule also implies that the actual significance level is greater than .05. In fact, in this case it is .075. When we combine these two procedural rules, we find that in this data base, the vote counters are in fact accepting as a successful replication any study that achieves a significant departure from the chance level at the .075 level on at least one of the five indices: direct hits, binary hits, sum of ranks, ratings, and binary coding.

A Simulation to Estimate the Error Rate

It would be easy to estimate the actual error rate for this rule if the indices were independent. But clearly the direct hits, binary hits, and sum of ranks must be intercorrelated. And it is reasonable to assume that these three indices will be highly correlated with the rating index. Because Palmer *et al.* (Study 11) report that they found no correlation between the binary coding and their rating score, I will assume that binary coding is relatively independent of the other four indices. By making a few reasonable assumptions, I was able to generate a set of simulated experiments to estimate the effective error rate.[2]

In the simulation, each experiment had the following characteristics:

1. The number of trials was fixed at 30 because the median number

of trials per study in the current data base is 30.

2. For each trial, an integer from 1 to 4 was randomly generated. This represented the subject's ranking of the actual target for that trial (assuming the target was randomly selected from a set of four candidates).

3. In addition, a standardized rating of the target was generated for each trial. This was done by generating four random integers from 0 to 100, standardizing these four to a mean of zero and a standard deviation of 1, and then selecting as the target rating that rating whose rank order matched the ranking assigned to the target for that trial.

For each study, I obtained four statistics: (a) the number of direct hits; (b) the number of binary hits; (c) the sum of ranks; and (d) the mean of the normalized ratings. Because three of the measures are discretely distributed, it was not possible to set the significance levels exactly to .075 (.05 for psi-hitting and .025 for psi-missing). The actual levels used turned out to be .0613 for direct hitting, .0708 for binary hitting, .064 for sum of ranks, and .075 for ratings.

Two separate batches of 1,000 simulated studies were conducted. Each batch yielded the following data: (a) the intercorrelations among the statistical indices; (b) the number of "significant" outcomes on each of the four indices; (c) the number of studies with at least one significant statistic.

If the four indices were independent, we would expect the probability of obtaining at least one significant outcome per experiment to be .24. In fact, the intercorrelations among these four indices ranged from approximately .62 between direct hits and binary hits to .95 between sum of ranks and ratings. And the actual probability of achieving at least one significant outcome per study on these four measures is approximately .152. Assuming that the binary coding index is uncorrelated with these other four indices, I estimate that the probability of achieving a significant outcome on at least one of these measures is approximately .22.

In other words, by using the procedural rule that appears to be followed by the vote counters on this data base, we obtain an effective level of significance of .22, or more than four times the assumed level of .05.

At this point, the objection might be raised that it is unrealistic to charge each study with the usage of five different indices. The binary coding system, for example, can be used only with the special set of slides created by Honorton and his coworkers; and, in fact, only a handful of studies actually used it. And in some studies, they used it in a way that shows it was clearly the only possible index they could compute. In still other studies, the data were collected so as to preclude either the calculation of a rating score, or a sum of ranks, or both.

Such an objection has merit, but it also raises again the problem of assigning error rates on the basis of the primary analysis conducted by the original investigator, the secondary analysis conducted by a reviewer, and the meta-analysis produced by combining the results of several studies on some assumed common metric. The procedural rules used by the vote counters of the ganzfeld psi studies, accepting as they do the actual index used by the original investigator (rather than attempting to reanalyze the results, where possible, to put them on a common footing), logically imply this .22 error rate.

Multiple Indices

The problem raised by multiple indices is just one of a number of ways in which multiple testing can occur. I shall mention some of the other ways shortly. However, the different forms of multiple testing intertwine, and it is difficult to consider them in isolation. Also, as I have just indicated, it is difficult to keep separate the error rate for the testing by the original investigator from the error rate for the subsequent uses of the original study by others. In the case of multiple indices, 55% of the original experimenters actually used two or more such indices, and no one actually used more than three. It is possible to assign a separate error rate, based on the simulations, to each study and then to compute an average error rate per study in terms of the criteria used by the original investigator. This error rate works out to approximately .10 per study.

It is important to keep in mind that this error rate applies only to the usage of two or more of the five common indices. As we will see, other factors contribute to inflating the actual error rate well beyond this level. But even if we consider an error rate based only on the use of multiple indices, this estimate is probably too low. Rarely did an investigator make it clear that he had decided on his primary index or test prior to conducting the study. And it is only in those studies in which the authors have given us sufficient documentation that we can be sure we know all the indices that were considered and perhaps later discarded. For some of the studies that were published only as an abstract in *Research in Parapsychology,* Honorton supplied me with a longer, unpublished version. In one or two of these, the longer report contained information that was missing from the shorter, published version. For example, if I had to rely only on the report in York (Study 42), I would not have assigned it a flaw in the category of "multiple indices" because the published report is written as if only direct hits were scored and tested. The longer, unpublished account, however, makes it clear that the primary measure was intended to be a rating score and that the direct hits were intended to be only a secondary index. It is possible that many of the other reports have not fully reported all the indices they actually tried or would have tried had their original index not worked out.

Some other indications in the current data base seem to support this last speculation. For example, Honorton and his colleagues have uniformly used either direct hits or binary coding in their studies (Studies 7, 8, 32). However, Terry and Honorton (Study 38) inexplicably departed from past practice and used binary hits as their primary index. This usage seems especially peculiar because their customary measure, direct hits, did not achieve significance in this study; and in their very next study (Study 39), described in the same report, the authors reverted to direct hits as the primary measure, with no further mention of binary hits. Even though Honorton (1979) later tried to justify this behavior, it cannot help but reinforce suspicions that even more potential multiple testing is going on than appears on the surface.

Honorton's sudden switch of dependent variable is also inconsistent with his own professed standards. For example, Braud and Wood (Study 3) used both binary coding and their customary binary hits. In a previous study involving the same two investigators (Study 2), Honorton justified using the significant outcome on binary hits rather than the nonsignificant outcome on direct hits to classify the study because the "Brauds have always used 'binary hits' as their primary measure." In the second study, Braud and Wood failed to find significance with their customary binary hits, but did find it (in one of 12 ganzfeld conditions) on the binary coding measure. Consistency would dictate classifying this study as nonsignificant. But Honorton classifies it, without explanation, as significant. Not only is such inconsistency perplexing to the outsider, but it also greatly strengthens the suspicion that the multiple options due to the availability of several indices of psi are underestimated by my assignments in the Appendix.

Considerations such as these suggest that the error rate per study in this data base, on the basis of the use of multiple indices, is at least .10 and almost certainly higher. But the use of multiple indices is just one of several ways that multiple testing occurs in this data base.

Multiple indices was but one of six formal categories of multiple testing on which I judged the studies in the data base. As indicated, over half the studies clearly used multiple indices without taking this into account in computing their statistical significance. A flaw was also assigned on one of the following categories of multiple testing, if it occurred without corresponding adjustments in the significance level.

Alternative tests. In five studies (12% of the total), the experimenters used more than one statistical test on the same index. For example, Raburn (Studies 16, 17) applied both Fisher's exact test and the chi-square test (which is an approximation to the exact test) to the direct hits in her studies. The results of such tests will be highly intercorrelated, but they do increase the actual level of significance above the assumed .05 level. In a few cases, the assignment to this category could just as well have been made to the category "groupings."

Multiple baselines. For the most part, the investigators in this data base tested their index of psi against a theoretical baseline. But many also included control groups of various kinds and tested the same index against the control comparison. Such use of multiple baselines occurred in 17 (40%) of the 42 studies. As one example, Terry *et al.* (Study 40) used both a ganzfeld psi condition and a control (guessing) condition. The number of binary coding hits for each of these conditions was tested separately against the chance baseline, with significance being obtained for the ganzfeld but not for the guessing conditions. The numbers of hits for each condition were also tested for significance against one another, with a nonsignificant outcome. Although this is counted as a significant outcome, one can just as logically argue that if the hitting in the ganzfeld condition is to be attributed to psi we should demand that it be significantly greater than a control condition in which the hitting is apparently due entirely to guessing. For our purposes, however, the point is that having the option of testing for psi by testing an index against both a theoretical and an empirical baseline effectively increases the true significance level beyond the .05 level used for each test separately.

Multiple dependent variables. Only three (7%) of the studies were assigned this flaw. In retrospect, because of the small frequency of occurrence, it might have been better to absorb this category into one of the others. As one example, Stanford (Study 35) had targets matched not only against the entire transcript but also against only the second half of the transcript. Again this increases the number of options for obtaining a significant result.

Multiple groupings. This cause of multiple testing was the most frequent one in this data base (27, or 64% of the studies). The possibility for this form of multiple testing exists whenever the study has more than one condition. Smith, Tremmel, and Honorton (Study 32), as one example, tested their two conditions separately as well as pooled.

Independent judges. The typical ganzfeld psi study (as contrasted with the typical remote-viewing experiment, for example) uses the percipients as their own judges. Some of the studies used independent judges instead. The use of independent judges was scored as a flaw here only if they were used in addition to subjects acting as their own judges in such a way as to produce unadjusted multiple testing. In this data base, 5 (12%) of the studies exhibited this flaw.

No significant differences on any of these six categories of multiple testing exist between the studies classified as "significant" and those classified as "nonsignificant." Nor can I think of any good reasons to expect such differences. One could imagine a scenario in which some investigators habitually indulge in multiple testing whereas others rigorously avoid it. We would then expect to find a greater proportion of multiple-testing flaws among the significant studies. However, we could just as easily imagine a scenario in which the typical investigator uses one option at a time until he either obtains a significant outcome or exhausts all the available options. In the latter scenario, we would predict a greater proportion of multiple-testing flaws in the nonsignificant studies. And, in still a third scenario, we might suppose that the data base contains a mix of the first two scenarios: In this case, one would not predict a difference among the significant and nonsignificant studies on these flaws.

The True Error Rate

The various flaws attributable to multiple testing in this data base and the arguments made in this section suggest that the true error rate is much higher than the assumed .05 level. The question is, how much higher? Unfortunately, we can only make some crude guesses at this time. One problem involves how to reconcile the probable error rate under which the individual experimenter was operating with the error rate that the secondary or meta-analyst is using. The typical experimenter in this data base seems to be operating at the .10 level of significance if we consider just the problem of multiple indices. But the vote counters, who are trying to find a consistent pattern in the total set of experimenters, are operating at the .22 level or higher if we consider their criteria for accepting individual studies as successful replications of one another.

These two estimates, made on the basis of computer simulations, use just one of the six ways that multiple testing occurs in this data base. How much more should these estimates be enlarged to take into account the additional five flaws? Perhaps some additional computer simulations based on various plausible assumptions could set some upper and lower bounds on these figures. And perhaps I or some other interested investigators will conduct such investigations in the future. But I think it is important to emphasize that the outcome of such investigations is likely to be surprising and somewhat counterintuitive to many investigators.

I shall use an example to indicate why I believe that the actual effective error rate is probably much higher than anyone has previously suggested. Consider the Braud and Wood study (Study 3); and to keep matters simple, I shall omit the four practice sessions through which they conducted their two groups. They ran two independent groups of subjects through pre-treatment and posttreatment ganzfeld psi sessions. They used two indices of psi: the number of binary hits, and the number of hits on the binary coding scale. The test for psi was made within each of the four conditions, the two pretreatment and the two posttreatment sessions. The test on each index can be considered to be at the .075 level for reasons already indicated (there seems little doubt that the typical experimenter will test for psi-missing if the number of hits is substantially less than chance). In addition, these two indices—binary coding and binary hitting—are apparently uncorrelated. This means that there is a probability of .144 of obtaining at least one significant result in a given condition just by chance. Furthermore, under the reasonable assumption that the tests in each of the four cells are independent, the probability that significance will be found in at least one of the four conditions becomes .464.

But this estimate of the effective significance level in this case is still too low. The experimenter also has the option of pooling the data over the pretreatment and posttreatment trials within each group (indeed, this was actually done). Although these new tests are not independent of the previous ones, they further increase the effective error rate, almost surely beyond .50. We still have to consider the option, used by Honorton, of pooling the data over both conditions and over all trials to make a further statistical test. In addition, we have the options, actually used by Braud and Wood, of testing the conditions not only against the chance baseline, but also against one another. And for simplicity, I omitted eight treatment conditions that could also be considered replications of the ganzfeld study.

In other words, this one study can be considered to be operating under a true significance level of well over .50. Indeed, if we consider the eight intervening practice conditions, the chances of coming up with a significant outcome are well over .80! And this is just one of many studies in this data base that exhibit such complex options, either explicitly or implicitly.

One possible protest against my treatment of the Braud and Wood study might be that the logic of the study suggests that they were predicting a significant outcome mainly in the posttreatment condition, which had been preceded by practice sessions with feedback. But this would be a feeble protest for a number of reasons. Significance was obtained only with the binary-coding index. The binary-hitting index, which Braud had consistently relied on in the past, was insignificant. No hint was given in the write-up that Braud and Wood had suddenly found grounds for predicting success on binary coding and not on their favored measure. At any rate, the outcome again raises questions about what constitutes a successful replication.

What if significance had been obtained in one of the pretrial conditions rather than one of the posttreatment conditions? Would Braud and Wood or Honorton have considered this a failure to replicate? This is highly unlikely when it is realized that the pretreatment conditions are closer replicas of the original Honorton–Harper study than either of the posttreatment conditions. And what if the posttreatment condition without the preceding feedback practice had been the only significant condition? Again, this surely would have been considered a successful replication since it is a closer replica of the original ganzfeld psi study than is the one condition for which significance was claimed.

Summary

In the paper I presented to the combined meetings of the Society for Psychical Research and the Parapsychological Association in August 1982, I estimated that the effective error rate was closer to .25 than to .05. Honorton attacked this estimate as based on subjective speculation. He also suggested it was based on a worst case scenario. Any estimate of the effective error rate is, of course, speculative. But I believe the arguments I have made in this section make a strong case that the overall effective error rate per study could easily be this high or higher. When taken together with the arguments in the preceding section on the actual rate of success, the claims made for the ganzfeld psi data base have been premature, to say the least. Many considerations indicate that the actual rate of successful replication is less than 30%. And the arguments in this section strongly suggest that this rate of "successful" replication is probably very close to what should be expected by chance, given the various options for multiple testing exhibited in this data base.

Procedural Flaws

As parapsychologists as well as their critics have frequently remarked, the evidence for psi consists of statistically significant deviations from a chance baseline. Presumably, parapsychologists, like critics, would agree that before such deviations are interpreted as being due to psi, certain elementary safeguards must be met. These safeguards are as follows: (a) randomization of targets and conditions in such a way as to guarantee, on the chance hypothesis, that the resulting distribution of hits and misses will be consistent with the assumptions underlying the statistical tests; (b) given the underlying assumptions, the use of appropriate statistical tests in such a way as to guarantee that the assumed error rate is, in fact, the actual one; and (c) use of experimental controls to eliminate obvious possibilities for sensory leakage.

The last section listed several reasons for concluding that insufficient attention had been given to the second safeguard. At most, 3 of the 42 studies in the data base were entirely free of multiple-testing flaws. I did not try to assign a flaw for an additional aspect of this safeguard—the need to ensure that sampling units are independent. The potential violation of independence was extremely widespread in the data base. The most common violation was the indiscriminate pooling over the within- and between-subject trials. But pooling also took place over separate experimental conditions without any attempt to segregate within- and between-condition variance. And a very common practice was to include within a single experimental condition trials in which agents were friends of the percipient along with trials in which agents were members of the laboratory staff. Just how serious such violations of independence are is difficult to decide. One can imagine possible models in which they make no difference. But all such models assume that randomization has been optimal and that, on the null hypothesis, no psi exists.

Procedural Categories

The first and third safeguards entail what I will designate as procedural safeguards. These involve conducting the study in such a way as to ensure proper randomization and to eliminate obvious possibilities for sensory communication between target and percipient. To these safeguards, I have added two other components: reporting the results in such a way that the reader can tell if the safeguards have been used, and conducting the statistical analyses correctly. I assigned flaws to the studies (see Appendix) if they were deficient on any of the following six procedural categories:

Randomization (R). Typically, the ganzfeld psi study uses a number of target pools. Each pool contains, say, four pictures or slides that are candidates for the target on a given trial. On a given trial, a pool is selected. Then, a target within that pool is chosen. Later, all the members of the pool are given to the subject or the judge for evaluation. Randomization refers to the procedure for making the selection at the first two stages. (I include problems of replacing the target among the other members of its pool for judging under the category *Feedback.*) The most critical aspect of the randomization procedure is the selection of the target from its pool. When the experimenter reported using an inadequate measure of randomization, such as hand shuffling of cards or reels, or tossing coins, I assigned the study an "R–." I also assigned this flaw to studies in which no randomization at all was used for selecting the target. For example, in Studies 7, 8, 38, and 39, the experimenter simply took the uppermost reel in a packet of four slide reels as the target. Altogether, 15 (36%) studies were assigned this flaw. When the experimenter reported using a table of random numbers or a random number generator to select the specific target from a pool, I assigned the study an "R+." Only 11 (26%) of the studies met this minimal standard. The remaining 16 studies were assigned an "R?" to indicate that they supplied insufficient information about how they were randomized. Because adequate randomization is so basic, one might assume that it can be taken for granted that an investigator has properly carried it out. So the failure to describe fully how the target was selected perhaps ought not to be tallied as a "flaw." But the fact that in those studies in which the target selection is fully described, 58% use a clearly inadequate method of randomization suggests that it would be unwise to assume that randomization was adequate in the questionable cases. For purposes of subsequent analysis, then, I have assumed that randomization was suboptimal in all those studies (74% of the total) in which it is not clear that it was conducted adequately. Fortunately, all of the correlations with this index come out in the same direction regardless of whether I use this stringent criterion or simply use only the studies that clearly describe their procedures. Only the studies involving Stanford (Studies 31, 35, 36) seem to treat the problem of randomization as something to be taken seriously.

Single Target (ST). Obviously, the use of the same target that has been separated from its pool and later replaced for judging purposes allows various possibilities for sensory leakage. At least, it was obvious to a critic such as myself when I first encountered the Honorton and Harper study (Study 8) (Hyman, 1977). Yet, it was not until 1980 that this flaw disappeared from ganzfeld psi studies. I assigned the flaw "ST" to each of the 23 studies (55% of the total) that used a single target.

Feedback (FB). The 10 studies to which I assigned this flaw, in addition to possible handling cues because of the use of a single target, typically did not use an adequate procedure to ensure that the target was properly randomized among the other candidates in the pool before being presented for judging. Although only 24% of the total data base exhibited this flaw, the flaw could occur only in those cases in which a single target was used. Of these cases, 43% exhibited this flaw.

Documentation (DOC). This could refer to inadequate reporting of many critical details needed for assessing the adequacy of the procedures. But most of the assignments of this flaw had to do with failure to report the number of times the agent was a friend of the percipient or to provide data on whether this made a difference in those studies in which subjects were encouraged to bring their own agents. As might be expected, this flaw was much more prevalent in the unpublished studies. Inadequate documentation was a serious problem in 81% of the unpublished studies as opposed to 38% of the published studies.

Security (SEC). The prototypical ganzfeld psi study corresponds to what Rhine and Pratt (1957) refer to as "the two-experimenter plan." With one experimenter monitoring the agent and one monitoring the subject, there is increased security against a variety of potential threats to the validity of the study. But some of the studies depart from this safeguard. In the study by Braud *et al.* (Study 2), a single person, an undergraduate student, plays the role of both experimenters as well as the agent—roles that are enacted by three different individuals in the typical study. A single person also plays this part in Studies 19 and 41. Such departures from the prototype lessen security. I assigned SEC to studies for other reasons also, such as failing to monitor the agent or rolling a clay ball over the target, etc. A total of 10 (24%) studies were assigned this flaw.

Statistics (STAT). I assigned 12 (29%) studies the flaw STAT because of what appeared to be an erroneous use of the statistical procedure. Apparently some investigators used Fisher's exact test without adding in the probabilities of getting results even more extreme than the actual outcome (Studies 16, 17, 31, 33). Such a mistake can greatly exaggerate the actual significance. In one study, this error was compounded because a two-tailed test had clearly been intended. The other studies involved inappropriate pooling over trials and using wrong degrees of freedom. As mentioned previously, inappropriate pooling and violations of independence were quite common in this data base. But I assigned a statistical error only in the most blatant violations—those in which the correct alternative should have been applied.

Additional Problems

The assignment of flaws according to the preceding six categories was conservative on a number of grounds. The occurrence of some flaws, for example, is contingent on other circumstances. For example, the FB flaw could occur only in studies that also have the ST flaw. And in some of the early studies, the absence of this flaw did not mean that the experimenter had taken the appropriate precautions, but rather that the procedure— the use of the binary coding method—made it irrelevant. Most of the statistical flaws occurred because of inappropriate handling of between- and within-subject trials. Such an error cannot occur in a simpler study that has a single condition and no repeated measures. Thus, the absence of some statistical flaws may not indicate that the experimenter was statistically sophisticated but rather that the simplicity of the design precluded committing certain types of mistake.

I did not systematically score a variety of flaws because they either depended on suspicions or hard-to-objectify criteria, or were not too common. I have already mentioned the "retrospective study," which can be charged to at least three studies but probably includes several more. Another problem was the fact that several studies used inconstant conditions. One changed the procedure halfway through the study, but did not include this change as a variable. Several studies allowed percipients to bring their own agents, but supplied an agent for those who did not. These potentially different conditions were typically not analyzed separately.

In any case, the existence of so many elementary defects in this data base is both disturbing and surprising. Only two studies were entirely free of the six procedural flaws. And if we include multiple-testing errors, not a single study in this data base was flawless. It is important to realize that the defects being discussed are not obscure or subtle. Rather, I suspect that a typical parapsychologist would spontaneously list them as being unacceptable in a psi experiment. Given the central role of statistical assumptions, it is distressing to discover that only 26% of the studies in this data base clearly used appropriate randomization. And, further, it should be of little comfort to find that 29% made statistical blunders.

I would like to emphasize that I do not view the existence of these flaws as causal in the sense that their presence accounts for the significant results. Rather, I see them as symptoms. I know, and have a great deal of respect for, the experimental competence of many of the investigators in this data base. I have little doubt that most of them know full well how to conduct a planned and well-controlled study. I believe that just about all of them would agree that the use of random numbers or random generators is superior to hand shuffling of cards. Yet, despite the universal availability of such optimal procedures, several experiments use suboptimal procedures.

Meta-Analysis of Flaws and Successful Outcomes

The surprising number of defects in the ganzfeld psi studies have been pointed out by critics within the field of parapsychology (Akers, 1984; Ballard, unpublished; Kennedy, 1979a, 1979b; Parker & Wiklund, 1987; Sargent, 1980a, 1980b). However, I have not heard any reasons offered for the occurrence of these defects. Instead, attempts have been made to dismiss the criticisms on the grounds that the flaws, in fact, make no difference. Characteristic of this approach to minimizing the defects is that of Honorton (1979, 1981).

Honorton argues that if a critic wishes to fault a study because of the possibility of handling cues, for example, then he is obliged to demonstrate empirically that such cues do, in fact, make a difference. Honorton deals specifically with the flaw I have called *Single Target (ST)*, which allows the possibility of handling cues. Honorton first reviews some studies that suggest that even when deliberately introduced, subliminal or sensory cues are rarely exploited. Then he demonstrates that, if anything, there is a slight tendency for ganzfeld studies that do not have this flaw to produce higher Z scores on overall hits.

My analysis agrees with Honorton in showing no correlation between the use of single targets and significance. In the current data base, 52% of the significant studies were assigned ST as compared with 58% of the nonsignificant studies. But this empirical relationship hardly justifies retrospectively sanctifying studies that committed this blunder. Honorton (1981) concludes:

> Since there was no difference in the results of the two groups of studies, the handling cue hypothesis was rejected. As John Stuart Mill put it, "A difference, in order to be a difference, must make a difference." . . . The moral here is simply this: Disputes over empirical claims can only be resolved through empirical methods. This is the hallmark of science and what differentiates it from other approaches to knowledge such as religion. (p. 159)

But such a defense will not do. Even if a first-order correlation is zero between a flaw and significance, this does not mean that no relationship exists or that a causal connection is absent. Much can depend on how the flaws intercorrelate with each other and other variables. For example, if, when all other factors are controlled, ST correlates positively with significance and we also have a second flaw that not only correlates highly with significance but also correlates negatively with ST, then we could easily find that the first-order correlation between ST and significance is zero or even negative. This is just one of the many problems of trying to use statistics to substitute for empirical controls.

In addition, correlation deals with symmetrical relationships and overlooks more complicated possibilities. For example, ST and FB are intercorrelated in this sample, but the relationship is asymmetric. Because of the way I scored it, FB can occur only if ST has also occurred. The probability of FB when ST is absent is zero, but is approximately .43 in this sample, given that ST is present. Furthermore, FB does seem to be correlated with significance. Of the significant studies that have ST, eight (or 67%) were assigned FB. Of the nonsignificant studies that were assigned ST, two (or 18%) were also assigned FB. In other words, even though, by Honorton's criterion, ST does not correlate with significance, its presence enables the occurrence of another flaw that does seem to correlate with significance.

In addition to the previous two considerations, as already indicated, such flaws are signs that the study was probably not carefully planned or properly carried out.

Dependent Variables for the Meta-Analysis

Although the retrospective correlation between flaws and experimental outcomes cannot be used to salvage improperly executed studies, it still may be helpful to follow Honorton's lead and, in the spirit of a meta-analysis (Glass *et al.,* 1981), examine the pattern of relationships among indices of success and various flaws. Such an examination should be taken in the spirit of exploratory data analysis, and its goal is to suggest hypotheses about what may be going on. For the purposes of this analysis, I used the following dependent variables:

1. Honorton's original classification as significant or nonsignificant. Using Honorton's orginial criterion (personal communication, November 30, 1981), I assigned the notation SIG-1 to studies he deemed to be significant overall and NSIG-1 to the remaining studies (see Appendix for these assignments).

2. Honorton's second classification after adjusting for multiple testing. Here I used Honorton's classification of June 2, 1982 (personal communication) to assign the notation SIG-2 to those studies that still achieved significance at the .05 level after adjustment of significance levels for multiple testing. The remaining studies were assigned NSIG-2.

3. Effect size in degrees (E). One problem with Honorton's classifications of significance is that he accepts the original investigator's primary index even though the index varies from experimenter to experimenter. This not only logically commits Honorton and the other reviewers who keep box scores in this manner to an absurdly high error rate, but it also violates the spirit of meta-analysis, which seeks to find a common index or scale by which to compare different studies. In addition, vote counting based on significance ignores the fact that different studies vary in number of trials (and, hence, power). Consequently, meta-analysis tries to focus on a common index of effect size rather than level of significance.

I needed an index that could be used to characterize most of the studies in this data base. The index I chose was the number of direct hits. When it was impossible to obtain the number of direct hits for a given study, I used binary hits instead. In a few cases, I used the number of hits on the binary coding scale when nothing else was available. I omitted six studies from this meta-analysis because they did not supply data that would enable me to compute an index comparable to the number of direct hits.

To convert the hits into a reasonably comparable measure of effect size, I used the Freeman-Tukey arc sine transformation for binomial proportions (Freeman & Tukey, 1950) on both the number of hits and the expected number of hits. The effect size was then the difference between these two transforms in degrees. In the Appendix, when BH or BC appears in parentheses after the effect size, this indicates that it was computed on the basis of binary hits or binary coding, respectively. If no such designation is given, then the effect size was calculated on the basis of direct hits.

Z score. The Freeman-Tukey transform supplies, as a side benefit, a theoretical standard deviation for each sample size. This was used to obtain a *Z* score for each effect size. The *Z* score can be referred to the tables of the normal curve for computing significance.

Absolute effect size and Z score. Finally, in many of the analyses, the absolute effect size and *Z* score were also used because graphic examination seemed to indicate that on some comparisons—say, effect size with sample size—the relationship was in terms of variance rather than algebraic mean.

Independent Variables

The 12 formal categories of flaws served as the major source of independent variables for finding correlates of effect size and significance. In addition, other variables were studied, such as number of trials, published or unpublished results, investigator, and year of report.

Because the 12 flaws are scored only as dichotomies, the first step was to find some rational or empirical means of combining the flaws into relatively continuous scales. For this purpose, I discarded three of the categories—Alternative Tests, Multiple Dependent Variables, and Independent Judges—because their frequency of occurrence was too low. I then obtained the intercorrelations (point-biserial *r*) between each pair of the remaining nine flaws and carried out both a factor analysis and a cluster analysis on the resulting matrix. Fortunately, both the cluster analysis and the factor analysis agreed in partitioning the nine flaw measures into three overlapping factors or clusters. For each cluster, I obtained the first principal component and used this as a basis for obtaining regression weights to use for combining the indices for each cluster into a single composite cluster score. On the basis of the weights, I gave each of the cluster scores a title:

Cluster I: "General security." This cluster was composed of five indices, but the major contributors were ST, FB, and SEC. These all seemed to be related to problems of security or possibilities of sensory leakage. The actual indices and their weights were:

$$C\text{-}I = -.33MI + .52ST + .54FB + .47SEC + .31STAT$$

Cluster II: "Statistics." This cluster also consisted of five indices, with the three strongest contributors being Multiple Baselines, Multiple Groupings, and Statistics. All these seem to be flaws that contribute to an inflated level of significance. The indices and their weights were:

$$C\text{-}II = .42MB + .48MG - .41MI - .41R + .51STAT$$

Cluster III: "Controls." This cluster consisted of four indices, with the strongest contributions coming from R, FB, and DOC. The simplest word I could find to characterize this dimension was *Controls.* The common aspect seems to be a lack of care in carrying out various procedural controls. The indices and their weights were:

$$C\text{-III} = .16MI + .64R + .48FB + .57DOC$$

Correlations Between Flaws and Significance

Of the three cluster scores, only Controls correlates significantly with both the original and adjusted classifications of significance. The group of studies that were significant in both classifications had the highest mean score on this index of flaws. The group that was significant on the original but not on the revised classification had the second highest mean score. And the group that was significant on neither classification had the lowest score on this cluster. This finding is confirmed by the meta-analysis. The correlation between effect size and the Controls cluster was .37, and that between Z score and the Controls cluster was .44 (both significant).

The individual flaws that seem to correlate (using conventional significance levels as a convenient criterion) with the three different measures of significance are Randomization, Feedback, Documentation, and Statistics. The more likely a study was to be assigned any of these flaws, the more likely it was to be classified as significant. The same pattern, but somewhat weaker, is to be found in the case of effect size. In the case of this latter index, the two best single predictors are Feedback and Documentation. Interestingly enough, the fewer the trials in an experiment, the *larger* the effect size!

Experimenter Effects

Parker (1978) has written, "The present crisis in parapsychology is that there appear to be few if any findings which are independent of the experimenter. Indeed, it can be claimed that the experimenter effect is parapsychology's one and only finding." Because several experimenters appeared in more than one study in the current data base, some of my analyses examined the relationship of variables such as flaws, effect size, and significance to experimenter. In this data base, experimenters tend to be quite consistent in their experimental designs from study to study. Indeed, most of the variation and covariation between studies is due to differences in experimenters. An analysis of variance on effect size with investigators as the independent variable yielded a significant outcome. Seven investigators who had two or more studies in the meta-analysis were included as levels. An additional level was constructed by combining the eight remaining studies in which the experimenters appeared only once. For the group of 36 studies as a whole, the average effect size was 5.98 degrees, which corresponds to a direct hit rate of 35% (as compared with the chance rate of 25%). However, four experimenters who contributed 18 studies, or 50% of the total data base, accounted for almost all of this effect size. These four experimenters (Honorton, Sargent, Sondow, and Raburn) reported results whose average effect size was 11.31 degrees, which corresponds to a direct hit rate of 44%. The remaining studies yielded an average effect size of 0.76 degrees, which corresponds to a hit rate of 26%.

Other analyses confirm that an experimenter effect does exist in these studies. Indeed, two experimenters account for much of the apparent success of this paradigm. Honorton and his coworkers dominate the successes in the first 4 years of the studies. In the past few years, Sargent and his coworkers have carried the burden. Strangely, no contributions have come from Honorton and his laboratory during the latter 4 years of the span covered by the present data base.

The experimenter effect is confounded with the fact that the experimenters also differ significantly in their patterns of flaws. Honorton's studies, which have the highest average effect size, also have the highest score on the Controls flaw cluster. Palmer's studies, which have the lowest average effect size (in fact, slightly negative), also have the lowest score on the Controls flaw factor. Therefore, it would be premature, to say the least, to look for the source of the experimenter effect in either the personality of the investigator or the social context in which he or she operates. The first place to look, it would seem, is in the differences in the way the investigators carry out their studies, such as use of a single condition or multiple conditions, care in procedural details, emphasis on security, and the like.

Factor Analysis of Variables

Several other relationships were examined. Because most of the findings seem to be captured by a factor analysis I conducted on several variables, I shall use the results of that analysis to summarize my findings from the meta-analysis. The factor analysis used 17 variables—the three cluster flaw scores, the logarithm of the number of trials, the year of the report, whether repeated measures were used, the five investigators with the largest number of studies in the data base (Honorton, Sargent, Rogo, Palmer, and W. G. Braud), effect size, Z score, the absolute values of the latter two indices, and a dummy variate to take into account that effect sizes on binary hits and binary coding tend to be lower than those for direct hits.

Four factors were extracted (using principal components and the varimax method of rotation). One factor was characterized by a high positive loading (0.85) on year and a high negative loading on the General Security cluster (–0.88). This reflects the fact that security, as measured by the increasing use of duplicate target sets, has been increasing in the past few years. Indeed, the possibility of sensory leakage owing to the use of a single target set has now disappeared. A second factor has high loadings on all the measures of effect size and significance level along with a positive loading (0.49) for the statistics cluster. The two indices with highest loading on this factor are absolute effect size (0.74) and absolute value of Z score (0.82). A third factor involves the number of trials. The major loadings on this third factor are logarithm of trials (0.91), cluster score on Statistics (0.53), and repeated measures (0.57). Part of this is consistent with other analyses that strongly suggest that statistical flaws that unwittingly inflate the significance level tend to increase with the complexity of the study. (Complexity is measured here by number of trials and use of repeated measures.)

But it is the fourth factor that holds most interest in the present context. The key loadings are effect size (0.55), Z score (0.59), and cluster score on Controls (0.81). In addition, this factor contrasts the experimenters Honorton (0.54) and Palmer (–0.71). This factor is simply consistent with the other analyses that indicate that both effect size and significance are correlated with the existence of flaws that indicate insufficient care with respect to experimental procedures. And it is also consistent with the prior findings that experimenters who pay the most attention to such controls also report the smallest effects.

Predicted Significance and Effects for Flawless Studies

The average Z score for this data base is 1.04. The composite Z score (using the method suggested by Rosenthal, 1978) is 6.27, which would suggest that for all practical purposes the possibility of getting such a combined result by chance is zero. In addition, the average effect size is 5.98, which corresponds to a direct hit rate of 34%. Another way to emphasize the magnitude of this composite picture, one favored by Honorton, is to use Rosenthal's (1979) procedure for dealing with the "file-drawer problem." The idea is to use the composite Z score to estimate the number of unknown or unreported studies with nonsignificant results that would have to exist to make the present 36 studies simply a selection from a population with zero effects. In this instance, the procedure informs us that it would take 486 such studies. Such considerations seem to indicate that the data base provides a robust and compelling argument for the existence of psi.

But, as we have seen, both Z score and effect size, in this data base, correlate with the cluster score on Controls. The three flaws that contribute most to this score are Randomization (R), Feedback (FB), and Documentation (DOC). These are scored as dichotomies, a "1" indicating the presence of the given flaw and a "0" indicating its absence. A regression equation relating these dummy variates to both Z score and effect size separately was computed to predict what the corresponding Z scores and effect sizes might be for studies that were free of these flaws. A dummy variate for Z scores and effect sizes that were not based on direct hits was also included in the equations to take into account the fact that binary coding and binary hits tended to give smaller effect sizes in this data base.

The regression equation for the Z score gave the following weights:

$$Z' = 0.03 + 0.74R + 0.28FB + 0.91DOC - 1.27D(BH/BC)$$

with a multiple correlation of .53. The corresponding equation for effect size was:

$$E' = 1.52 + 2.55R + 3.68FB + 4.50DOC - 7.40D(BH/BC)$$

with a multiple correlation of 0.48.

These equations should cause us to reconsider the seemingly impressive implications of the composite Z score and the estimates based on the file-drawer problem. The first equation informs us that for studies in which the flaws R, FB, and DOC are eliminated, we can expect the Z score based on direct hits to be zero. The second equation, when properly translated, tells the same story. It predicts an effect size of 1.52 degrees for experiments that have none of these three flaws. Such an effect size corresponds, in terms of direct hits, to a hit rate of 27%, which is well within the statistical neighborhood of the 25% chance rate.

Published Versus Unpublished Studies

About half of the studies in the data base actually were published. The rest appeared as abstracts or papers presented at meetings of the Parapsychological Association. Unlike the findings of meta-analyses in other bodies of research literature (Glass et al., 1981), no difference in effect size or other variables, with one exception, between published and unpublished studies showed up in this sample. The one exception was documentation. As would be expected, unpublished studies were much more likely to lack adequate documentation than published ones.

Conclusions

By now it is clear that I believe that the ganzfeld psi data base, despite initial impressions, is inadequate either to support the contention of a repeatable study or to demonstrate the reality of psi. Whatever other value these studies may have for the parapsychological community, they have too many weaknesses to serve as the basis for confronting the rest of the scientific community. Indeed, parapsychologists may be doing themselves and their cause a disservice by attempting to use these studies as examples of the current state of their field.

I have no doubt that most of the investigators who have contributed to this data base are fully capable of conducting well-planned and relatively flawless studies. Whatever the reasons, the 42 studies in the present data base cannot by any stretch of the imagination be characterized as flawless, and I suspect that most of them were not well planned. If these investigators wish to impress outsiders and critics with their efforts, they will have to present them with studies that have reasonable controls against sensory leakage, adequate procedures to ensure that the underlying statistical assumptions have been met, and evidence that the advertised error rate is, in fact, the actual one. If a body of such studies can be carried out, and the results come out as successful as many parapsychologists believed the ganzfeld psi studies were, then the time will have come for the scientific community to sit up and take notice.

Exploratory Versus Confirmatory Studies

One problem with the current data base seems to be a confusion between exploratory and confirmatory studies. In fact, many of the authors explicitly announce their studies as exploratory. In responding to Sargent's (1980b) critique of her study, Sondow (1980) says, "Finally, I must point out that asking more than one question in an exploratory study is hardly a 'shortcoming' " (p. 272). Indeed, asking many questions in carrying out exploratory data analysis is greatly to be encouraged. But such exploratory investigations should be used as the basis for generating testable hypotheses, not for both generating and testing the hypotheses. Any findings from an exploratory data analysis need to be confirmed with new data that are collected for the explicit purpose of testing one or more given hypotheses under a controlled and specified error rate.

One suggestion might be for the Parapsychological Association to attempt to draw up a set of standards for designating studies as confirmatory. Ideally, exploratory studies, as such, should not be published, except possibly as the context for a confirmatory study that was a consequence of the exploratory study. By requiring confirmatory studies both to be labeled as such and to conform to a given set of standards, the parapsychological community will not only help to dispel much confusion, but it will also help both parapsychological and critical reviewers to select the appropriate studies to include in a meta-analysis.

Comments on the Individual Flaws

Would data bases in other fields of research withstand the same sort of scrutiny to which I have put the ganzfeld psi data base? I suspect, for example, that if I devoted the same effort to a critical evaluation of a set of studies in an area of psychology, I would find many of the same sorts of flaws. I am almost certain, based on my years as a referee for several scientific journals, that I would find the same sorts of multiple-testing flaws that I report in the ganzfeld psi studies. This is because parapsychologists have been trained as psychologists, biologists, and physicists and have been taught statistics from the same textbooks. And it is sad to report that most of this training is inadequate and even inconsistent in dealing with the problem of simultaneous statistical inference. Both textbooks and journal editors seem to have no hesitation, for example, in allowing investigators to test the several separate lines of an analysis of variance table each at the .05 level. Yet, when the same investigators attempt to compare the individual means within a given line of that same table, they are often required to use post hoc tests that penalize them for the implicit number of comparisons that might be made.

In other words, the problem of multiple testing and inflated error rates is by no means unique to the ganzfeld psi data base. But this should be of little comfort to the parapsychologist. Nor should this lessen the force of my arguments based on the existence of these inflated significance levels. In addition, an argument might be made that parapsychologists should be more vigilant in this regard than scientists in other areas. After all, the argument for psi is currently based on the assumption that the statistical probabilities as reported are reasonably close to what is actually the case.

Again, a body such as the Parapsychological Association might lessen the seriousness of multiple testing by establishing guidelines. And the various journals might make it clear to potential authors that such guidelines must be followed for all papers that are submitted as confirmatory studies. As well as setting a model for other fields to emulate, the development of such guidelines might also break new ground in other ways. One would be to suggest ways that authors can most efficiently and legitimately make multiple comparisons and tests and appropriately take this into account in drawing their conclusions.

I am not so sure about how much the procedural flaws in this data base would also characterize studies in other fields. I suspect that randomization in many areas of psychology is a casual affair. As such, it would be considered "flawed" by my criterion. But again, appropriate randomization is more critical in a parapsychological study than it probably is in a learning or perceptual study. The very definition of psi involves a statistically significant departure from a value in a specified distribution. Both the meaning of the departure and the interpretation of the significance level depend crucially on the underlying assumptions being correct. And careful attention to randomization is one of the few ways to guarantee the adequacy of such assumptions.

Again, perhaps the Parapsychological Association in conjunction with various journal editors can lead the way in emphasizing the critical importance of randomization. The one investigator in the current sample who seems to realize the importance of randomization is Stanford (Studies 31, 35, 36). The three studies in which he was investigator or coinvestigator were the only ones about which I was confident that randomization had truly been carried out correctly. The indication that inadequate randomization in this sample is correlated with significance further stresses the importance of making it clear to future investigators that this is not a casual matter.

One promising trend in this data base is the significant reduction over the 8 years in the flaws relating to security. Most of this reduction is due to the replacement of single target sets with duplicate ones. But the parapsychologists ought not to be content simply to point out that this flaw has been banished. In my opinion, they ought to ask themselves why this flaw was allowed to persist so long. Studies continued exhibiting this flaw through 1979. Only in the last 2 years of the data base did it finally disappear. Why did it take the parapsychological community 6 years to finally recognize and abolish this flaw that so readily strikes the eye of an outsider? If such an obvious flaw can persist in a major body of parapsychological literature for 6 years, what other, perhaps more subtle, flaws still abound?

The flaws classified as Statistics (STAT) raise other challenges. Twelve, or 28%, of the studies were faulted for such mistakes. This could be an underestimate for several reasons. I could detect some of the errors only when enough data were provided for me to recalculate the statistics. In some cases I suspected that the reported statistics could not be correct, but I was unable to verify this suspicion because of insufficient data. And because the occurrence of this flaw was correlated with the size and complexity of the study, it could be the case that other experimenters might also have exhibited such errors if they had conducted more complicated studies.

All this suggests that parapsychologists no longer should rest content with Burton Camp's 1937 assertion that for Rhine's work "the statistical analysis is essentially valid" (cited in Mauskopf & McVaugh, 1979). Because there is no common curriculum for those who end up as parapsychologists, it is probably not safe to assume that a parapsychologist automatically knows how to conduct and compute the appropriate statistical analysis properly. As paradigms change and complexity increases, statistical competence that was adequate for previous research may no longer apply. Again, both the Parapsychological Association and journal editors might take the lead in trying to ensure that future work uses correct statistical analyses.

Here, too, is an opportunity to break new ground. In many of the ganzfeld psi studies, there is a gray area in which it is unclear what the appropriate sampling unit should be. Many questions arise about when it is safe to pool over conditions, trials, subjects, and other potentially correlated dimensions. Both theoretical and empirical work could be useful here in establishing some guidelines.

It is no surprise that unpublished abstracts often are inadequately documented. But 38% of the published papers were also faulted for insufficient documentation. Much of this involves the introduction of changes or variations in conditions without the inclusion of information about the effects of these changes. This is closely related to another problem, for which I did not create a formal category, but which strongly suggest that these studies were conducted on a rather informal basis. Percipients, for example were often encouraged to bring friends as agents. For those who did not, the experimenter supplied an agent. Here we have a variable treated as a constant because, with one or two exceptions, all these situations were treated as a single condition.

In conclusion, the current data base has too many problems to be seriously put before outsiders as evidence for psi. The types of problems exhibited by this data base, however, suggest interesting challenges for the parapsychological community. I would hope that both parapsychologists and critics would wish to have parapsychological studies conducted according to the highest standards possible. If one goal is to convince the rest of the scientific community that the parapsychologist can produce data of the highest quality, then it would be a terrible mistake to use the current ganzfeld psi data base for this purpose. Perhaps the Parapsychological Association can lead the way by setting down guidelines for what should constitute an adequate confirmatory study. And then, when a sufficient number of studies that meet these guidelines have accumulated, they can be presented to the rest of the scientific community as an example of what parapsychology, at its best, can achieve. If studies carried out according to these guidelines also continue to yield results suggestive of psi, then the outside scientific community should be obliged to take notice.

Notes

1. When a reference is cited for general or historical purposes, it is followed as usual by the year of publication in parentheses and is listed in the Reference section. For the 42 reports in the data base, however, study *numbers* are used (e.g., Study 1) and are referenced in the Appendix.

2. Ron Friedland aided me with both the programming and the running of the computer simulations. The program was written in Pascal.

References

Akers, C. (1984). Methodological criticisms of parapsychology. In S. Krippner (Ed.), *Advances in parapsychological research* (Vol. 4). Jefferson, N.C.: McFarland.

Ballard, J. A. (1981). *Relaxation and the ganzfeld as psi-conductive states.* Unpublished manuscript.

Blackmore, S. (1980). The extent of selective reporting of ESP ganzfeld studies. *European Journal of Parapsychology, 3,* 213–219.

Freeman, M. F., & Tukey, J. W. (1950). Transformations related to the angular and the square root. *Annals of Mathematical Statistics, 21,* 607–611.

Glass, G. V., McGaw, B., & Smith, M. L. (1981). *Meta-analysis in social research.* Beverly Hills, Calif.: Sage Publications.

Hansel, C. E. M. (1980). *ESP and parapsychology: A critical reevaluation.* Buffalo, N.Y.: Prometheus Books.

Hedges, L. V., & Olkin, I. (1982). Analyses, reanalyses, and meta-analysis [Review of *Meta-analysis in social research*]. *Contemporary Education Review, 1,* 157–165.

Honorton, C. (1978). Psi and internal attention states: Information retrieval in the ganzfeld. In B. Shapin & L. Coly (Eds.), *Psi and states of awareness* (pp. 79–90). New York, N.Y.: Parapsychology Foundation.

———. (1979). Methodological issues in free-response experiments. *Journal of the American Society for Psychical Research. 73,* 381–394.

———. (1981). Beyond the reach of sense: Some comments on C. E. M. Hansel's *ESP and parapsychology: A critical reevaluation. Journal of the American Society for Psychical Research, 75,* 155–166.

Honorton, C., & Harper, S. (1974). Psi-mediated imagery and ideation in an experimental procedure for regulating perceptual input. *Journal of the American Society for Psychical Research, 68,* 156–168.

Hyman, R. (1977, November/December). The case against parapsychology. *The Humanist, 37,* 47–49.

Kennedy, J. E. (1979a). Methodological problems in free-response ESP experiments. *Journal of the American Society for Psychical Research, 73,* 1–15.

———. (1979b). More on methodological issues in free-response psi experiments. *Journal of the American Society for Psychical Research, 73,* 395–401.

Light, R. J., & Smith, P. V. (1971). Accumulating evidence: Procedures for resolving contradictions among different research studies. *Harvard Educational Review, 41,* 429–471.

Mauskopf, S. H., & McVaugh, M. R. (1979). The controversy over statistics in parapsychology, 1934–1938. In S. H. Mauskopf (Ed.), *The reception of unconventional science* (pp. 105–123). Boulder, Colo.: Westview Press.

Palmer, J. (1983, August). In defense of parapsychology: A reply to James E. Alcock. *Zetetic Scholar,* No. 11, 39–70.

Parker, A. (1978). A holistic methodology in psi research. *Parapsychology Review,* **9** (2), 1–6.

Parker, A., & Wiklund, N. (1982). *The ganzfeld: A methodological evaluation of the claims for a repeatable ESP experiment.* Manuscript submitted for publication.

———. (1987). Ganzfeld experiments: toward an assessment. *Journal of the Society for Psychical Research,* **54,** 261-265.

Rhine, J. B., and Pratt, J. G. (1957). *Parapsychology: Frontier Science of the Mind.* Springfield, Ill.: C. C. Thomas.

Rogo, D. S. (1977, November/December). The case for parapsychology. *The Humanist,* **37,** 40–44.

Rosenthal, R. (1978). Combining results of independent studies. *Psychological Bulletin,* **85,** 185–193.

———. (1979). The "file drawer problem" and tolerance for null results. *Psychological Bulletin,* **86,** 638–641.

Sargent, C. L. (1980a). Exploring psi in the ganzfeld. *Parapsychological Monographs,* No. 17. New York: Parapsychology Foundation.

———. (1980b). [Letter to the editor]. *Journal of the American Society for Psychical Research,* **74,** 265–267.

Sondow, N. (1980). [Letter to the editor]. *Journal of the American Society for Psychical Research,* **74,** 267–272.

Appendix: The Ganzfeld Psi Data Base

The data base consists of 42 separate ganzfeld psi studies as defined by Charles Honorton (personal communication, November 30, 1981). These include all the studies conducted between 1974 and 1981 known to Honorton and meeting his criteria of acceptable ganzfeld psi studies. The studies are numbered for referencing in the text of the article. They are listed alphabetically. Because the same report sometimes describes more than one study, the reference is repeated separately for each study.

A list of coded descriptors follows each entry. These are defined briefly here but are described more fully in the text:

AT. Alternate tests used without adjusting significance.

DOC. Inadequate documentation, usually with respect to trials that differ on how the agent is related to the percipient.

E. Effect size defined as the difference in degrees between the transformed proportion of hits and transformed proportion expected by chance. Proportions were converted to degrees by the Freeman-Tukey arc sine transformation for binomial proportions (Freeman & Tukey, 1950). When the effect size is followed by a BH or a BC in parentheses, this indicates that it was calculated either on the basis of binary hits or binary coding, respectively. When neither of these descriptors is given, the effect size is based on direct hits. Where no effect size is given, it indicates that the report gave insufficient data for calculating an effect size.

FB. Inadequate randomization of target and foils at judging, or inadequate precautions against communication from percipient to agent at feedback.

IJ. Independent judges used in addition to subjects as own judges without adjusting significance.

MB. Multiple baselines (testing the same index against both a chance and a control baseline without adjusting significance).

MDV. Multiple dependent variables used without adjusting significance.

MG. Multiple groupings in testing for psi against control comparisons without adjusting significance.

*MI.*Multiple indices used without adjusting significance.

*NSIG-1.*Not classified as significant on the first (November 1981) data base.

*NSIG-2.*Not classified as significant after the June 1982 adjustments.

R(+). Appropriate randomization.

R(-). Inadequate randomization.

R(?). Randomization procedures inadequately described.

*SEC.*Inadequate security, usually in monitoring crucial phases of the study or in having only one experimenter.

*SIG-1.*Classified as significant overall on the primary index by Honorton at the .05 level as of November 30, 1981.

*SIG-2.*Classified as significant by Honorton after adjusting for multiple testing (personal communication, June 2, 1982).

*ST.*Single target used, allowing sensory cueing.

*STAT.*Inappropriate statistics, such as wrong degrees of freedom or failing to calculate *p* for Fisher's exact test appropriately.

*Z.*Critical ratio or normal deviate based on the effect size E and its theoretical standard deviation.

The Studies

1. Ashton, H. T., Dear, P. R., Harley, T. A., & Sargent, C. L. (1981). A four-subject study of psi in the ganzfeld. *Journal of the Society for Psychical Research,* **51,** 12–21. [Experiment 4 of Sargent, 1980]

SIG-1, NSIG-2, AT, MG, MI, R(?), DOC, E = 11.03, Z = 2.19

2. Braud, W. G., Wood, R., & Braud, L. W. (1975). Free-response GESP performance during an experimental hypnagogic state induced by visual and acoustic ganzfeld techniques: A replication and extension. *Journal of the American Society for Psychical Research,* **69,** 105–113.

SIG-1, SIG-2, MB, MI, R(?), ST, FB, SEC, E = 8.08, Z = 0.91

3. Braud, W. G., & Wood, R. (1977). The influence of immediate feedback on free-response GESP performance during ganzfeld stimulation. *Journal of the American Society for Psychical Research,* **71,** 409–427.

SIG-1, SIG-2, MB, MDV, MG, MI, R(?), ST, DOC, STAT, E = -2.82 (BH),
Z = -0.77

4. Child, I. L., & Levi, A. (1979). Psi-missing in free-response settings. *Journal of the American Society for Psychical Research,* **73,** 273–289.

SIG-1, NSIG-2, R(?), ST, FB, SEC, STAT, E = -20.43, Z = -2.71

5. Dunne, B. J., Warnock, E., & Bisaha, J. P. (1977). Ganzfeld techniques with independent rating for measuring GESP and precognition. In J. D. Morris, W. G. Roll, & R. L. Morris (Eds.), *Research in parapsychology, 1976* (pp. 41–43). Metuchen, N.J.: Scarecrow Press.

SIG-1, NSIG-2, MI, R(-), DOC

6. Habel, M. M. (1976). Varying auditory stimuli in the ganzfeld: The influence of sex and overcrowding on psi performance. In J. D. Morris, W. G. Roll, & R. L. Morris (Eds.), *Research in parapsychology, 1975* (pp. 181–184). Metuchen, N.J.: Scarecrow Press.

NSIG-1, NSIG-2, MG, R(?), ST, DOC, E = -0.63(BH), Z = -0.21

7. Honorton, C. (1976). Length of isolation and degree of arousal as probable

factors influencing information retrieval in the ganzfeld. In J. D. Morris, W. G. Roll, & R. L. Morris (Eds.), *Research in parapsychology 1975* (pp. 184–186). Metuchen, N.J.: Scarecrow Press.

  SIG-1, SIG-2, R(-), ST, FB, DOC, E = 32.76, Z = 3.13

  8. Honorton, C., & Harper, S. (1974). Psi-mediated imagery and ideation in an experimental procedure for regulating perceptual input. *Journal of the American Society for Psychical Research,* **68,** 156–168.

  SIG-1, SIG-2, R(-), ST, FB, DOC, SEC, E = 10.77, Z = 2.08

  9. Keane, P., & Wells, R. (1979). An examination of the menstrual cycle as a hormone related physiological concomitant of psi performance. In W. G. Roll (Ed.), *Research in parapsychology, 1978* (pp. 72–74). Metuchen, N.J.: Scarecrow Press.

  SIG-1, NSIG-2, MB, MDV, MG, R(+), DOC, STAT

  10. Palmer, J., & Aued, I. (1975). An ESP test with psychometric objects and the ganzfeld: Negative findings. In J. D. Morris, W. G. Roll, & R. L. Morris (Eds.), *Research in parapsychology, 1974* (pp. 50–53). Metuchen, N.J.: Scarecrow Press.

  NSIG-1, NSIG-2, MB, MG, MI, R(+), ST, SEC, E = -2.68, Z = -0.60

  11. Palmer, J., Bogart, D. N., Jones, S. M., & Tart, C. T. (1977). Scoring patterns in an ESP ganzfeld experiment. *Journal of the American Society for Psychical Research,* **71,** 121–145.

  NSIG-1, NSIG-2, MI, IJ, R(+), ST, E = -1.07, Z = -0.21

  12. Palmer, J., Khamashta, K., & Israelson, K. (1979). An ESP ganzfeld experiment with Transcendental Meditators. *Journal of the American Society for Psychical Research,* **73,** 333–348.

  NSIG-1, NSIG-2, MB, MI, IJ, R(+), ST, E = -10.67, Z = -1.69

  13. Palmer, J. Whitson, T., & Bogart, D. N. (1980). Ganzfeld and remote viewing: A systematic comparison. In W. G. Roll (Ed.), *Research in parapsychology, 1979,* (pp. 169–171). Metuchen, N.J.: Scarecrow Press.

  NSIG-1, NSIG-2, MG, R(+)

  14. Parker, A. (1975). Some findings relevant to the change in state hypothesis. In J. D. Morris, W. G. Roll, & R. L. Morris, (Eds.), *Research in parapsychology, 1974* (pp. 40–42). Metuchen, N.J.: Scarecrow Press.

  NSIG-1, NSIG-2, MG, R(?), ST, SEC, E = -7.48(BH), Z = -1.44

  15. Parker, A., Millar, B., & Beloff, J. (1977). A three-experimenter ganzfeld: An attempt to use the ganzfeld technique to study the experimenter effect. In J. D. Morris, W. G. Roll, & R. L. Morris (Eds.), *Research in parapsychology, 1976*(pp. 52–54). Metuchen, N. J.: Scarecrow Press.

  NSIG-1, NSIG-2, MG, R(+), DOC

  16. Raburn, L. (1975). *Expectation and transmission factors in psychic functioning.* Unpublished honors thesis, Tulane University, New Orleans, La. [Experiment 1 = Cell with informed Ss and an agent].

  SIG-1, SIG-2, AT, MG, R(-), ST, FB, DOC, SEC, STAT, E = 37.20, Z = 4.21

  17. *Ibid.* [Experiment 2 = Cell with informed subjects but no agent]

  NSIG-1, NSIG-2, AT, MG, R(-), ST, FB, DOC, SEC, STAT, E = 8.33, Z = 0.94

  18. Rogo, D. S. (1976). ESP in the ganzfeld: An exploration of parameters. In J. D. Morris, W. G. Roll, & R. L. Morris, (Eds.), *Research in parapsychology, 1975* (pp. 174–176). Metuchen, N.J.: Scarecrow Press. [Experiment 1]

  NSIG-1, NSIG-2, MI, R(-), ST, DOC, E = 2.21, Z = 0.41

  19. *Ibid.* [Experiment 2]

  NSIG-1, NSIG-2, MI, R(-), ST, DOC, SEC, E = 8.33, Z = 0.94

  20. Rogo, D. S. (1977). A preliminary study of precognition in the ganzfeld. *European Journal of Parapsychology,* **2** (1), 60–67.

  NSIG-1, NSIG-2, AT, MG, R(+), E = -3.72(BC), Z = -1.84

21. Rogo, D. S., Smith, M., & Terry, J. (1976). The use of short-duration ganzfeld stimulation to facilitate psi-mediated imagery. *European Journal of Parapsychology,* **1,** 72–77.
    NSIG-1, NSIG-2, MI, R(–), ST, FB, DOC, E = 5.93, Z = 0.94
*22. Roney-Dougal, S. M. (1982). A comparison of psi and subliminal perception: A confirmatory study. In *Research in parapsychology, 1981* (pp. 96–99). Metuchen, N.J.: Scarecrow Press.
    SIG-1, NSIG-2, MB, MG, MI, IJ, R(?), DOC, SEC, STAT, E = 6.09, Z = 1.35
23. Sargent, C. L. (1980). Exploring psi in the ganzfeld. *Parapsychological Monographs,* No. 17. [Experiment 1]
    NSIG-1, NSIG-2, MI, R(–), E = -3.53, Z = 0.63
24. *Ibid.* [Experiment 2]
    SIG-1, SIG-2, MI, R(?), E = 11.51, Z = 1.82
25. *Ibid.* [Experiment 3]
    SIG-1, NSIG-2, MI, R(?), E = 11.51, Z = 1.82
26. *Ibid.* [Experiment 5]
    SIG-1, SIG-2, MB, MI, R(?), E = 16.33, Z = 3.15
27. *Ibid.* [Experiment 6]
    NSIG-1, NSIG-2, MB, MG, MI, R(?), E = 5.10, Z = 1.07
*28. Sargent, C. L., Bartlet, H. J., & Moss, S. P. (1982). Rsesponse structure and temporal incline in ganzfeld free-response GESP testing. In W. G. Roll, R. L. Morris, & R. A. White (Eds.), *Research in parapsychology, 1981* (pp. 79–81). Metuchen, N.J.: Scarecrow Press.
    SIG-1, NSIG-2, MG, MI, IJ, R(?), DOC, E = 1.95, Z = 0.39
29. Sargent, C. L., Harley, T. A., Lane, J., & Radcliffe, K. (1981). Ganzfeld psi-optimization in relation to session duration. In W. G. Roll, & J. Beloff (Eds.), *Research in parapsychology, 1980* (pp. 82–84). Metuchen, N.J.: Scarecrow Press.
    NSIG-1, NSIG-2, MB, MG, MI, R(?), DOC, E = 1.58. Z = 0.35
*30. Sargent, C., & Matthews, G. (1982). Ganzfeld GESP performance in variable duration testing. In W. G. Roll, R. L. Morris, & R. A. White (Eds.), *Research in parapsychology, 1981* (pp. 159–60). Metuchen, N.J.: Scarecrow Press.
    SIG-1, SIG-2, MB, MG, MI, R(?), DOC, E = 12.28, Z = 2.21
31. Schmitt, M., & Stanford, R. G. (1978). Free-response ESP during ganzfeld stimulation: The possible influence of the menstrual cycle phase. *Journal of the American Society for Psychical Research,* **72,** 177–182.
    SIG-1, SIG-2, MB, MG, R(+), ST, STAT, E = 19.74, Z = 3.12
32. Smith, M., Tremmel, L., & Honorton, C. (1976). A comparison of psi and weak sensory influences on ganzfeld mentation. In J. D. Morris, W. G. Roll, & R. L. Morris (Eds.), *Research in parapsychology, 1975* (pp. 191–194). Metuchen, N.J.: Scarecrow Press.
    SIG-1, SIG-2, MG, R(–), DOC, STAT, E = 3.01(BC), Z = 2.10
33. Sondow, N. (1979). Effects of associations and feedback on psi in the ganzfeld: Is there more than meets the judge's eye? *Journal of the American Society for Psychical Research,* **73,** 123–150.
    SIG-1, SIG-2, AT, MB, MG, IJ, R(–), ST, FB, DOC, STAT, E = -9.70, Z = 3.40
*34. Sondow, N., Braud, L., & Barker, P. (1982). Target qualities and affect measures in an exploratory psi ganzfeld. In W. G. Roll, R. L. Morris, & R. A. White (Eds.),

---

*At the time this report was written, I had access to the paper as submitted rather than the version published in *Research in Parapsychology.* I assume that the two versions differ in no essential respect.

Research in parapsychology, 1981 (pp. 82–85). Metuchen, N.J.: Scarecrow Press.
  SIG-1, NSIG-2, MB, MG, MI, R(+), DOC, STAT, E = 4.62, Z = 1.03

35. Stanford, R. G. (1979). The influence of auditory ganzfeld characteristics upon free-response ESP performance. *Journal of the American Society for Psychical Research,* **73,** 253–272.
  NSIG-1, NSIG-2, MB, MDV, MG, R(+), STAT

36. Stanford, R. G., & Neylon, A. (1975). Experiential factors related to free-response clairvoyance performance in a sensory uniformity setting (ganzfeld). In J. D. Morris, W. G. Roll, & R. L. Morris (Eds.), *Research in parapsychology, 1974* (pp. 89–93). Metuchen, N.J.: Scarecrow Press.
  NSIG-1, NSIG-2, MB, MG, R(+), ST

37. Terry, J. C. (1976). Comparison of stimulus duration in sensory and psi conditions. In J. D. Morris, W. G. Roll, & R. L. Morris (Eds.), *Research in parapsychology, 1975* (pp. 179–181). Metuchen, N.J.: Scarecrow Press.
  NSIG-1, NSIG-2, MG, R(–), E = –0.34(BC), Z = –0.22

38. Terry, J. C., & Honorton, C. (1976). Psi information retrieval in the ganzfeld: Two confirmatory studies. *Journal of the American Society for Psychical Research,* **70,** 207–217. [Experiment 1]
  SIG-1, SIG-2, MG, MI, R(–), ST, FB, DOC, E = 9.28, Z = 1.70

39. *Ibid.* [Experiment 2]
  SIG-1, SIG-2, MG, MI, R(–), ST, FB, DOC, E = 11.91, Z = 3.23

40. Terry, J., Tremmel, L., Kelly, M., Harper, S., & Barker, P. L. (1976). Psi information rate in guessing and receiver optimization. In J. D. Morris, W. G. Roll, & R. L. Morris (Eds.), *Research in parapsychology, 1975* (pp. 194–198). Metuchen, N.J.: Scarecrow Press.
  SIG-1, SIG-2, MB, R(–), DOC, STAT, E = 4.19(BC), Z = 1.80

41. Wood, R., Kirk, J., & Braud, W. (1977). Free response GESP performance following ganzfeld stimulation vs. induced relaxation, with verbalized vs. nonverbalized mentation: A failure to replicate. *European Journal of Parapsychology,* **1,** 80–93.
  NSIG-1, NSIG-2, MB, MG, MI, R(–), ST, DOC, SEC, E = -2.76, Z = -0.67

42. York, M. (1977). The defense mechanism test (DMT) as an indicator of psychic performance as measured by a free-response clairvoyance test using a ganzfeld technique. In J. D. Morris, W. G. Roll, & R. L. Morris (Eds.), *Research in parapsychology, 1976* (pp. 48–49). Metuchen, N.J.: Scarecrow Press.
  SIG-1, SIG-2, MI, R(?), ST, DOC, E = 11.07, Z = 2.72

A Joint Communiqué:
The Psi Ganzfeld Controversy*

(with Charles Honorton)

ABSTRACT: Instead of continuing with another round of our debate on the psi ganzfeld experiments, we decided to collaborate on a joint communiqué. The Honorton-Hyman debate emphasized the differences in our positions, many of these being technical in nature. But during a recent discussion, we realized that we possessed similar viewpoints on many issues concerning parapsychological research. This communiqué, then, emphasizes these points of agreement. We agree that there is an overall significant effect in this data base that cannot reasonably be explained by selective reporting or multiple analysis. We continue to differ over the degree to which the effect constitutes evidence for psi, but we agree that the final verdict awaits the outcome of future experiments conducted by a broader range of investigators and according to more stringent standards. We make recommendations about how such experiments should be conducted and reported. Specific recommendations are about randomization, judging and feedback procedures, multiple analysis and statistics, documentation, and the growing role we believe meta-analysis will play in the evaluation of research quality and the assessment of moderating variables. We conclude that psi researchers and their critics share many common goals, and we hope that our joint communiqué will encourage future cooperation to further these goals.

The *Journal of Parapsychology* had planned to publish one more exchange between us on the debate that we initiated in the March 1985 issue (Honorton, 1985; Hyman, 1985). In fact, one of us had already written and submitted

---

Journal of Parapsychology 50 (December 1986), 351–64. Reprinted by permission.

his reply, and the other was preparing a rejoinder when we encountered each other at the 1986 meeting of the Parapsychological Association. The idea of replacing another round of exchanges with this joint communiqué emerged from a discussion during a luncheon meeting.[1] During the discussion we realized that each of us had not fully and accurately understood the other's position on some of the major issues dividing us.[2] In addition, much of our disagreement at this stage involves technicalities and differences of opinion about the proper ways to assign and rate studies on specific attributes. To put emphasis on these details detracts from the broader and more important propositions, on which we find ourselves in agreement.

These propositions relate in general to how psi researchers and critics can work together toward the resolution of their differences. Specifically, they relate to how we believe psi ganzfeld experiments should be conducted and reported in the future.

General Areas of Agreement

As in any other area of scientific inquiry, research in parapsychology requires continual scrutiny and criticism. Both critics and parapsychologists want parapsychological research to be conducted according to the best possible standards. Critics can contribute to this need only if their criticisms are informed, relevant, and responsible.

As to the psi ganzfeld data base, we agree, as our earlier exchanges indicate (Honorton, 1983, 1985; Hyman, 1983, 1985), that the experiments as a group departed from ideal standards on aspects such as multiple testing, randomization of targets, controlling for sensory leakage, applicaton of statistical tests, and documentation. Although we probably still differ about the extent and seriousness of these departures, we agree that future psi ganzfeld experiments should be conducted in accordance with these ideals. In the second section of this joint communiqué, we shall make a number of specific recommendations about the conduct and documentation of future psi ganzfeld studies. It is our hope that these recommendations will lay the groundwork for a new round of studies that will serve to resolve the differences remaining between us.

Although we probably still differ on the magnitude of the biases contributed by multiple testing, retrospective experiments, and the file-drawer problem, we agree that the overall significance observed in these studies cannot reasonably be explained by these selective factors. Something beyond selective reporting or inflated significance levels seems to be producing the nonchance outcomes. Moreover, we agree that the significant outcomes have been produced by a number of different investigators.

Whereas we continue to differ over the degree to which the current ganzfeld data base contributes evidence for psi,[3] we agree that the final verdict awaits the outcome of future psi ganzfeld experiments—ones conducted by a broader range of investigators and according to more stringent standards.

The strongest disagreements between us might appear to be over the relationship in the data base between "flaws" and study outcome. Honorton finds no significant correlation between indices of study quality and study outcome. Hyman agrees that there is no significant correlation between study outcome and some procedural indicators, such as multiple analysis, sensory leakage, statistics, and security. But he finds a positive correlation between study outcome and other procedural indicators, such as suboptimal randomization, feedback, and inadequate documentation.

Which correlation one obtains depends on how the "flaws" are assigned to individual studies, how one orders the seriousness of flaws when constructing scales, how many different attributes are included as flaws, and similar judgments. But these differences, no matter how controversial, should not be allowed to obscure our agreement that the present data base does not support any firm conclusion about the relationship between flaws and study outcome. Our disagreements about the actual correlation only emphasize this point.

If psi is responsible for the outcomes obtained in this data base, then the ganzfeld experiment should continue to produce successful outcomes when the various problems that Hyman pointed out are eliminated. Indeed, what differentiates the ganzfeld debate from many earlier controversies between psi researchers and critics is that the claim is one of replicability. Consequently, the best way to resolve the controversy between us is to await the outcome of future ganzfeld psi experiments. These experiments, ideally, will be carried out in such a way as to circumvent the file-drawer problem, problems of multiple analysis, and the various defects in randomization, statistical application, and documentation pointed out by Hyman. If a variety of parapsychologists and other investigators continue to obtain significant results under these conditions, then the existence of a genuine communications anomaly will have been demonstrated. The demonstration of an anomaly, of course, does not explain it. Such a demonstration would, however, be very important because it would require acknowledgment that there is, indeed, something to be explained, and the debate would then shift toward such efforts. Whether the anomaly is ultimately to be considered "paranormal" will, as Palmer (1986) suggests, depend on further developments such as the extent to which the findings can be brought under lawful control and the construction of a positive theory of the paranormal.

On the other hand, if the findings can all be attributed to various artifacts, this too is important to determine. Discovering the nature of such artifacts and how they are produced could have important methodological implications for all scientific inquiry. Thus, we agree that further research in this area is important, not only for parapsychology, but for science generally. And we believe it is essential, in order to develop a clear picture of what is actually going on, that the research should be conducted not only by parapsychologists, but by a range of investigators with diverse opinions concerning psi. Studies conducted by investigators who are skeptical of the psi hypothesis would be particularly useful from a number of perspectives. It is possible, for instance, that such studies might reveal potential sources of artifact that have been overlooked or that are not obvious from analysis of existing research reports. Further, investigators favoring conventional explanations of parapsychological findings could contribute substantially to a resolution of the psi controversy by systematically testing and delimiting the explanatory power of various proposed alternative hypotheses (Palmer, 1986).

Finally, before moving on to our recommendations for future psi ganzfeld studies, we believe it is appropriate to say a few words about the process in which we are engaged. As is evident from what has been said above, there are areas in which we continue to disagree. We agree to disagree. Even though our continuing disagreements about the degree to which the existing studies in this area contribute evidence for psi, for example, are not inconsequential, we fully respect each other's position and we disassociate ourselves from the more strident advocates on both sides of the psi controversy who would label those with opposing views by such pejoratives as "prejudiced," "credulous," and "irrational."

Recommendations for Future Psi Ganzfeld Experiments

Although much of what we say in this section might also apply to other areas of parapsychological research, we will make our recommendations specific to the ganzfeld psi experiment and its data base that we discussed previously (Honorton, 1985; Hyman, 1985). The recommendations are intended to illustrate what a parapsychologist and a critic might accomplish when trying to seek common grounds for agreement. What follows are specific recommendations to parapsychologists and other investigators who intend to conduct a ganzfeld psi experiment.

Control for Sensory Leakage

We agree that future investigators should strive to eliminate all possibilities for sensory communication between sender and receiver—both during the ganzfeld session and at judging. The typical two-experimenter psi ganzfeld experiment effectively eliminates sensory leakage during the actual ganzfeld period. The use of duplicate target pools or the binary coding system (Honorton, 1975) guards against sensory leakage at the time of judging. Proper attention to monitoring and recording the actual target should undermine the possibility, suggested by Hyman, of leakage from receiver to sender during feedback. Fortunately, the use of single target pools has disappeared in recent ganzfeld psi experiments.

Randomization of Targets

We agree that more careful attention needs to be given to the procedures for selecting targets and that the procedures should be thoroughly documented.

The method of target selection should be described in full. The following details should be included: (a) the person performing the randomization, (b) the specific source of randomness, (c) the method of sampling the random source (*i.e.,* obtaining entry points for random number tables, seeds for pseudorandom generators, or specific values for hardware random generators). To illustrate what we agree would constitute adequate documentation of randomization procedures for each of the above random sources, consider a hypothetical ganzfeld experiment involving 20 target pools of four pictures each:

> Target preparation was performed by R. H., a member of the laboratory staff who was not otherwise involved in the experiment. . . .
> *Random number tables.* Pools and targets were selected using the RAND tables (RAND Corporation, 1955). An entry point into the RAND table was obtained for each session as follows. The first digit of the row was determined by coin toss ("heads" = 0, "tails" = 1). A deck of numbered cards (0–9) was then shuffled and cut four times. The uppermost card for each iteration provided subsequent digits for the row. The block (0–9) was then determined by again shuffling the numbered deck. Cards bearing the digits 6–9 and 0 were then removed from the deck, which was again shuffled to determine the specific column (1–5) within the block. The first two digits within the range 01–20 thus provided the pool for the session. R. H. then removed the appropriate judging pool and left it where it could be retrieved by the experimenter. Only after this was done was the actual target for the session determined. This was done by repeating the above procedure and obtaining the first digit within the range 1–4.
> *Pseudorandom generators.* Pools and targets were selected using the random number generator function in the Applied Statistics module of a Texas Instruments TI 59 Programmable Calculator (Texas Instruments, 1977). The seed was obtained by subtracting the six digits composing the subject's birthdate from the six digits composing the date of the session. A uniform random number within the range of 1–20 provided the pool

for the session. R. H. then removed the appropriate judging pool and left it where it could be retrieved by the experimenter. Only after this was done was the actual target for the session determined. The next random digit within the range of 1–4 was the target.

Hardware random number generators. The targets were selected using a PsiLab II random number generator interfaced to an Apple II computer (Psychophysical Research Laboratories, 1984). A BASIC program sampled the RNG, such that the first byte value returned within the range of 1–20 was the pool. R. H. then removed the appropriate judging pool and left it where it could be retrieved by the experimenter. Only after this was done was the actual target for the session determined. This was done by repeating the above procedure and obtaining the first digit within the range of 1–4.

Although random number generators are often today more convenient than tables of random numbers, several caveats are in order regarding their use in serious research applications. In general, we do not recommend use of microcomputer random functions. The algorithms used are generally not documented, and some have been shown to produce spurious results (*e.g.,* Hansen, 1986). A good discussion of the characteristics of some of the more widely used pseudorandom algorithms is given in Radin (1985). Hardware random number generators can have design flaws or may develop intermittent problems that will lead them to fail. And even though a brief description of the circuitry and its theory of operation is desirable, technical descriptions of the hardware cannot be substituted for empirical tests of the output. Ideally, randomness tests would be done on the actual targets used in an experimental series. However, owing to the typically small sample of psi ganzfeld studies, such tests would be of little value. Control tests should be reported to ensure adequate randomness of the targets. Because ganzfeld experiments involve only one target selection per session, sequential bias is not likely to be an issue as it could be in other areas of psi research, and the ganzfeld investigator can restrict his or her attention to a frequency analysis allowing assessment of the degree to which targets occur with equal probability. A good discussion of randomness tests is given by Davis and Akers (1974).

Hyman believes that the best way to assure adequate randomization is to include empirical, in addition to the usual theoretical, baselines. One way to do this would be to systematically compare the percipient's first choice both against the intended target and against the intended target for a control trial (which could be the actual trial for another percipient). If the randomization procedure is adequate, the control comparisons should produce observed means and standard deviations consistent with the theoretical distribution on the null hypothesis. This recommendation is identical to the "cross check" method used in the early card-guessing experiments (Rhine *et al.,* 1940/1966, p. 46).

Judging and Feedback

We agree that the judging and feedback procedures should be presented in greater detail than has generally been the practice in past ganzfeld studies. Specifically, the report should explicitly document the following procedures: (a) the manner in which persons knowing the identity of the actual target (*i.e.,* the sender and sender's experimenter) remain isolated from the receiver and receiver's experimenter until completion of judging; (b) the instructions given to the receiver for judging; (c) how the judging pool is presented to the subject; (d) the manner in which the subject's ranks or ratings are recorded; and (e) how feedback to the actual target is delivered at completion of the subject's judging.

Multiple Analysis

The problem of multiple analysis pervades all the sciences. Determining the size of the total critical region is often difficult even when the investigator has conscientiously set out in advance the tests that will be made. More typically the investigator has a more or less general idea of the hypotheses to be tested, but the precise details have not been worked out in advance. Under these conditions, the precise indices, cutting points, and tests are constructed after the data have been collected and assembled. The temptation is strong to tailor the specifics of the testing to the peculiarities of the data.

Even though it is not possible to make a generalized recommendation that will meet all contingencies, clearly investigators should specify all the confirmatory tests, as well as the precise critical region in advance of collecting the data, and such specification of confirmatory tests should be explicitly stated in the experimental report. Adherence to this recommendation should not be taken as being inconsistent with exploratory data analysis. The point of the recommendation is to prevent confusion between confirmatory tests and suggestive findings that require confirmation by future experiments. When multiple tests are planned, appropriate adjustments should be made to keep the total overall error rate within the commonly accepted region. One approach involves using the Bonferroni inequality (*e.g.,* Rosenthal & Rubin, 1984).

We recommend that future investigators consider the possibility of increasing statistical power by using, with appropriate adjustments, two or more of the several indices that have been used as indicators in psi ganzfeld experiments.

Hyman believes either theoretical or empirical investigations might suggest that a linear combination of two or more of these indices could usefully increase statistical power. Or, it might turn out that more power can be achieved by performing separate tests on two or more of these indicators and then adjusting the overall level of significance appropriately. It is not clear at this time what might be the best combination. If the investigator decides to use just two indices, for example, statistical considerations might suggest choosing those two that are least correlated. This would argue for using both direct hits and binary hits. Simulation studies by Hyman indicate that these two measures correlate 0.61, whereas the intercorrelations between any other pair of the most common indicators are approximately 0.80 or higher. On the other hand, the studies in the current data base that used binary hits rather than direct hits appeared to yield less impressive results. Those studies that used the special slide pool allowing use of Honorton's binary coding system (Honorton, 1975) indicate that the resulting index is uncorrelated with the four major indices of direct hits, binary hits, sum of ranks, and normalized ratings. However, the binary coding index also seems to yield smaller and less significant effects (Hyman, 1985).

Honorton believes a good case can be made for using both direct hits and sum of ranks measures. Because the two measures are discretely distributed, the penalty required for using both is minimal. Consider, for example, a study involving 20 trials and a hit probability of .25. If alpha is set to .05 and the direct hits measure alone is used, a significant outcome will be achieved with 9 or more direct hits (p = .041). If the sum of ranks measure alone is used, significance will be achieved with a sum of ranks equal to or less than 41 (p = .036). If both indices, adjusted by the Bonferroni method, are used, significance will be achieved by either 10 direct hits or a sum of ranks equal to 40. Thus, the added flexibility achieved by allowing use of either measure is, in this case, purchased at a cost amounting to one additional direct hit. The Bonferroni method is overly conservative. As Hyman's simulation shows, direct hits and sum of ranks are highly correlated. Hansen (1986) has recently reported a simulation study involving these two measures and is preparing tables for various sample sizes that will provide more accurate p levels for the use of both direct hits and sum of ranks.

File-Drawer and Retrospective Experiments

Given the Parapsychological Association's policy of actively discouraging the selective reporting of "positive" results, the file-drawer problem is probably less acute in parapsychology than it is in many other scientific disciplines. Certainly reports of nonsignificant outcomes are far more common in the parapsychological literature than in other areas of psychology. This is not to imply, however, that the file-drawer problem is nonexistent in parapsychology. Investigators should bear in mind that registration of statistically nonsignificant outcomes is essential to the development of a realistic appraisal of a research area and that a study's value is independent of its statistical significance.

As to Hyman's suggestion concerning "retrospective" experiments, we recommend that along with specifying the critical region, the investigator should also specify in advance the status of the experiment. Designations such as *classroom exercise, confirmatory experiment,* or *process-oriented* will help future reviewers to classify and properly evaluate the results.

Statistics

Over 20% of the experiments in the meta-analytic sample of 28 studies contained errors in the use of statistical tests. Although some of these errors may not have had serious consequences, their existence should be a cause for concern to the parapsychological community. We believe that the parapsychological journals, along with the authors, share responsibility for ensuring the adequacy of statistical tests used in empirical contributions and that some of these problems could be avoided if authors adhered to the following recommendations printed on the inside back cover of the *Journal of Parapsychology:*

> 1. State concisely the precise statistical formulation of the hypothesis being tested and list it in advance of the results section. It is recommended that the type of statistical tests that are planned be given along with the hypothesis.
> 2. For any statistical analysis that was not preplanned, give a brief statement of why it was done; the probability value should be placed close enough to this statement that its association is obvious.
> 3. When statistical analyses are done, report not only the inferential statistics (e.g., t values) but also the descriptive statistics for the data evaluated (e.g., group means and standard deviations). Also, report the actual values of correlation coefficients, not simply that a correlation is significant or nonsignificant.
> 4. Have the data and statistical analyses independently rechecked before submitting the paper.

Documentation

In general, we believe that readers (including research analysts and prospective replicators) should be able to reconstruct the author's procedures from the descriptions provided in the experimental report. Although this is not common practice in science generally, we believe it is important in areas such as parapsychology where routine replicability cannot be taken for granted. More detailed exposition of methods and procedures should serve not only to aid evaluation of research quality, but also to increase the likelihood that other investigators will be able to replicate the original investigator's results successfully. As for future ganzfeld psi experiments, we recommend that, in addition to the procedural details described above, investigators routinely supply information on the following: the training, supervision, and qualifications of student experimenters; information on the subject population, including sources of subject recruitment and prior psi-testing experience; the individual ranks and target selection; the acquaintanceship of sender and receiver; the status of the experiment (confirmatory, exploratory, exercise, etc.); and similar information that is germane to the evaluation and replication of the study.

The Role of Meta-Analysis

The standards and recommendations we have discussed so far, for the most part, apply to the individual experiment. Indeed, almost all the guidelines for doing good research are aimed at the individual experiment. And the statistical procedures have been developed and taught with the idea that they apply to the evaluation of a single experiment. But scientific inquiry is cumulative, and the outcome of a single experiment rarely, if ever, determines the acceptance or rejection of laws and theories. Science progresses by the cumulative outcomes of many experiments done by many investigators.

This fact has been recognized in the contemporary interest in the development of formal techniques for the statistical integration of a series of experiments. The field of meta-analysis is still in its infancy and somewhat controversial. Some of the controversy, as reflected in our debate, deals with the extent to which meta-analysis can compensate for the individual inadequacies of the specific experiments that are included in the data base.

Nevertheless, meta-analysis realistically emphasizes that scientific evidence rests on the consistency of results across many experiments. Before the focus on meta-analysis, the individual investigator designed, conducted, and reported the results with little, if any, consideration of how this particular experiment fit into a larger series of experiments.

Our next recommendation takes into account the growing role we believe meta-analysis will play, both in the evaluation of research quality and in the assessment of moderating variables. We urge parapsychological investigators to plan and report their experiments with the idea that their single experiment will contribute to a future meta-analysis. Much of this information could be encapsulated in summary tables at the end of the research report, as illustrated by Table 1.

Table 1
Illustrative Study Summary

				Subject information						
Session	ID	Recru	Belief	Pract	Test	Gz	Acq	Tgt	Resp	Rank
1	1	AD	7	1	1	0	0	3B	3D	2
2	2	ST	2	0	0	0	0	11A	11A	1
3	3	OS	5	1	0	0	0	6C	6B	3
4	4	EA	3	0	1	1	1	1D	1D	1
5	5	VI	6	1	1	0	2	17C	17A	4
•	•	•	•	•	•	•	•	•	•	•
•	•	•	•	•	•	•	•	•	•	•
•	•	•	•	•	•	•	•	•	•	•
•	•	•	•	•	•	•	•	•	•	•

Note. Abbreviations are defined as follows:
ID = subject ID.
Recru = source of subject recruitment.
AD = response to newspaper ad.
ST = student volunteer.
OS = recruited by other subjects.
EA = acquaintance or friend of experimenter.
VI = laboratory visitor.
Belief = belief in psi (1 = low, 7 = high).
Pract = practices such as meditation (0 = no, 1= yes).
Test = prior psi-testing experience; not ganzfeld (0 = no, 1 = yes).
Gz = prior psi ganzfeld experience.
Acq = sender/receiver acquaintance.
    0 = none; sender is laboratory staff member not previously acquainted with subject.
    1 = lab friend; subject is a friend/acquaintance of laboratory staff member serving as sender.
    2 = friend; sender is a friend/acquaintance of the subject.
Tgt = pool and target for session (e.g., 3A = Pool 3, element 'A').
Resp = pool element selected as first choice by subject.

Conclusion

In making these recommendations, we recognize the need to distinguish between ideals and practicality. We believe that the above recommendations are consistent with what is realistically attainable given the current resources of parapsychology. The psi ganzfeld paradigm is now over a decade old, and though the need for innovation and individual creativity is as great as ever, we believe there is also a need for greater discipline and standardization. We hope that parapsychological investigators and journal editors will welcome our suggestions and view them as a constructive step forward—one that, with their active cooperation, could lead to a broader based consensus on at least the basic empirical "facts."

Our final recommendation, unlike the others, is probably not feasible under present circumstances, but it is proposed here only to indicate how many of the problems under debate could be avoided if certain ideals could be achieved.

Many of the problems we encountered in evaluating the ganzfeld psi experiments could be avoided in future experiments if the reviewers could be sure that they were dealing with the entire population of relevant studies and could ensure the internal validity of those studies. Ideally, the best way to achieve this would be to sponsor a systematic replication series under the auspices of a neutral agency such as the National Science Foundation. The sponsoring agency would establish guidelines and rules based on the joint recommendations of successful investigators and knowledgeable critics. The guidelines would then delimit the experimental designs, the investigator-base, and the time frame for the experimental series, as well as the basic framework for a subsequent meta-analysis of the series as a whole.

The writing of this joint communiqué convinces us that, despite obvious differences, parapsychologists and their critics share many common objectives. These commonalities rarely are noticed in the debates, which focus on the differences. Yet such commonalities hold the key for how the parapsychologist and the critic can join forces to achieve the ends to which they both aspire.

Notes

1. Marcello Truzzi participated in this discussion. We would like to thank him for his encouragement and suggestions.

2. To the best of our knowledge, this is the first time a parapsychologist and a critic have collaborated on a joint statement of this type. Hyman prepared the first draft and we continued exchanging drafts until we had one we were both satisfied with. For those who are interested, the final product is draft 4.

3. The term *psi phenomena* was introduced by Thouless and Wiesner as a neutral label denoting unexplained interactions between organisms and their environment. Their intention was to avoid the surplus meaning associated with terms such as *extrasensory perception*. Although this usage is generally understood within parapsychology, the term *psi* has unfortunately taken on broader connotations within the popular culture. Even within parapsychology, the terms *psi* and *paranormal* are sometimes used interchangeably

and in a way that confuses description with explanation.

Consistent with the original usage, the term *psi* in this paper simply denotes a communications anomaly. No particular explanation of the anomaly is intended, nor do we believe any is warranted at the present time. We suggest that communication between parapsychologists and other scientists could be improved if this distinction were maintained.

References

Davis, J. W., & Akers, C. (1974). Randomization and tests for randomness. *Journal of Parapsychology, 38,* 393–407.

Hansen, G. (1986). *Monte Carlo methods in psi research.* Paper presented at the 29th Annual Convention of the Parapsychological Association.

Honorton, C. (1975). Objective determination of information rate in psi tasks with pictorial stimuli. *Journal of the American Society for Psychical Research, 69,* 353–359.

Honorton, C. (1983). Response to Hyman's critique of psi ganzfeld studies. In W. G. Roll, J. Beloff, & R. A. White (Eds.), *Research in parapsychology 1982* (pp. 23–26). Metuchen, N.J.: Scarecrow Press.

Honorton, C. (1985). Meta-analysis of psi ganzfeld research: A response to Hyman. *Journal of Parapsychology, 49,* 51–91.

Hyman, R. (1983). Does the ganzfeld experiment answer the critics' objections? In W. G. Roll, J. Beloff, & R. A. White (eds.), *Research in parapsychology 1982* (pp. 21–23). Metuchen, N.J.: Scarecrow Press.

Hyman, R. (1985). The ganzfeld psi experiment: A critical appraisal. *Journal of Parapsychology, 49,* 3–49.

Palmer, J. (1986). Progressive skepticism: A critical approach to the psi controversy. *Journal of Parapsychology, 50,* 29–42.

Psychophysical Research Laboratories. (1984). *PsiLab II user's manual,* Princeton, N.J.: Psychophysical Research Laboratories.

Radin, D. (1985). Pseudorandom number generators in psi research. *Journal of Parapsychology, 49,* 303–328.

RAND Corporation. (1955). *A million random digits with 100,000 normal deviates.* New York: The Free Press.

Rhine, J. B., Pratt, J. G., Smith, B. M., Stuart, C. E., & Greenwood, J. A. (1940/1966). *Extra-sensory perception after sixty years.* Boston: Bruce Humphries.

Rosenthal, R., & Rubin, D. B. (1984). Multiple contrasts and ordered Bonferroni procedures. *Journal of Educational Psychology, 76,* 1028–1034.

Texas Instruments. (1977). *Applied Statistics.* Lubbock, Tex.: Texas Instruments Inc.

Parapsychological Research: A Tutorial Review and Critical Appraisal*

ABSTRACT: Beginning in the 1850s, some eminent scientists, such as Robert Hare, Alfred Russel Wallace, and Sir William Crookes, investigated the claims of spiritualist mediums and believed that they had demonstrated scientifically the existence of psychic phenomena. Critics, without examining the evidence, dismissed the claims out of hand and charged the offending scientists with gross incompetence or fraud. Encouraged by the work of these early psychical researchers, a group of scholars founded the Society for Psychical Research in London in 1882. In spite of this beginning, psychical research remained an amateur and uncoordinated set of activities until the publication of Rhine's *Extra-Sensory Perception* in 1934. The card-guessing experiments featured in Rhine's book became the model for experimental parapsychology for the next forty years. Since the 1970s Rhine's paradigm has been replaced by a number of research programs such as remote viewing, the ganzfeld experiment, and psychokinetic investigations using random event generators. The present paper examines examples of what were considered, in their time, the best examples of scientific evidence for paranormal phenomena. Each generation of parapsychologists has set aside the work of earlier generations and offered up as sufficient scientific evidence the best work of its own day. As a result, parapsychology lacks not only lawful and replicable phenomena, but also a tradition of cumulative evidence. Two systematic evaluations of the best contemporary research programs in parapsychology revealed that the experiments departed from the minimal standards of adequate randomization of targets, appropriate use of statistical inference, and controls against sensory leakage. The historical survey in this paper suggests that the same themes and inadequacies that haunted the very earliest investigations still characterize contemporary parapsychological research. Both proponents and critics, throughout the 130 years of the controversy over psychical research,

*© 1986 IEEE. Reprinted, with permission, from *Proceedings of the IEEE.* Vol. 74, No. 6, pp. 823-849, June 1986.

have deviated greatly from those standards of fair play and rationality that we would like to believe characterize the best scientific arguments. Some encouraging signs for progress towards resolving some of the issues raised by the controversy have recently appeared. The criticism of the parapsychological claims is becoming more informed and constructive. Many younger parapsychologists have been working for higher standards within their field. The best lines of systematic research in parapsychology are not of sufficient quality to be put before the scrutiny of the rest of the scientific community. However, with the recent increase in constructive criticism and with the growing awareness within the parapsychological community that it needs to specify minimal standards and set its own house in order, there is hope that in the near future either the parapsychologists will fail to find evidence for psi or will be ready to challenge the scientific community with the sort of evidence that it cannot ignore.

Robert Jahn, dean of the School of Engineering and Applied Science at Princeton University, can be taken as a representative example of what happens when an eminent and established scientist takes the time to examine carefully the evidence for paranormal phenomena. About seven years ago, an undergraduate requested him to supervise her investigation of psychic phenomena [1].

> Although I had no previous experience, professional or personal, with this subject, for a variety of pedagogical reasons I agreed, and together we mapped a tentative scholarly path, involving a literature search, visits to appropriate laboratories and professional meetings, and the design, construction, and operation of simple experiments. My initial oversight role in this project led to a degree of personal involvement with it, and that to a growing intellectual bemusement, to the extent that by the time this student graduated, I was persuaded that this was a legitimate field for a high technologist to study and that I would enjoy doing so.

As a result of his own survey of the field as well as his own initial experiments in parapsychology, Jahn concluded that [1]:

> once the illegitimate research and invalid criticism have been set aside, the remaining accumulated evidence of psychic phenomena comprises an array of experimental observations, obtained under reasonable protocols in a variety of scholarly disciplines, which compound to a philosophical dilemma. On the one hand, effects inexplicable in terms of established scientific theory, yet having numerous common characteristics, are frequently and widely observed; on the other hand, these effects have so far proven qualitatively and quantitatively irreplicable, in the strict scientific sense, and appear to be sensitive to a variety of psychological and environmental factors that are difficult to specify, let alone control.

Jahn, like many of his predecessors who took a serious look at the evidence for the paranormal, finds the phenomena to be erratic, evasive, and ephemeral. Indeed, he admits that when judged according to strict scientific standards, the evidence for the actual existence of the phenomena is not "fully persuasive." But he is intrigued. Like his predecessors, he is optimistic that with the right application of technology and scientific ingenuity the phenomena can be captured and made lawful.

This is one of a number of justifiable reactions one can have as a result of examining fairly the case of psychical research. Jahn is willing to risk his time and reputation on the possibility that careful and diligent investigation will bring some lawfulness to this unruly area of inquiry. Jahn's research into anomalous phenomena began over seven years ago, but it will be several more years before we know whether it has managed to progress much beyond previous attempts to bring scientific order into the field.

During the 130-year history of psychical research many other scholars and scientists have initiated investigations of psychic phenomena with equally high hopes of taming the phenomena. One was the philosopher Henry Sidgwick, who was the first president of the Society for Psychical Research founded in 1882. According to William James, Sidgwick and his colleagues

> hoped that if the material were treated rigorously and, as far as possible, experimentally, objective truth would be elicited, and the subject rescued from sentimentalism on the one side and dogmatizing ignorance on the other. Like all founders, Sidgwick hoped for a certain promptitude of result; and I heard him say, the year before his death, that if anyone had told him at the outset that after twenty years he would be in the same identical state of doubt and balance that he started with, he would have deemed the prophecy incredible. It appeared impossible that the amount of handling evidence should bring so little finality of decision [2].

James, who made this observation in his last article on psychical research in 1909, continued as follows [2]:

> My own experience has been similar to Sidgwick's. For twenty-five years I have been in touch with the literature of psychical research, and have had acquaintance with numerous "researchers." I have also spent a good many hours (though far fewer than I ought to have spent) in witnessing (or trying to witness) phenomena. Yet I am theoretically no "further" than I was at the beginning; and I confess that at times I have been tempted to believe that the Creator has eternally intended this department of nature to remain *baffling,* to prompt our curiosities and hopes and suspicions all in equal measure, so that, although ghosts and clairvoyances, and raps and messages from spirits, are always seeming to exist and can never be fully explained away, they also can never be susceptible of full corroboration.
> The peculiarity of the case is just that there are so many sources of

possible deception in most of the observations that the whole lot of them *may* be worthless, and yet that in comparatively few cases can be aught more fatal than this vague general possibility of error be pleaded against the record. Science, meanwhile needs something more than bare possibilities to build upon; so your genuinely scientific inquirer—I don't mean your ignoramus "scientist"—has to remain unsatisfied.

Some 67 years after James's final word on the matter, the philosopher Antony Flew summed up his 25 years of interest in parapsychology with remarkably similar sentiments [3]:

My long-out-of-print first book was entitled, perhaps too rashly, *A New Approach to Psychical Research.* . . . When I reviewed the evidential situation at that time it seemed to me that there was too much evidence for one to dismiss. Honesty required some sort of continuing interest, even if a distant interest. On the other hand, it seemed to me then that there was no such thing as a reliably repeatable phenomenon in the area of parapsychology and that there was really almost nothing positive that could be pointed to with assurance. The really definite and decisive pieces of work seemed to be uniformly negative in their outcome.

It is most depressing to have to say that the general situation a quarter of a century later still seems to me to be very much the same. An enormous amount of further work has been done. Perhaps more has been done in this latest period than in the whole previous history of the subject. Nevertheless, there is still no reliably repeatable phenomenon, no particular solid-rock positive cases. And yet there still is clearly too much there for us to dismiss the whole business.

Sidgwick was assessing the first 50 years of psychical research. James was evaluating the same period with another ten years or so added. Flew based his assessment on an additional 67 years of inquiry. Yet, all three agree that they could detect no progress. In each case, after a quarter of a century of personal involvement, the investigator found the evidence for the paranormal just as inconclusive as it had been at the beginning. James openly concedes that *all* the claimed phenomena might be the result of self-deception or fraud. Yet he, and the other two philosophers, cannot quite shake the conviction that, despite all this inconclusiveness, "there might be something there."

Over this same span of history, the critics have consistently insisted that "there is nothing there." All the alleged phenomena of telepathy, clair-voyance, psychokinesis, levitation, spirit materialization, and premonitions can be accounted for in terms of fraud, self-delusion, and simple gullibility. The proponents have naturally resented such dismissals of their claims. They have argued that the critics have not fairly examined the evidence. They have accused the critics of attacking the weakest evidence and of ignoring the stronger and better supported evidence in favor of the paranormal.

Unfortunately, as any reading of the history of psychical research quickly reveals, the psychical researchers are correct in their appraisal of their critics. Too often, the major critics have attacked straw men and have not dealt with the actual claims and evidence put forth by the more serious researchers. The fact that most of the criticism of the psychical research has been irrelevant and unfair, however, does not necessarily mean that the psychical researchers have a convincing case.

Indeed, the message that we get from Sidgwick, James, Flew, and Jahn is that the evidential base for psychic claims is very shaky at best. At most, these scholars, after carefully weighing all the evidence available to them, are claiming only that they cannot help feeling that, despite the inconsistencies and nonlawfulness of the data, that "there must be something there."

As will be discussed later in this paper, both the critics and the proponents subscribe to what I refer to as the *false dichotomy*. When scientists or scholars, after investigating possible psychic phenomena, conclude that the phenomena are real, the assumption is that either their conclusion is justified or they are delinquent in some serious way—being either incompetent or subject to some pathology. When critics deny that the claim is justified, the proponents feel that their integrity or competence is being challenged. And the critics, sharing in this assumption, feel that they must show that the claimants are incompetent, gullible, or deficient in some serious way [4].

I consider this a false dichotomy because competent and honest investigators can make serious judgmental errors when investigating new phenomena. Competence and expertise in any given field of endeavor are bounded. Cognitive psychologists, historians of science, and sociologists of knowledge have been gathering data that demonstrate how thinking is guided by conceptual frameworks and paradigms within which the thinker operates. Successful scientific thinking, for example, is not successful because it operates according to abstract, formal rules of evidence. Rather, it succeeds because the thinker is guided by the often implicit rules and procedures inherent within the specific content and practices of the narrow field of specialization within which the problem is being pursued. These "heuristics" or guidelines for successful thinking are not foolproof, and under changed circumstances they can trap the thinker into erroneous convictions. In other words, competence in a given scholarly or scientific discipline and high intelligence are no barriers to becoming trapped into asserting and defending erroneous positions.

In this paper, I agree with Sidgwick, James, Flew, and Jahn in the most general sense that "something" is indeed going on. However, I do not see any need to assume that this "something" has anything to do with the paranormal.

I think we should not lightly dismiss the fact that for 130 years some of our best scholars and scientists have seriously carried out psychical research and have become convinced that they have demonstrated the existence of a "psychic force" or a supernatural realm occupied by intelligent and superior beings. As far as I can tell, these proponents were competent scholars, sane, and highly intelligent. They made every apparent effort to employ what they believed to be objective and scientific standards in observing, recording, and reporting their findings.

Yet, as I will argue, contrary to Jahn's assessment, the total accumulation of 130 years' worth of psychical investigation has not produced any consistent evidence for paranormality that can withstand acceptable scientific scrutiny. What should be interesting for the scientific establishment is not that there is a case to be made for psychic phenomena, but rather that the majority of scientists who decided to investigate seriously *believed* that they had made such a case. How can it be that so many outstanding scientists, including several Nobel Prize winners, have convinced themselves that they have obtained solid, scientific evidence for paranormal phenomena?

If they are wrong, what has made them wrong? Does this suggest weaknesses or limitations of scientific method and training? And if these investigators have not actually encountered psychic phenomena, what is it that they have discovered?

I am not sure that I can provide satisfactory answers to these questions. But I believe that it will help to look at some selected cases in which investigators believed that they had obtained adequate scientific evidence for the reality of psychic phenomena. I will start at the beginning by describing the sort of evidence that convinced the first scientists who took psychical claims seriously. Even some contemporary parapsychologists believe these early scientists may have been wrong, but their cases are still worth examining because in them we will find many of the same issues and problems that characterize contemporary parapsychological research. These early investigators tested spiritualistic mediums who were noted for their ability to produce powerful psychic phenomena such as levitations, materializations, and other physical feats.

Psychical research became transformed into what is now called parapsychology when the focus shifted, after the first half-century of investigation, to the study of extrasensory perception and psychokinesis in ordinary individuals by means of standardized testing materials and procedures. I will examine what was, at the time, considered to be the most rigorous and successful application of this form of parapsychological research—the now notorious investigations by Soal on Shackleton and Mrs. Stewart. Again, the purpose is not to beat a dead horse but to abstract out principles and issues that still haunt contemporary parapsychology.

The card-guessing experiments begun by Rhine in the 1930s established the paradigm that dominated parapsychology for the next 40 years. New technology and interest in altered states resulted in departures from Rhine's paradigm beginning about 1970. Experiments with random event generators, remote viewing, and the ganzfeld technique have been the strongest contenders for providing parapsychology with its long-sought-for repeatable experiment. I will argue that a fair and objective assessment of this latest work strongly suggests that, like its predecessors, it still does not stand up to critical scrutiny.

Scientists and Psychics

The first major scientist to test experimentally a psychic claim was Michael Faraday in 1853. As will be described in more detail in the next section, Faraday concluded that the phenomena he had investigated, table turning, had a normal explanation. Robert Hare, an American chemist, at first agreed with Faraday's conclusion. But, then, after personal investigations of his own he changed his mind and openly supported the claims of spiritualistic mediums. A decade later, Alfred Russel Wallace, the cofounder with Darwin of the theory of evolution by natural selection, and Sir William Crookes, the discoverer of thallium, astounded their scientific colleagues by openly endorsing paranormal claims. Wallace and Crookes believed, as had Hare, that their own inquiries had established scientific proof to support their paranormal claims.

Hare, Wallace, and Crookes were the first of a succession of eminent scientists who have endorsed paranormal claims as a result of their experimental tests of alleged psychics. These scientists have established a tradition that has played a major role in the development of psychical research. The first half-century of psychical research consisted mainly of testing paranormal claims within this tradition. Beginning in the 1930s a second approach—experimental investigations according to standard protocols and using unselected subjects—became the dominant approach under the name of parapsychology. Today parapsychology includes both approaches.

In the first half of the present paper, I will focus on the first approach. The research of Sir William Crookes will be used as an example of this approach. In the second half of the paper, I will deal with the second approach. Again, I will use the research of a single investigator to bring out the more general issues and problems with the field of parapsychology. In both parts of the paper I will also briefly mention other investigators and lines of research that bring out the same themes illustrated by the more detailed examples. Finally, I will briefly look at the contemporary situation in parapsychology to argue that the concerns and difficulties that haunted the earlier investigations still persist.

Table Turning and Psychical Research

Modern spiritualism began when unaccountable raps were heard in the presence of two teen-age girls, Margaret and Kate Fox, in 1848. By using a code, the girls' mother was able to converse with the raps and concluded that they originated from the spirit of a peddler who had been murdered in the very house in which the Fox family then lived. Word of this miraculous communication spread quickly, and soon a variety of means for communicating with the unseen spirits via "the spiritual telegraph" were developed in the United States and then spread to Europe. The individuals through whom the spirits produced their phenomena and communicated with mortals were called *mediums.* The mediums, at first, displayed phenomena such as rapping sounds, movements of tables and objects, playing of musical instruments by unseen agencies, and the occurrence of strange lights in the dark. Later, more elaborate phenomena were produced, such as the levitation of objects or the medium; the disappearance or appearance of objects; the materialization of hands, faces, or even of complete spirit forms; spirit paintings and photographs; and written communications from the spirit world [5], [6].

By the early 1850s, table turning (also called table tilting or table rapping) had become the rage both in the United States and in Europe. A group of individuals, usually called *sitters,* would arrange themselves around a table with their hands resting flat upon the tabletop. After an extended period of waiting a rap would be heard or the table would tilt up on one leg. Sometimes the table would sway and begin moving about the room, dragging the sitters along. On some occasions, sitters would claim that the table actually levitated off the floor under the conditions in which all hands were above the table. Reports even circulated that sometimes the table levitated when no hands were touching it. Table turning was especially popular because it could occur with or without the presence of an acknowledged medium. Any group of individuals could get together and attempt to produce the phenomenon in the privacy of their own living room.

Table turning plays an important role in the history of psychical research because it was what first attracted the attention of serious scientists to alleged paranormal phenomena [6]. The phenomenon had become so widespread in England by the summer of 1853 that several scientists decided to look into it. Although the prevailing explanation for the table's movements favored the agency of spirits, other explanations at the time were electricity, magnetisim, "attraction," Reichenbach's Odyllic Force, and the rotation of the earth. Electricity—which in the public mind was then considered to be an occult and mystical force—was especially popular. Indeed, many spiritualists probably thought that the spirits operated by electricity.

In June 1853, a committee of four physicians held seances to investigate table turning. They found that the table did not move at all when the sitters' attention was diverted and they had not formed common expectations about how the table should move. In another condition they found that the table would not move if half the sitters expected it to move to the right and the other half expected it to move to the left. "But when expectation was allowed free play, and especially if the direction of the probable movement was indicated beforehand, the table began to rotate after a few minutes, although no one of the sitters was conscious of exercising any effort at all. The conclusion formed was that the motion was due to muscular action, mostly exercised unconsciously" [6]. Other investigators came to similar conclusions.

But by far the most publicized and influential investigation was that by England's' most renowned scientist, the physicist Michael Faraday. Faraday obtained subjects who were "very honorable" and who were also "successful table-movers"[7]. Faraday found that he could obtain movements of the table in a given direction with just one subject sitting at his table in the laboratory. His first tests were designed to eliminate as explanations well-known forces such as magnetism and electricity. He demonstrated that substances such as sandpaper, millboard, glue, glass, moist clay, tinfoil, cardboard, vulcanized rubber, and wood did not interfere with the table turning. He could find no traces of electrical or magnetic effects. "No form of experiment or mode of observation that I could devise gave me the slightest indication of any peculiar force. No attractions, or repulsion, . . . nor anything which could be referred to other than the mere mechanical pressure exerted inadvertently by the turner."

Although Faraday suspected the the sitter was unconsciously pushing the table in the desired direction, the sitter adamantly insisted that he was not the agency but, instead, was pulled in the expected direction by some force within the table. Faraday created some ingenious arrangements to see if the sitter's claim was true. He placed four or five pieces of slippery cardboard, one over the other, on the tabletop. The pieces were attached to one another by little pellets of a soft cement. The lowest piece was attached to a piece of sandpaper that rested on the tabletop. The edges of the sheets overlapped slightly, and on the under surface, Faraday drew a pencil line to indicate the position. The table turner then placed his hands upon the upper card and waited for the table to move in the previously agreed-upon direction (to the left). Faraday then examined the packet. "It was easy to see, by displacement of the parts of the line, that the hand had moved farther than the table, and that the latter had lagged behind— that the hand, in fact had pushed the upper card to the left and that the under cards and the table had followed and been dragged by it" [7].

In another arrangement, Faraday fixed an indicator to two boards on the tabletop such that if the sitter was pulled by the table the indicator would slope to the right, but if the sitter pushed the table, the indicator would slope to the left. The table moved as before as long as the sitter could not see the indicator. But as soon as the sitter was able to watch the indicator, which gave him immediate feedback when his hands pushed in the expected direction, all movements of the table ceased.

> But the most valuable effect of this test-apparatus . . . is the corrective power it possesses over the mind of the table-turner. As soon as the index is placed before the most earnest, and they perceive—as in my presence they have always done—that it tells truly whether they are pressing downwards only or obliquely; then all effects of table-turning cease, even though the parties persevere, earnestly desiring motion, till they become weary and worn out. No prompting or checking of the hands is needed—*the power is gone;* and this only because the parties are made conscious of what they are really doing mechanically, and so are unable unwittingly to deceive themselves [7].

Faraday's investigation convinced several scientists that table turning was the result of self-deception resulting from unconscious motor movements guided by expectation. His report is even credited with dampening the enthusiasm, for a few years, for spiritualism in England [6]. But several spiritualists and table turners were not convinced by Faraday's arguments. And this brings up another issue that invariably accompanies the controversy over paranormal claims. Whenever a skeptic demonstrates how an alleged psychic phenomenon can be duplicated by mundane means, the claimant usually responds, "It's not the same thing!"

To many spiritualists and those who had witnessed table turning, Faraday's explanation appeared hopelessly inadequate. Professional mediums, for example, while sitting at the table could provide meaningful answers by means of table rapping to questions that sitters put to their assumed spirit communicators. In addition, the table often moved in a variety of ways that seemingly could not be explained by simple muscular pressure applied by the sitters. For example, the table often levitated above the floor with all the sitters' hands resting on the top surface. And some reports claimed that the table moved and levitated when no human was in contact with it.

Faraday's explanation dealt with only one important cause of the table turning. He did not attempt to account for the various ways in which the table could be moved and levitated by trickery. Nor did he deal with the problem of the notorious unreliability of eyewitness testimony. Nor did he and his fellow skeptics realize that an abstract, even if correct, explanation of table turning was impotent when matched against the personal and powerfully emotional experience of a sitter who has been converted during an actual table-turning session. These same limitations on any attempt to "explain away" an alleged paranormal event by a mundane account continue to provide loopholes whereby the proponent can maintain the reality of a paranormal claim.

Two striking illustrations of the power of the experience that "it is not the same thing" can be found in the conversions to spiritualism of the next two major scientists to investigate psychic phenomena. Both Robert Hare and Alfred Russel Wallace were familiar with Faraday's research and explanation when they first investigated spiritualistic phenomena by means of table turning. And both were immediately convinced that their personal experiences could not be accounted for by Faraday's theory. In these instances, the forewarning, rather than serving to forearm, actually disarmed. And this, too, is a recurring theme in the history of psychical research.

Sir William Crookes

Faraday, the first major scientist seriously to investigate spiritualistic phenomena, concluded that self-deception was sufficient to explain what he observed. As a result, he remained skeptical and critical of all further claims of paranormal phenomena. Faraday's scientific colleagues were obviously grateful for his investigation and conclusions. But within the next two decades three other major scientists also investigated paranormal claims and concluded, contrary to Faraday, that they had witnessed truly paranormal phenomena.

Robert Hare began his inquiry into spiritualistic phenomena in 1853 immediately after Faraday's investigation. Alfred Russel Wallace initiated his investigations in 1865. And Sir William Crookes began his investigations in 1869. All three had already achieved reputations as outstanding scientists before they surprised their scientific colleagues with their assertions of having witnessed psychic phenomena. Their colleagues were disturbed and puzzled by such assertions from obviously competent scientists. Their reactions, unfortunately, were not always rational and tended to make a confusing situation worse.

I believe it is important to try to understand how these otherwise competent scientists became convinced that they had acquired evidence sufficient to justify the belief in paranormal phenomena. The investigations of these scientists can be credited with the initiation of psychical research as a field with scientific aspirations. And many of the same issues of scientific justification of claims for the paranormal that we find in their work are still with us today.

Robert Hare was professor emeritus of chemistry at the University of

Pennsylvania and 72 years of age when circumstances conspired to launch him on a new career as a psychic investigator in 1853 [8]. Hare, the author of more than 150 scientific papers, had invented the oxy-hydrogen blowpipe, which was the predecessor of today's welding torch [9]. According to Asimov, Hare was "one of the few strictly American products who in those days could be considered within hailing distance of the great European chemists" [10].

Both Hare and his critics took it for granted that a competent scientist could carry out observations and experiments on a variety of phenomena and, as a result, come to trustworthy and sound conclusions. Until he announced his conversion to the spiritualistic hypothesis, Hare's colleagues did not doubt his competence as an observer and experimenter. When he announced that he had not only experimentally verified paranormal phenomena, but also had been communicating with the spirits of his departed relatives and also with George Washington, John Quincy Adams, Henry Clay, Benjamin Franklin, Byron, and Isaac Newton, this placed his incredulous colleagues in a quandary [8].

For half a century, the scientific world had accepted Hare's scientific papers and conclusions with respect and admiration. His scientific accomplishments were widely recognized and honored. But now this respected fellow scientist, by using apparently the same observational and experimental skills that had earned him his renown, was claiming to have demonstrated the reality of phenomena that scientists felt were just too preposterous to be true. Instead of examining Hare's arguments and evidence, his colleagues reacted emotionally and rejected his conclusions out of hand. Furthermore, they treated him as a traitor to the scientific enterprise and refused to allow him to present his case in the regular scientific forum.

From Hare's perspective this reaction was both unfair and unscientific. His arguments were being rejected without even being given a hearing. In his last few years he turned away from his scientific colleagues and confined his social interactions entirely to his spiritualistic associates. From the perspective of the scientific establishment, Hare had suddenly gone insane or had suffered some other form of pathology. Here we see the false dichotomy in action. And this same false dichotomy will be found throughout the story of psychical research right up to the present.

Alfred Russel Wallace's conversion to spiritualism began in the same way that Hare's did—sitting at an animated table during a seance. Wallace's experience, just as Hare's did, convinced him that Faraday's explanation of the table's antics would not do. Unlike Hare, however, Wallace was not 72 and at the end of his career. Instead he was 42 years old and in the middle of a long and productive career. Only seven years earlier, Wallace had independently conceived the theory of evolution by natural selection, the very same theory that Darwin had been secretly working on for many years [11]-[13].

Critics have found it easy to dismiss the psychical evidence of Hare on the basis of old age and of Wallace on the assertion that, while he was a great naturalist and observer, he was not an experimenter [11]. Neither criticism can be applied, however, to William Crookes, who was the next great scientist to investigate and endorse the reality of paranormal phenomena. Crookes was generally acknowledged, even by many who opposed his psychic beliefs, as one of the preeminent chemists and physicists of his day. Crookes—the discoverer of thallium, inventor of the radiometer, developer of the Crookes tube, pioneer investigator of radiation effects, and a contributor to photography and other fields—was elected a Fellow of the Royal Society at age 31, was later knighted, and received just about every honor available to a scientist of his time.

When Crookes began attending seances with Mrs. Marshall (the same medium who helped convert Wallace) and J.J. Morse in 1869, he was 37 years of age. He had been very upset by the death of his youngest brother and apparently believed he had received spirit communications from him through the services of these mediums. In July 1870 Crookes announced his intention to conduct a scientific inquiry into spiritualistic phenomena. He wrote, "I prefer to enter upon the inquiry with no preconceived notions whatever as to what can or cannot be, but with all my senses alert and ready to convey information to the brain; believing, as I do, that we have by no means exhausted all human knowledge or fathomed the depths of all physical forces" [15].

Although most of the scientific community assumed that Crookes was undertaking the investigation as a skeptic, his biographer wrote, "But it is certain, at all events, that when in July 1870 Crookes, at the request, it is said of a London daily paper, announced his intention of 'investigating spiritualism, so-called,' he was already much inclined towards spiritualism. What he really intended to do was to furnish, if possible, a rigid scientific proof of the objectivity and genuineness of the 'physical phenomena of spiritualism,' so as to convert the scientific world at large and open a new era of human advancement" [16].

Crookes packed almost all his research into psychical phenomena into the four-year period 1870–74 [17]. When he failed to sway his scientific colleagues—and as a result of bitter attacks by his critics—Crookes quietly dropped this work and devoted his scientific efforts from 1875 onwards to more mainstream subjects. But he never gave up his beliefs and he never severed his ties with the field. In his final years, he began attending seances again and believed, near the end, that he had finally found proof of survival when he obtained a spirit photograph of his dead wife [15].

By today's standards, the investigations that come closest to being "scientific" were those that Crookes carried out with the celebrated medium

Daniel Dunglas Home. Home is probably the most colorful and enigmatic psychic in the history of spiritualism [6], [9]. In one session, which took place at Crookes's home on May 31, 1871, Home held an accordion (which had just been purchased by Crookes for this occasion) by one end so that the end with the keys hung down towards the floor. The accordion was placed in a special cage under the table, which just allowed Home's hand to be inserted to hold the accordion. Home's other hand was visible above the table. The individuals sitting on either side of Home could see his hand as well as the accordion in the wire cage. "Very soon the accordion was seen by those on each side to be moving about in a somewhat curious manner, but no sound was heard." After putting the accordion down, Home picked it up again. This time several notes were heard. Crookes's assistant crawled under the table and said that he saw the accordion expanding and contracting, but Home's hand was quite still [15].

At the same session Crookes reported an experiment that he regarded as even "more striking, if possible, than the one with the accordion." A mahogany board, 3 ft long, with one end resting on a table and the other end supported by a spring balance, was in a horizontal position. Home, while "sitting in a low easy-chair" placed the tips of his fingers lightly on the extreme end of the board, which was resting on the table. "Almost immediately the pointer of the balance was seen to descend. After a few seconds it rose again. This movement was repeated several times, as if by successive waves of the Psychic Force. The end of the board was observed to oscillate slowly up and down during the experiment" [15].

To see if it were possible to produce an effect on the spring balance by ordinary pressure, Crookes stood on the table and pressed one foot on the end of the board where Home had placed his fingers. By using the entire weight of his body (140 lb), Crookes was able to get the index to register at most 2 lb. Home had apparently achieved a maximum displacement of 6 lb.

Because of such results Crookes concluded that "these experiments appear conclusively to establish the existence of a new force, in some un-known manner connected with the human organisation which for con-venience may be called the Psychic Force" [15]. The skeptics were not convinced. They raised a variety of objections to the experiment measuring the movement of the board. Crookes thought some of the criticisms were unfair and irrelevant. But he repeated the experiment with additional controls. To avoid direct contact with the board, he altered the apparatus slightly in a manner that had previously been used by Robert Hare in some of his experiments. A bowl of water was placed on the end of the board not supported by the spring scale. Inside the bowl of water was lowered a "hemispherical copper vessel perforated with several holes at the bottom."

The copper vessel was suspended from a large iron stand, which was separate from the rest of the apparatus. Home placed his fingers lightly in the water in the copper bowl. Presumably, this prevented him from having direct contact with the board. Yet, under these conditions Home managed to cause the other end of the board to sway up and down.

Finally, Home was removed a few feet away from the apparatus and his hands and legs were held. Even under these conditions, Crookes was able to record movements of the board, although the displacement was less the farther Home was from the apparatus. In further answer to critics, Crookes described similar experiments carried out successfully by other researchers including Robert Hare. Crookes also got similar results using a lady who was not a professional medium in place of Home.

This series of experiments is by far the most impressive, from a scientific viewpoint, of any that Crookes conducted. Indeed, so far as I can tell, although these were among the very first serious attempts by a scientist to test a psychic, they have not been exceeded in degree of documentation and experimental sophistication during the subsequent 114 years. This is despite the fact that, following Crookes's example, eminent scientists during almost every decade since Crookes's experiments have conducted tests of famous psychics.

The comments in the preceding paragraph should not be taken as an endorsement of Crookes's results. His experiments on the "Psychic Force" are superior *relative* to what has been reported by other scientists, including contemporary ones, in their tests of psychic superstars. On an absolute scale of judgment the experiments still leave much to be desired. A major problem is documentation. Crookes omits many details which, from today's perspective at least, seem important in assessing what might have taken place.

Responding to the accusation that his witnesses were not reliable, Crookes wrote, "Accustomed as I am to have my word believed without witnesses, this is an argument which I cannot condescend to answer. All who know me and read my articles will, I hope, take it for granted that the *facts* I lay before them are correct, and that the experiments were honestly performed, with the single object of eliciting *the truth*"[15].

Here Crookes raises an important issue. When he reported finding a green line in a spectrum where one had never been reported, and followed this up with various analyses and controls to support the assertion that he must have discovered a new element (thallium), his scientific colleagues did not insist that he import skeptical witnesses, nor did they question his observations. The reported observation was made by using standard apparatus and recording procedures. The necessary controls and possibilities of error in such a context were well known to workers in the field and it could be safely assumed that any trained chemist in this situation would behave according to both implicit and explicit rules.

But Crookes and his critics seriously err when they assume that similar confidence and trust can be placed in observations made in a field outside the investigator's training and one in which no standardization exists for devising instrumentation, making observations, instituting controls, recording the data, and reporting the results. The difficulties are compounded further when the observations are made, not of inanimate and reasonably passive materials, but of events involving humans who have a capacity to anticipate the experimenter's objectives and alter their behavior accordingly.

I recently discovered that Podmore, back in 1902, anticipated most of my reservations about Crookes's experiment on the movements of the balance [6]:

> The experiment as it stands, even without the modifications introduced later by Mr. Crookes in deference to his scientific critics, seems, indeed, conclusive against the possibility of Home's affecting the balance by any pressure on his end of the board. But, tested by the canons laid down by Mr. Crookes himself at the outset of his investigations, we shall find the conditions of the experiment defective in one important particular. Mr. Crookes had shown that it is the province of scientific investigation, not merely to ascertain the reality of the alleged movements and measure their extent, but to establish their occurrence under conditions which render fraud impossible. In the passage quoted on page 183 it is implicitly recognized that such conditions are to be secured by eliminating the necessity for continuous observation on the part of the investigator. The proof of the thing done should depend upon something else than the mere observation of the experimenters, however skilled.
>
> Now in the experiment quoted these conditions were not fulfilled. On the contrary, we are expressly told that all present guarded Home's feet and hands. It is pertinent to point out that a duty for which the whole company were collectively responsible may well at times have been intermitted. Moreover, Dr. Huggins and Mr. Crookes had to watch the balance also, and Mr. Crookes had to take notes. Again, the experiment described was not the first of the kind; it occurred in the middle of a long series. It is indeed stated that Home was not familiar with the apparatus employed. But as similar apparatus had been employed, probably at previous trials by Mr. Crookes himself, certainly by earlier investigators—amongst them Dr. Hare, with whose published writings on Spiritualism we cannot assume Home was unacquainted—the statement carries little weight. Further, a point of capital importance, there had apparently been many previous trials with various modifications of the apparatus and many failures; in Mr. Crookes's own words, "the experiments I have tried have been very numerous, but owing to our imperfect knowledge of the conditions which favor or oppose the manifestations of this force, to the apparently capricious manner in which it is exerted, and to the fact that Mr. Home himself is subject to unaccountable ebbs and flows of the force, it has but seldom happened that a result obtained on one occasion could be subsequently confirmed

and tested with apparatus specially contrived for the purpose."

The real significance of this statement is that Home—a practiced conjurer, as we are entitled to assume—was in a position to dictate the conditions of the experiment. By the simple device of doing nothing when the conditions were unfavorable he could ensure that the light (gas in the present instance) was such and so placed, the apparatus so contrived, and the sitters so disposed, as to suit his purpose, and that in the actual experiment the attention of the investigators would necessarily be concentrated on the wrong points. Under such conditions, as ordinary experience shows, and as the experiments described in the last chapter have abundantly demonstrated, five untrained observers are no match for one clever conjurer.

Podmore is referring, in the last sentence, to the dramatic experiments on eyewitness testimony conducted by S.J. Davey [18]. Davey had been converted to a belief in spiritualistic phenomena by the slate-writing demonstrations of the medium Henry Slade. Subsequently, Davey accidentally discovered that Slade had employed trickery to produce some of the phenomena. Davey practiced until he felt he could accomplish all of Slade's feats by trickery and misdirection. He then conducted his well-rehearsed seance for several groups of sitters, including many who had witnessed and testified to the reality of spiritualistic phenomena. Immediately after each seance, Davey had the sitters write out in detail all that they could remember having happened during his seance. The findings were striking and very disturbing to believers. None of the sitters had suspected Davey of using trickery. Sitters consistently omitted crucial details, added others, changed the order of events, and otherwise supplied reports that would make it impossible for any reader to account for what was described by normal means.

Podmore has much more to say about this experiment. His reference to "untrained" observers is not meant to question Crookes's scientific competence.

But his previous training did not necessarily render him better qualified to deal with problems differing widely from those presented in the laboratory. To put it bluntly, if Home was a conjurer, Mr. Crookes was probably in no better position for detecting the sleight-of-hand than any other man his equal in intelligence and native acuteness of sense. Possibly even in a worse position; for it may be argued that his previous training would prepare the way for Home's efforts to concentrate attention on the mechanical apparatus, and thus divert it from the seemingly irrelevant movements by which it may be conjectured the conjurer's end was attained.

Finally, Podmore points out ways in which the report is incomplete. He then speculates about one possible way Home might have tricked Crookes.

He describes a scenario in which Home could have employed a thread, which he attached to the apparatus, probably the hook of the scale. Some further points could be mentioned, such as the fact that Crookes's unpublished notes suggest that the experiment was much more informal and involved many more distractions than the published version indicates [15].

Crookes held many seances not only with Home but also with almost every major spiritualistic medium who was in England during the years 1869 through 1875. He reported having observed a variety of phenomena that he argued could not have been produced by normal means: movement of heavy bodies with contact but without mechanical exertion; raps and other sounds; the alteration of weights of bodies; movements of heavy substances at a distance from the medium; the rising of tables and chairs off the ground, without contact of any person; the levitation of human beings; the appearance of hands, either self-luminous or visible by ordinary light; direct writing; and phantom forms and faces [18]. His documentation for such phenomena, however, falls far short of what he has supplied us for the movements of the balance.

As was the case with Hare and Wallace, Crookes was bitterly attacked for his views. The eminent physiologist, William Carpenter, led the opposition. Carpenter openly questioned Crookes's competence as a scientist, wrongly stated that Crookes's election to the Royal Society had been questionable, and made several other unwarranted insults [16], [17]. Like Wallace, Crookes tried to get his scientific colleagues and critics to witness his experiments with Home and other psychics. But none of them accepted his invitations.

Difficulties in Testing Alleged Psychics

Hare, Wallace, and Crookes were the first of many eminent scientists who have investigated and endorsed psychics. Their work inspired many later scientists also to take time away from their regular scientific activities to investigate the paranormal claims of mediums or self-professed psychics [4], [19]–[29]. Yet, I suspect that many parapsychologists will object to using the work of these psychic investigators as part of a general evaluation and critique of parapsychology. The objection would be- based on two arguments.

First, today, most parapsychologists would not include the reports of Hare, Wallace, and Crookes in their case for the reality of *psi* (the current term to refer to extrasensory perception and psychokinesis). And, second, even the reports by more recent scientists on psychics do not form part of the primary data base of parapsychology. Instead, today's parapsychologists want to base their argument on evidence emerging from laboratory experiments with unselected subjects and which use standardized tasks.

However, I believe there are five good reasons for focusing on these early investigators:

1. At the time they were reported, these investigations were considered to be the strongest evidence for the paranormal. From 1850 to 1866 Hare's research consituted practically the entire "scientific" case upon which proponents could base their claims. From 1870 until the founding of the Society for Psychical Research in 1882, it was the work of Crookes and Wallace that proponents put forth as the best scientific justification for their paranormal claims.

2. The psychical research of these three eminent scientists served as the model for all later investigations of psychics by scientists. Although sometimes the latest technological developments are brought into the investigations, no change in approach or improvements in methodology for such investigations have occurred during the 130 years since Hare first reported his findings [23]. In terms of adequacy of documentation, for example, it is difficult to find any improvement over Crookes's reports on his experiments with Home in the subsequent accounts by such psychic investigators as Richet, Barrett, Lodge, Lombroso, Zoellner, Eisenbud, Targ, Puthoff, Hasted, and the many others.

3. The work of this early trio served as an important impetus for the subsequent founding of the Society for Psychical Research in 1882. In his presidential address to the first general meeting of the Society for Psychical Research on July 17, 1882, Henry Sidgwick went out of his way to acknowledge the importance and evidential value of the work of these pioneer researchers [30]:

> I say that important evidence has been accumulated; and here I should like to answer a criticism that I have privately heard which tends to place the work of our Society in a rather invidious aspect. It is supposed that we throw aside *en bloc* the results of previous inquiries as untrustworthy, and arrogate to ourselves a superior knowledge of scientific method or intrinsically greater trustworthiness—that we hope to be believed, whatever conclusions we may come to, by the scientific world, though previous inquirers have been uniformly distrusted. Certainly I am conscious of making no assumption of this kind. I do not presume to suppose that I could produce evidence better in quality than much that has been laid before the world by writers of indubitable scientific repute—men like Mr. Crookes, Mr. Wallace, and the late Professor de Morgan. But it is clear that from what I have defined as the aim of the Society, however good some of its evidence may be in quality, we require a great deal more of it. I do not dispute,— it is not now time to dispute—with any individual who holds that reasonable persons, who have looked carefully into the evidence that has been so far

obtained, ought to be convinced by that evidence; but the educated world, including many who have given much time and thought to this subject, are not yet convinced, and therefore we want more evidence.

Sidgwick makes it clear that he and the other founders of the Society for Psychical Research consider the findings of Wallace and Crookes as scientifically sound. Sidgwick has no doubt that Wallace's and Crookes's reports *should* convince reasonable members of the scientific community. But he pragmatically makes the distinction between what *should* and what *will* convince the critics. "What I mean by *sufficient evidence* is evidence that will convince the scientific world, and for that we obviously require a good deal more than we have so far obtained" [30]. In other words, Sidgwick does not aspire to improve the quality of the preceding scientific investigators. Rather he wants to acquire more of the same quality.

4. The investigations of these original psychical researchers bring out many of the same issues of evidence, testimony, and proof that still characterize current controversies in parapsychology. Unfortunately, not much in the way of further clarification or resolution of these issues has occurred since their efforts first stimulated the debate. I have already mentioned some of these issues in my discussions of the individual cases.

Many of the issues involve the problem of competency. To what extent, for example, does competency in one branch of inquiry transfer, if at all, to a different branch? Can scientists, no matter how competent and well-intentioned, initiate inquiries into a previously unstructured and unstandardized area and single-handedly produce results that bear the same scientific status as the results they have produced in their original area of expertise? Elsewhere, I have given my reasons for answering this question in the negative [23].

One important issue is perhaps worth bringing up at this point. The scientists who have defended the trustworthiness of their psychical research have typically insisted that the observations and evidence of their reports of psychic happenings do not differ in quality from that which characterizes their more orthodox investigations.

Yet, at the same time, these same investigators acknowledge an important difference between their inquiries into physics and biology and their investigations of psychics. Hare, Wallace, and Crookes, as well as the later psychical researchers, insisted that the psychics being tested must be treated with proper respect and concern for their feelings. If the investigator is overly skeptical or otherwise betrays distrust of the alleged psychic this could adversely affect the paranormal performance. Thus these scientists try to convey the impression that they conduct their tests using every precaution against fraud and deception, but at the same time making sure not to take any step or include any condition that meets with the disapproval of the alleged psychic. Skeptics such as myself, who both have experience in conducting experiments with humans and have been trained in conjuring, believe this is an impossible task. The twin goals of preventing trickery on the part of the alleged psychic and of ensuring that this same person will be satisfied with all the experimental arrangements are mutually incompatible.

But scientists who have testified to the paranormal powers of their subjects confidently insist they have simultaneously achieved both goals. A contemporary version of this theme has been eloquently put forth by a group of scientists, including two of England's outstanding physicists, in describing their experiments on the psychokinetic powers of Uri Geller [31]:

> We have come to realize that in certain ways the traditional ideal of the completely impersonal approach of the natural sciences to experimentation will not be adequate in this domain. Rather, there is a personal aspect that has to be taken into account in a way that is somewhat similar to that needed in the disciplines of psychology and medicine. This does not mean, of course, that is not possible to establish facts on which we can count securely. Rather, it means that we have to be sensitive and observant, to discover what is a right approach, which will properly allow for the subjective element and yet permit us to draw reliable inferences. One of the first things that reveals itself as one observes is that psychokinetic phenomena cannot in general be produced unless *all* who participate are in a relaxed state. A feeling of tension, fear, or hostility on the part of any of those present generally communicates itself to the whole group. The entire process goes most easily when all those present actively want things to work well. In addition, matters seem to be greatly facilitated when the experimental arrangement is aesthetically or imaginatively appealing to the person with apparent psychokinetic powers.
>
> We have found also that it is generally difficult to produce a predetermined set of phenomena. Although this may sometimes be done, what happens is often surprising and unexpected. We have observed that the attempt to concentrate strongly in order to obtain a desired result (e.g., the bending of a piece of metal) tends to interfere with the relaxed state of mind needed to produce such phenomena. . . . Indeed, we have sometimes found it useful at this stage to talk of, or think about, something not closely related to what is happening, so as to decrease the tendency to excessive conscious concentration on the intended aim of the experiment. . . .
>
> In the study of psychokinetic phenomena, such conditions are much more important than in the natural sciences, because the person who produces these phenomena is not an instrument or a machine. Any attempt to treat him as such will almost certainly lead to failure. Rather, he must be considered to be one of the group, actively cooperating in the experiment, and not a "subject" whose behavior is to be observed "from the outside" in as cold and impersonal manner as possible. . . .
>
> In such research an attitude of mutual trust and confidence is needed; we should not treat the person with psychokinetic powers as an "object"

to be observed with suspicion. Instead, as indicated earlier, we have to look on him as one who is working with us. Consider how difficult it would be to do a physical experiment if each person were constantly watching his colleagues to be sure that they did not trick him. How, then, are we to avoid the possibility of being tricked? It should be possible to design experimental arrangements that are beyond any reasonable possibility of trickery, and that magicians will generally acknowledge to be so. In the first stages of our work we did, in fact, present Mr. Geller with several such arrangements, but these proved to be aesthetically unappealing to him. From our early failures, we learned that Mr. Geller worked best when presented with many possible objects, all together on a metal surface; at least one of these objects might appeal to him sufficiently to stimulate his energies. . . .

Nevertheless, we realize that conditions such as we have described in this paper are just those in which a conjuring trick may easily be carried out. We understand also that we are not conjuring experts, so if there should be an intention to deceive, we may be as readily fooled as any person. Moreover, there has been a great deal of public criticism, in which the possibility of such tricks has been strongly suggested. For this reason it has often been proposed that a skilled magician should be present to help to see that there will be no possibility of deception. It is in the nature of the case, however, that no such assurance can actually be given. For a skilled magician is able to exploit each new situation as it arises in a different and generally unpredictable way. . . . In principle, we would welcome help of this kind in decreasing the possibility of deception. It has been our observation, however, that magicians are often hostile to the whole purpose of this sort of investigation, so they tend to bring about an atmosphere of tension in which little or nothing can be done. Indeed, even if some magicians were found who were not disposed in this way, it does not follow that their testimony will convince those who are hostile, since the latter can always suppose that new tricks were involved, beyond the capacity of those particular magicians to see through them. Because of all of this, it seems unlikely that significant progress towards clearing up this particular question could be made by actually having magicians present at the sessions, though we have found it useful to have their help in a consultative capacity. . . . We recognize that there is a genuine difficulty in obtaining an adequate answer to criticisms concerning the possibility of tricks, and that a certain healthy skepticism or doubt on the part of the reader may be appropriate at this point. . . . However, we believe that our approach can adequately meet this situation.

These investigators close this discussion of the difficulties of carrying out such research with an optimistic prognosis: "We feel that if similar sessions continue to be held, instances of this kind might accumulate, and there will be no room for reasonable doubt that some new process is involved here, which cannot be accounted for, or explained, in terms of the laws of physics at present known. Indeed, we already feel that we have very nearly reached this point." These hopeful words were written in 1975. Neither they nor other scientists have yet managed to present scientific evidence that Uri Geller or his many imitators can bend metal paranormally. Although at least one major physicist continues his investigations of paranormal metal bending [20], a decade of research on Uri Geller by scientists who adhered to the advice of treating the metal bender as a respected colleague and catering to his aesthetic sensibilities has only succeeded to demonstrate that Geller can bend metal under conditions that allow him to do it by cheating [21].

Hare, Wallace, and Crookes, as well as subsequent psychic researchers, insisted they had guarded against the possibility of trickery while, at the same time, acknowledging the necessity to treat their subjects in the special way described by Hasted *et al.* Unfortunately, as Hasted *et al.* concede, this special treatment increases the difficulties of preventing deception. But, like their predecessors in psychical research, they express confidence that their scientific skills can overcome the difficulty. In fact, the suggested procedure gives the alleged psychic veto power over any arrangement that impedes trickery and also supplies a ready excuse for not producing phenomena when the dangers of detection suddenly seem too high. The conditions that the scientists report as ideal for the production of psychical phenomena are just those that are also ideal for the production of the same phenomena by trickery.

5. As already discussed, Hare, Wallace, and Crookes were bitterly attacked by their skeptical scientific colleagues. And the same sorts of attacks and defenses have characterized subsequent cases. Both critics and defenders still implicitly subscribe to the same false dichotomy. And both the critics and the defenders, in different ways, do not emerge as rational, objective, scientific, or otherwise admirable in their exchanges. Worse, no lessons from the past seem to have been either learned or carried over to the current controversies. If the critical exchanges had been more constructive and rational at the time of Hare, Wallace, and Crookes, today we might be closer to understanding what was really going on to make such eminent scientists put forth such seemingly outrageous claims.

Hare, Wallace, and Crookes had no success in inducing their critics to come and examine the evidence for themselves. It is possible that if Huxley and Carpenter had accepted Wallace's invitation to attend at least six seances, no phenomena would have taken place. On the other hand, it would be useful to have the accounts of such skeptical observers before us if, say, Miss Nichol did produce the flowers in their presence. And it certainly would have helped if Carpenter and Stokes had accepted Crookes's invitation to watch his experiments with Home and the balance.

The Creery Sisters

For its first 30 years, psychical research consisted of individual and un-coordinated investigations by scholars or scientists such as Hare, Wallace, and Crookes. During this period some feeble and unsuccessful attempts were made to form research societies and coordinate the research [32]. The first successful attempt to institutionalize psychical research was the founding of the Society for Psychical Research in London in 1882. Four of the principal leaders of this society—the philosopher Henry Sidgwick, the physicist William Barrett, the literary scholar Edmund Gurney, and the classicist Frederic Myers—had been encouraged, in addition to their own investigations of telepathy and mediums, by the research of such scientists as Wallace and Crookes. The founders of the society clearly believed that they possessed solid scientific evidence for the reality of thought transference. At the first general meeting of the society in London on July 17, 1882, Henry Sidgwick ended his presidential address with the following words [30]:

> We must drive the objector into the position of being forced either to admit the phenomena as inexplicable, at least by him, or to accuse the investigators either of lying or cheating or a blindness or forgetfulness incompatible with any intellectual condition except absolute idiocy. I am glad to say that this result, in my opinion, has been satisfactorily attained in the investigation of thought-reading. Professor Barrett will now bring before you a report which I hope will be only the first of a long series of similar reports which may have reached the same point of conclusiveness.

Before looking at the experimental results whose "conclusiveness" Sidgwick believed was beyond reasonable doubt, I would like to call the reader's attention to the use of the false dichotomy in Sidgwick's strategy. The goal is to report evidence that is so compelling that the critic either has to admit that psychic phenomena have been demonstated or that the investigator is deliberately lying, afflicted with a pathological condition, or incredibly incompetent. Sidgwick does not allow for the possibility that an investigator could be competent, honest, sane, and intelligent, and still wrongly report what he believes to be "conclusive" evidence for the paranormal. Unfortunately, as seen in the cases of Hare, Wallace, and Crookes and as typifies succeeding cases, the critics, in responding to paranormal claims, have implicitly accepted the false dichotomy. When confronted with paranormal claims by otherwise competent investigators, many critics have taken the bait and have tried to discredit the offending investigators by questioning their competence, insinuating fraud, or suggesting pathology.

The "conclusive" evidence with which Sidgwick wanted to confront the objector came from a series of experiments on thought transference conducted by his colleagues William Barrett, Edmund Gurney, and Frederic Myers [33]. The investigators introduced this series as follows [33]:

> In the correspondence we have received there were two cases which seemed, upon inquiry, to be free from any *prima facie* objections, and apparently indicative of true thought-reading. One of these cases is given in the Appendix . . . but as we cannot from personal observation testify to the conditions under which the trials were made, we simply leave it aside. The other case was that of a family in Derbyshire, with whom we have had the opportunity of frequent and prolonged trials.
>
> Our informant was Mr. Creery, a clergyman of unblemished character, and whose integrity indeed has, it so happens, been exceptionally tested. He has a family of five girls, ranging now between the ages of ten and seventeen, all thoroughly healthy, as free as possible from morbid or hysterical symptoms, and in manner perfectly simple and childlike. The father stated that any one of these children (except the youngest), as well as a young servant-girl who had lived with the family for two years, was frequently able to designate correctly, without contact or sign, a card or other object fixed on in the child's absence. During the year which has elapsed since we first heard of this family, seven visits, mostly of several days' duration, have been paid to the town where they live, by ourselves and several scientific friends, and on these occasions daily experiments have been made.

The preceding quotation was taken from the "First report on Thought-Reading," which was read at the first meeting of the society. Several more experiments were conducted with the Creery sisters and the results included in the second and third reports [34], [35]. Notice the emphasis placed upon Reverend Creery's "unblemished character" and integrity. Within the Victorian society of Sidgwick and his colleagues this emphasis on character had a special significance. According to Nicol, many flaws in the investigative reports of the Society were due to "a *double standard* of evidence."

> The Society's double standard of evidence arose in the following way. The Society's leaders were members of the middle and upper middle strata of society. When faced with the problem of estimating the value of evidence, they divided the world into two classes: (a) Members of their own class (Ladies and Gentlemen in the Victorian sense) whom they tended to treat trustingly; (b) Members of the lower classes, whom for brevity we may call the Peasants: them they treated with suspicion [36].

The experiments with the Creery sisters were all variants of the popular Victorian pastime known as the "willing game" [37].

> The game admits of many variations, but is usually played somewhat as follows. One of the party, generally a lady, leaves the room, and the rest determine on something which she is able to do on her return—as to take

a flower from some specified vase, or to strike some specified note on the piano. She is then recalled, and one or more of the "willers" place their hands lightly on her shoulders. Sometimes nothing happens; sometimes she strays vaguely about; sometimes she moves to the right part of the room and does the thing, or something like the thing, which she has been willed to do. Nothing could at first sight look less like a promising starting-point for a new branch of scientific inquiry.

Barrett, Gurney, and Myers go to great lengths to assure their readers that they are aware of the many nonparanormal ways in which information from the senders can be communicated to the percipient. Subtle unconscious pushes by the "willer," for example, can guide the percipient to the correct place. And there is always the possibility of secret codes being employed [33], [37]. Nevertheless, they relate incidents from their own experience with the game which they believe cannot be handled by such obvious explanations.

In their typical experimental procedure, one child would be selected to leave the room. When she was out of the room, the remaining participants would select a playing card or write down a number or name. "On re-entering she stood—sometimes turned by us with her face to the wall, oftener with her eyes directed towards the ground, and usually close to us and remote from her family—for a period of silence varying from a few seconds to a minute, till she called out to us some number, card, or whatever it might be" [33]. Before leaving the room, the child was always informed of the general category, such as playing cards, from which the target item was to be chosen.

The authors obviously felt that their knowledge of the various ways that inadvertent and deliberate signaling of the percipient could occur somehow made them immune from such errors. As an added precaution, however, they conducted several trials in which either members of the family were absent or only the experimenters knew the chosen object (unfortunately they do not distinguish among trials on which only the experimenters were informed of the target but the family was present and trials on which only the experimenters were present). The investigators claim that keeping the family uninformed did not appreciably lower the proportion of above-chance correct guesses.

The results were quite striking. Looking only at the results of those trials on which members of the committee alone knew the card or number selected, the investigators summarize their findings as follows [35]:

260 Experiments made with playing cards; the first responses gave 1 quite right in 9 trials; whereas the responses, if pure chance, would be 1 quite right in 52 trials. 79 Experiments made with numbers of two figures; the first responses gave 1 quite right in 9 trials; whereas the responses, if pure chance, would be 1 quite right in 90 trials.

The experimenters also summarize the results of the much larger number of trials in which the family members were not excluded. Two points are worth noting about the results reported above. By ordinary statistical criteria the odds against such an outcome being due just to chance are enormous. But the calculation of such odds assumes that, in the absence of telepathy, we know the expected value and distribution of hits. The way experimenters can ensure the appropriate conditions for the application of the statistical tests is to include careful procedures for randomizing the targets on each trial such that each target has an equal chance of being selected and that the selected object on a given trial is independent of the selection on the next. But nowhere in the three reports do we find any mention of how the playing card or number was chosen on each trial. We do not know if the deck was shuffled even once, let alone between trials. The number selection is even more disturbing because if, as seems to be the case, a committee member simply thought of any two-digit number that came to mind, we know that some numbers are much more likely than others. And the same few numbers that are favored by the sender are likely to be those that come to the mind of the percipient. These most probable numbers, known as "mental habits" in the older literature, are called "population stereotypes" by Marks and Kammann [25].

The second peculiarity, which was noted by Coover, is that the proportion of successful hits in these experiments seems to be independent of the chance probability [38]. Thus the hit rate is 1 out of 9 trials regardless of whether cards or numbers are being guessed. To Coover this suggests the use of a code rather than the imperfect transmission of psychic signals.

As already indicated, the founders of the Society for Psychical Research believed that, with the experimental results on the Creery sisters, they had finally succeeded in scientifically establishing telepathy as a valid phenomenon. As just one example of the importance attached to these experiments, Gurney's statement in the society's first major monograph, *Phantasms of the Living,* can be cited: "I have dwelt at some length on our series of trials with the members of the Creery family, as it is to those trials that we owe our own conviction of the possibility of genuine thought-transference between persons in a normal state" [39].

Despite this confidence in the conclusiveness of the Creery experiments, critics quickly pointed out perceived flaws [38], [40], [41]. It was charged that the authors grossly underestimated the extent to which sophisticated coding could take place between the girls in the experimental situation. The critics also suggested that the experimenters were naive in assuming that they could prevent inadvertent cueing just by being aware of the possibility.

Concerning the trials in which only the investigators knew the chosen object, the critics complained about inadequate documentation. The experimenters never state how the card or object was chosen; whether the members of the family were present during the selection (even though they were presumably kept ignorant of the choice): whose deck of playing cards was used; and so forth.

As can be seen, even on this brief account, we encounter a number of the issues that characterized earlier psychical research. The investigators assume that to be forewarned is to be forearmed. For example, they devote six pages of their first report to a discussion of the various types of errors that, if not excluded, could invalidate their research [33]. The purpose is to assure the reader that because they are keenly aware of the possibilities of such errors the errors could not have occurred. As previously mentioned, one way the investigators tried to preclude giving the girl any involuntary muscular cue was simply for the investigator to be consciously aware of such a possibility and consciously prevent himself from displaying such cues. Not only is such a precaution useless [42], but it was unnecessary since one could more directly prevent unwitting bodily cues by simply screening those who know the target from the percipient. This tendency to substitute *plausible* (to the investigator) reasons for discounting a possible source of error for actual experimental controls to guard against the error characterizes psychical research from its inception to the present.

A second theme is that prior experience in investigating paranormal claims automatically qualifies one as an expert who can be trusted not to make mistakes or be susceptible to trickery in future situations. This theme is closely related to the false dichotomy issue.

The report on the Creery sisters also illustrates another recurring theme in psychical research—the *patchwork quilt fallacy*. As Giere points out, the "patchwork quilt fallacy" gets its name because "the hypothesis, initial conditions, and auxiliary assumptions are pieced together in such a way that they logically imply the known facts" [43]. Telepathy or psi always seems to be just that mysterious phenomenon that produced all the peculiar patterns that we happened to observe in our data. On some days the Creery sisters performed no better than chance. This variability among days became, in the minds of the investigators, a property of the phenomenon [35]:

> It may be noted that the power of these children, collectively or separately, gradually diminished during these months, so that at the end of 1882 they could not do, under the easiest conditions, what they could do under the most stringent in 1881. This gradual decline of power seemed quite independent of the tests applied, and resembled the disappearance of a transitory pathological condition, being the very opposite of what might have been expected from a growing proficiency in code-communication.

The fact that alleged psychics inevitably seem to lose their powers under continued investigation has become known as the *decline effect,* which can occur in a variety of patterns and guises. Gurney and his colleagues propose the decline as additional support for the genuineness of the telepathy because it is not what might be expected if the girls were becoming more proficient in using a code. The cynic, of course, views this decline in just the opposite way. Presumably the investigators are also becoming more proficient in knowing what to look for, especially in the face of continuing criticism, and, as a result, they have made it more difficult for the girls to get away with their tricks.

As it turns out the investigators later caught the girls cheating. The girls, at least on this occasion, had used a simple code. This brings up an additional theme in psychical research that we might, for short, label the *problem of the dirty test tube.* Gurney revealed the deception in a brief note that appeared in the *Proceedings of the Society for Psychical Research* in 1888 [44]. Hall thinks it is very significant that Gurney's fellow investigators did not sign this revelation [41].

In the note, Gurney reminds his readers

> that the earliest experiments in Thought-transference described in the Society's *Proceedings* were made with some sisters of the name of Creery. The important experiments were, of course, those in which the "agency" was confined to one or more of the investigating Committee. . . . But though stress was never laid on any trials where a chance of collusion was afforded by one or more of the sisters sharing in the "agency," nevertheless some results contained under such conditions were included in the records. It is necessary, therefore, to state that in a series of experiments with cards, recently made at Cambridge, two of the sisters, acting as "agent" and "percipient," were detected in the use of a code of signals; and a third has confessed to a certain amount of signaling in the earlier series to which reference has been made [44].

Gurney then describes both the visual and auditory codes used by the girls. He continues as follows [44]:

> The use of the visual code was very gratuitous on the part of the sisters, since it had been explained to them that we did not attach any scientific value to the experiments in which they acted as agent and percipient in sight of each other, the possibility of success under these conditions having been abundantly proved. The object of our experiments at Cambridge on this occasion was, if possible, to strengthen the evidence for Thought-transference (1) when no members of the family were aware of the thing to be guessed, and (2) when the sister acting as agent was in a different room from the one acting as percipient. The experiments in which the codes were used were intended merely as amusement and encouragement with a view to increase the chance of success in the more difficult ones—which

were all complete failures. The account which was given as to the earlier experiments, conducted under similar conditions, is that signals were very rarely used; and not on specially successful occasions, but on occasions of failure, when it was feared that visitors would be disappointed. But of course the recent detection must throw discredit on the results of all previous trials in which one or more of the sisters shared in the agency. How far the proved willingness to deceive can be held to affect the experiments on which we relied, where collusion was excluded, must of course depend on the degree of stringency of the precautions taken against trickery of other sorts—as to which every reader will form his own opinion.

This manner of treating the discovery of cheating illustrates a number of interwoven themes. The finding of a "dirty test tube" ordinarily implies that all the results of the experiment are brought into question. Gurney argues that only those results clearly attached to the "dirty test tube" should be discarded. Since the girls could not have used their code, in his judgment, in those trials in which only investigators knew the chosen object, those trials still retain their evidential value. Related to this is what the early psychical researchers called the problem of "mixed mediumship." Psychics and mediums are under constant pressure to produce results, yet they have little direct control over their fickle powers. Therefore, in order not to disappoint their followers or from fear of losing the attention that goes with mediumship, they learn to supplement their real powers with tricks to simulate the phenomena. Still another variant of this exploits the apparent fact that many mediums and psychics are apparently in a trance or altered state when performing. In such a state they are highly suggestible and behave in ways expected of them. If skeptics are among the onlookers, they will sometimes cheat because this is what is expected of them. The onus for the consequent cheating is by this means placed upon the skeptic rather than the cheater.

The dirty test tube problem has been with psychical research from its beginning and, as we will see, is still very much a part of the contemporary scene. The medium Eusapia Palladino's long career was noteworthy for the number of times she was caught cheating. She readily acknowledged that she would cheat if the investigators gave her the opportunity. Despite this record of cheating, many psychical researchers, including some of today's leaders in the field, have no doubt that on many other occasions she displayed true paranormal powers [19]. On the contemporary scene, parapsychologists are willing to admit that the controversial metal bender Uri Geller often cheats, but that, on occasion, he exhibits real paranormal powers [45]. And parapsychologists blamed me, rather than Geller, for the fact that Geller cheated in my presence because, as they put it, I did not impose sufficiently stringent conditions to prevent him from cheating [22].

Despite this attempt to save some of the evidence from the Creery experiments, the leaders of the Society for Psychical Research quietly removed the experiment from their evidential data base. But Sir William Barrett refused to go along with this demoting of the experiment. According to Gauld, this incident sparked dissension between Barrett and the other founders [32]. "Barrett had been the first to experiment with these girls, and they were his special proteges. . . . Barrett would never agree that the later and crude cheating invalidated all the earlier results; he considered that his 1876 experiments, together with his experiments with the Creerys had established his claim to be the discoverer of thought-transference, and he remained bitter towards the Sidgwicks for the rest of his life."

Not only did Barrett continue to defend the evidential value of the Creery experiments, but so did later parasychologists. In his classic monograph of 1934 on *Extra-Sensory Perception,* J. B. Rhine included this experiment as among the most evidential of the early research. "On the whole the early experiments in E.S.P. were admirably conducted . . . as one would expect from the array of highly impressive names connected with them. The experiments with the Creery sisters, for instance, were conducted by Professors William Barrett, Henry Sidgwick and Balfour Stewart, by Mrs. Henry Sidgwick, Frederic Myers, Edmund Gurney and Frank Podmore. . . . In all this work the results were sufficiently striking to leave no doubt as to the exclusion of the hypothesis of chance" [46].

Despite these attempts to salvage something from the Creery experiments, I believe it is fair to say that today the experiments are not part of the case that parapsychologists would make in support of psi. Indeed, my perusal of several contemporary books and histories of parapsychology indicates that the experiments are rarely, if ever, mentioned.

The same fate befell the very next major experiment on telepathy conducted by the same investigators. In their "Second Report on Thought-Transference," Gurney and his colleagues describe the first of their experimental findings in which two young men, Smith and Blackburn, were apparently able to communicate telepathically under conditions that prevented normal communication. If anything, the investigators placed even more reliance upon these later experiments than in those with the Creery sisters.

As was the case with the Creery sisters, Smith and Blackburn soon lost their powers. Smith was then hired by the society to assist in the conduct of several successful telepathic experiments. In 1908, Blackburn, thinking that Smith was dead, publicly confessed as to how he and Smith had tricked the investigators during the experiments. Smith, who was very much alive and still employed by the society, denied the charges. In the ensuing debate, the society's leaders defended Smith. Good accounts of this amazing incident can be found in [38] and [41]. Today, the Smith-Blackburn experiments are no longer considered part of the parapsychological case for psi.

J. B. Rhine

The founding of the Society for Psychical Research in 1882 was an attempt to organize and professionalize psychical research. Other societies, such as the American Society for Psychical Research, quickly followed. Journals and proceedings were published and international congresses were held. Despite these steps towards institutionalization, psychical research continued for the next 50 years to be an uncoordinated activity of amateurs. No agreed-upon program or central body of concepts characterized the field.

During this period, psychic researchers disagreed among themselves on issues involving subject matter, methodology, and theory. On one side were those, perhaps the majority, who supported the spiritist hypothesis that psychic phenomena reflected the activity of departed spirits or superintelligent beings. Opposed to these were psychic researchers like Nobel laureate Charles Richet who defended the position that the phenomena could be explained in terms of a "psychic force" without assuming survival of spirits [47].

Another division had on one side those who felt that psychical research should confine itself to mental phenomena such as telepathy, premonitions, and clairvoyance. Opposed to these were those who felt that the physical phenomena such as levitation, materialization, poltergeist events, and psycho-kinesis should be the focus of inquiry. The majority of psychical researchers believed in telepathy but were dubious about clairvoyance. But a strong minority, led by Richet, believed that clairvoyance not only existed but was the basic phenomenon underlying telepathy.

Possibly the most divisive issue of all was the question of what sort of a research program was appropriate for psychical investigation. A small but vocal minority wanted psychical research to become a rigorous experimental science. A larger group felt that the natural-historical method was more appropriate because so many of the important phenomena were spontaneous and not observable in the laboratory. Opposed to both these groups were members of the societies who felt that the quantification and rigor of the natural sciences were irrelevant to the study of psychical phenomena.

The event that is credited with providing psychical research with a common focus and a coherent research program was the publication in 1934 of J. B. Rhine's monograph *Extra-Sensory Perception* [46]. Mauskopf and McVaugh [47] provide an excellent survey of the period from 1915 to 1940, which they treat as the period when psychical research made the transition from a preparadigmatic to a paradigmatic research program.

Rhine pulled together the various strands already existing in psychical research and coordinated them into a coherent program. He also coined the terms *parapsychology* to refer to the new experimental science that descended from psychical research and *extra-sensory perception* to refer to the basic phenomenon to be studied. In agreement with Richet, and in disagreement with the British parapsychologists, Rhine viewed clairvoyance as on the same footing with telepathy. Later, precognition was also put under the rubric of extra-sensory perception (ESP). ESP became defined as "knowledge of or response to an external event or influence not apprehended through known sensory channels" [48]. This included telepathy, clairvoyance, precognition, and retrocognition. The psychic phenomena not involving reception of information were included under the term *psychokinesis* (PK), which is defined as "the influence of mind on external objects or processes without the mediation of known physical energies or forces" [48]. Today both ESP and PK are included under the more general term *psi*, which is "a general term to identify a person's extra-sensorimotor communication with the environment" [48].

Rhine's 1934 monograph deals only with clairvoyance and telepathy. In 1934 he also began research programs on precognition and psychokinesis. Apparently, he was reluctant to publicize these latter programs too soon for fear of making parapsychology too controversial and unacceptable to mainstream science [48]. He waited until 1938 before he published anything on precognition and until 1943 for the first reports on his PK results.

The major innovation introduced by Rhine was the use of the five target designs: circle, cross, wavy lines, square, and star. These patterns were printed on cards,, and the standard ESP deck consisted of 5 cards of each symbol for a total of 25 cards. Rhine also introduced standard procedures for using these target materials. The two most common were the Basic Technique and the Down Through Technique. In the Basic Technique (B.T.), the deck is shuffled and placed face down; the percipient guesses the value of the top card; this is then removed and laid aside; the percipient guesses the value of the second card; the second card is then removed and laid on top of the first; the percipient now guesses the third card; etc. This procedure is continued until all 25 cards have been used. At the end of such a "run," a check is made to see how many guesses were hits. If the procedure was supposed to test telepathy, then an agent would look at each card at the time the percipient was trying to guess its symbol. If clairvoyance was being tested, no one would look at each card as it was placed aside. The Down Through Technique (D.T.) tested clairvoyance by having the percipient guess the symbols from top to bottom before any of them were removed for checking against the call. The D.T. technique is considered to be superior methodologically in that it better protects against inadvertent sensory cues from the backs of the cards.

Extra-Sensory Perception attracted the attention of both the psychical researchers and the skeptics for two reasons. Rhine's data base consisted of 91,174 separate trials or guesses over a three-year period using a number of nonprofessional individuals as percipients. More important was the unprecedented level of success he reported. Of the 85,724 guesses recorded using the five-symbol ESP decks, 24,364 were "hits." This was 7,219 more hits than the 17,145 that would be expected just by chance. The odds against this being just an accident are calculated as being practically infinite. His subjects averaged 7.1 hits per run of 25 as against the chance expectation of 5. Although this is only 2 extra hits per 25, such consistency over this huge number of trials and different subjects had no precedent in the prior history of psychical research.

Rhine's best subject, Hubert Pearce, averaged 8 hits per run over a total of 17,250 guesses. As Rhine notes [46]:

> Most people are more impressed by a spectacular series of successive hits than by lower but cumulative scoring. Pearce's scoring 25 straight hits under clairvoyant conditions, in my presence, and Zirkle's 26 straight hits in pure telepathy with my assistant, Miss Ownbey, are the best instances of these. Other subjects have approached these. Linzmayer scored 21 in 25 clairvoyance, in my presence; Miss Ownbey herself, unwitnessed, scored 23, pure clairvoyance. Miss Turner's score of 19 in distance P.T. [pure telepathy] work stands out because of the 250 miles between her and the agent. Miss Bailey scored 19 in P.T. in the same room with the agent, as did also Cooper. The odds against getting one series of 25 straight hits by mere chance would be 5^{25} which is nearly 300 quadrillions—just one score of 25! A small part of our 90,000 trials.

Rhine's work provided the model for most parapsychological work from 1934 to around 1970. Using card guessing with the five ESP symbols, an astonishing variety of questions about ESP were investigated [48]. Because of its huge data base, its claims to statistical and experimental sophistication, and its unprecedented rate of success Rhine's research gained the attention of scientific and popular audiences [47]. At first scientists were at a loss about how to react. Many scientists, as a result of reading Rhine's work, were encouraged to try to replicate the results. A few got encouraging results, but most failed.

The first attacks by the critics were aimed at Rhine's statistical procedures. As it turned out, some of Rhine's statistical procedures were technically incorrect, but, for the most part, his results could not be explained away as due to inappropriate statistical procedures. The critics turned out to be wide off the mark in many of their accusations. On the whole, however, the statistical debate led to constructive developments and improved clarification about the proper use of statistical procedures in such experiments [47].

Having essentially lost the statistical battle, the critics then turned to Rhine's experimental controls. Here, he was much more vulnerable. And,

ironically, it was the British psychical research community that had anticipated the critics and provided the sharpest critiques of Rhine's methods
[47]. The British parapsychologists were astonished both by Rhine's apparent
ease in finding successful percipients as well as his claims that clairvoyance
worked as well as telepathy. With only a few exceptions, they had found
only evidence for telepathy. And their experience had convinced them that
telepathic powers were very rare. While they welcomed Rhine's contribution,
they were quick to point out many of its defects, especially Rhine's inadequate
description of his procedures and the seeming casualness of his experiments.

During the 1930s, nevertheless, Rhine's work, as reported in *Extra-
Sensory Perception,* was hailed by parapsychologists as the best scientific
case for ESP ever put before the world. Today, as I understand it, most
parapsychologists, although they acknowledge its seminal influence on the
development of the field, dismiss much of Rhine's earlier work as non-
evidential because of its loose controls, poorly made target materials, and
inadequate documentation.

S. G. Soal

Rhine's strongest critic among the British parapsychologists was the mathematician S. G. Soal. Just prior to the appearance of Rhine's monograph,
Soal had conducted a huge series of card-guessing experiments with only
chance results. But the experiments for which Soal became most renowned
began as a direct response to Rhine's monograph.

After five years of heroic research, Soal was sure that he had succeeded
only in demonstrating the laws of chance. A colleague, however, persuaded
him to check for a certain trend in his data. And this resulted in a new
series of experiments that for almost 25 years was hailed as the most
convincing and fraud-proof demonstration of ESP ever achieved. Because
the experiment and results seemed so impressive, some critics—in a way
reminiscent of Carpenter's attacks upon Wallace and Crookes and within
the spirit of Sidgwick's false dichotomy—openly accused Soal of fraud on
no other basis than that his results were too good. Other critics attacked
him on grounds that were irrelevant. As it turns out the critics were right,
but for the wrong reasons!

As soon as Soal heard about Rhine's successful American research,
he began an ambitious program to replicate Rhine's findings in England.
Soal started late in 1934 and continued his experiments for five years. At
the end he had accumulated 128,350 guesses for 160 percipients. This is
almost 30 percent more guesses than Rhine had accumulated for his 1934
monograph. Soal was sure that he had removed all the flaws and weaknesses

that had characterized Rhine's work. Unfortunately, Soal found that this enormous effort yielded "little evidence of a direct kind that the persons tested, whether considered as individuals or in the mass, possessed any faculty for either clairvoyance or telepathy" (quoted in [49]).

Soal reported these results to a stunned parapsychological world in 1940. At the same time another British parapsychologist, Whately Carington, reported the results of telepathy experiments that seemed to show a "displacement effect." Instead of achieving hits on the target, his subjects seemed to achieve above-chance matches when their guesses were matched with either the immediately preceding or the next target in the series. Carington asked Soal to check his data to see whether he, too, might find such a displacement effect [49].

Soal was reluctant to do so. He told Goldney that he thought Carington's request was preposterous and he wasn't going to waste his time going through his huge batch of records. But Carington persisted, and Soal finally agreed. Soal found, among the records of his 160 percipients, two who seemed to show Carington's displacement effect. Although this finding was published, presumably Soal realized that such a post hoc finding had to be replicated [49].

Fortunately, one of his two percipients, Basil Shackleton, was available for testing during the years 1941 through 1943. With the collaboration of K.M. Goldney, 40 sittings that yielded a total of 11,378 guesses were obtained with Shackleton during this difficult period when England was at war. As had been the case with the original testing, Shackleton's guesses were at chance level when compared with the actual target, but when compared with the symbol coming up immediately after the target (precognitive hitting), Shackleton's guesses yielded 2,890 successes as compared with the 2,308 expected by chance. The odds against this being a chance occurrence were calculated to be more than 10^{35} to 1 [50].

In 1945 Soal was able to begin experimenting on the second percipient who had displayed the displacement effect in the original data, Mrs. Gloria Stewart. He was able to accumulate a total of 37,100 guesses during 130 separate sittings. Unlike Shackleton's or her own previous performance, her hitting this time was on the actual target rather than on the immediately preceding or following trial. She managed to achieve 9,410 hits, which were 1,990 more hits than would be expected by chance. The odds against such a result were calculated as 10^{70} to 1 [50].

Soal's stated objective was to make these experiments completely error-free and fraud-proof. The basic procedure, which was varied slightly on occasion, was as follows. The percipient—Basil Shackleton or Gloria Stewart —sat in one room monitored by one of the experimenters (EP). In an adjoining room, the sender or agent sat at table opposite the second experimenter (EA). The door between the rooms was slightly open so that the percipient could hear EA's call as to when to make his or her guess. The percipient, of course, could see neither the agent nor EA. A screen with a small aperture separated the agent and EA. For each block of 50 trials EA had before him a list of randomized numbers that determined the target for each trial. Each number could range from 1 to 5. If the target number for the first trial was, say, 3, EA would hold up a card with the number 3 on it so that it could be seen by the agent through the aperture. The agent had, lying before him in a row, five cards. Each card had a different drawing of an animal on it: elephant, giraffe, lion, pelican, and zebra. Before each block of trials, the agent shuffled the order of the picture cards. If EA held up a card with 3 on it, the agent would turn up the third card and concentrate upon the animal depicted on it. The percipient would then try to guess which animal was being "sent" and write his guess for that trial in the corresponding place on the response sheet. After every block of 50 trials, the agent reshuffled the target cards so that, for that block, only the agent knew which animal corresponded with which number.

In addition to this rather elaborate arrangement, independent observers were invited to attend many of the sittings. Several professors and a member of Parliament were among the observers. On some blocks of trials, unknown to the percipient, the agent did not look at the symbols. This was a test for clairvoyance. Other variations were introduced from time to time. The experiments with Gloria Stewart, while following the same pattern, were admittedly not as carefully controlled. Special precautions were also introduced to ensure that the prepared target sequences could not be known to agent or percipient in advance. And careful safeguards were introduced during the recording of the results and the matching of the targets against the guesses. Duplicates of all records were made and posted immediately after each session to a well-known academic.

Never before had so many safeguards been introduced into an ESP experiment. With so many individuals involved, and with prominent observers freely observing, any form of either unwitting cueing or deliberate trickery would seem to be just about impossible. If fraud of any sort were to be suspected, it would seemingly require, under the stated conditions, the active collusion of several prominent individuals. Beyond these safeguards, Soal randomized his targets, instituted sophisticated checks for randomness, and used the most appropriate statistical procedures. Despite these elaborate precautions, the two subjects managed to consistently score above chance over a number of years.

Soal's findings were hailed as definitive by the parapsychological community and were so good that the rest of the scientific community, including the skeptics, could not ignore them. Here was one of Rhine's severest critics, a man who had spent many years meticulously conducting enormous card-guessing experiments with only chance results, a man who was by profession a mathematician, and an experimenter who had seemingly taken every known precaution to guard against every loophole and possibility of error, who suddenly demonstrated highly successful telepathic and precognitive results over sustained periods of time with two percipients.

Whately Carington, the parapsychologist who convinced Soal to re-examine his seemingly unsuccessful results, wrote (as quoted in [51]):

> Mr. Soal is a most remarkable man, for whose work I have the highest possible admiration. Possessed of a more than Jobian patience, and a conscientiousness, thoroughness which I can only describe as almost pathological, he worked in various branches of the subject for many years with nothing but a succession of null results to show for it. . . . Hoping to repeat Rhine's experiments in England, he tested 160 persons, collecting 128,350 Zener card guesses singlehanded, and using the most elaborate precautions against every possible source of error. . . . If I had to choose one single investigation on which to pin my whole faith in the reality of paranormal phenomena, or with which to convince a hardened skeptic (if this be not a contradiction in terms), I should unhesitatingly choose this series of experiments, which is the most cast-iron piece of work I know, as well as having yielded the most remarkable results.

Similar sentiments were expressed by virtually every parapsychologist who commented on this work. As just one illustration, R. A. McConnell [52] phrased it as follows: "As a report to scientists this is the most important book on parapsychology since the 1940 publication of *Extra-Sensory Perception After Sixty Years.* If scientists will read it carefully, the 'ESP controversy' will be ended."

G. R. Price's Critique

Ironically, some critical scientists did read it carefully, but, contrary to McConnell's prognosis, the controversy did not end. Indeed, one of the first major reviews in a scientific journal raised the controversy to new heights. Although the Shackleton experiments had originally been reported by Soal and Goldney in the *Proceedings of the Society for Psychical Research* in 1943, the scientific world did not become aware of those experiments until they·were reported along with the later experiments with Gloria Stewart in the 1954 book *Modern Experiments in Telepathy* by Soal and Bateman [50].

What fueled the controversy was an unprecedented review article, nine pages in length, appearing in *Science,* the prestigious journal of the American Association for the Advancement of Science. On August 26, 1955, George

R. Price's article on "Science and the Supernatural" was the only feature article for that issue. Price, who as far as I can tell had never before written on parapsychology, was described as being a research associate in the Department of Medicine at the University of Minnesota.

Price began his controversial article by stating that "believers in psychic phenomena—such as telepathy, clairvoyance, precognition, and psychokinesis—appear to have won a decisive victory and virtually silenced opposition" [53]. Price writes that such a victory has seemed close in the past, but always critics have managed to find flaws. But Price sees the time at which he is writing as unique because practically no scientific papers had attacked parapsychology during the preceding 15 years [53].

> The victory is the result of an impressive amount of careful experimentation and intelligent argumentation. The best of the card-guessing experiments of Rhine and Soal show enormous odds against chance occurrence, while the possibility of sensory clues is often eliminated by placing cards and percipient in separate buildings far apart. Dozens of experimenters have obtained positive results in ESP experiments, and the mathematical procedures have been approved by leading statisticians.
>
> I suspect that most scientists who have studied the work of Rhine (especially as it is presented in *Extra-Sensory Perception After Sixty Years*), . . . and Soal (described in *Modern Experiments in Telepathy*), . . . have found it necessary to accept their findings. . . . Against all this evidence, almost the only defense remaining to the skeptical scientist is ignorance, ignorance concerning the work itself and concerning its implications. The typical scientist contents himself with retaining in his memory some criticism that at most applies to a small fraction of the published studies. But these findings (which challenge our very concepts of space and time) are—if valid— of enormous importance, both philosophically and practically, so they ought not to be ignored.

Price then elaborates upon a suggested scheme, using redundancy coding, which would make ESP useful, even if it is a very weak and erratic form of communication. He then presents his version of Hume's argument against miracles. He quotes Tom Paine's more succinct version of the same argument: "Is it more probable that nature should go out of her course, or that a man should tell a lie?"

To justify using Hume's argument as his only grounds for accusing the parapsychologists of cheating, Price first tries to show that if ESP were real it would violate a number of fundamental principles underlying all the sciences. Some of these principles are that the cause must precede the effect, signals are attenuated by distance, signals are blocked by appropriate shielding, and so forth. ESP, according to Price, if it exists, violates all these principles. Then Price puts forth reasons why he considers ESP to be a principle of magic rather than merely a previously undiscovered new law of nature. "The essential characteristic of magic is that phenomena occur that can most easily be explained in terms of action by invisible intelligent beings. . . . The essence of science is mechanism."

These lengthy considerations back up Price's solution to coping with the challenge of parapsychological claims [53]: "My opinion concerning the findings of the parapsychologists is that many of them are dependent on clerical and statistical errors and unintentional use of sensory clues, and that all extrachance results not so explicable are dependent on deliberate fraud or mildly abnormal mental conditions."

Actually, nothing is novel or startling about Price's opinion. The same opinion, stated in just about the same words, probably is held by all skeptics. Price has carried his opinion beyond skepticism, however. The thrust of his article is that the *best* research in parapsychology as exemplified in the work of Rhine and Soal *cannot* be dismissed on the basis of "clerical and statistical error and unintentional use of sensory clues." Therefore, he concludes that the results of this otherwise exemplary research *must* be due to fraud. He does not feel that he requires any evidence of fraud. Hume's argument against miracles gives him sufficient license. Price's position, of course, no longer belongs to skepticism, but rather to dogmatism. His position seemingly is that no research, no matter how well done, can convince him of ESP.

But Price does not want to go to quite that extreme. He says that he still can be convinced *provided that* the parapsychologists can supply him with just one successful outcome from a truly fraud-proof experiment. "What is needed is one completely convincing experiment—just one experiment that does not have to be accepted simply on the basis of faith in human honesty. We should require evidence of such nature that it would convince us even if we knew that the chief experimenter was a stage conjurer or a confidence man."

But does not the Soal experiment with Shackleton and Stewart meet this criterion? No, says Price, because he can imagine scenarios in which cheating could have taken place. Price then presents a number of possible ways that he feels cheating *could* have occurred in the Soal experiments [53].

> I do not claim that I know how Soal cheated if he did cheat, but if I were myself to duplicate his results, this is how I would proceed. First of all, I would seek a few collaborators, preferably people with good memories. The more collaborators I had, the easier it would be to perform the experiments, but the greater would be the risk of a disclosure. Weighing these two considerations together, I'd want four confederates to imitate the Shackleton experiments. For imitating the Stewart series, I'd probably want three or four—although it is impossible to be certain, because the

Stewart sittings have not been reported in much detail. In recruiting, I would appeal not to desire for fame or material gain but to the noblest motives, arguing that much good to humanity could result from a small deception designed to strengthen religious belief.

After providing a sampling of scenarios in which cheating could have occurred, all involving the collusion of three or more investigators, participants and onlookers, Price supplies some designs of what he would consider to be a satisfactory test. The key to all his designs involves a committee. "Let us somewhat arbitrarily think of a committee of 12 and design tests such that the presence of a single honest man on the 'jury' will ensure validity of the test, even if the other 11 members should cooperate in fraud either to prove or disprove occurrence of psi phenomena."

Perhaps if some enterprising group of scientists collaborated and conducted an ESP experiment with positive results according to Price's approved designs, the outcome might very well convince *him*. But I do not think it would, nor should it, convince the majority of skeptical scientists. Without going into all its other faults, a single experiment—no matter how elaborate or allegedly fraud-proof—is simply a unique event. Scientific evidence is based on cumulative and replicable events across laboratories and investigators. The rubbish heap of scientific history contains many examples of seemingly airtight experiments whose results have been discarded because later scientists could not replicate the results. The experiments on mitogenetic radiation would be just one example. No one has found fault with the original experiments. But since later experimenters could not replicate the results, the original experiments have been cast aside. Can anyone doubt that this would not also happen to a successful, but nonreplicable, ESP outcome from one of Price's "satisfactory tests"?

Price tells us "that I myself believed in ESP about 15 years ago, after reading *Extra-Sensory Perception After Sixty Years,* but I changed my mind when I became acquainted with the argument presented by David Hume in his chapter 'Of miracles' in *An Enquiry Concerning Human Understanding."* So Hume supplies him with his escape hatch.

But all this seems unnecessarily dramatic. Price has fallen into a particularly stark version of the false dichotomy. He has been forced into the very position that Henry Sidgwick wanted for the critics. The best ESP evidence is so good that either the critic must admit the reality of psi or accuse the proponents of lying and fraud. In falling into this trap— one that critics from the days of Hare and Crookes right up to the present keep falling into—Price has needlessly attributed to the Rhine and Soal results a level of evidential value that they cannot carry. At the same time, Price has implied that he is sufficiently expert in parapsychological research that he can infallibly judge when a given outcome unquestionably supports the conclusions of the experimenters. In fact, I doubt that even the parapsychologists are ready to give such power to a single experiment, even one so seemingly well-conducted as Soal's.

Price writes as if, when confronted with experimental evidence for psi, such as can be obtained by reading *Extra-Sensory Perception After Sixty Years* or *Modern Experiments in Telepathy,* he must immediately (a) find ways to reject the findings on the basis of possible sensory leakage, statistical artifacts, or loose experimental controls; or (b) accept the outcome as proof of psi; or (c) accuse the investigators of fraud if he can imagine some scenario, no matter how complex and unlikely, under which fraud *could* have occurred. Price just does not understand either parapsychological research or scientific research in general if he truly believes these are the only alternatives open to him. Unfortunately, Price is behaving like many of the other outspoken critics of psychical research. To Price's credit, he has at least tried to make his basis for action explicit.

Both Rhine and Soal, in their responses to Price's critique, eagerly accepted Price's implicit endorsement of their experimental procedures. Soal commented that "it is very significant and somewhat comforting to learn that Price admits that 'most of Soal's work' cannot be accounted for by any combination of statistical artifact and sensory leakage" [54]. Soal also examined in detail Price's various proposed schemes for faking the experiments [54]:

> Price goes to great length in devising variations on this theme, but they all depend on the Agent being in collusion with the chief Experimenter or with the Percipient. Now four of the Agents with whom Mrs. Stewart was highly successful were lecturers of high academic standing at Queen Mary College in the University of London. Two were senior lecturers and the other two were mathematicians who had done distinguished creative work. A fifth Agent who was brilliantly successful over a long period was a senior civil servant, in fact an assistant director of mathematical examinations in the Civil Service. Now is it plausible to suppose that I, as chief Experimenter, could persuade any of these men to enter into a stupid and pointless collusion to fake the experiments over a period of years? What had any of them to gain from such deplorable conduct? If I had gone to any of them and suggested (as Price recommends) that in a good cause a little deception would be no harm, I know quite plainly that the result would have been a first-class scandal in university circles.

Rhine found even more solace in Price's attack. "Strange though it may seem, the publication of the George Price paper . . . is, on the whole, a good event for parapsychology" [55]. For one thing, it was a way of getting a lot of instruction on parapsychology before the scientific community.

Rhine also felt Price's vivid portrayal of the potential importance of ESP was valuable. He welcomed Price's effective rebuttal against the standard criticisms against ESP. And Rhine especially liked the fact that Price focused on the point that psi was incompatible with the materialism of science [55]:

> [Price], even more than any other critical reviewer, gives indication of having felt the force of the evidence for ESP. When he turns then—albeit a bit too emotionally—and says that, according to the current concept of nature, ESP is impossible and therefore the parapsychologists must all be fakers, he at least draws the issue where it can be squarely met. The answer of the parapsychologist is: "Yes, either the present mechanistic theory of man *is* wrong—that is, fundamentally incomplete—or, of course, the parapsychologists *are* all utterly mistaken."*One* of these opponents is wrong; take it, now, from the pages of *Science!* This recognition of the issue gives point to the findings of parapsychology in a way none can easily miss.

Notice that Rhine and Price agree on some aspects of this controversy. Both Rhine and Price believe that if the claims of parapsychology are correct the foundations of science are seriously threatened. Rhine welcomes such a destruction of what he calls materialism. Price seems willing to take the most drastic measures to avoid this overthrow of what he calls the basic limiting principles. (Not all parapsychologists agree with Rhine that the acceptance of psi need be inconsistent with scientific materialism.) One issue involves what it means for contemporary science to accept the reality of psi. This concerns matters that are currently controversial among philosophers of science, so it is probably not fruitful to attempt to deal with them here.

Rhine and Price also agree that the standard arguments against parapsychological evidence do not hold up. According to reasonable scientific criteria, the evidence for psi is more than adequate. And so it is at this point that both Rhine and Price want to have the showdown. Price, as a defender of the materialistic faith, puts all his money on the hope that the parapsychologists have faked the data. He has no evidence to back this claim. But if he can invent possible scenarios whereby trickery *might* have been committed in a given experiment, then he believes he can, under license from David Hume, assume that fraud must have taken place. He is not completely dogmatic about this. If the parapsychologist can come up with positive results in at least one experiment conducted under what Price considers to be fraud-proof conditions, then Price has committed himself to accept the consequences.

Many issues are raised by Price's dramatic confrontational posturing. At this point, I will mention just one. Price goes beyond conventional scientific practice when he empowers a given experiment with the ability to prove the existence of psi. Once we realize that no experiment by itself definitely establishes or disproves a scientific claim, then Price's extreme remedies to save his image of science become unnecessary. No matter how well-designed and seemingly flawless a given experiment, there is always the possibility that future considerations will reveal previously unforeseen loopholes and weaknesses.

Indeed, a careful analysis of the Soal experiment will reveal a variety of weaknesses. For example, in spite of the number of observers and experimenters, Soal always had control over the prepared target sequences or over the basic recording. And both Shackleton and Stewart only produced successful results when Soal was present. On one occasion, without informing Soal, his co-investigator Mrs. Goldney conducted a sitting with Shackleton. The outcome was unsuccessful. The American parapsychologist J. G. Pratt ran a series of experiments with Mrs. Stewart without Soal's presence. No evidence for psi was found. And whereas all Rhine's results showed no difference between telepathic and clairvoyance trials, both Shackleton and Mrs. Stewart produced successful results only on telepathic trials. Furthermore, in spite of the much-vaunted measures to guard against sensory leakage, the actual experimental setup, when carefully considered, offered a variety of possibilities for just such unwitting communication.

None of the foregoing considerations, in themselves, account for Soal's findings. But they make superfluous, I would argue, the hasty assumption that the findings can only be explained either by psi or some elaborate form of dishonest collusion.

The Discrediting of Soal

As it turns out, if Soal did cheat—and it now seems almost certain that he did—he almost certainly did so in ways not envisaged by either Price or Hansel. The scenarios generated by these two critics involved collusion among several of the principals. Soal apparently managed the fraud entirely on his own or, at most, with the collusion of one other person. Furthermore, he probably used a variety of different ways to accomplish his goals.

If it had not been for a series of seemingly fortuitous events, Soal's experiment might still occupy the honored place in the parapsychologists' exhibits of evidence for psi [56]–[60]. The discrediting of Soal's data occurred through a number of revelations during the period from 1955 through 1978. Up until 1978 the accumulation of evidence suggested that something was highly suspicious about the records in the Shackleton experiments. The case was strong enough to discredit Soal's results in the judgment of some leading parapsychologists, but many others still defended Soal's findings.

The final blow to the credibility of Soal's results came in 1978 when

Betty Markwick published her article "The Soal-Goldney Experiments with Basil Shackleton: New Evidence of Data Manipulation" [60]. As with the previous revelations of peculiarities in the data, Markwick's stunning findings arose out of a series of fortuitous incidents.

The story is much too complicated to relate here. Essentially, Markwick had begun a rather elaborate project to clear Soal of accumulating charges that he had tampered with the data. Her plan involved searching the records with the aid of a computer to find subtle patterns, which, if they existed, would account for the anomalies found by the critics and would vindicate Soal. Markwick did not find such patterns. Instead, she discovered previously unnoticed patterns that could be accounted for if one assumed that Soal had used a sophisticated plan for inserting "hits" into the records while he was apparently summarizing and checking the results. Reluctantly, she was forced to conclude that only the hypothesis of deliberate tampering with the data could explain her findings [60].

> Protestations to the effect that Soal, a respected scientist, would not have cheated in his own experiments—and that anyway the rigorous experimental conditions in the Shackleton series precluded fraud—seem to me to carry little weight in the face of the evidence. We can rarely fathom how conjurors achieve *their* feats, and perhaps Soal was as clever. It is futile to argue that the prison cell is escape-proof when the inmate has clearly gone.

Markwick, obviously dismayed at having discovered that Soal almost certainly faked his data, suggests two possible explanations for why he might have done so. One of her hypotheses made use of the well-known fact that Soal sometimes did automatic writing in a dissociated state. Markwick suggested the possibility that Soal may have had a split personality and that the cheating was done by his other self.

Markwick's second hypothesis involved data massage and has more universal psychological plausibility (although it is not necessarily inconsistent with her first hypothesis). She assumes that Soal's enormous accumulation of negative ESP findings were obtained legitimately. She also assumes that his *post hoc* finding of consistent displacement effects in the data of Basil Shackleton and Gloria Stewart was also legitimate [60]. "Having embarked upon the Shackleton series, one may imagine the scoring rate begins to fade (as ESP scores are wont to do after the initial flush of success). Soal, seeing the chance slipping away of gaining scientific recognition for Parapsychology, a cause in which he passionately believes, succumbs to the temptation of 'rectifying' a 'temporary' deficiency."

Markwick's second scenario is consistent with known patterns in which scientists have tampered with their data [61], [62]. The components appear to be: (1) the investigator believes, on the basis of previous experience, that the phenomenon under investigation is "real"; (2) for some unknown reason his current research fails to reveal the phenomenon; (3) if he reports negative results his readers might wrongly believe that the phenomenon does not exist; (4) as a result, the "truth" and assumed positive consequences of the phenomenon might be lost to humanity. Given these ingredients, it takes a very small step for the investigator to convince himself that he is helping both the truth and a good cause along by doctoring his data.

William James, with reference to his experiences in psychical research, suggested that cheating in order to convince others of the "reality" you know to be the case might be defensible. James discussed the matter in his last essay on psychical research. He referred to the policy of English investigators to consider a medium who has been caught cheating as one who always cheats. He indicated that he thought this had generally been a wise policy [2].

> But, however wise as a policy the S.P.R.'s maxim may have been, as a test of truth I believe it to be almost irrelevant. In most things human the accusation of deliberate fraud and falsehood is grossly superficial. Man's character is too sophistically mixed for the alternative of "honest or dishonest" to be a sharp one. Scientific men themselves will cheat—at public lectures—rather than let experiments obey their well-known tendency toward failure.

James gave two examples of such cheating. And then revealed the following about his own behavior [2]:

> To compare small men with great, I have myself cheated shamelessly. In the early days of the Sanders Theater at Harvard, I once had charge of a heart on the physiology of which Professor Newell Martin was giving a popular lecture. This heart, which belonged to a turtle, supported an index-straw which threw a moving shadow, greatly enlarged, upon the screen, while the heart pulsated. When certain nerves were stimulated, the lecturer said, the heart would act in certain ways which he described. But the poor heart was too far gone and, although it stopped duly when the nerve of arrest was excited, that was the final end of its life's tether. Presiding over the performance, I was terrified at the fiasco, and found myself suddenly acting like one of those military geniuses who on the field of battle convert disaster into victory. There was no time for deliberation; so, with my forefinger under a part of the straw that cast no shadow, I found myself impulsively and automatically initiating the rhythmical movements which my colleague had prophesied the heart would undergo. I kept the experiment from failing; and not only saved my colleague (and the turtle) from humiliation that but for my presence of mind would have been their lot, but I established in the audience the true view of the subject. The lecturer was stating this; and the misconduct of one half-dead specimen of heart ought not to destroy the impression of his words. "There is no worse lie than a truth misunderstood," is a maxim which I have heard ascribed to a former venerated

President of Harvard. The heart's failure would have been misunderstood by the audience and given the lie to the lecturer. It was hard enough to make them understand the subject anyhow; so that even now as I write in cool blood I am tempted to think that I acted quite correctly. I was acting for the *larger* truth, at any rate, however automatically. . . . To this day the memory of that critical emergency has made me feel charitable towards all mediums who make phenomena come in one way when they won't come easily in another. On the principles of the S.P.R., my conduct on that one occasion ought to discredit everything I ever do, everything, for example, I may write in this article—a manifestly unjust conclusion.

I wonder if James would have approved of the way William Crookes covered up the cheating of the medium Mary Showers in behalf of "the larger truth"? Mary Showers, a young medium, conducted at least one joint seance with Florence Cook in the Crookes's home. Apparently Crookes had several other sittings with Mary. Daniel Home presumably heard rumors that Crookes might be having an affair with the young Mary Showers. Crookes wrote a letter to Home explaining how the scandal had originated [63].

According to Crookes he had obtained a complete confession from Mary Showers in her own handwriting that her phenomena were wholly dependent upon trickery and the occasional use of an accomplice. Crookes said, however, that he had undertaken not to reveal the fact that Mary was fraudulent even to her mother, because of "the very great injury which the cause of truth would suffer if so impudent a fraud were to be publicly exposed."

The Post-Rhine Era

Rhine's card-guessing paradigm dominated experimental parapsychology from 1934 to at least the 1960s. Since the 1960s card-guessing experiments have played a minor role. Contemporary parapsychologists have deviated from Rhine's paradigm in a variety of ways. In Rhine's paradigm both the possible targets and the possible responses are severely restricted. The targets consist of five, deliberately neutral and simple, symbols. And, on each trial, the percipient is restricted to calling out the name of one of these possible five symbols. From a strictly methodological viewpoint these restrictions have several advantages. Most percipients have no strong preferences for any of the symbols; randomizing of targets is straightforward; scoring of hits and misses is unambiguous; and the statistical calculations are fairly standard.

But these same features have been blamed by contemporary investigators for the lack of impressive findings since the spectacular scoring reported by Rhine in 1934 [46]. Because the symbols are relatively meaningless and uninteresting, the repetitive guessing over many trials is boring and, according to the parapsychologists, contributes to both a lack of motivation and emotional involvement that might be needed for the effective functioning of psi.

As a result, one break with the past is the increased use of more complex and meaningful targets such as reproductions of paintings, travel slides, geographical locations, and emotionally laden photographs. In addition, instead of the forced-choice procedure of the card guessing, most experimenters allow free responding on the part of their percipients. Percipients are encouraged, on a given trial, to free associate and describe, both in words and in drawings, whatever comes to mind. The use of free responses complicates enormously the problems of scoring and statistical analysis. But parapsychologists believe the added complications are a small price to pay if the newer procedures produce better psychic functioning.

Along with the free-response designs, parapsychologists have renewed their interest in the possibility that psychic functioning may be enhanced in altered states such as dreaming, hypnosis, meditation, sensory-deprived states, and progressive relaxation. The basic idea is that these altered states greatly reduce or block attention to external sensory information while, at the same time, increasing attention to internal mentation. Under such conditions it is hypothesized that the psi signal is easier for the percipient to detect because it has less competition from sensory inputs [64]. One survey of 87 experiments in which percipients were in an altered state found that 56 percent reported significant hitting of targets [65].

Another departure from the Rhine paradigm was stimulated by developments in electronic technology. Psi experiments employing random event generators began in the 1970s. Electronic equipment could be used to generate random targets as well as automatically record the percipient's responses and keep running tallies of the hits. Although such equipment has been used to test ESP, the most widespread use has been in the study of psychokinesis. In such experiments an operator or "psychic" attempts to bias the output of a random event generator by mental means alone. In 1980, May, Humphrey, and Hubbard found reports of 214 such experiments, "74 of which show statistical evidence for an anomalous perturbation—a factor of nearly seven times chance expectation" [66].

A third major departure has been the so-called "remote viewing" paradigm [22], [24], [28], [67], [68]. The claims made for the ability of this procedure to consistently demonstrate ESP with a variety of percipients are perhaps the strongest ever put forth by parapsychologists [28].

> Our laboratory experiments suggest to us that anyone who feels comfortable with the idea of having paranormal ability can have it. . . . In our experiments, we have never found anyone who could not learn to perceive scenes, including buildings, roads, and people, even those at great distances and

blocked from ordinary perception. . . . We have, as of this writing, carried out successful remote viewing experiments with about twenty participants, almost all of whom came to us without any prior experience, and in some cases, with little interest in psychic functioning. So far, we cannot identify a single individual who has not succeeded in a remote viewing task to his own satisfaction.

In a more recent assessment of remote viewing, Targ and Harary assert, "In laboratories across this country, and in many other nations as well, forty-six experimental series have investigated remote viewing. Twenty-three of these investigations have reported successful results and produced statistically significant data, where three would be expected" [68].

A fourth emphasis has been the study of personality correlates of the alleged psi ability [48].

In addition to the experimental programs on altered states, random event generators, remote viewing, and personality correlates, contemporary parapsychologists have been actively doing research in other areas. The various chapters in the *Handbook of Parapsychology* provide a good idea of the range of topics [48]. The research on reincarnation, survival after death, paranormal photography, psychic metal bending, poltergeist phenomena, hauntings, and faith healing, while admittedly colorful, does not deserve the attention of scientists—at least not in its current state. I suspect that most serious parapsychologists would also not want to rest their case on such research.

Today the parapsychologists who want the scientific establishment to take their work seriously do not offer for inspection the evidence that previous generations of psychic researchers believed was sufficient—the findings of Hare, Wallace, Crookes, Gurney, Rhine, or Soal. Nor do they offer up the reports on reincarnation, psychic healing, paranormal photography, spoon bending, psychic detection, and the related phenomena that so readily appeal to the media and the public. Instead, they ask us to look at the trends and patterns they find in research programs carried out in a variety of parapsychological laboratories.

Two aspects of this new type of claim are worth noting. One is the admission that a single investigation, no matter how seemingly rigorous and fraud-proof, cannot be accepted as scientific evidence. The idea of a single "critical experiment" is a myth. The second and related aspect is that replicability is now accepted as the critical requirement for admission into the scientific marketplace.

Both proponents and critics have previously assumed, either tacitly or explicitly, that the outcome of a single investigation could be critical. Sidgwick believed that the results of the investigation of the Creery sisters were of this nature. The evidence was so strong, he argued, that the critics now had either to accept the reality of telepathy or to accuse the investigators of fraud [30]. Carpenter, rather than withhold judgment until independent investigators had either succeeded or failed in attempts to replicate Crookes's experiments with Home, acted as if he had either to agree to Crookes's claim or to prove that Crookes had been duped. Both Price and Hansel insisted that it would be sufficient for Rhine and Soal to convince them of ESP if a parapsychologist could perform successfully a single "fraud proof" experiment.

The myth of the single, crucial experiment has resulted in needless controversy and has contributed to the false dichotomy. Flew is just one who has argued convincingly that a single, unreplicated event that allegedly attests to a miracle is simply a historical oddity that cannot be part of a scientific argument [3].

Apparently not all parapsychologists are convinced that the achievement of a repeatable psi experiment is either necessary or desirable for the advancement of parapsychology. The late J. G. Pratt argued that "psi is a spontaneous occurrence in nature, and we can no more predict precisely when it is going to occur in our carefully planned and rigorously controlled experiments than we can in everyday life psychic experiences. . . . Predictable repeatability is unattainable because of the nature of the phenomena" [69].

Pratt argued that parapsychology should give up the quest for the replicable experiment—an impossible goal in his opinion—and concentrate upon accumulating enough data on anomalous happenings to convince scientists and the public that psi is real. Other parapsychologists, however, realize that scientists are not going to be convinced until some semblance of replicability has been achieved. The late Gardner Murphy, while noting that replicability was not necessary for scientific acceptability in some areas of science, argued that for supporting claims for such irrational phenomena as psi, replicability was necessary. And, speaking as one of the dominant figures in parapsychology in 1971, he made it clear that he felt that parapsychology had a long way to go before it achieved replicable results [70].

Perhaps Honorton's position represents the contemporary position of the major parapsychologists [71]: "Parapsychology will stand or fall on its ability to demonstrate replicable and conceptually meaningful findings. Future critics who are interested in the resolution rather than the perpetuation of the psi controversy are advised to focus their attention on systematic lines of research which are capable of producing such findings."

Psi and Repeatability

As the preceding quotation indicates, Honorton believes that critics should focus on "systematic lines of research" that apparently display replicable and/or "conceptually meaningful" findings. And, as we have seen, contemporary parapsychologists have offered us a number of such systematic lines to demonstrate that they have, in fact, already achieved the goals of repeatability and conceptual meaningfulness. The claims put forth on behalf of the altered state, random event generator, and remote viewing paradigms have already been cited. Similar claims have been made for work on correlates of psi such as attitudes and personality [72].

What can we expect if a critic, in an effort to be open-minded and responsible, accepts the challenge of Honorton and his fellow parapsychologists to examine the accumulated evidence from one or more of the "systematic lines" of inquiry? This challenge opens up a variety of possibilities. Which experiments should be included in the evaluation? It is impractical to consider all the experiments in parapsychology because even in this relatively sparsely populated area the number is by now enormous. In considering a subset of experiments in the ESP area, for example, Palmer covered approximately 700 experimental reports [72]. Including PK as well as ESP, I would estimate that, today, a determined critic who wants to evaluate exhaustively all available experimental reports might have to cope with upwards of 3,000 experiments. Given my recent experience in trying to do justice to just 42 experiments on the ganzfeld psi phenomenon [73], I would estimate that it could take a responsible critic over five years of almost full-time effort to properly evaluate this material.

Another problem facing both the proponent and critic is, once a suitable sample of experiments has been selected, how to make an overall judgment about what patterns, trends, strengths, and weaknesses characterize the sample. Up until recently, such a review of a body of literature has been an unstructured and highly subjective affair. Understandably, two individuals surveying the same body of literature could, and often did, come up with diametrically opposed conclusions.

As cognitive psychologists have emphasized, the capacity of humans to handle mentally a number of items is severely limited. What constitutes an "item" varies greatly with the structure of the material and the individual's previous familiarity and expertise in a given field of knowledge. Even within his or her field of specialty, a scientist would have great difficulty in trying to comprehend patterns in over a dozen or so reports without external aids and a systematic procedure.

When nonparapsychologist critics try to make sense of a large body of parapsychological literature, they are at a great disadvantage. Their critical capacities have not been trained to pick out relevant from irrelevant details in seeking interrelationships. Lacking concrete experience with many of the experimental designs, they are at a decided disadvantage in knowing what things could go wrong and which sorts of controls would be critical.

And when the number of separate reports is more than a dozen or so, they cannot be expected to be able to grasp the total picture without help from systematic and quantitative summarization procedures.

Yet, so far as I can tell, only two critical evaluations of "systematic lines" of parapsychological research have ever been carried out with any procedure approximating systematic, explicit, and quantitative guidelines. Both of these were carried out fairly recently. One was by Charles Akers, a former parapsychologist with both experience and publications in the field [74]. The other was by myself, acting as an external critic who accepted the parapsychologists' challenge to evaluate fairly a systematic line of research that they feel represents their strongest case for the repeatable experiment [73], [75].

Akers's Methodological Criticisms of Parapsychology

Akers's methodological evaluation of contemporary parapsychological research represents a landmark in parapsychological criticism. Akers, who holds a Ph.D. degree in social psychology, has worked as a parapsychologist in Rhine's laboratory and knows the contemporary scene from the inside.

After a careful selection procedure, Akers arrived at a sample of 54 ESP experiments. These experiments had all been cited in the *Handbook of Parapsychology* or other parapsychological literature as exemplars of the evidential data base. The selection was restricted to studies in which significant results had been claimed for a sample of relatively unselected percipients. He excluded unpublished reports, studies that were reported only as abstracts or convention reports, and studies that were exploratory or preliminary to a stronger replication. He also excluded experiments that produced scores in the wrong direction ("psi missing") [74]. "The final sample of 54 experiments is fairly complete. If it is not inclusive, it is at least representative of findings in altered state and personality research."

Akers then screened all his 54 studies sequentially through each of his several criteria to see how many could pass through all of them. He first looked at how many of the studies used inadequate randomization of the targets. Although he found almost half of the studies used inferior methods to randomize targets, he considered this to be a "minor contaminant." In his opinion, such randomization failures as he observed would not be sufficient to account for the above-chance results that each of these studies obtained.

Next he looked at the possibility of sensory leakage. For example, in several of the ganzfeld experiments the agent handled the slide or picture that served as the target. Later the percipient was given that very same target along with some foils and asked to select which item had been the target. In such a stiuation either inadvertent or deliberate cueing is clearly a possibility. A parapsychologist should not be entitled to claim ESP as the explanation for a successful selection by the percipient under such circumstances. Akers assigned a flaw to any experiment that had this or one of his other categories of possibilities for sensory leakage. As many as 22 of the 54 experiments were cited for having at least one flaw of the sensory leakage kind (some had more than one kind).

In a similar fashion, Akers checked for security problems, recording errors, optional stopping, data selection, inadequate documentation, multiple testing, and some additional flaws of a technical nature. On each criterion, Akers assigned a flaw only if, in his opinion, the defect was sufficient to account for the above-chance hitting actually reported [74].

> Results from the 54-experiment survey have demonstrated that there are many alternative explanations for ESP phenomena; the choice is not simply between psi and experimenter fraud. . . . The numbers of experiments flawed on various grounds were as follows: randomization failures (13), sensory leakage (22), subject cheating (12), recording errors (10), classification or scoring errors (9), statistical errors (12), reporting failures (10). . . . All told, 85 percent of the experiments were considered flawed (46/54).

In other words, only 8 of the 54 experiments—all of which were selected to be best cases—were free of at least one serious flaw on Akers's criteria. But Akers points out a number of reasons to be concerned about the adequacy of even these "flawless" studies [74]. "In conclusion, there were eight experiments conducted with reasonable care, but none of these could be considered as methodologically strong. When all 54 experiments are considered, it can be stated that the research methods are too weak to establish the existence of a paranormal phenomenon."

Akers's conclusion is especially damaging to the case for psi because he leaned over backwards to give the benefit of doubt to the experimenters. In some cases where the documentation was incomplete, Akers assumed that the investigator had taken the proper precautions against sensory leakage. And Akers did not assign flaws to the experiments if their randomization procedures were less than optimal (he considered this to be only a "minor contaminant"). Experiments that were deficient on his other criteria such as optional stopping and others were not assigned flaws if, on Akers's judgment, the deficiency on that criterion was insufficient to have caused the total number of hits. In other words, Akers was not judging whether the experiment had met standards of scientific acceptability, but rather, he was assigning flaws if a given deficiency *by itself* was sufficient to have accounted for the results. And, finally, Akers did not consider the possibility that *combinations* of deficiencies, each in themselves being insufficient, might have been more than enough to account for the reported findings.

Hyman's Critique of the Ganzfeld Experiments

Although Akers's and my critiques were conducted independently, and although our samples and procedures differed in many important ways, we came to essentially the same conclusion. In spite of claims for both scientific confirmation of psi and repeatability within certain systematic lines of research, both Akers and I concluded that the best contemporary research in parapsychology does not survive serious and careful scientific scrutiny. Parapsychology is not yet ready to bring its case before the general scientific public.

My approach was to look for a research program in parapsychology that consisted of a series of experiments by a variety of investigators and that was considered by parapsychologists as especially promising. I quickly discovered a systematic body of research that many of the leading parapsychologists considered to be the most promising one on the contemporary scene. This research program was based on the ganzfeld/psi paradigm.

The word *ganzfeld* is German for total field. It is used to describe a technique in the study of perception that creates a visual field with no inhomogeneities. The motivation for creating such a visual field stems from certain theoretical predictions of gestalt psychology. A recently developed and simple procedure for creating such a ganzfeld is to tape halves of ping-pong balls over the eyes of subjects. A bright light is then directed to the covered eyes. The percipient experiences a visual field with no discontinuities and describes the perceptual effect as like being in a fog.

The parapsychologists became interested in the ganzfeld when it was reported that subjects who experience the ganzfeld quickly enter into a pleasant, altered state. They adopted it as a quick and easy way to place percipients into a state that they felt would be conducive to the reception of psi signals. In a typical ganzfeld/psi experiment, the percipient has the ping-pong balls taped over his or her eyes and then is placed in a comfortable chair or reclines on a bed. In addition to a bright light shining on the halved ping-pong balls, white noise or the sound of ocean surf is fed into the percipient's ears through earphones.

After 15 minutes or so in this situation, the percipient is presumed ready to receive the psi signal. An agent, in another room or building, is given a target that is randomly selected from a small pool, say, of four pictures (the pool of pictures has been selected, in turn, by random means from a large collection of such pools). The agent concentrates or studies the target during a predetermined time interval. At the same time the percipient, isolated in a relatively sound-proofed chamber, freely describes all the associations and impressions that occur to him or her during the sending interval.

At the end of the session the halved ping-pong balls are removed. The pool of pictures for that trial, including the target, are brought to the percipient. The percipient then indicates, by ranking or rating, how close each of the items in the pool is to the impressions that occurred to him or her during the ganzfeld session. The most typical scoring procedure classifies the outcome as a "hit" if the percipient correctly judges the actual target as closest to the ganzfeld impressions.

In the typical experiment a pool of four target candidates is used on each trial. Over a number of trials, the percipients would be expected to achieve hits on 25 percent of the trials just by chance. If the actual rate of hitting is significantly above this chance level, then it is assumed, given that proper experimental controls have been employed, that ESP has probably operated.

Charles Honorton, the parapsychologist who first published a ganzfeld/psi experiment [76] and who also has strongly defended the paradigm as "psi conducive," responded to my request for cooperation by undertaking to supply me with copies of every relevant report between 1974—the date of the first published ganzfeld/psi experiment—and the end of 1981—the year I made the request. In January 1982 I received a package containing 600 pages of reports on the ganzfeld/psi experiment.

The experiments in the data base given to me for examination were extracted from 34 separate reports written or published from 1974 through 1981. By Honorton's count, these 34 reports described 42 separate experiments. Of these, he classified 23 as having achieved overall significance on the primary measure of psi at the 0.05 level. This successful replication rate of 55 percent is consistent with earlier estimates of success for this paradigm, which ranged from 50 to 58 percent [73]. Approximately half of these experiments had been published in refereed journals or monographs. The remainder had appeared only as abstracts or papers delivered at meetings of the Parapsychological Association. The studies had been authored by 47 different investigators, many of them prominent members of the Parapsychological Association.

The details of my analysis and my conclusions have been published in the *Journal of Parapsychology* [73]. The same issue of that journal contains Honorton's detailed rebuttal to my critique [77]. Here I will merely supply the bare bones of my critique.

1. I first examined the claim that the proportion of successful replications of the ganzfeld/psi experiment was 55 percent. This estimate, it turned out, was based upon a number of questionable assumptions. Much ambiguity exists as to what the unit of analysis should be. In some cases,

the individual experimental conditions within a single complicated experiment were each counted as separate "experiments." In other cases, the pooled data over a number of separate experimental conditions were counted as a single unit. That this can make a difference is shown by the fact that when I tried to supply a consistent criterion to the data base for determining individual units, I came up with a success rate closer to 30 than to 50 percent. Other considerations such as unknown experiments led me to conclude that the actual success rate, defining "success" according to Honorton's criterion, was probably around 30 percent.

2. But even a success rate of 30 percent is impressive if the actual rate of success to be expected by chance was the assumed 5 percent. I pointed to a variety of examples in which multiple tests were applied to the same data in such a way as to inflate the actual probability for success just by chance over the assumed rate. Taking into consideration a number of factors, I estimated that the actual chance level could easily be 25 percent or higher.

3. In addition to analyses that inadvertently inflated the significance levels, I noted a number of other departures from optimal experimental procedure that could have artificially contributed to the outcomes. These flaws could be clustered into three categories: *security, statistical,* and *procedural.* Security flaws included failure to preclude sensory cues as well as loose monitoring of critical aspects in the experiment. Statistical flaws consisted of wrong use of statistical procedures. Procedural flaws consisted of inadequate randomization of targets, incomplete documentation, and possible problems of feedback. What was both surprising and dismaying to me was that not a single experiment in the data base was free from at least one of these defects. These defects were chosen to be those that I assume most parapsychologists would agree should not be part of a well-conducted experiment.

4. I tried to make it clear that I was not assuming that these flaws were the cause of the observed results. Rather, I assumed that the presence of such defects could be taken as a symptom that the experiment had not been conducted with adequate care. Indeed, it was clear that at least some of the experiments in the data base had been intended to serve only as pilot or preliminary experiments. Nevertheless, I did look at the correlation between the three clusters and success of the experiment. Although the security and the statistical clusters did not correlate with outcome, the procedural cluster did correlate with the probability of obtaining a significant outcome. Honorton strongly disagrees with this conclusion [77].

As a result of my detailed examination of the claims for the ganzfeld/psi findings, I concluded my long report as follows [73]:

In conclusion, the current data base has too many problems to be seriously put before outsiders as evidence for psi. The types of problems exhibited by this data base, however, suggest interesting challenges for the parapsychological community. I would hope that both parapsychologists and critics would wish to have parapsychological experiments conducted according to the highest standards possible. If one goal is to convince the rest of the scientific community that the parapsychologists can produce data of the highest quality, then it would be a terrible mistake to employ the current ganzfeld/psi data base for this purpose. Perhaps the Parapsychological Association can lead the way by setting down guidelines as to what should constitute an adequate confirmatory experiment. And, then, when a sufficient number of studies have accumulated which meet these guidelines, they can be presented to the rest of the scientific community as an example of what parapsychology, at its best, can achieve. If studies carried out according to these guidelines also continue to yield results suggestive of psi, then the outside scientific community should be obliged to take notice.

Honorton, not surprisingly, disagrees with my conclusions [77]. After my critique was completed, Honorton carried out a revised and different analysis of the data base. He claims his new analysis eliminates my criticisms about inflated significance levels. Honorton also developed his own scale for evaluating the methodological quality of each experiment. According to his ratings, there is no correlation between quality of the experiment and its outcome.

The problem that both of us face when judging the quality of the individual experiments is that we are doing this after the fact. Although we agree on several of our ratings, we tend to disagree in ways that suggest our presumed biases. Honorton tends to find more defects in the unsuccessful experiments than I do. On the other hand, I tend to find more defects in the successful experiments than Honorton does. In the absence of double-blind ratings, this aspect of our disagreement represents a stalemate.

However, whether one uses Honorton's or my ratings the number of departures from accepted methodological procedure is unacceptably high for this data base. Although Honorton and I disagree on whether the observed flaws weaken the case for psi, we do not disagree that they exist. So far as I can tell, no parapsychologist has provided an explanation of why almost all of the experiments in this data base have at least one of these flaws.

Conclusions

With the exception of the contemporary parapsychological literature, the evidence for psi reviewed in this paper comes from investigations that today's parapsychologists would not put before us as part of their strongest case for psi. Many of these parapsychologists might believe I was being unfair in dwelling upon these castoffs from the past. But it is just this fact—that the cases I have examined are now castoffs—that brings up important questions about how to approach the contemporary evidence.

The cases from the past that I have discussed were, in their own time, considered by the parapsychologists of that day to be examples of scientifically sound evidence for psi. It is only subsequent generations, for the most part, who have set the preceding exemplars aside. In some cases the reasons for the abandonment of what was once a foundation stone in the case for psi are clear. Subsequent investigators or critics found previously unrecognized defects in the studies or strong suspicions of fraud had been generated. Other experimental paradigms have disappeared from the data base for less obvious reasons.

Some previously successful paradigms have disappeared because they no longer seem to yield significant results. Others, such as the sheep-goats design, seem to have simply gone out of fashion. One major parapsychologist once told me that it seems to be the ultimate fate of every successful paradigm eventually to lose its ability to yield significant results. He believed this was related to the fact that psi depends upon both the novelty of the design and the motivations of the experimenter. At first a new paradigm generates excitement and optimism. But after it has been around for a while, the initial excitement and enthusiasm abate and the experimenter no longer communicates the original emotions that accompanied the paradigm when it was still relatively new.

But, whatever the reason, each generation's best case for psi is cast aside by subsequent generations of parapsychologists and replaced with newer, more up-to-date best cases. Not only does the evidence for psi lack replicability, but, unlike the evidence from other sciences, it is noncumulative. It is as if each new generation wipes the slate clean and begins all over again. Consequently, the evidential data base for psi is always shifting. Earlier cases are dropped and replaced with newer and seemingly more promising lines of research. [One of the readers of this paper argues that it is only partially true that parapsychological research is noncumulative. Although his argument might have some validity, I do not think it changes the point I am making here.]

The late J. G. Pratt, in challenging his parapsychological colleagues' hopes for a repeatable experiment, wrote [69]:

> One could almost pick a date at random since 1882 and find in the literature that someone somewhere had recently obtained results described in terms implying that others should be able to confirm the findings. Among those persons or groups reflecting such enthusiasm are the S.P.R. Committee on Thought-Transference; Richard Hogson (in his investigation of Mrs.

Piper); Feilding, Baggally, and Carrington (in their Palladino investigations); J. B. Rhine (work reported in *Extra-Sensory Perception*); Whately Carington (in his work on paranormal cognition of drawings); Gertrude Schmeidler (in her sheep-goat work); Van Bussbach, and Anderson and White (in their research on teacher-pupil attitudes); the Maimonides dream studies; the Stepanek investigators; the investigators of Kulagina's directly-observable PK effects; research using the ganzfeld technique; and the SRI investigators ("remote viewing"). One after another, however, the specific ways of working used in these initially successful psi projects have fallen out of favor and faded from the research scene—except for the latest investigations which, one may reasonably suppose, have not yet had enough time to falter and fade away as others before them have done.

When Pratt wrote those words in 1978, the "latest investigations" included the ganzfeld/psi experiments, the remote viewing investigations, and the PK research using random event generators. These would have been among the contemporary investigations that, given Pratt's pessimistic extrapolations, "one may reasonably suppose, have not yet had enough time to falter and fade away as others before them have done." Today, signs do seem to indicate that these seemingly "successful" lines of research may be much weaker than had been previously advertised [24], [74], [75].

However, as always, new and more promising lines of work seem to be ready to take their place. Honorton and his colleagues at the Psychophysical Research Laboratories in Princeton, N.J., seem to be developing a number of very promising lines of research [78]. They have been developing a completely automated version of the ganzfeld experiment that eliminates many of the problems raised by my critique. They have also been perfecting a "transportable" experiment—one that can be carried out by any investigator who has access to an Apple personal computer. The experiment, also completely automated, is a variation of the random event generator paradigm but with a variety of built-in safeguards that apparently eliminate almost all the options for multiple testing.

Nearby, but completely independent of the work going on at the Psychophysical Research Laboratories, is the research on anomalous phenomena being carried out by Robert Jahn and his associates in the School of Engineering and Applied Science at Princeton University [1], [79], [80]. For more than five years Jahn and his associates have been perfecting the instrumentation and experimental designs for conducting sophisticated variations of both the remote viewing paradigm and the PK work with random event generators. Although they have collected a large data base for each of these paradigms, most of the work has been reported only in technical reports. The reported findings do seem impressive, but they have yet to be described in sufficient detail for a full-scale evaluation. And, given both the scale of the effort and the sophistication of the methodology and instrumentation, it will be many years before adequate replications in independent laboratories will be possible.

As promising as this most recent work by Honorton and Jahn might seem to be, none of it has reached a stage where it is ready for a full-scale critical evaluation. Already, the sharp-eyed critic can detect both inconsistencies with previous findings in the same lines of research and departures from ideal practice. As the history of parapsychology teaches us, we will have to wait for several more years before we can adequately judge if somehow these latest efforts can avoid the fate that all their promising predecessors have suffered.

Perhaps, however, history does not have to repeat itself in all its depressing aspects. And I can see some encouraging signs of breaks with previous patterns in the way proponents carry out and defend their findings and the way critics respond.

Since its inception as an institutionalized undertaking, psychical research has suffered from the lack of relevant, informed, and constructive criticism. This particular deficiency seems to be changing. For one thing, the younger generation of parapsychologists have produced some internal critics who are both knowledgeable and effective. In addition to Akers, there are others, such as Susan Blackmore, Adrian Parker, Gerd Hövelmann, and J. E. Kennedy, who have recognized the current deficiencies of parapsychological research and have a strong commitment to raising the standards. Although it is still difficult to find external critics who are both informed and constructive, one can see some indications that this situation may also improve.

Another positive sign is the attempt to replace subjective, impressionistic evaluations of the parapsychological literature with more systematic, explicit assessments. Both Honorton [77] and I [73] have used "meta-analysis" in our dispute over the adequacy of the ganzfeld/psi data base. *Meta-analysis* is a term coined to describe the approach to reviewing a body of research that makes the various phases as explicit and quantitative as feasible [81], [82].

> The approach to research integration referred to as "meta-analysis" is nothing more than the attitude of data analysis applied to quantitative summaries of the individual experiments. By recording the properties of studies and their findings in quantitative terms, the meta-analysis of research invites one who would integrate numerous and diverse findings to apply the full power of statistical methods to the task. Thus it is not a technique; rather it is a perspective that uses many techniques of measurement and statistical analysis [81].

Meta-analysis is by no means a panacea. Much subjectivity remains on such matters as which studies to include and exclude from the sample, how to score the "effect size" or degree of success of a study, what variables to include, how to assign studies values on the variables, and what should be the sampling unit. In addition, many serious problems have to be resolved about how to cope with the fact that individual studies are not independent and the analyses are conducted *post hoc*. Yet, it has many advantages over the previously unstructured and subjective assessments. The reviewer is forced to make many more of his or her standards and procedures explicit. The resulting debate can be more focused, and the specific areas of disagreement can be pinpointed more accurately. In addition, the use of quantitative summaries often brings out patterns and relationships that would ordinarily escape the unaided reviewer's cognitive limits.

Along with an increase in informed and constructive criticism there are signs that the parapsychological community is responsive and willing to change both its procedures and claims in line with some of the criticisms. Although we still disagree strongly on many of the issues, Honorton has made many changes in his claims and procedures in a sincere effort to take some of my criticisms into account [73], [77]. At its 1984 annual meetings in Dallas, Texas, the Parapsychological Association established a committee that will attempt to establish guidelines for the performance of acceptable experiments in various lines of parapsychological research. Along with some major parapsychologists such as Honorton, the committee includes both internal critics such as Akers and external ones such as myself.

My survey of psychical research from the time of Hare and Crookes to the present has suggested that, although the specific evidence put forth to support the existence of psi changes over time, many of the key issues and controversies have remained unchanged. The parapsychologists still employ similar stratagems seemingly to enable them to stick to their claims in the face of various inconsistencies. And the critics, sharing many assumptions with the proponents, still behave in rather emotional and irrational ways. Indeed, the level of the debate during the preceding 130 years has been an embarrassment for anyone who would like to believe that scholars and scientists adhere to standards of rationality and fair play.

I suspect it is because the quality of the criticism has been so poor and its content so obviously irrelevant that parapsychologists have managed to live so long with the illusion that the quality of their evidence was so much better than it really was. Both Akers and I were surprised to find how defective, in terms of the most elementatry standards, the best of the contemporary parapsychological research really was. I know that some parapsychologists have been surprised to realize how far the current status of psi research departs from the professed standards of their field. And I would not be surprised if most of the rest of the parapsychological community, in the absence of systematic and critical surveys, had assumed that their data base was of a much higher quality than it, in fact, is.

All this suggests, as I have already indicated, that the parapsychological evidence, despite a history of more than 130 years of inquiry, is not ready to be placed before the scientific community for judgment. The parapsychologists' first order of business should be to get their own house in order. They no longer can safely assume that the typical parapsychologist has the competence to use statistical tools correctly, design appropriate investigations, carry out these investigations correctly, or write them up properly. Indeed, the evidence suggests the opposite. Both the Parapsychological Association and the parapsychological journals have to establish explicit guidelines and minimal standards. Then they have to make sure that members of their profession become fully aware of these standards and recognize the necessity for living up to them.

References

[1] R. G. Jahn, "The persistent paradox of psychic phenomena: an engineering perspective," *Proc. IEEE,* vol. 70, pp. 136-170, Feb. 1982.

[2] G. Murphy and R.O. Ballou, *William James on Psychical Research.* New York: Viking Press, 1969.

[3] A. Flew, "Parapsychology revisited: laws, miracles, and repeatability," in *Philosophy and Parapsychology,* J. Ludwig, Ed., Buffalo, N.Y.: Prometheus Books, pp. 263-269.

[4] R. Hyman, "Pathological science: Towards a proper diagnosis and remedy," *Zetetic Scholar,* no. 6, pp. 31-39, July 1980.

[5] R. L. Moore, *In Search of White Crows: Spiritualism, Parapsychology and American Culture.* New York: Oxford Univ. Press. 1977.

[6] F. Podmore, *Mediums of the 19th Century.* New Hyde Park, N.Y.: University Books, 1963 (two volumes).

[7] M. Faraday, "Experimental investigation of table-moving." *The Athenaeum,* pp. 801-803, July 2, 1853.

[8] R. Hare, *Experimental Investigation of the Spirit Manifestations, Demonstrating and Existence of Spirits and their Communion with Mortals: Doctrine of the Spirit World Respecting Heaven, Hell, Morality, and God. Also, the influence of Scripture on the Morals of Christians.* New York: Partridge & Brittan, 1855.

[9] L. Shepard, Ed., *Encyclopedia of Occultism and Parapsychology.* Detroit, MI: Gale Research Co., 1978.

[10] I. Asimov, *Asimov's Biographical Encyclopedia of Science and Technology.* New York: Equinox, 1976.

[11] W. George, *Biologist Philosopher: A Study of the Life and Writings of Alfred Russel Wallace.* New York: Abelard-Shuman, 1964.

[12] M. J. Kottler, "Alfred Russel Wallace, the origin of man, and spiritualism," *Isis,* vol. 65, pp. 145-192, 1974.

[13] F. M. Turner, *Between Science and Religion: The Reaction to Scientific Naturalism in Late Victorian England.* New Haven, Conn.: Yale Univ. Press, 1974.

[14] A. R. Wallace, *My Life: A Record of Events and Opinions.* New York: Dodd, Mead, & Co., 1906.

[15] R. G. Medhurst, Ed., *Crookes and the Spirit World: A Collection of Writings by or Concerning the Work of Sir William Crookes, O.M., F.R.S., in the Field of Psychical Research.* New York: Taplinger, 1972.

[16] E. E. F. D'Albe, *The Life of Sir William Crookes.* New York: D. Appleton and Co., 1924.

[17] J. Palfreman, "William Crookes: Sprititualism and science." *Ethics Sci. Med.,* vol. 3, pp. 211-227, 1976.

[18] S. J. Davey, "The possibilities of mal-observation and lapse of memory from a practical point of view: Experimental investigation," *Proc. Soc. Psychical Res.,* vol. 4, pp. 405-495, 1887.

[19] E. J. Dingwall, *Very Peculiar People: Portrait Studies in the Queer, the Abnormal and the Uncanny.* New Hyde Park, N.Y.: University Books, 1962.

[20] J. Hasted, *The Metal-Benders.* London, England: Routledge & Kegan Paul Ltd., 1981.

[21] R. Hyman, [Review of *The Geller Papers*]. *The Zetetic [The Skeptical Inquirer].* vol. 1, pp. 73-80, Fall/Winter 1976.

[22] ———. "Psychics and scientists: 'Mind-Reach' and remote viewing." *The Humanist,* vol. 37, pp. 16–20, May/June 1977.

[23] ———. "Scientists and psychics," in *Science and the Paranormal,* G. O. Abell and B. Singer, Eds. New York: Scribner's, 1981, pp. 119–141.

[24] ———. "Outracing the evidence: The muddled 'Mind Race'." *The Skeptical Inquirer,* vol. 9, pp. 125–145, 1984–1985.

[25] D. Marks and R. Kammann, *The Psychology of the Psychic.* Buffalo, N.Y.: Prometheus Books, 1980.

[26] J. Palfreman, "Between scepticism and credulity: A study of Victorian scientific attitudes to modern spiritualism," in *On the Margins of Science: The Social Construction of Rejected Knowledge,* R. Wallis, Ed. Staffordshire, England: University of Keele, 1979, pp. 201–236.

[27] C. Panati, Ed., *The Geller Papers: Scientific Observations on the Paranormal Powers of Uri Geller.* Boston, Mass.: Houghton Mifflin, 1976.

[28] R. Targ and H. E. Puthoff, *Mind Reach: Scientists Look at Psychic Ability.* New York: Delacorte, 1977.

[29] J. C. F. Zöllner, *Transcendental Physics.* New York: Arno Press, 1976 [Reprint of 1888 edition published by Colby & Rich, Boston].

[30] H. Sidgwick, [Presidential Address], *Proc. Soc. Psychical Res.,* vol. 1, pp. 7–12, 1882–1883.

[31] J. B. Hasted, D. Bohm, E. W. Bastin, and B. O'Regan, "Experiments on psycho-kinetic phenomena," in *The Geller Papers,* C. Panati, Ed. Boston, Mass.: Houghton Mifflin, 1976, pp. 183–196.

[32] A. Gauld, *The Founders of Psychical Research.* New York: Schocken, 1968.

[33] W. F. Barrett, E. Gurney, and F. W. H. Myers, "First report on thought-reading," *Proc. Soc. Psychical Res.,* vol. 1, pp. 13–34, 1882–1883.

[34] E. Gurney, F. W. H. Myers, and W. F. Barrett, "Second report on thought-transference," *Proc. Soc. Psychical Res.,* vol. 1, pp. 70–89, 1882–1883.

[35] E. Gurney, F. W. H. Myers, F. Podmore, and W. F. Barrett, "Third report on thought-transference," *Proc. Soc. Psychical Res.,* vol. 1, pp. 161–181, 1882–1883.

[36] F. Nicol, "The Founders of the S. P. R.," *Proc. Soc. Psychical Res.,* vol. 55, pp. 341–367, 1972.

[37] W. F. Barrett, E. Gurney, and F. W. H. Myers, "Thought-reading," *The Nineteenth Century,* vol. 11, pp. 890–900, June 1882.

[38] J. E. Coover, *Experiments in Psychical Research.* Stanford, Calif.: Stanford Univ. Press, 1917.

[39] E. Gurney, F. W. H. Myers, and F. Podmore, *Phantasms of the Living.* London, England: Trubner's, 1886.

[40] G. S. Hall, [Reviews of the *Proceedings of the English Society for Psychical Research,* July, 1882 to May, 1887, and of *Phantasms of the Living*], *Amer. J. Psychol.,* vol. 1, pp. 128–146, 1887–1888.

[41] T. H. Hall, *The Strange Case of Edmund Gurney.* London, England: Duckworth, 1964.

[42] O.Pfungst, *Clever Hans.* New York: Holt, 1911.

[43] R. N. Giere, *Understanding Scientific Reasoning.* New York: Holt, Rinehart & Winston, 1979.

[44] E. Gurney, "Note relating to some published experiments in thought-transference," *Proc. Soc. Psychical Res.,* vol. 5, pp. 269–270, 1898.

[45] C. Tart, [Review of *The Magic of Uri Geller* by the Amazing Randi; *The Geller Papers* edited by Charles Panati; and *My Story* by Uri Geller], *Psychol. Today,* pp. 93–94, July 1976.

[46] J. B. Rhine, *Extra-Sensory Perception.* Boston, Mass.: Bruce Humphries, 1935 [Originally published in 1934 by the Boston Society for Psychic Research].

[47] S. H. Mauskopf and M. R. McVaugh, *The Elusive Science: Origins of Experimental Psychical Research.* Baltimore, Md.: The Johns Hopkins Press, 1980.

[48] B. Wolman, Ed., *Handbook of Parapsychology.* New York: Van Nostrand-Reinhold, 1977.

[49] K. M. Goldney, "The Soal-Goldney experiments with Basil Shackleton (BS): A personal account," *Proc. Soc. Psychical Res.,* vol. 56, pp. 73–84, 1974.

[50] S. G. Soal and F. Bateman, *Modern Experiments in Telepathy,* 2nd ed. New Haven, Conn.: Yale Univ. Press, 1954.

[51] K. M. Goldney, "Obituary: Dr. S. G. Soal, M. A., D. Sc.," *J. Soc. Psychical Res.,* vol. 48, pp. 95–98, 1975.

[52] R. A. McConnell, [Review of *Modern Experiments in Telepathy*], *J. Parapsychol.,* vol. 18, pp. 245–258, 1954.

[53] G. R. Price, "Science and the supernatural," *Science,* vol. 122, pp. 359–367, 1955.

[54] S. G. Soal, "On 'Science and the supernatural,' " *Science,* vol. 123, pp. 9–11, 1956.

[55] J. B. Rhine, "Comments on 'Science and the supernatural,' " *Science,* vol. 123, pp. 11–14, 1956.

[56] C. Scott and P. Haskell, "Fresh light on the Shackleton experiments?" *Proc. Soc. Psychical Res.,* vol. 56, pp. 43–72, 1974.

[57] R. G. Medhurst, "The fraudulent experimenter: Professor Hansel's case against psychical research," *J. Soc. Psychical Res.,* vol. 44, pp. 217–232, 1968.

[58] C. E. M. Hansel, *ESP: A Scientific Evaluation.* New York: Scribner's, 1966.

[59] ——, *ESP and Parapsychology: A Critical Re-Evaluation.* Buffalo, N.Y.: Prometheus Books, 1980.

[60] B. Markwick, "The Soal-Goldney experiments with Basil Shackleton: New evidence of data manipulation," *Proc. Soc. Psychical Res.,* vol. 56, pp. 250–277, 1978.

[61] W. Broad and N. Wade, *Betrayers of the Truth.* New York: Simon & Schuster, 1982.

[62] J. Hixson, *The Patchwork Mouse.* New York: Doubleday, 1976.

[63] T. Hall, "Florence Cook and William Crookes: A footnote to an enquiry," *Tomorrow,* vol. 11, pp. 341–359, Autumn 1963.

[64] C. Honorton, "Psi and internal attention states: Information retrieval in the ganzfeld," in *Psi and States of Awareness,* B. Shapin and L. Coly, Eds. New York: Parapsychology Foundation, pp. 79–90, 1978.

[65] ——, "Psi and internal attention states," in *Handbook of Parapsychology,* B. B. Wolman, Ed. New York: Van Nostrand-Reinhold, pp. 435–472, 1977.

[66] E. C. May, B. S. Humphrey, and G. S. Humbard, "Electronic system perturbation techniques," SRI Int., Final Rep., Sept. 30, 1980.

[67] H. E. Puthoff and R. Targ, "A perceptual channel for information transfer over kilometer distances: Historical perspective and recent research," *Proc. IEEE,* vol. 64, pp. 329–354, 1976.

[68] R. Targ and K. Harary, *The Mind Race: Understanding and Using Psychic Abilities.* New York: Villard Books, 1984.

[69] J. G. Pratt, "Prologue to a debate: Some assumptions relevant to research in parapsychology," *J. Amer. Soc. Psychical Res.,* vol. 72, pp. 127–139, 1978.

[70] G. Murphy, "The problem of repeatability in psychical research," *J. Amer. Soc. Psychical Res.,* vol. 65, pp. 3–16, 1971.

[71] C. Honorton, "Beyond the reach of sense: Some comments on C. E. M. Hansel's *ESP and Parapsychology: A Critical Re-Evaluation,"J. Amer. Soc. Psychical Res.,* vol. 75, pp. 155–166, 1981.

[72] J. Palmer, "Extrasensory perception: Research findings," in *Advances in Parapsychological Research,* vol. 2: *Extrasensory Perception,* S. Krippner, Ed. New York: Plenum, pp. 59–243, 1978.

[73] R. Hyman, "The Ganzfeld Psi experiment: A critical appraisal," *J. Parapsychol.,* vol. 30, pp. 76–82, 1985.

[74] C. Akers, "Methodological criticisms of parapsychology," in *Advances in Parapsychological Research,* vol. 4, S. Krippner, Ed. Jefferson, N.C.: McFarland, 1984.

[75] R. Hyman, "Does the Ganzfeld experiment answer the critics' objections?" in *Research in Parapsychology,* W. G. Roll, J. Beloff, and R. A. White, Eds. Metuchen, N.J.: Scarecrow Press, pp. 21–23, 1983.

[76] C. Honorton and S. Harper, "Psi-mediated imagery and ideation in an experimental procedure for regulating perceptual input," *J. Amer. Soc. Psychical Res.,* vol. 68, pp. 156–168, 1974.

[77] C. Honorton, "Meta-analysis of psi ganzfeld research: A response to Hyman," *J. Parapsychol.,* vol. 49, pp. 51–91, 1985.

[78] Psychophysical Research Laboratories, *1983 Annual Report,* Princeton, N.J.

[79] R. D. Nelson, B. J. Dunne, and R. G. Jahn, "An REG experiment with large data base capability, III: Operator related anomalies," Tech. Note, School of Eng./Appl. Sci., Princeton Univ., Princeton, N.J., Sept. 1984.

[80] B. J. Dunne, R. G. Jahn, and R. D. Nelson, "Precognitive remote perception," Tech. Note, School of Eng./Appl. Sci., Princeton Univ., Princeton, N.J., Aug. 1983.

[81] G. V. Glass, B. McGaw, and M. L. Smith, *Meta-Analysis in Social Research.* Beverly Hills, Calif.: Sage Publ., 1981.

[82] L. V. Hedges and I. Olkin, "Analyses, reanalyses, and meta-analysis [Review of *Meta-Analysis in Social Research]." Contemp. Educ. Rev.,* vol. 1, pp. 157–165, 1982.

Psi Experiments:
Do the Best Parapsychological
Experiments Justify the Claims for Psi?*

SUMMARY. Since the founding of the Society for Psychical Research in 1882, psychical researchers have, in each generation, generated research reports that they believed justified the existence of paranormal phenomena. Throughout this period the scientific establishment has either rejected or ignored such claims. The parapsychologists, with some justification, complained that their claims were being rejected without the benefit of a fair hearing. This paper asks the question of how well the best contemporary evidence for *psi*—the term used to designate ESP and psychokinetic phenomena—stands up to fair and unbiased appraisal. The results of the scrutiny of the three most widely heralded programs of research—the remote viewing experiments, the psi ganzfield research, and the work with random number generators—indicates that parapsychological research falls short of the professed standards of the field. In particular, the available reports indicate that randomization is often inadequate, multiple statistical testing without adjustment for significance levels is prevalent, possibilities for sensory leakage are not uniformly prevented, errors in use of statistical tests are much too common, and documentation is typically inadequate. Although the responsible critic cannot argue that these observed departures from optimal experimental procedures have been the sole cause of the reported findings, it is reasonable to demand that the parapsychologists produce consistently significant findings from experiments that are methodologically adequate before their claims are taken seriously.

The Society for Psychical Research was founded in London in 1882 to investigate scientifically that large group of debatable phenomena designated by such terms as mesmeric, psychical, and Spiritualistic.[16] From the

*Experientia 44 (1988), 315–22. Reprinted by permission.

founding of this society through the present, the major psychical researchers have carried out investigations they claim have met the standards of scientific evidence and whose results support the conclusion that paranormal phenomena have been demonstrated. However, during this same period the majority of the scientific establishment has either ignored or rejected the claims of the psychical researchers. Along with their rejection of the claims, the skeptical scientists have insisted that the evidence was inadequate.

Today, *parapsychologists* (the contemporary term for psychical researchers) conduct experiments, which they publish in several refereed parapsychological journals. These parapsychologists, for the most part, have been trained in one or more of the recognized natural or social scientific disciplines. The experiments feature the same types of methodological controls, sophisticated instrumentation, and statistical analyses that one finds in the more orthodox scientific disciplines.

Despite this apparent sophistication in methodology and continual publication of experimental findings purporting to confirm the existence of *psi* (ESP and psychokinetic phenomena), the majority of the scientific establishment still does not accept the claims. Indeed, in many ways the relationship between psychical research and the scientific establishment has remained the same from 1882 to the present. Each new generation of psychical investigators puts before the scientific community experimental results that it claims proves the existence of paranormal phenomena. And each new generation of orthodox scientists either ignores the evidence or dismisses it out of hand.

One aspect of this relatively static relationship that particularly frustrates the parapsychologists is that the members of the scientific community often judge the parapsychological claims without firsthand knowledge of the experimental evidence. Very few of the scientific critics have examined even one of the many experimental reports on psychic phenomena. Even fewer, if any, have examined the bulk of the parapsychological literature that appears regularly in *The Journal of Parapsychology, The Journal of the Society for Psychical Research, The Journal of the American Society for Psychical Research,* and *The European Journal of Parapsychology.*

Consequently, parapsychologists have justification for their complaint that the scientific community is dismissing their claims without a fair hearing. The parapsychologists have consistently maintained that their research has to conform to standards that are more stringent than one finds in psychology and other, related fields of inquiry. And they have asserted that if scientists would examine their experimental reports with an open mind the scientific community would have to admit that the evidence justifies the parapsychological claims.

This paper deals with the question: Does an impartial and objective evaluation of the best contemporary research in parapsychology justify the claims for paranormal phenomena? In the past few years a few critics have taken the time and trouble to evaluate carefully some of the best research programs in current parapsychology. Two critics, Akers[1] and this author[4], applied systematic criteria for evaluating the quality of a well-defined and carefully selected segment of the parapsychological literature.

The critical evaluation of the parapsychological literature strongly suggests that the quality falls far short of what the parapsychological community has believed and claimed. As a result of independent surveys, both Akers[1], a former parapsychologist, and I[4], an outside critic, came to the same conclusion: the best parapsychological research is sufficiently flawed that it cannot support any conclusions about the existence of paranormal phenomena.

What Constitutes Evidence for Psi?

Parapsychologists use the term *psi* to refer "to a person's extrasensorimotor communication with the environment. Psi includes ESP and PK." (The definitions in this paragraph can be found in the back of any issue of *The Journal of Parapsychology.*) By *ESP* or *extrasensory perception,* parapsychologists refer to the "experience of, or response to, a target object, state, event, or influence without sensory contact." By *PK* or *psychokinesis,* parapsychologists refer to "the extramotor aspect of psi; a direct (*i.e.,* mental but nonmuscular) influence exerted by the subject on an external physical process, condition, or object." Although these definitions are neat and tidy, no acceptable positive theory of psi exists. Parapsychologists recognize that until such a theory has been developed, both the definition of, and evidence for, psi have to be negative.

The parapsychologist John Palmer has characterized the situation in the following words: "How do parapsychologists define psi? . . . One [definition] which I think most of us would accept is the following: Psi is a statistically significant departure of results from those expected by chance under circumstances that mimic exchanges of information between living organisms and their environment, *provided that,* A) proper statistical models and methods are used to evaluate the significance, and B) reasonable precautions have been taken to eliminate sensory cues and other experimental artifacts."[12]

To this characterization I would add (in addition to his A and B) that C) reasonable steps have been taken to ensure that the assumptions of the statistical model being used have been met (assumptions such as independence of sampling units, appropriate randomization of targets, and the like).

This characterization, then, implies the minimal criteria needed to demonstrate psi. Requirement C indicates that special care must be taken to ensure that any statistical conclusions are valid. Requirement A is needed to assure us that the observed number of successful "hits" is significantly better than chance. And requirement B certifies that the nonchance results could not be due to sensory cues or other artifacts. If an experiment can be faulted on any of these three requirements, then both parapsychologists and their critics should agree that it cannot be used as evidence for psi.

At this general level, then, I think that parapsychologists and their critics can agree. To demonstrate psi, an experiment must be so designed and conducted that the statistical tests can be legitimately interpreted and that the possibilities for normal sensory communication between target and subject have been eliminated. When disagreement arises, it rarely, if ever, concerns these three general requirements. Rather, disagreements tend to focus on whether one or more of these requirements was adequately achieved in a given experiment.

The reason why the experimental approach has become dominant in parapsychology is just because it provides the only known way to guarantee that these minimal criteria have in fact been met. Only the well-controlled experiment can provide us with all the safeguards needed to eliminate possible alternatives to psi. Data obtained from nonexperimental situations or from incompletely controlled experiments always allow for nonparanormal explanations. Some of these nonparanormal alternatives may be more or less plausible. And, indeed, parapsychologists have often put forth flawed data as evidence for psi on the grounds that the conceivable normal alternatives were highly implausible. Such arguments replace reliance on strict experimental control with arguments based on plausibility. Unfortunately, plausibility is a highly subjective criterion. And to skeptics, even highly implausible possibilities may appear relatively more likely than the even greater implausibility (to them) of the paranormal.

The criteria I have been discussing up to now are "local" in the sense that they apply to the evaluation of a single experiment. As is true in other areas of scientific inquiry, most of the explicit concern with methodology deals with adequacy of the individual experiment. Such emphasis on local criteria seems inconsistent with the fact that scientific inquiry is a cumulative process. A single experiment, no matter how well conducted, never suffices to establish a conclusion, especially one that is novel or surprising in the light of contemporary theories. Rather, laws and theories are based on the cumulative trends of many experiments carried out in several independent laboratories and which tend to converge upon a coherent set of findings.

I will refer to standards that apply to groups of experiments as "global" criteria. With one major exception, most of the debates on the adequacy of parapsychological experiments have focused on local criteria, such as the adequacy of the statistics and the possibilities for sensory leakage. The major exception has been the issue of replicability. Another exception has been the suspicion that many unsuccessful experiments go unreported, thereby inflating the apparent proportion of successful outcomes. This latter concern is known as the *file-drawer problem*.

But global criteria include much more than the replicability and file-drawer problems. There is the matter of lawfulness. It is one thing to argue that a certain proportion of the experiments in a given area yields significant departures from chance. It is another, and scientifically more important, question whether the results of the different experiments yield consistent and lawful patterns. A related matter is cumulativeness. Do today's experimental findings build upon and extend the findings of the previous generations of the experimenters in the field? Parapsychology seems to be alone among the various areas of inquiry that claim scientific status in that it lacks such cumulativeness. As I have argued elsewhere, each new generation of parapsychologists discards the findings of the previous generation and essentially starts from scratch with new paradigms.[5] Other important, but even vaguer, global criteria could be mentioned, such as theoretical productivity and paradigmicity.

Although global criteria, in the long run, play a more important role in the development and acceptance of scientific claims, they are much more difficult to specify than the local criteria. Indeed, until the recent efforts to devise objective procedures for summarizing the trends in a body of research, the assessment of global criteria was an informal and subjective matter. Despite the development of tools for combining probabilities over sets of experiments and for performing meta-analyses, the assessment of the impact of a set of experiments, as opposed to the evaluation of the quality of a single experiment, is still a highly subjective and idiosyncratic activity.

An unfortunate consequence of the fact that we lack standardized, objective methods for assessing the impact of a series of experiments is that different reviewers can and do draw opposite conclusions from the same body of research. Consequently we should not be surprised to discover that on the very few occasions when parapsychologists and critics have tried to evaluate the same set of experiments, they have disagreed sharply on the conclusions to be drawn.

The interrelationship between local and global criteria has played an interesting role in the debates between critics and parapsychologists. The emphasis on local criteria has led some critics, such as Hansel[2], to challenge the parapsychologists to produce a single, fraud-proof experiment that could demonstrate psi. The idea that the existence of psi could be determined by a single experiment, no matter how faithfully it fulfilled all of the local criteria, is quite unrealistic, as the parapsychologists have been quick to point out. No field of scientific inquiry decides such important matters on the basis of a single "critical" experiment. The key to scientific justification is the ability to produce consistent findings across a number of independent investigations. And this is, of course, a global criterion.

On the other hand, many parapsychologists have resurrected a version of the ancient faggot theory by asserting that global criteria could somehow compensate for inadequacies in local criteria.[9] When recent critics, both from within as well as without the parapsychological community, pointed out serious flaws at the local level in some recent parapsychological experiments, the response was interesting. Although the existence of the flaws was not questioned, the defenders of the experiments argued that the flaws were irrelevant because global criteria suggested that they were not responsible for the successful outcomes. In other words, the existence of deficiencies in individual experiments could be dismissed as irrelevant because of overall patterns that cut across all the experiments. Whether there is any sense in which flaws in individual experiments can be compensated for by systematic patterns in the total set of experiments is highly questionable. At any rate we can be sure that the scientific community is not going to accept the reality of paranormal phenomena on the basis of experiments that are individually flawed.

What Can We Conclude from the Best Psi Experiments?

Given these preliminary observations on some of the issues involved in evaluating the current status of parapsychological research, what conclusions about psi, if any, are justified on the basis of the best contemporary parapsychological research? Fortunately, there seems to be a consensus in the parapsychological community as to which research programs currently display the strongest case for psi. In this respect, three programs stand out. The experiments on remote viewing, which began in 1972, have received the most publicity outside of the parapsychological community.[15] Within the parapsychological community the so-called ganzfeld experiments have been considered most evidential. Finally, the experiments using random number generators, expecially those involving psychokinesis, have been very influential.

My comments on the remote viewing experiments will be brief because Christopher Scott has provided a detailed methodological critique.* I will

---

Experientia 44 (1988), pp. 322–326.

also be brief with my comments on the experiments with random number generators because, as will be noted, I can rely upon the systematic survey of a parapsychologist.

The principal basis for my conclusions will be the only two relatively systematic and objective critical surveys of contemporary parapsychological research that are known to me. One was my own attempt to assess the quality of the experiments in the ganzfeld research program.[4] The other is Akers's systematic evaluation of 54 of the best parapsychological experiments that yielded successful outcomes.[1]

Remote Viewing

As Christopher Scott's critique indicates, the remote viewing experiments have serious weaknesses. Both the experiments with random number generators and the ganzfeld experiments also are characterized by methodological deficiencies. Unlike these latter two cases, however, the deficiencies in the remote viewing experiments provide a highly plausible and normal alternative explanation for the results. The flaws in the ganzfeld and random number generator experiments violate accepted standards for parapsychological research. But they do not necessarily supply a plausible alternative account of the findings.

Just about all the serious weaknesses with the remote viewing experiments can be attributed to two important aspects of the procedure. In each experiment, a single percipient or subject supplies all the data for the sequence of trials. A single trial consists of the percipient, who is isolated with an experimenter, attempting to describe the target site, which is being visited by one or more members of a target team. Neither the percipient nor the experimenter who is with him or her has any normal means of knowing the particular target site at the time the description is provided. Immediately after each trial, the target team returns to the laboratory and then returns to the target site with the percipient. This gives the percipient immediate feedback concerning the target site for that trial.

In addition to the feedback after each trial, the remote viewing experiments are characterized by a lack of independence among the successive trials. This comes about because after the experiment is completed a judge is given a set of all the target descriptions and a list of all the targets. These have previously been randomized so that the judge supposedly has no normal clues as to which description goes with which target site. The judge visits each target site in turn. At each site, he or she rank orders the entire set of descriptions from best to worst in terms of how well each apparently describes the particular target site. These rankings serve as the primary data for the later statistical analyses upon which the conclusions are based.

The combination of the immediate feedback and the interdependence of the trial descriptions creates a fatal flaw in the procedure. It is this flaw that has allowed the sort of overt cueing in the transcripts discussed by Marks and Kammann.[8] This same flaw also produced overly optimistic statistical analyses in the early experiments. And it is this flaw that, I have repeatedly argued, enables the possibility of more pervasive cueing that cannot be corrected by any amount of post hoc analyses or editing.

The underlying flaw that I am talking about involves the lack of independence among the trials. This concept of independence is highly technical, and I find that it is not easy to explain it to the uninitiated. However, I think I can provide an example that might make some of its implications evident. Imagine that we are dealing with a remote viewing experiment that consists of only three trials. Three trials would ordinarily be too few for a meaningful statistical analysis, but it is much less complicated to discuss. The basic principles are the same when we add more trials. Now further imagine that the experiment varies from the standard procedure for remote viewing experiments in that the judge does not rank all three descriptions against each target site. Instead, for each trial, the experimenters generate a separate pool of three possible sites, one of which is randomly selected as the actual target. Instead of ranking all three descriptions against each site, the judge visits all the sites in a given target pool and rank orders the three sites in terms of how well each matches the description for that trial.

In this latter procedure, which is the more typical of parapsychological experiments using free responses, there is a one-third chance that the actual target site will receive the top ranking for each trial. Given three trials, this would mean that there would be one chance in 27 of having the actual target site correctly ranked for each trial. Such an outcome would be suggestive that something other than just chance provided the successful matchings.

Now compare the procedure in the preceding two paragraphs with the one that is actually used in remote viewing experiments. Here the judge visits each target site and ranks all three descriptions against each target site. Because the concept of independence can be subtle, the investigator may tend to treat the statistical analysis the same as I did for the preceding method. If the corresponding description turned out to be ranked one for each of the targets, he might calculate the chance level as again 1 in 27 on the grounds that there was just one chance in three for the description to be ranked first for each of the three sites.

But the probability of correctly ranking all three descriptions is much greater than 1 in 27. This is because of the lack of independence in the judging procedure. Almost certainly the judge will not rank the same description as first for more than one target. Indeed, if the judge believes, as he or she should, that each description goes with a single target, he or she is apt to judge accordingly. Because the number of possible rankings is much more restricted in the latter case, the probability of getting all three correct is probably closer to 1 in 6 rather than 1 in 27. In fact, the early remote viewing experiments provided overly optimistic estimates of the significance of the results because they failed to realize the lack of independence among the trials. Kennedy[7] noted that 7 out of the 8 earliest remote viewing experiments were reported as yielding significant outcomes when the experimenters used a statistical test that assumed independence among trials. When Kennedy applied a more conservative test that took lack of independence into account, the number of significant outcomes was reduced from 7 to 3.

The lack of independence among the trials can be circumvented by using a more conservative statistical test, as Kennedy has demonstrated. In theory it might be possible to compensate for the overt clues in the transcripts of the type that Marks and Kammann[8] uncovered by careful editing. In practice it is not clear that this can be accomplished to the satisfaction of all critics. However, as I have repeatedly argued, the possibility for nonparanormal matching of descriptions to target sites is an ineradicable feature of the way the remote viewing experiments are designed.

The combination of immediate feedback and dependence among the trials makes it plausible that the percipient's descriptions will contain sufficient information, for entirely normal reasons, to enable the judge to match descriptions to target sites without error. To see how this could come about, imagine that the first target site was the Hoover Tower on the Stanford University campus. Immediately after having provided her description, the percipient is taken to the target site. At her second trial, it is reasonable to assume that the percipient will avoid describing anything that would specifically match the Hoover Tower. Assume that the second target site is the Palo Alto train station. On the third trial it is highly unlikely that the percipient will include in her description anything that directly matches either the Hoover Tower or the Palo Alto train station. Each successive description can be expected to lack descriptors that uniquely match any of the preceding target sites. In this way, it is easy to believe that the transcripts could be matched successfully to the target sites without having to assume paranormal powers. This flaw is fatal, because I do not see any way of compensating for its effects as long as the experiments continue to be run in the present way. [Against this argument, however, is the fact that well-controlled experiments, which allow feedback and interdependence of judges' rankings, but which prevent sensory leakage to judges of target order or transcript positioning, have not in practice yielded statistically significant results.]

Experiments with Random Number Generators

Schmidt, a quantum physicist by training, has probably been the individual most responsible for making the experiments with random number generators (RNGs) a major paradigm in contemporary parapsychology.[14] Schmidt began his experiments in 1969 and has continued doing them ever since. At first, the RNGs were used in ESP-type experiments. But quickly the use of RNGs in psychokinesis (PK) experiments became more common. The typical RNG randomly generates a sequence of binary outputs such as 0's and 1's. If the RNG is unbiased, the successive outputs will be independent of one another, and the 0's will tend to occur 50% of the time. In a PK experiment, the subject or "operator" sits before the RNG and tries to influence the output mentally so that the frequency of 1's will either become greater than or less than the expected 50%. During the past 15 years, in fact, many parapsychologists have reported results that they believe prove that operators can mentally bias the output of RNG devices.

The two most influential programs of research on this type of PK together account for approximately 60% of all the known experiments with RNGs. In addition to Schmidt's research program, Jahn began a program in the late 1970s, when he was dean of the School of Engineering and Applied Science at Princeton University. The research programs initiated by these two physical scientists are not only among the most highly respected ones in parapsychology, but are also the most consistently successful in achieving significant outcomes.

When trying to assess the strength of the evidence for PK from such experiments, we should realize that the purported effects are extremely small. Over the years, Schmidt's subjects have "produced" an average of 50.5% hits in comparison with the expected chance level of 50%. Jahn and his colleagues have come up with an even lower rate of success than Schmidt's. In their "formal" series of 78 million trials, the percentage of hits in the intended direction was only 50.02%. Such extremely weak effects can yield strong statistical significance when considered over several million trials.

But even an extremely weak PK effect, if real, violates some currently accepted principles about the physical universe. An extremely weak effect— one that takes millions of trials to document—may also suggest unknown, but very small, biases, which only emerge when we average over an enormous number of trials. The statistical tests that are typically used in scientific experiments, for example, require certain assumptions about how the world operates. A typical experiment in biology or psychology, for example, may use fewer than 100 trials, or sometimes a few hundred trials, but rarely anything much higher. Under these conditions, empirical and theoretical studies by statisticians have found that the statistical tests in use are reasonably "robust." By this term, they mean that even though the assumptions underlying the statistical tests do not strictly hold, the results of the tests are still reasonably accurate. In other words, even though the underlying distributions are rarely strictly normal and the population variances are not always equal, such departures from the ideal rarely make a serious difference in the interpretation of the statistical tests. But the situation could be quite different when we jump from experiments with relatively large effects and a small number of trials to experiments with extremely small effects and millions of trials. So far as we know, even the slightest departure from the assumptions might suffice to produce artificially significant outcomes.

Such considerations indicate that we have to be even more vigilant to ensure that any evidence for PK effects on RNGs was obtained under conditions that stringently adhere to the standards of good scientific practice. Unfortunately, as was the case for remote viewing, the experiments using RNGs have typically been conducted under rather casual and poorly documented circumstances.

By ordinary standards, the accumulated results from RNG experiments seem impressive. A recent survey counted 332 separate "experiments" published during the years 1969 through 1984.[13] Approximately 57% of these 332 experiments had been reported in refereed journals or conference proceedings. If we assume that these latter experiments have some claim to scientific status, then around 31% of the scientifically reported RNG experiments produced significant results as compared to the 5% that would be expected by chance. (For the entire set of 332 experiments, 21% produced significant results at the traditional 0.05 level.)

Such a success rate suggests that the successful outcomes probably cannot be entirely attributed to the reporting of only successful experiments. Although it does look as if successful experiments in this area are somewhat more likely to be reported than unsuccessful ones, the probability that all the apparent significance could have come about in this manner is quite low.

On the other hand, the use of these results to argue for the reality of PK depends upon how successfully other alternative explanations have been eliminated. The most obvious alternatives have to do with possible biases in outputs of the RNGs or of other factors such as temperature, humidity, and transients upon the outputs. The quality of any RNG experiment has to be judged by how well the investigator has ensured that such alternatives have been successfully eliminated.

As May and his colleagues make clear,[10] the RNG experiments up to 1979 all are inadequate on one or more key details, such as controls for transients, tests of randomness, supervision of the operator, and documentation of procedures. As far as can be determined, this situation has not improved since that report. Today, the most impressive body of research on RNGs, both in quantity and apparent quality of the experimentation, is that of Jahn and his colleagues.[11] Jahn's research presents the usual problem that an outsider has in trying to reach a fair conclusion concerning the implications of the reported results. The data base includes an accumulation of trials from a small number of operators over a period of more than six years. The procedures and instrumentation used in the Princeton Anomalies Laboratory are unique. They differ in many ways from those used in other parapsychological laboratories. Indeed, these procedures and technologies have changed over time during the experiments. Presumably, the earlier trials were conducted under conditions that were relatively more informal and less fail-safe than those currently employed. But it is not clear if the data for the various conditions can be separated and analyzed separately. This problem is especially critical because of the extremely small size of the effect being claimed.

Another problem is that the various operators do not contribute equally to the data base. One subject, for example, is apparently responsible for 23% of the total data base. This subject's hit rate was 50.05%. If we eliminated that subject's data from the data base, the remaining data yield a hit rate of 50.01%, which is not only extremely close to 50%, but is no longer significantly different from chance.

Given the implications of the claims being made, it becomes imperative to provide data from these experiments in which the operators have been adequately monitored and the specific experimental arrangements have been consistent throughout. If such experimentally adequate trials continue to yield positive and significant results, then we would want to see replication in independent laboratories.

As is the case with the remote viewing experiments, the RNG experiments, upon close inspection, suffer from a variety of defects at both the local and global level. In the case of remote viewing, the flaws are such that they suggest a plausible, normal alternative to account for the results. We do not have such an obvious plausible alternative to account for the results of the RNG experiments. Most of the experiments lack adequate tests of the randomness of the RNG being used. But, in most such experiments, it is not clear how any systematic biases could account for the results, since such systematic biases presumably would affect control and experimental trials in the same way. Similar problems face the critic who wants to argue that the specific flaws in a given RNG experiment could, in fact, have accounted for the results.

On the other hand, the critic can rightfully insist that it is not his or her responsibility to provide an alternative account. It is sufficient to point out that the given experiment violates one or more criteria that the parapsychologists themselves have asserted are necessary for a sound parapsychological experiment. Yes, we do not have an obvious account of how inadequate randomization could have produced the reported results. On the other hand, we have no way of assessing the meaning of the reported results unless we can be sure that the reported statistical levels of significance are correct. And we can only have confidence in the statistical conclusions when we know that the underlying assumptions for their interpretation have been met. Yet this is just what we do not know. In other words, the only reasonable conclusion to draw from the existing body of data from the RNG experiments is that we do not know what to make of it. We cannot say that the results were definitely the result of some artifact. On the other hand we cannot say that they were not. The only way we will be able to draw meaningful conclusions from such experiments is when they have been conducted according to the standards that both the parapsychologists and their critics assert ought to be met by any acceptable parapsychological experiment.

The Ganzfeld Psi Experiments

The ganzfeld psi experiments, which began at roughly the same time as the remote viewing experiments, seemingly have produced a stronger case for psi. Because of this, I undertook a careful and systematic review of this data base.[4] The ganzfeld psi experiments are named after the term *ganzfeld,* which was used by gestalt psychologists to designate the entire or whole visual field. For theoretical purposes, the gestalt psychologists wanted to create a situation in which the subject or observer could view a homogeneous visual field, one with no imperfections or boundaries. They called such a field the *ganzfeld.* Later psychologists discovered that when individuals are put into a ganzfeld situation they tend quickly to experience an altered state of consciousness.

In the early 1970s, some parapsychologists decided that.the use of the ganzfeld would provide a relatively safe and easy way to create an altered state in their experimental subjects. They believed that such a state was more conducive towards picking up the elusive psi signals. In a typical psi ganzfeld experiment, subjects (or percipients) have halved ping-pong balls taped over their eyes. They then recline in a comfortable chair while white noise occurs in the earphones attached to their head. A bright light shines in front of their face. When seen through the translucent ping-pong balls, the light is experienced as a homogeneous fog-like field. When so prepared, almost all subjects report experiencing a pleasant altered state within 15 minutes.

While an experimenter is preparing the subject for the ganzfeld state, a second experimenter randomly selects a target pool from a large set. The target pool typically consists of four possible targets, usually reproductions of paintings or pictures of travel scenes. One of these four candidates is randomly chosen to be the target for that trial. The target is given to an agent or sender who tries to communicate its substance psychically to the subject who is in the ganzfeld state. After a designated period, the subject is removed from the ganzfeld state and presented with the four candidates from the target pool. The subject then ranks the four candidates in terms of how well each matched the experience of his or her ganzfeld period. If the actual target is ranked first, the trial is designated as a "hit." An actual experiment consists of several trials. In the example, the probability is that one out of every four trials will produce a hit. If the number of hits significantly exceeds the expected 25%, then the result is considered to be evidence for the existence of psi.

What sorts of flaws did I find in this data base?[4] All but three of the 42 experiments used multiple analyses that artificially inflated the chances of obtaining significant outcomes. Only 11 (26%) of the studies contained evidence of having adequately randomized the target selections. As many as 15 (36%) clearly used inferior randomization, such as hand shuffling, or no randomization at all. The remaining 16 experiments did not supply sufficient information on how they had chosen the targets. As many as 23 of the experiments (55%) used only one target pool, which meant that the subject was handed for judging the very same target that the percipient had used. This allowed for the possibility of sensory cueing. Although the argument for psi is mainly a statistical one, the reports of 12 experiments (29%) revealed statistical errors. A variety of other departures from optimum practice were also found.

Honorton's rebuttal questioned many of my flaw assignments, provided a re-analysis of the data base, which he claimed overcame many of the statistical weaknesses of the original experiments, and argued that the existing flaws were not sufficient to have accounted for the findings.[3] He does not deny that the experiments departed from optimal design, but he argues that such departures were insufficient to have accounted for the results.

Honorton and I subsequently published a joint paper to emphasize those points on which we agree.[6] Some of the key points of agreement were expressed by us in the following words:

As to the psi ganzfeld data base, we agree, as our earlier exchanges indicate
. . . that the experiments as a group departed from ideal standards on aspects
such as multiple testing, randomization of targets, controlling for sensory
leakage, application of statistical tests, and documentation. Although we
probably still differ about the extent and seriousness of these departures,
we agree that future psi ganzfeld experiments should be conducted in
accordance with these ideals. . . .

Although we probably still differ on the magnitude of the biases
contributed by multiple testing, retrospective experiments, and the file-drawer
problem, we agree that the overall significance observed in these studies
cannot reasonably be explained by these selective factors. Something beyond
selective reporting or inflated significance levels seems to be producing the
nonchance outcomes. Moreover, we agree that the significant outcomes
have been produced by a number of different investigators.

Whereas we continue to differ over the degree to which the current
ganzfeld data base contributes evidence for psi, we agree that the final verdict
awaits the outcome of future psi ganzfeld experiments—ones conducted
by a broader range of investigators and according to more stringent standards.

Akers's Critique

The systematic evaluation of the contemporary parapsychological literature
by Akers,[1] a former parapsychologist, is interesting because it used a strategy
different from mine. My approach was to evaluate the entire data base
of a single research paradigm, including both successful and unsuccessful
outcomes. Akers confined himself to the best contemporary ESP experiments that had produced significant results with unselected subjects. I
assigned flaws to experiments without regard for whether each flaw, by
itself, could have caused the observed outcome. Akers was more conservative.
He charged a flaw to a study only if he thought it could plausibly have
been sufficient to produce the observed result. Akers chose a sample of
54 parapsycholgical experiments from areas of research that had been
previously reviewed by one of two major parapsychologists, Honorton or
Palmer. The intent was to choose experiments that could be viewed as
the current best evidence for the existence of psi. Akers then evaluated
the experiments in terms of a number of possible flaws. An experiment
was eliminated as evidential only if it was so seriously defective on a given
flaw that the defect could plausibly have caused the observed outcome.
As a result of this exercise, Akers concluded:

Results from the 54-experiment survey have demonstrated that there are
many alternative explanations for ESP phenomena; the choice is not simply between psi and experimenter fraud. . . . The number of experiments
flawed on various grounds were as follows: randomization failures (13),

sensory leakage (22), subject cheating (12), recording errors (10), classification or scoring errors (9), statistical errors (12), reporting failures (10). . . . All told, 85% of the experiments were considered flawed (46/54). This leaves eight experiments where no flaws were assigned. . . . Although none of these experiments has a glaring weakness, this does not mean that they are especially strong in either their methods or their results. . . . In conclusion, there were eight experiments conducted with reasonable care, but none of these could be considered as methodologically strong. When all 54 experiments are considered, it can be stated that the research methods are too weak to establish the existence of a paranormal phenomenon.[1]

Conclusions on the Scientific Evidence

The parapsychologists whom we have cited as well as their critics agree that the best contemporary experiments in parapsychology fall short of acceptable methodological standards. The critics conclude that such data, based on methodologically flawed procedures, cannot justify any conclusions about psi. The parapsychologists argue that, while each experiment is individually flawed, when taken together, the composite body of data suffices to justify that psi exists.

We should distinguish between three degrees of criticism of a given parapsychological finding. The first is what we might refer to as the *smoking gun*. This is the type of criticism that asserts or strongly implies that the observed findings were due to factor X. Such a claim puts the burden of proof on the critic. To back up such a claim, the critic must provide evidence that the results were in fact caused by X. Many of the bitterly contested feuds between critics and proponents have often been the result of the proponent correctly or incorrectly assuming that this type of criticism was being made.

The second type of criticism can be termed the *plausible alternative*. Here the critic does not assert that the result was due to factor X. Instead, he or she asserts that the obtained result *could have been* due to factor X. Such a stance also places a burden on the critic, but one not so stringent as the smoking gun assertion. The critic now has to make a plausible case for the possibility that factor X was sufficient to have caused the result. Optional stopping, for example, can bias the results. But the bias is a small one, and it would be a mistake to assert that an outcome was due to optional stopping if the probability of the outcome is extremely low. Akers's critique,[1] which was previously discussed, is an example based on the plausible alternative.

The third type of criticism can be called the *dirty test tube*. In this case the critic points out that the experiment departs from accepted methodological standards of the field in certain ways. The critic, in this case, does not claim to know that the results have been produced by some artifact. Rather, he or she points out that the results have been obtained under conditions that fail to meet generally accepted standards. The strength of this latter type of critique is that test tubes should not be dirty when doing careful and important scientific research. To the extent that the test tubes were dirty, it suggests that the experiment was not carried out according to acceptable standards. Consequently, the results remain suspect even though the critic cannot demonstrate that the dirt in the test tubes was sufficient to have produced the outcome.[4]

It is in this latter sense—the dirty test tube sense—that the best parapsychological experiments fall short. To be fair, we do not have a smoking gun, nor have we demonstrated a plausible alternative. But we suspect that even the parapsychological community must be concerned to discover that their best experiments still fall far short of the methodological adequacy they themselves would profess.

Under the circumstances, it seems reasonable to withhold judgment at this time. But can we not make at least a provisional conclusion based on the tendencies in the data that have been accumulated up to now? We would argue that it would be counterproductive even to try to draw a tentative conclusion because the data lack *robustness*. By this term, we mean that even relatively small changes in the data base are capable of reversing any conclusion we might wish to make. For example, Honorton[3] and I[4] differed on whether to assign a flaw on randomization to Sargent's experiments. With Honorton's assignment, the studies with adequate randomization do not differ in significance of outcome from those with inadequate randomization. On Hyman's assignment, the experiments with inadequate randomization significantly have more successful outcomes than do those with adequate randomization. A simple disagreement on one experimenter's research can thus make a huge difference as to whether we conclude that this flaw contributed or did not contribute to the observed outcomes. Several other similar examples could be cited to illustrate the extreme sensitivity of this data base to slight changes in flaw assignments.

References

1. Akers, C., "Methodological criticisms of parapsychology," in: *Advances in Parapsychological Research,* vol. 4. Ed. S. Krippner. McFarland, Jefferson, N.C. 1984.
2. Hansel, C. E. M., *ESP and parapsychology: A critical re-evaluation.* Prometheus Books, Buffalo, N.Y. 1980.
3. Honorton, C., "Meta-analysis of psi ganzfeld research: A response to Hyman."

J. Parapsychol. 49 (1985) 351–364.

4. Hyman, R., "The ganzfeld psi experiment: A critical appraisal." *J. Parapsychol. 49* (1985) 3–49.

5. Hyman, R., "A critical historical overview of parapsychology," in: *A Skeptic's Handbook of Parapsychology,* pp.3–96. Ed. P. Kurtz. Prometheus Books. Buffalo, N.Y. 1985.

6. Hyman, R., and Honorton, C., "A joint communiqué: The psi ganzfeld controversy." *J. Parapsychol. 50* (1986) 351–364.

7. Kennedy, J. E., "Methodological problems in free-response ESP experiments." *J. Am. Soc. Psych. Res. 73* (1979) 1–15.

8. Marks, D. F., and Kammann, R., "Information transmission in remote viewing." *Nature 274* (1978) 680–681.

9. Marks, D. F., "Investigating the paranormal." *Nature 320* (1986) 119–124.

10. May, E. C., Humphrey, B. S., and Hubbard, G. S., "Electronic System Perturbation Techniques." SRI International (Final Report) Menlo Park, Calif. 1980.

11. Nelson, R. D., Dunne B. J., and Jahn, R. G., "An RNG experiment with large data base capability, III: Operator related anomalies." Technical Note PEAR 84003, Princeton Engineering Anomalies Research, Princeton University, 1984.

12. Palmer, J., "In defense of parapsychology: A reply to James E. Alcock." *Zetetic Scholar* (1983) 39–70.

13. Radin, D. I., May, E. C., and Thomson, M. J., "Psi experiments with random number generators: Meta-analysis part 1." SRI International, Menlo Park, Calif., 1985.

14. Schmitdt, H., "A PK test with electronic equipment." *J. Parapsych. 34* (1970) 175–181.

15. Targ, R., and Puthoff, H. E., "Information transmission under conditions of sensory shielding." *Nature 252* (1974) 602–607.

16. "The Society for Psychical Research: Objects of the society." *Proc. Soc. Psych. Res 1* (1882–83) 3–6.

Reviews

Modern Experiments in Telepathy, Second Edition.
S. G. Soal and Frederick Bateman.
New Haven, Conn.: Yale University Press, 1954. Pp. xv, 425.*

Two minds can communicate with each other, according to *Modern Experiments in Telepathy,* without the intervention of normal sensory channels. Such communication seems to be just as effective when 500 miles, rather than the usual dozen feet, separate agent and percipient. And even more intriguing is the claim that the percipient can be aware of a thought *before* the agent has concentrated upon it.

Confronted with such claims, the skeptical scientist is apt to ask himself, "Is extra-sensory perception fact or artifact? And if it is a fact what consequences, if any, does it foreshadow for me and my work?"

Clearly, the scientist views the possibility of extra-sensory perception with misgivings. The concepts of telepathy and precognition, especially with their historical origins in spiritualism and psychic investigation, suggest a return to the animism and magic from which modern science supposedly has freed itself. When a carefully documented work such as *Modern Experiments in Telepathy,* therefore, attempts to place extra-sensory perception on a scientific footing, the scientist will scrutinize the argument for possible loopholes.

Soal and Bateman base their conclusions upon more than 60,000 guesses obtained from two gifted subjects. These guesses were made in the following experimental situation. An *experimenter,* on each trial, relays a number to an *agent.* The agent, in turn, encodes this number into one of five symbols.

---

*This review was published in *American Statistical Association Journal* 52 (1957), 607–10. Reprinted by permission.

Only the agent knows which symbol corresponds to which number, and he changes this code after every block of 25 trials. The agent concentrates upon the appropriate symbol while the *percipient,* in an adjoining room, tries to guess which one it is. A typical experimental session consists of 400 such guesses. All told, the results of the Shackleton-Stewart series comprise 170 sessions.

The telepathy displayed by the two subjects was not the dramatic "mind reading" of folklore and conjuring. The communication between agent and subject was of a very rudimentary kind, being detectable only in the form of a slight, but statistically significant, excess of correct guesses. Basil Shackleton consistently guessed better than expectation, over a period of 2¼ years, with odds against chance quoted at 10^{35} to 1. This was true, however, not when his guess was matched against the target symbol, but only when it was matched against the next symbol in the series. Mrs. Stewart, over a period of 4 years, guessed the target symbol sufficiently often to make the odds against chance 10^{70} to 1.

Soal and Bateman, anticipating negative reactions to their work, have fortified these odds with sophisticated arguments and evidence to the effect that their positive results are not due to recording errors, optional stopping, improper selection of data, ad hoc tests of hypotheses, wrong statistical models, inadequate randomization of target symbols, or deliberate signaling between agent and percipient.

In addition to these painstaking efforts to avoid statistical and methodological pitfalls, the book raises many other issues to frustrate hasty attempts to "explain away" the findings as artifact. The features that make the Soal and Bateman argument one of the most formidable in the annals of psychic research, in this reviewer's opinion, can be summarized under four points.

1. *Consistency of scoring rate.* Despite changes in personnel, procedures, symbols, locale, etc., the scoring rates remained remarkably stable from session to session for both Basil Shackleton and Mrs. Stewart.

2. *Empirical checks on the adequacy of randomization procedures.* Soal and Bateman systematically applied the following cross check to each block of 50 target stimuli and guesses. The first 25 guesses were matched against the last 25 target symbols, and the last 25 guesses were matched against the first 25 target symbols. This cross check yielded results in accord with the probability model. A cross check on 33,500 guesses made by Mrs. Stewart, for example, registered 6,711 correct hits as against a binomial expectation of 6,700. When the same guesses were matched against their intended targets, the actual number of correct guesses was 8,694 hits or 27 standard deviations above chance.

3. *The difference between telepathic and interspersed clairvoyant trials.* During some sittings the authors alternated blocks of telepathic trials (in

which the agent looks at the designated symbol) with clairvoyant trials (in which the agent does not look at the designated symbol). Both Shackleton and Mrs. Stewart maintained their significantly positive scoring rates on the telepathic trials while guessing no better than chance on the interspersed clairvoyant trials.

4. *The long distance experiment with Mrs. Stewart.* A series of 6 sessions, in which Mrs. Stewart was separated from the agent by 500 miles, was very successful with results comparable to those obtained at regulation distance.

How do such results stand up to the criticisms of skeptics? This reviewer was able to classify all the major attempts to dismiss the findings of Soal and Bateman under one of three headings: possibility of sensory cues, defects in the probability model, or an incompatibility of extra-sensory perception with the presuppositions of modern science. As we shall see, none of these criticisms, with the exception of the imputation of fraud to the investigators and subject, succeeds in finding a plausible alternative that encompasses all four points.

Possibility of sensory cues. One obvious place to seek a flaw is in the possibility of actual sensory communication between agent and percipient. The "double whispering" theory of D. H. Rawcliffe, which Soal and Bateman brand as "preposterous," invokes involuntary whispering and hypersensitive hearing as the links between the agent and the experimenter, on one hand, and the agent and the percipient on the other hand. Although Rawcliffe's suggestion is needlessly complex, it is obviously less "preposterous" to most scientists than is the alternative of extra-sensory perception.

When we consider the conditions under which most of the sittings were conducted (in the percipient's own home, inadequate separation of experimenter from agent and percipient, subjectively timed trials, vocal announcements of trial numbers, etc.), a simple explanation in terms of subliminal sensory cues does seem quite reasonable. Communication between agent and experimenter, who were seated at the same table with only half a screen separating them, in the form of sensory cues transmitting partial or complete information about the code, is well within the bounds of possibility. And communication between the experimenter, who vocally announces each trial number, and the percipient is even more plausible.

But this hypothesis runs into serious difficulty when it encounters the successful series in which Mrs. Stewart was separated from the agent by the English Channel. Unless a more detailed description of these 6 sittings uncovers unsuspected loopholes, Soal and Bateman can righteously ignore the accusation of actual sensory contact between agent and percipient. This successful long distance series is indeed fortunate for the argument of Soal and Bateman. It is only because of the outcome of this series, in this reviewer's opinion, that the entire set of 170 sittings becomes plausible evidence for nonsensory communication.

Defects in the probability model. Almost as curious as the phenomenon of extrasensory perception, itself, is the proposition that the deviations from chance imply a bias that results when the probability model is used in conjunction with published tables of random numbers (Brown in *Nature,* 25 July 1953; Boring in *American Scientist,* January 1955; Bridgman in *Science,* 6 January 1956). In essence, the argument implies that Soal and Bateman make all their comparisons against an *a priori* baseline and that this baseline may be too low because of biases in randomization procedures.

Just how such a suggestion could arise in connection with the work in *Modern Experiments in Telepathy* is puzzling, indeed. For one of the outstanding virtues of this work is the empirical cross check on the randomization procedures. Both the cross check and the results of the clairvoyance trials yielded empirical numbers of hits that agreed well with the probability model. And the number of correct guesses by Shackleton and Mrs. Stewart was far in excess of the empirical as well as the *a priori* baselines.

It certainly must be a peculiar bias, as Soal and Bateman point out, that operates only on telepathic calls and suspends activity on interspersed clairvoyant calls and on empirical cross checks.

Incompatibility of extra-sensory perception with the basic presuppositions of modern science. Some scientists view extra-sensory perception as incompatible with science. And the parapsychologists, themselves, have furthered this impression by holding up their findings as arguments against the "materialism," "mechanism," and "physicalism" of modern science. Further, this incompatibility has been seized upon as sufficient grounds for dismissing the evidence for extra-sensory perception (Price, *Science,* 26 August 1955).

Such an approach shifts the emphasis away from the empirical evidence and brings us face to face with complex psychological and philosophical questions. One question is how fundamental is the causality concept to science. And just where one stands on this issue—the role of causality in science; whether it be invariant temporal sequence, functional relation, statistical regularity; whether it need imply spatiotemporal contiguity; etc.—depends upon which philosopher of science one prefers to read.

There are other complex ramifications of such a position. Are these basic principles of science of such a universality that we must assume them to hold even in areas not previously explored by science? And, to get back to the empirical plane, how do we know that extra-sensory perception violates such principles? The answer to the latter question depends partly upon definitions and partly upon the accumulation of more data than is currently available.

It seems to this reviewer that the attempt to deny extra-sensory perception the status of "fact" on purely *a priori* grounds exaggerates the universality and status of the basic presuppositions concerning space, time, and causality. And, as a corollary, it enhances the significance of parapsychological findings beyond anything warranted by the paucity and crudity of the data.

Rather than argue the question at a philosophical level—a level at which there is little agreement concerning definitions and ideals—Soal and Bateman's data, like other scientific evidence, should be evaluated on their empirical merits. And at this level, it seems, most critics are willing to concede that the findings were obtained according to the same rules of procedure we use in orthodox inquiries.

The real question, then, is not whether the phenomenon (or phenomena) uncovered by Soal and Bateman is a "fact"—for by current empirical standards it is a fact—but what kind of a fact is it? What significance does this "fact" have for the rest of science?

The phenomenon called extra-sensory perception does seem to be a peculiar fact. Among other things the evidence suggests that it is elusive and not repeatable by prescription; it is rare; it is beyond conscious control; it is unpredictable; it is detectable only by subtle and indirect means; and it is shy in the presence of skepticism. Just how characteristic such features are is a moot question. Soal and Bateman's data more than adequately demonstrate the existence of the phenomenon; but too many things were varied simultaneously from session to session to enable one to isolate factors that correlate with scoring rate.

For all practical purposes, then, extra-sensory perception behaves very much like what the scientist calls errors of measurement. In the quest for repeatable, systematic relationships the scientist lumps all factors that "cause" "random" fluctuations in measurements from experiment to experiment under the broad category of variable errors. Extra-sensory perception, even if it were to enter into the scientist's measurements, would do so as a random error. From what we know about the phenomenon, it would certainly not produce any long-range bias.

What about the theoretical status of this phenomenon? As far as this reviewer can see (and, judging from published reactions to this book, there are many who would disagree), the walls of science will not come tumbling down if we admit the phenomenon to be a fact. For, at the moment, it is nothing but an isloated fact. It fits into no scientific scheme; it can be deduced from no current theoretical system. With more evidence concerning the antecedent conditions and correlated factors, it may persist in remaining an isolated fact—one with little significance beyond itself. Or it may force a duality upon us concerning human behavior and physics; or it may force us to revise our basic premises concerning science; or it may—after all the heated controversy—turn out to be something that is compatible and consistent with our present presuppositions about the physical world.

It is too soon to judge. We need many more facts than the parapsychologists have supplied us. And judging from the difficulties that lie ahead for them, it will be a long time before we will be in a position to judge.

In some ways the present situation in parapsychology reminds one of the "explanatory crisis" that Bridgeman saw posed by relativity and quantum phenomena (*Logic of Modern Physics,* 1928). "Whenever experience takes us into new and unfamiliar realms, we are to be at least prepared for a new crisis. . . . It seems to me that the only sensible course is to . . . wait until we have amassed so much experience of the new kind that it is perfectly familiar to us, and then to resume the process of explanation with elements from our new experience included in our list of axioms."

Is the phenomenon of extra-sensory perception a fact that we should be concerned about? The answer to this question must wait upon this amassing of "so much experience of the new kind." For, as Boring has put it, "Of its importance in the developing scientific skein, posterity will be able to judge, and you cannot hurry history."

"The Case for Parapsychology." D. Scott Rogo. *The Humanist* 37 (November–December 1977), 40–44.*

"The Case for Parapsychology" has provided a welcome service. D. Scott Rogo has supplied us with a convenient classification of the arguments against parapsychology. For each criticism he has supplied a rebuttal. He has also been extremely helpful by indicating which, in his opinion, are the best examples of good parapsychological research.

Parapsychologists are doing much more sophisticated research than many critics and indifferent scientists realize; and if nonparapsychologists took the time to read the current parapsychological journals, most of them would discover that the field contains a solid core of dedicated, serious, and competent experimenters. Furthermore, it is difficult to read through this literature without coming to the conclusion that "something" is there.

This much we can concede to Rogo. But the real issue is, does it matter? And if so, in what way? Why should I, as a scientist or as a human, be concerned about what the parapsychologists are doing and claiming?

---

*This review appeared under the title, "The Case Against Parapsychology," in *The Humanist* (November–December 1977), 47–49. Reprinted by permission.

It is with respect to these questions that I find Rogo's arguments unconvincing. I do not think that Rogo or parapsychology has produced sufficient evidence to claim our attention.

I think I can best justify my case against parapsychology by referring to the same criticisms that Rogo discusses and attempts to rebut. Three of these criticisms—that the parapsychologist is biased in favor of his results, that psi is *a priori* impossible, and that parapsychological findings are irrelevant to science—according to Rogo, "are not logical criticisms, but emotional charges or value judgments."

Rogo is partly correct. These charges are often leveled against parapsychology in irrational ways. Parapsychologists probably *are* very much biased in favor of believing in psi. Why else would an individual risk his or her reputation to pursue a frustratingly elusive and unpredictable phenomenon? But such a bias, in itself, does not make the data and arguments untrustworthy. The argument that psi is *a priori* impossible is a complex one and partly semantic. Even some parapsychologists believe that *all* data must eventually have a *normal* explanation. But I agree that we cannot rule out certain kinds of data on purely logical grounds.

I disagree strongly, however, with Rogo's assertion that the third criticism—that parapsychological findings are irrelevant to science—is irrational. If parapsychologists want to argue that their findings and concepts are relevant to other areas of science, they have to make a much stronger case than is currently available. Apparently some of Rogo's fellow parapsychologists agree with me. To take one example, in "Parapsychology and Education" (*Education in Parapsychology*, ed. by B. Shapin and L. Coly), M. Johnson, the parapsychologist at the University of Utrecht, said:

> I must confess that I have some difficulties in understanding the logic of some parapsychologists when they proclaim the standpoint, that findings within our field have wide-ranging consequences for science in general, and especially for our world picture. . . . I believe that we should not make extravagant and, as I see it, unwarranted claims about the wide-ranging consequences of our scattered, undigested, indeed rather 'soft' facts, if we can speak at all about facts within our field.

For similar sentiments, see "The Study of the Paranormal as an Educative Experience," by J. Beloff, in *Education in Parapsychology;* "Laws, Miracles, and Repeatability," in the *New Humanist* (November 1975); and "The Problem of Repeatability in Psychical Research" and "Recent Criticisms of Parapsychology: A Review," in the *Journal of the American Society for Psychical Research* (1971).

Rogo asserts that two other criticisms—inappropriate statistics and inadequate methodology—"have been adequately answered time and time again over the past years." Well, yes and no. The debates over the statistics and methodologies have covered a wide range of issues. Some of the original criticisms were shown to be wrong or irrelevant. Others produced changes and improvements in both the conduct of the experiments and the analyses of the data. But Rogo's dismissal of these criticisms is somewhat misleading. He says that "as far back as 1937, the American Institute of Mathematical Statistics certified that the statistics used in parapsychology were totally valid." Rogo is referring to a press release dated December 30, 1937, that said: "Dr. Rhine's investigations have two aspects: experimental and statistical. On the experimental side, mathematicians of course have nothing to say. On the statistical side, however, recent mathematical work has established the fact that assuming the experiments have been properly performed, the statistical analysis is essentially valid. If the Rhine investigation is to be fairly attacked, it must be on other than mathematical grounds." The statement was signed by Burton H. Camp, president of the Institute of Mathematical Statistics, and appears in "Notes," in the *Journal of Parapsychology* (1937).

I don't know who Mr. Camp is or what the Institute of Mathematical Statistics is. But the statement says little more than that Rhine and his coworkers, when they compute the critical ratio, are employing the correct formula and referring to the appropriate probability tables. Camp clearly implies that the question of statistical appropriateness cannot be separated from methodological issues in general. A given statistical test assumes, under the assumption of chance results, a certain theoretical distribution. The test is appropriate when it can be safely assumed that all the underlying assumptions have been met. There is no way that Mr. Camp or anyone else can certify that "the statistics used in parapsychology were totally valid." Nor does such a certification made in 1937 guarantee that all is well in 1977. In fact, the appropriateness of any statistical technique has to be justified separately for each experiment.

As a result of the debates over statistical techniques during the 1930s and 1940s, parapsychologists learned a number of valuable lessons. A most important one was that the experimenter cannot rely upon hand shuffling or intuitive human mixing to ensure the sort of randomness that is assumed by the accepted statistical techniques. That is why Schmidt and others have developed highly sophisticated means for randomizing target selections. Yet it is easy to find examples of blatant disregard of such lessons in the current parapsychological literature. For example, Russell Targ and Harold Puthoff, in their recent book, *Mind-Reach*, comment that some referees of their paper published in *Nature* objected to their method of target selection in experiments with Uri Geller. The "referees felt that this method of target selection might not be sufficiently random, a spurious argument in our estimation." Just why they did not use a more appropriate method of randomization is not known. But the statistical calculations they make, based on the results of this experiment, become meaningless.

In their book, Targ and Puthoff refer to an exact statistical procedure developed by Robert Morris, which they apply to the judge's rankings in their remote viewing experiments. This is an appropriate statistic when certain assumptions are fulfilled, such as ensuring that each target description is independent of the preceding one. But this assumption is violated in their experiments, because immediately after each description the subject is taken to the target site. The subject begins his or her description of the next target with knowledge of preceding targets. It is possible that such descriptions inadvertently contain information about the preceding targets. Such cueing is obviously present in the transcripts of the experiments with Pat Price that appeared in *Mind-Reach* and in *The Search for Superman*, by J. L. Wilhelm. In one transcript, for example, Targ, who is in the laboratory with Price, says: "I've been trying to picture it in my mind and where you went yesterday out on the nature walk. . . ." This tells an alert judge two things. It tells him or her that the present target is *not* the nature walk. Furthermore, it tells what the correct target is, since the judge knows the order in which the targets are judged. So the statistic, which would have been appropriate had such inappropriate leakage not been possible, now becomes inappropriate and the impressive statistical odds become meaningless.

Unfortunately, we find a surprising lack of sensitivity to ensuring that the statistical tools will be appropriate in the series of experiments that Rogo happens to select to illustrate a "good" ESP experiment. In the "ganzfeld" experiment made by C. Honorton and S. Harper and described in their article "Psi-mediated Imagery and Ideation in an Experimental Procedure for Regulating Perceptual Input," published in the *Journal of the American Society for Psychical Research,* three sorts of randomization are required for the experiment. One of thirty-one sets of four View-Master reels is selected by shuffling and cutting a deck of numbered cards. In the selected set, the particular reel that is used as the target is chosen by simply hand shuffling the four reels and placing them in the holder. And, finally, another deck of cards is shuffled and cut to decide which time interval will be employed to transmit the target. Why such crude randomization procedures were employed in an otherwise sophisticated experiment is not explained. Since the agent handles the target reel and then shuffles it with the other three before the four reels are given to the subject, there is the clear-cut possibility of sensory cues—inadvertent or deliberate— between subject and agent. All this suggests that Rogo's claim that this experiment meets his standards of being fraud- and error-proof and that it is statistically valid is somewhat premature, to say the least.

Rogo is probably correct in claiming that statistical and methodological standards are generally quite high in current parapsychological research. But my perusal of recent parapsychological journals suggests that papers with sophisticated methodology and analyses can be found side by side with papers with glaring deficiencies. (A recent issue of the *Journal of the American Society for Psychical Research,* for example, contained a report on Sai Baba that I am sure would have been rejected as totally inadequate by the original founding fathers of psychical research.) And even within the same article we can find, as in the Honorton and Harper study, commendable sophistication side by side with primitive and inadequate procedures.

The one remedy for such errors and possibilities of fraud is for parapsychology to overcome its most serious problem—the problem of generating repeatable results that will hold up across independent laboratories. I will return to this matter at the conclusion of this article.

Rogo feels he has eliminated most of the criticisms of parapsychological research as being irrational or irrelevant. This, in his opinion, leaves two valid criticisms—fraud and misinterpretation of the results. He dismisses both of these with the assertion that neither can account for today's results. As parapsychologists point out, the problems of fraud and self-deception are not unique to parapsychology. But deception is a much more serious problem in parapsychology than it is in any of the natural sciences. In those areas of inquiry the only source of fraud would be the experimenter. But parapsychology is unique in that the material being studied is handled by conscious agents who can be reactive to the experimenter and who are often motivated to succeed.

As I have said, many of the criticisms would be adequately met if parapsychology could cope with its most serious problem—repeatability. Rogo makes a valiant effort to "correct another myth about parapsychology; namely that the findings of specific ESP and PK experiments are rarely replicated." Both his argument and his irrelevant reference to failure of psychologists to publish replications of their experiments hardly deal with the issue. Yes, the ganzfeld experiments and the sheep-goat effect have been successfully replicated. So far as I know at this writing, the ganzfeld experiment has been successfully replicated twice (or three times, depending upon how you count separate experiments), once in an independent laboratory. But three attempts at replication have failed. The last attempt, reported by J. Palmer, D. M. Bogart, S. M. Jones, and C. T. Tart in "Scoring Patterns in an ESP Ganzfeld Experiment," in the *Journal of the American Society for Psychical Research* (no. 71), was especially noteworthy in that the authors went out of their way to ensure all the conditions that para-psychologists believe *ought* to enhance the effect.

The sheep-goat effect is very weak. J. Palmer makes a good case in his survey of all the experiments between 1947 and 1970 for the reality of the effect. (See Palmer's "Scoring in ESP Tests as a Function of Belief in ESP, Part I, The Sheep-Goat Effect," in the *Journal of the American Society for Psychical Research* [No. 65, 1971].) Of the seventeen experiments that meet his standards, six give significant results in the expected direction. Thirteen give results in the appropriate direction. Palmer argues from this that the effect is real and replicable. But he admits to serious weaknesses in his argument, especially when considering the unpublished cases.

The issue, then, is not that there are no successful replications. Admittedly, both in the sheep-goat and the ganzfeld experiments there are some successful repeats. The issue, as far as Gardner Murphy and other parapsychologists have put it, is that we cannot specify in advance the conditions under which the effect will occur. For each successful replication there are one or more failures. Beloff, Flew, Johnson, Murphy, and Ransom are just some of the parapsychologists who apparently agree with the critics that parapsychology cannot expect to gain the ear of the other sciences until it has, as a minimum, at least some phenomena for which it can spell out conditions sufficient to guarantee their occurrence.

Handbook of Parapsychology. Benjamin B. Wolman (Ed.)
Laura A. Dale, Gertrude R. Schmeidler, and
Montague Ullman (Associate Eds.)
New York: Van Nostrand-Reinhold, 1977. Pp. xxi + 967.*

According to Wolman, "The aim of the *Handbook* was to describe in a most rigorous and scholarly way what is presently known of that field which has been exploited for too long a time by incompetent and sometimes fraudulent individuals" (personal communication). Despite some disappointments and some authors who did not fulfill their obligations, the resulting product is impressive indeed. A total of 32 contributors produced 35 separate chapters (including the introduction), along with useful appendices on suggested readings and a glossary. These chapters are grouped under such headings as "History of Parapsychology," "Research Methods," "Perception, Communication, and Parapsychology," "Parapsychology and Physical Sys-

*This review appeared in *Contemporary Psychology* 23 (9) (1978), 644–46, copyright 1978 by the American Psychological Association. Reprinted by permission of the publisher.

tems," "Parapsychology and Altered States of Consciousness," "Parapsychology and Healing," "Survival of Bodily Death," "Parapsychology and Other Fields," "Parapsychological Models and Theories," and "Soviet Research in Parapsychology."

As might be expected, the chapters vary in level of difficulty, usefulness, relevance, and assumed expertise of the reader. The chapter on "Parapsychology and Physics," complete with equations and matrices, will be comprehensible, I fear, only to theoretical physicists. The chapter on statistics, although highly technical, is an original contribution and should be useful to many researchers outside the field of parapsychology. Some of the other chapters, such as one on healing and another on altered states of consciousness, could just as well have appeared in nonparapsychological contexts.

The *Handbook* poses a challenge to skeptics and critics of parapsychology, among whom I include myself. The determined skeptic can find many reasons for challenging the sort of evidence that is offered in the chapters on reincarnation, survival, poltergeists, paranormal photography, and spontaneous phenomena. But the critic will be surprised by both the quantity and quality of the evidence presented in the chapters on experimental results. The obvious and usual charges of misuse of statistics, selection of data, inadequate experimental controls, fraud, or other common artifacts do not appear sufficient to account for the entire array of findings summarized in the chapters on personality correlates, intrasubject effects, experimental psychokinesis, and internal attentional states.

The procedure employed in these summaries, either implicitly or explicitly, can be called "the box-score method." A number of separate experiments on the same problem are reviewed. Then the reviewer tallies how many came out significant or in the same direction. Both Palmer and Honorton actually calculate probabilities on this basis. For example, Honorton reviews 16 published studies on the ganzfeld effect and psi. He finds that 8 are significant and reports the combined significance of all 16 as 2.1×10^{-9}. By broadening his criterion to include any sort of attempt to reduce external sensory input, he finds 87 separate studies, 49 of which produced significant results. The combined odds against such an occurrence happening just by chance are astronomical. Such a box-score approach explicitly acknowledges the individual experiment as the appropriate unit for evaluating parapsychological results (one reason is that psi scores are notoriously unreliable).

Such summaries of the hard-core laboratory data in favor of psi convince me that "something" is there. And furthermore, this "something" is sufficiently important that it ought to engage the attention of philosophers, historians of science, scientists, and especially social scientists. The parapsychologists are sharply divided over the potential nature and import of this "something." As Beloff points out, some parapsychologists see "psi" as merely a synonym for ignorance, and when we come to understand it, it will turn out to be perfectly compatible with the rest of the sciences. The majority of parapsychologists, however, maintain that "psi" signals the limitations of the scientific view and indicates a realm of existence that lies outside science's grasp. It seems to me that a nonparapsychologist can also believe that there is "something" there and that this "something" when fully understood may prove no threat to the general conceptions of reality that come out of contemporary science. My guess is that this "something" will tend to have methodological, rather than theoretical or substantive, import for the way we do science in the future.

Although the data summarized in this volume provide challenges to the skeptics, challenges also exist for the parapsychologist. The case for psi and for its correlations with other variables is not as strong as the tidy box-score summaries imply. The astronomical odds that Honorton and Palmer calculate from such summaries are totally meaningless. This is so for a variety of reasons. Only published studies get included in the tallies. And the criteria for including studies are somewhat arbitrary and post hoc. The studies vary in quality and other details. Most of the studies were testing more than one hypothesis with the same set of data. The studies are not independent, many originating from the same laboratory and from the same investigators. (Since only some laboratories get results, the argument could be made that the laboratory, not the individual study, should be the appropriate unit of analysis.) These are just some of the reasons why such calculated odds are almost certainly highly exaggerated.

I make no pretense of having consulted many of the original journal articles on which the box-score summaries are based. I did, however, go back and read some of the original studies, especially in the ganzfeld series. What I read confirmed my belief that there is typically a discrepancy between the ideal and the actual experiment. Inevitably, we have to compromise. In spite of many sophisticated aspects, the ganzfeld experiments show such deviations from the ideal in using hand shuffling to randomize stimuli and allowing possibilities for sensory leakage. Now, as I understand it, parapsychologists have come forth with convincing arguments why such criticisms involving selective factors due to using only published reports, inadequate randomization, and the like, cannot *individually* account for their results. But what seems crucial is how such compromises with the ideal, when taken in combination, can affect the overall picture. Perhaps some computer simulations could be revealing for this situation.

But leaving such problems aside, the parapsychologists still face enormous problems, even if we acknowledge that what they have demonstrated is as they claim. Those parapsychologists who are convinced that psi has been demonstrated beyond doubt, also seem to agree about many of its properties. All agree that psi can occur only under "psi conducive" conditions. But, alas, no one can specify or provide these conditions. Many believe that the experimenter and his or her attitudes are critical and that psi can occur only in certain laboratories. Furthermore, psi has a disconcerting way of changing the mode in which it manifests itself—sometimes as psi-hitting or psi-missing, but other times as increased or decreased variability of hits around a chance baseline, or in displacement to nontargets, or as decline effects, and so on. Among other things, this creates the awkward possibility of the "privileged observer"—only certain subsets of the population of scientists will ever be able to observe psi, and then only at times that are infrequent and unpredictable.

By bringing together in one volume the best evidence for the various kinds of phenomena included under the rubric of psi, the editors and their contributors have placed a heavy burden on both the parapsychologists and their critics. The parapsychologists can now be in a position to take stock of where their field is and what it desperately needs in the way of coherent theory and systematic effects before it can seriously claim the attention of orthodox science. And the critics, if they are to be fair, must find ways to account for the virtually hundreds of experimental studies that are summarized herein before they summarily dismiss parapsychology as a pseudoscience.

Parapsychology: Science or Magic? A Psychological Perspective. James E. Alcock. New York: Pergamon Press, 1981. 244 pp.*

James Alcock tells us that his book is about "the problems involved in trying to tell the difference between reality and fantasy in our own personal experiences, in the testimony of others, and in evidence which is presented in the name of science" (p. 3). The particular domain in which he explores this problem, as the title indicates, is parapsychology. And the author makes it clear to the reader, right at the outset, where he stands on parapsychology. "I am a skeptic," he declares in his Foreword. "My own skepticism about the paranormal is based on more than a decade of following the parapsychological literature and on my knowledge, as a social psychologist, of the many sources of error both in the interpretation of everyday experience and in the carrying out of experimentation involving human subjects. Were there any persuasive evidence for any of the various paranormal phenomena

*This review appeared in *Parapsychology Review* 13 (March–April 1982), 24–27. Reprinted with permission of copyright owner, Parapsychology Foundation, Inc.

which are claimed to exist, I would, along with a large proportion of the psychological research community, leap to the study of what would be beyond doubt the most exciting, the most important psychological ability ever discovered. But, alas, the evidence is not there" (pp. viii–ix).

One more quotation will serve, I believe, to gain a preliminary overview of this book. The blurb on the back cover, presumably written by an anonymous editor, neatly captures the essence of Alcock's monograph with these words: "Every individual is prone to infer causality where none exists, to interpret certain classes of experience as extraordinary when they are in fact quite ordinary, to maintain erroneous beliefs even in the face of evidence to the contrary, and to embrace beliefs which give solace in the face of existential anxieties. This book explores these and other factors which contribute to belief in the paranormal. In addition, the so-called scientific evidence which has been adduced to support parapsychological claims is critically examined, and it is concluded that parapsychology, while wearing the cloak of science, has more in common with pseudo-science and magic."

When we add to these intimations of the book's substance the additional fact that Alcock relies heavily on Hansel for his case against parapsychology, I suspect that the typical reader of this journal will want to follow Theodore Rockwell's advice (cf. *Parapsychology Review,* May–June 1980) "not to waste precious effort in the foolish game of refuting such critics. . . . New ideas, new tools, and new channels of communication are opening up. Let us develop them, and 'the devil take the critics!' "

I do not think Alcock fits the model of the sort of critic that Rockwell wants you to ignore. Alcock is skeptical; he concludes that parapsychology is a pseudoscience and he attributes various forms of irrationality to parapsychologists. Yet it is clear that he tries to reach such conclusions in a responsible manner. And he obviously has done much of his homework. Indeed, the range of special subject matters that he tries to encompass is, to me, awesome. So far as I can tell, Alcock manages to cover every issue and perspective that could be relevant to evaluating the claims for psi. For this reason alone I think his book can be read with profit by believer and critic.

As the foregoing comments suggest, Alcock conducts his inquiry of parapsychology by asking two questions. Do the evidence and arguments put forth by parapsychologists justify the belief in psi? And, as already indicated, he concludes that they do not. This conclusion leads to the second question. What are the processes that generate and preserve a belief in psi in the absence of justifiable arguments? The book tackles these two questions in reverse order, starting out with four chapters which examine various reasons for falsely believing in psi and then examining the scientific case in chapters 6 and 7.

Alcock presents each of his chapters as another perspective on parapsychology. Chapter 2 on "Magic, Religion and Science" examines a variety of proposed theories about the contemporary interest in the supernatural and the paranormal. These are categorized under four rubrics: the religious void, distrust of science, the unfettered mind, and personal experience (of a "paranormal" type). After reviewing arguments and evidence for each of these explanations, Alcock wisely decides that no one of them adequately fulfills the job. He concludes that current belief in psi can be accounted for by some combination of one or more of these factors. This conclusion raises for me a question that kept recurring throughout my reading of the book. Whose beliefs is Alcock trying to account for? Those belonging to members of the Parapsychological Association? To all investigators of psychic phenomena? To the lay public?

The next chapter deals with "The Psychology of Belief." The theories and evidence that try to account for the origins, maintenance, and change of belief are surveyed. Alcock believes the data on personality and belief justify the conclusion "that believers in the paranormal, at least in the student population, tend to be more dogmatic in their beliefs and less skilled at critical thinking than are skeptics. In addition, the believer in the paranormal appears to be more open towards novel and unsubstantiated evidence which may involve transcendental forces than he is towards novel but non-transcendental material, suggesting the use of rules of evidence from two different belief systems."

Cognitive dissonance, selective exposure, and confirmatory bias are employed to account for why beliefs can persist in face of contradictory evidence. And Alcock makes the important point that scientists, "The Guardians of Rationality," are just as prone to these biases—especially when operating outside of their narrow domain of expertise—as the rest of us.

The chapter on "The Psychology of Experience" makes a point similar to the theme of Andrew Neher's *The Psychology of Transcendence*. Alcock phrases the matter in these words: "It is foolhardy to study the putatively paranormal unless we have educated ourselves about normal experience in all its diverse forms" (p. 64). This chapter surveys a variety of phenomena that have naturalistic origins, but which can produce compelling illusions of paranormality for those who do not understand the ways our unconscious and conscious psychological mechanisms operate and interact.

Chapter 5 on "The Fallibility of Human Judgment" catalogs a variety of forces that can deflect our cognitive operations from the straight and narrow path—the gambler's fallacy, regression to the mean, illusory correlation, the availability heuristic, the illusion of control, the illusion of validity, etc. With so many ways for our thinking to go astray it is a wonder that we ever arrive at rational and justifiable conclusions. It was the consideration of such fallacies that resulted in a colleague of mine labeling all humans as "cognitive cripples."

Up to this point Alcock has created a strong case for powerful, non-rational forces that can produce and preserve false beliefs. And, arguably, this could account for a large number of individuals and scientists believing in psi even if it did not exist. But Alcock realizes that the demonstration that many normal mechanisms could produce a false belief in psi does not answer the question of whether or not psi, in fact, exists. He tackles this question with two chapters: "Science or Pseudo-Science: The Case of Parapsychology" and "Parapsychology and Statistics."

Alcock's objective in the chapter on the scientific foundations of parapsychology is to set up criteria for distinguishing between a science and a pseudoscience and then apply these criteria to parapsychology. In the process, he manages to touch upon a wide range of philosophical issues. Popper's concept of corroboration and Kuhn's all-embracing construct of "paradigm" help structure the argument. Alcock also briefly discusses continental drift, Boltzmann's thermodynamics, conservation of energy, meteorites and absorption as premature ideas that met initial resistance, but were later accepted by the scientific community. Parapsychology, in Alcock's view, is not a premature idea with a prognosis similar to those classic examples. For one thing, the attempts to give parapsychology theoretical credibility by linking it to developments in modern physics is misguided and, according to Alcock, involves fundamental misunderstandings. The attempts to link psi to simultaneity, the Einstein-Podolsky-Rosen Paradox, the Heisenberg Uncertainty Principle, and Tachyons are briefly examined and declared in error. As he does in other parts of his book, Alcock manages to find a parapsychologist to quote in support of his particular criticism. In this case it is the physicist and parapsychologist Peter Phillips who argued that parapsychologists err in trying to tie psi to current physical theory *(Parapsychology Review,* July–August, 1979). William James, Anthony Flew, and John Beloff are also quoted to show that parapsychology lacks not only a coherent theory, but also a core of solid data. After evaluating parapsychology against each of seven criteria enumerated by the philosopher Bunge, Alcock concludes that the field fails on each test and is therefore a pseudoscience.

I find such an exercise both fascinating and futile. The current disputes among philosophers of science and the inability to find consensual criteria for demarcating science from nonscience have always intrigued me. That great minds can disagree has important implications for philosophy and psychology. But whether it makes sense to insist on unambiguously categorizing parapsychology as science or pseudoscience is questionable. At any rate, in the current confusion on demarcation among philosophers of science,

I doubt that parapsychology can be categorized with anything approaching a consensus. The categories of both science and pseudoscience are fuzzy, continually changing and probably not even mutually exclusive. Furthermore, what qualifies as membership in each of these categories changes with time, political climate, and cultural temperament. Finally, the relevant criteria—to the extent that there is an agreed-upon set—are continual rather than dichotomies and forms of inquiry rarely fall entirely within the boundaries of any philosopher's version of ideal science, but, rather, are apt to be more like science in some respects and less like it in other respects.

I readily grant that if society at large could agree on whether parapsychology should be labeled "science" or "pseudoscience" such a labeling could have important political and social consequences. But such a condition, itself, will result more from political-social factors than it will from arbitrarily setting up lists of criteria and, just as arbitrarily, deciding which ones do or do not apply.

For one thing, the exercise suffers from all the very problems that Alcock attributes to the defense of parapsychology. It looks very much like the criteria themselves were chosen in order to exclude parapsychology. And the decision about which ones apply was certainly not objective or "blind." I am sure that parapsychologists can dispute Alcock's judgment on each one.

But the issue is not whether parapsychology is clearly science or pseudoscience, but whether psi does or does not exist. And this brings up an issue that has bothered me. To what extent does the "scientific" status of parapsychology depend upon the intent and efforts of its practitioners, and to what extent is such a status beyond their control? Much of the emotional heat generated by the misguided attempts to defend parapsychology as "scientific" or to attack it as "pseudoscience," in my opinion, stems from the implicit assumption that the practitioners in a field can turn it into a science by their own efforts. If what they are doing somehow does not meet some of the properties of science it must reflect upon the competence and sincerity of the practitioners. But what if, as I believe, a field of inquiry cannot gain general acceptance as science unless it deals with lawful phenomena that are sufficiently robust to withstand scrutiny under varied conditions? If a group of investigators choose to investigate a phenomenon that does not have this required degree of robustness, then no matter how competent and conscientious they may be, they will not achieve general recognition as scientists. This failure, however, is beyond their control (other than the choice to persist in the study of the elusive phenomenon).

In his concluding chapter, Alcock asks a very provocative question. "What if parapsychologists are correct, what if psi exists and contemporary scientists are ignoring one of the most important potential advancements in knowledge of all time? What would the demonstrated existence of psi mean for the world, especially if as is claimed people can learn to develop psi abilities?"

Alcock reviews some of the positive applications that have been suggested by parapsychologists. These include medical diagnosis, space exploration, executive ESP, stock market predictions, and gambling. To these Alcock adds sight for the blind, prediction of earthquakes and disasters, breaking up hurricanes, and the like. But Alcock suggests that chaos could also result. We would have no privacy, dictators could know when followers are disloyal, and adversaries may square off against each other using PK.

But here I think Alcock has gone overboard. One reason for the emotional intensity in the debate between the believers and the critics, I suspect, is just this shared assumption that we know what psi will be like if it turns out to be real. Some of the believers seem to have visions of survival after death, validation of religious and mystical myths, unlimited human potential, and a sudden flowering of peace and love among people. And the critics have nightmares of the sudden loss of scientific objectivity, the return to supernaturalism, and the possibility that the entire scientific edifice is fundamentally in error.

But what would it mean if the parapsychologists are correct? Let's assume that the claimed phenomena of ESP and PK, as presumably demonstrated in the experiments published in the *Journal of Parapsychology* and the several other parapsychological journals, are valid. What does it add up to? We would have evidence of real, "paranormal" departures from chance that occur on a sporadic basis. At this point, several major parapsychologists suspect that such phenomena can only occur under "psi conducive" conditions, but no one can agree or confidently specify what these "psi conducive" conditions are. Indeed, the late J. G. Pratt was convinced that there were no such psi-conducive conditions. He believed that psi exists, but it is not subject to causal laws. No one will ever be able to specify conditions for its occurrence. It will always be something that happens on infrequent and completely random occasions—sort of like a cosmic hiccup. But even if we accept the characterization of psi put forth by the more optimistic parapsychologists such as Palmer, Honorton, and Tart, we would have no basis for expecting such an erratic and uncontrollable phenomenon to lead to the practical consequences that both believer and critic imagine.

Indeed, demonstrating that there is a phenomenon such as psi is little more than justifying the further attempt to elucidate and understand—and possibly tame—it. Until such a time, it is merely wild and irresponsible speculation to talk about predicting earthquakes, making medical diagnoses, or averting disaster. Not only has everyone so far failed to achieve anything at all lawful and with reasonable frequency with psi, but they have not even provided any evidence that the various demonstrations of psi are really manifestations of the same phenomenon. Maybe the various departures from statistical significance are due to a multitude of different phenomena, each unrelated to the other.

The mistake Alcock makes on this matter is to argue in one place that if psi exists, it is so weak and sporadic that it could have no practical consequences, and then complain, in his last chapter, that if psi exists it would lead to chaos and the undermining of the scientific method. Since no one knows what psi is, even if it does exist, it is premature, to say the least, to spell out futuristic scenarios based upon its existence. Perhaps it is these futuristic scenarios that lead Alcock to declare that if psi exists it would represent one of the most important breakthroughs in the science of man. Why could it not be the case that psi could exist and turn out to be of no particular consequence for human survival and living?

Another closely related, but different, question could be asked. What if parapsychologists could succeed in achieving their current goals other than the obvious one of capturing and taming psi? That is, what if establishment science embraced parapsychology as a fully legitimate science with full privileges of publication in journals such as *Science* and *Nature,* with academic departments and curricula, with equal opportunities for funding from various agencies, and with access to various forums and meetings? On the few occasions when I discussed this matter with parapsychologists I got varied and somewhat surprising answers. One major parapsychologist speculated that such sudden acceptance could have disastrous results on parapsychology as a unified discipline. Money might be spent unwisely and devoted to wasteful pursuits. Another indicated that parapsychology is not yet ready for such a blessing because the discipline has not yet gotten to the stage where it knows what its most important problems are. Still another informant thought that parapsychology would disappear and its various components would be absorbed into the relevant areas of physics, psychology, and biology. Some were sure that it would create major changes in the content of the current sciences, but would not lead to any fundamental revisions of the foundations. Yet, others were sure that science as we know it would disappear and be replaced with some new cosmology. So, just as it is not yet clear what, if anything, would change if psi turns out to be real, we have no basis for knowing what to expect if, by some quirk, parapsychologists suddenly achieve all their current goals.

How does this book compare with other recent critiques of parapsychology? Four other recent books immediately come to mind: Randi's *Flim-Flam!,* Hansel's *ESP and Parapsychology,* Marks and Kammann's *The Psychology of the Psychic,* and Neher's *The Psychology of Transcendence.*

Randi and Hansel are the most uncompromising and adversarial of these critics, while Alcock and Neher seem relatively more open and less prone to imply fraud and gross incompetence. Randi and Neher are more comprehensive in scope and include parapsychology as only one among a variety of occultisms and mystic practices. Hansel, Marks and Kammann, and Alcock focus specifically on parapsychology, but with Marks and Kammann restricting their treatment mainly to remote viewing and the investigations of Uri Geller. Both Randi and Hansel restrict their attack to arguments that allege loopholes, possibilities of fraud, and other defects of the evidence. The other three books go beyond the examination of the scientific case; they try to provide psychological reasons for belief in psi and the occult. Marks and Kammann provide us with a useful, if somewhat unsystematic, checklist of fallacies and psychological biases that could lead us into false belief. Neher does a similar job, but he focuses more on those physiological, psychological, and cultural forces that can produce transcendent experiences that, under certain circumstances, can be mistaken for paranormal experiences. Alcock overlaps both these latter books in this regard.

Of the five books, Alcock's is the most systematic and comprehensive. He manages to comment upon all the matters brought up in the other books, as well as include material not brought out by them. But his encyclopedic breadth comes at a price. None of the issues is followed through in depth. Several times I found myself frustrated because Alcock had gone on to another topic before I was satisfied that I had fully grasped his argument and points relating to the preceding topic. But to have pursued the variety of issues included to any depth would most likely have required a book many times the size of the current one. The alternative, a book that selectively probes a limited number of topics, would have been a different assignment. And perhaps this lack of closure on most of the issues can be a virtue for certain uses of the book. In a course or seminar, Alcock could be very stimulating in raising provocative questions, but in leaving it to the students to pursue and develop further those of special interest. For me, the book is especially valuable because it brings together under one set of covers just about all the important questions and issues about this controversial topic that need exploring. And in writing about these topics, Alcock has managed to refer to key sources on both sides of the issues.

Part Two

Scientists and the Paranormal

Introduction

The papers collected in Part II overlap with those in Part I. But there are important differences. The papers in Part I focus on laboratory experiments and criticize them on the basis of how well they meet technical criteria, such as appropriate use of statistics, adequate randomization of targets, control for sensory leakage, and the like. The papers in Part II deal with scientists—usually of the first rank—who take time out from their more orthodox pursuits to test specific psychic claims.

Laboratory experiments in parapsychology tend to have the trappings we associate with experimental science. They use standardized equipment and procedures. They also tend to use as subjects unselected individuals from the general population.

Since the 1850s, each decade has witnessed one or more accomplished scientists who have accepted the challenge to test a psychic claim. Usually the claim involves the alleged powers of a psychic superstar. What distinguishes such tests from the laboratory experiments discussed in Part I is that each one uses procedures specific to the claims of the alleged psychic who is being tested. The aura of science attaches to these tests because the examiner is a well-known scientist who often conducts the tests in a laboratory setting.

But such tests depart from normal science in important ways. As indicated, each test is unique. Standardized procedures and equipment are rarely involved. The investigation does not occur within a normal "disciplinary matrix" and thereby lacks the checks and safeguards that accompany normal scientific inquiries. In almost every case, the primary observations are made by investigators under incompletely specified circumstances. Despite the fact that social scientists and psychologists have a long history of experience in devising ways to standardize and check the reliability of such observations, not one of the many scientists who have made such observations on alleged psychics had made even a token gesture towards demonstrating that the observational procedures were reliable and free from bias.

Apparently, these scientists believe in the myth that scientific training and experience in one area of inquiry automatically transfer to any other area of inquiry. But this is not so. When the new area is the study of *ad hoc* claims by individuals who may be confidence artists or experienced swindlers, the problems created by this myth are aggravated. Much of the success of scientific inquiry depends on the phenomenon under investigation, however obscure, not changing its behavior as a result of what the scientist is doing. Because of their training and experience in orthodox science, scientists are often at a disadvantage when trying to use their typical modes of operation to study individuals who are intent on outwitting the investigators.

With the exception of Michael Faraday in his study of table turning, the scientists I have studied who have tested a psychic claimant have ended by endorsing the psychic claim. In most of these cases the subsequent evidence strongly indicates that the scientists were victimized by trickery. This raises interesting questions about how some of the best and brightest of human minds could go astray in this way.

The attempt to provide a sensible answer to this question occupies much of my writing in these papers. I point to what I call the *false dichotomy* as a contributing factor. I also discuss my concern that the scientific tendency to banish such embarrassments from further discussion may be self-defeating. If subsequent generations of scientists never learn about the mistakes of their predecessors, they cannot learn any lessons from those failures. They may continue to repeat the same mistakes because of this.

My paper on "Pathological Science: Towards a Proper Diagnosis and Remedy" stirred up a surprising amount of emotion, as indicated by the commentaries on it that follow the paper in this book. One reason for such heated reaction, especially from sociologists, is my use of the term *pathological science*. Sociologists of science, as I have since learned, are programmed to reject any attempt to draw the line between "good" and "bad" science. Indeed, they believe that the very attempt to draw such a line somehow reflects capitalistic decadence and other horrible social maladies. Their approach raises fascinating issues, but ones that are too complicated to discuss here. I hint at some of these issues in my reply to the commentators.

The reader will encounter some redundancy in this collection, since I use the same examples and make similar points in several papers. (This redundancy would have been even greater had we included several other of my papers on the same topics.) I can justify some of this redundancy on the grounds that many of the points are worth repeating and that I have sometimes used the same examples for slightly different purposes. Finally, I believe that I make some very important points in the two reviews included in Part II; these points are not repeated elsewhere in the book.

Psychics and Scientists*

Modern spiritualism began when unaccountable raps were heard in the presence of two girls, Margaret and Kate Fox, in 1848. By employing a code, the girls' mother was able to converse with the raps and concluded that they originated from the spirit or intelligence of an individual who had died some years earlier. Very quickly, various means for communicating with unseen spirits via "the spiritual telegraph" were developed in the United States and Europe. The individuals through whom the spirits produced their phenomena and communicated with individuals in this world were called *mediums*. At first the phenomena were rapping sounds, movement of objects such as tables, playing of musical instruments by unseen agencies, and the occurrence of strange lights in the dark. Later more elaborate phenomena developed, such as levitation of objects, disappearance or appearance of objects, levitation of the medium, materialization of the spirits, written communications from the spirits, and so forth (*cf.* Podmore, 1963).

By the early 1850s table tilting had become the rage in both the United States and England. A group of individuals, usually called *sitters,* would sit around a table, each with both hands flat upon the tabletop. After an extended period of waiting, a rap would be heard or the table would tilt up on one leg. Sometimes the table would sway and begin moving about the room, dragging the sitters along. On some occasions, sitters would claim that the table actually levitated off the floor under conditions in which all hands were above the table; at some seances the table moved or levitated when no hands were touching it. Table tilting was especially popular because it could occur with or without the presence of an acknowledged medium. Any group of individuals could get together and attempt to produce the phenomenon in the privacy of their own living room.

---

*Previously unpublished, this article was written in 1977.

The Scientists

By 1852, England's great physicist Michael Faraday became so concerned over the table-turning hysteria that he took time out from his researches to investigate the phenomenon. He obtained subjects who were "very honorable" and who were also "successful table-movers." By a series of ingenious experiments Faraday first demonstrated that no unusual forces or electricity were involved; the tables moved purely from a mechanical force. He next demonstrated conclusively that the force was applied by the hands of the sitters although the sitters were unaware that this was so. Faraday concluded that:

> It is with me a clear point that the table moves when the parties, though they strongly wish it, do not intend, and do not believe that they move it by ordinary mechanical power. They say, the table draws their hands; that it moves first, and they have to follow it—that sometimes it even moves from under their hands. Though I believe the parties do not intend to move the table, but obtain the result by a *quasi* involuntary action—still I had no doubt of the influence of expectation upon their minds, and through that upon the success or failure of their efforts (Faraday, 1853).

Robert Hare

Soon after Faraday's investigation, the American chemist Robert Hare was asked for his opinion as to the cause of table turning. Hare wrote a letter in answer to this query, which was published in the *Philadelphia Inquirer* on July 27, 1853. At that time Professor Hare, who was considered one of the most outstanding chemists in the United States, was seventy-two years of age. He effectively demolished the idea that some exotic force or electricity could account for the phenomenon. "I recommend to your attention, and that of others interested in this hallucination," he wrote, "Faraday's observations and experiments, recently published in some of our respectable newspapers. I entirely concur in the conclusions of that distinguished expounder of Nature's riddles" (Hare, 1855).

Hare died five years after this letter was written. If it had not been for a reply to his letter by a Mr. Amasa Holcombe and an invitation by a Dr. Comstock to "attend a circle," Hare might be remembered as one of the first great American scientists, the inventor of the blowpipe and a confirmed skeptic on psychical and spiritualistic phenomena. But Holcombe's letter convinced Hare that he might have been too hasty in his judgment, and his subsequent investigations of table turning and other spiritualistic phenomena converted him to the cause of spiritualism. The result was an unusual book with the bizarre title, *Experimental Investigation of the Spirit Manifestations, Demonstrating the Existence of Spirits and Their Communion with Mortals. Doctrine of the Spirit World Respecting Heaven, Hell, Morality, and God. Also, the Influence of Scripture on the Morals of Christians* (Hare, 1855).

Upon accepting Dr. Comstock's invitation, Hare was taken to a private house. Here is his own description of what took place:

> Seated at a table with half a dozen persons, a hymn was sung with religious zeal and solemnity. Soon afterwards tappings were distinctly heard as if made beneath and against the table, which, from the perfect stillness of every one of the party, could not be attributed to any one among them. Apparently, the sounds were such as could only be made with some hard instrument, or with the ends of fingers aided by the nails.
>
> I learned that simple queries were answered by means of these manifestations; one tap being considered as equivalent to a negative; two, to doubtful; and three, to an affirmative. With the greatest *apparent sincerity*, questions were put and answers taken and recorded, as if all concerned considered them as coming from a rational though invisible agent.
>
> Subsequently, two media sat down at a small table, (drawer removed) which, upon careful examination, I found to present to my inspection nothing but the surface of a bare board, on the under side as well as upon the upper. Yet the taps were heard as before, seemingly against the table. Even assuming the people by whom I was surrounded, to be capable of deception, and the feat due to jugglery, it was still inexplicable. But manifestly I was in a company of worthy people, who were themselves under a deception if these sounds did not proceed from spiritual agency.
>
> On a subsequent occasion, at the same house, I heard similar tapping on a partition between two parlours. I opened the door between the parlours, and passed to that adjoining the one in which I had been sitting. Nothing could be seen which could account for the sounds (Hare, 1855, p. 38).

Hare describes other examples of rappings that he could not account for on the basis of normal agency. During his first visit to the circle, for example, he held the table with all his energy, but was unable to keep the table from moving to and fro when two female mediums sat opposite him and merely placed their hands on the surface of the table. In another circle, table tilting was substituted for the sounds as a form of communication from the alleged spirit world. Messages could be spelled out by having a sitter pass his or her hand over an alphabetic pasteboard. A letter was selected when the table either tilted or tapped as the hand passed over it. A skeptical lawyer friend of Hare's remarked that the coherent messages that resulted from this procedure must be due either to "legerdemain" on the part of the medium or to the agency of some invisible intelligent being.

Hare's reply is interesting: "But assigning the result to legerdemain was altogether opposed to my knowledge of his character. This gentleman, and the circle to which he belonged, spent about three hours, twice or thrice a week, in getting communications through the alphabet, by the process to which the lines above mentioned were due. This would not have taken place, had *they* not had implicit confidence, that the information thus obtained proceeded from spirits" (Hare, 1855, p. 40).

The preceding quotation suggests that Hare was already convinced that the phenomena he had witnessed were spiritual in origin. But Hare was too much the careful scientist to commit himself just yet. He "contrived an apparatus which, if spirits were actually concerned in the phenomena, would enable them to manifest their physical and intellectual power independently of control by any medium." Hare took a circular pasteboard disk of somewhat more than a foot in diameter. He attached around its circumference the letters of the alphabet in a haphazard order. By means of pulleys, cords, weights, and other mechanisms, a medium could sit with her hands on a table without being able to see the letters of the alphabet on the pasteboard circle. Movements of the table would cause a pointer to move around the wheel and indicate various letters of the alphabet.

With an accomplished medium sitting at the table, Hare seated himself in front of the disk. Hare then began by asking any spirits present to indicate their presence by causing the letter *Y* to be under the pointer. Immediately the pointer moved to the letter *Y*. Hare next asked, "Will the spirit do us the favour to give the initials of his name?" The index pointed first to R and next to H. Hare immediately asked, "My honoured father?" The index pointed to *Y*. After a few more tests such as these, the onlookers urged that Hare admit the reality of spiritual agency. Hare must have still shown some hesitation, because the index spelled out, "Oh, my son, listen to reason!"

Hare's sense of scientific propriety kept him from committing himself prematurely. "I urged that the experiment was of immense importance, if considered as proving a spirit to be present, and to have actuated the apparatus; affording thus precise experimental proof of the immortality of the soul: that a matter of such moment should not be considered as conclusively decided until every possible additional means of verification should be employed."

Hare's companions accused him of extreme incredulity. His medium told him she "should not deem it worth while to sit for me again." But Hare managed to persuade her to relent, and a few days later she came to Hare's house to try out an improved version of his apparatus. The results confirmed the preceding experiment. Hare's father, mother, and sister all came through and said they were happy. Hare obtained similar results on the apparatus with other mediums.

Hare made many other tests and observations. He claims to have seen a table continue its movements even when every person in the room had withdrawn to a distance of about a foot. He reports tables rising from the floor when hands were placed flat on the top surface. Many of the tests that Hare devised were suggested to him by the spirits who were communicating through the raps and his alphabetic index. Hare indicates that the greatest difficulty in carrying out his research in this area was the necessity of making every observation under conditions that guaranteed he was not being deceived by the mediums. But when he himself acquired the powers of a medium, sufficient to converse directly with his spirit friends, Hare no longer felt "under the necessity of defending media from the charge of falsehood and deception. It is now my own character only that can be in question."

Alfred Russel Wallace

Although Hare was "one of the few strictly American products who in those days could be considered within hailing distance of the great European chemists" (Asimov, 1976), a critic might be tempted to attribute his conversion to spiritualism and testimonies to supernatural happenings to senility, since he was seventy-two years old when he began his investigations of mediums. But such an explanation will certainly not do for the next major scientist who became a convert to spiritualism as a result of his investigation of mediums. When Alfred Russel Wallace—the cofounder, along with Darwin, of the theory of evolution by natural selection, began his investigations of psychic phenomena in 1865, just ten years after Hare published his findings, he was forty-two years of age. Wallace was a materialist at the time, but he had already shown a willingness to consider seriously unorthodox phenomena when, at the age of twenty-one, he became interested in mesmerism and phrenology. He believed he had observed clairvoyance in his subjects, especially the phenomenon in which a mesmerized subject experiences all the sensations that the mesmerizer (in this case, Wallace) is experiencing (see Fodor, 1974; George, 1964; Kottler, 1974; Marchant, 1916; Wallace, 1906).

This early experience with two heresies that were being attacked by orthodox scientists at the time had a lasting effect upon Wallace. He said, "Knowing by my own experience that it is quite unnecessary to resort to trickery to produce the phenomena, I was relieved from that haunting idea of imposture which possesses most people who first see them, and which seems to blind most medical and scientific men to such an extent as to render them unable to investigate the subject fairly, or to arrive at any trustworthy conclusions in regard to it." He further explained: "The importance of these experiments to me was that they convinced me, once for all, that the antecedently incredible may nevertheless be true; and, further, that the accusations of imposture by scientific men should have no weight whatever against the detailed observations and statements of other men, presumably as sane and sensible as their opponents, who had witnessed and tested the phenomena, as I had done myself in the case of some of them" (Wallace, 1906).

Faraday's 1853 report had helped to curb temporarily the rise of spiritualism in England. But interest in spiritualism regained its momentum, and reports began reaching Wallace in the late 1850s while he was in the Far East. He writes that he was skeptical about what he heard. Some reports seemed to be "the raving of madmen. Others, however, appeared to be so well authenticated that I could not at all understand them, but concluded, as most people do at first, that such things *must* be either imposture or delusion" (Wallace, 1906). Nevertheless, he decided that he would look into these matters at the first opportunity after his return to England.

In July 1865 Wallace attended his first seances at the home of a skeptical friend. No medium was present at these seances. Wallace, his friend, and the friend's wife and two daughters sat at a large table. After a half hour, taps were heard and the table moved somewhat. The movements and the taps increased in intensity over time. "Then a curious vibratory motion of the table commenced, almost like the shivering of a living animal. I could feel it up to my elbows." After the session was over, Wallace and his friend found that the table could not be voluntarily moved in the same manner without great effort. They could discover no way to produce the taps with their hands upon the table.

Wallace participated in a number of such seances with these friends. He varied conditions to pin down further what was taking place. Raps occurred even when Wallace was sitting alone at the table." Wallace concluded from these initial table-turning sessions that "these experiments have satisfied me that there is an unknown power developed from the bodies of a number of persons placed in connection by sitting round a table with all their hands upon it" (quoted in Kottler, 1974).

In September 1865 Wallace attended his first seances with a medium. The medium was Mrs. Mary Marshall, who was one of England's best known mediums of this period. Wallace attended several seances accompanied by "one or more of my friends as skeptical and as earnest inquirers after fact as myself." Wallace regarded Mrs. Marshall as one of the best public mediums for physical phenomena that he had ever met. This was high praise, coming as it did in 1906, at a time when Wallace had sat with probably every well-known medium of the last half of the nineteenth century (Wallace, 1906). Wallace claimed that he and his friends "made whatever investigations we pleased, and tried all kinds of tests. We always sat in full daylight in a well-lighted room, and obtained a variety of phenomena of a very startling kind." Among these phenomena were tables levitating and moving around the room. Wallace also received messages, purportedly from the spirit world, including names, ages, and other information about departed relatives. Wallace was sure that such information could not have been known to Mrs. Marshall. Wallace also tried to lay traps and insert tests to check on the possibility of deception on the part of Mrs. Marshall. "However strange and unreal these few phenomena may seem to readers who have seen nothing of the kind, I positively affirm that they are the facts which really happened just as I have narrated them, and that there was no room for any possible trick or deception."

But the best was yet to come. A year later, in November 1866, a young medium, Agnes Nichol (later Mrs. Guppy), was discovered by Wallace's sister. Miss Nichol produced phenomena within his own home that Wallace considered as conclusive. Wallace described one session with Agnes Nichol in a letter to John Tyndall dated May 8, 1868:

> During the last two years I have witnessed a great variety of phenomena, under such varied conditions that each objection as it arose was answered by other phenomena. The further I inquire, and the more I see, the more impossible becomes the theory of imposture or delusion. I *know* that the facts are real natural phenomena, just as certainly as I know any other curious facts in nature.
>
> Allow me to narrate *one* of the scores of equally remarkable things I have witnessed, and this one, though it certainly happened in the dark, is thereby only rendered more difficult to explain as a trick.
>
> The *place* was the drawing-room of a friend of mine, a brother of one of our best artists. The *witnesses* were his own and his brother's family, one of two of their friends, myself, and Mr. John Smith, banker, of Malton, Yorkshire, introduced by me. The medium was Miss Nichol. We sat round a pillar-table in the middle of the room, exactly under a glass chandelier. Miss Nichol sat opposite me, and my friend, Mr. Smith, sat next her. We all held our neighbour's hands, and Miss Nichol's hands were both held by Mr. Smith, a stranger to all but myself, and who had never met Miss N. before. When comfortably arranged in this manner the lights were put out, one of the party holding a box of matches ready to strike a light when asked.
>
> After a few minutes' conversation, during a period of silence, I heard the following sounds in rapid succession; a slight *rustle,* as of a lady's dress; a little *tap,* such as might be made by setting down a wineglass on the table; and a very slight jingling of the drops of the glass chandelier. An instant after Mr. Smith said, "Miss Nichol is gone." The matchholder struck a light, and on the table (which had no cloth) was Miss Nichol *seated in her chair,* her head just touching the chandelier.

I had witnessed a similar phenomenon before, and was able to observe coolly; and the facts were noted down soon afterwards. Mr. Smith assured me that Miss Nichol simply glided out of his hands. No one else moved or quitted hold of their neighbour's hands. There was not more noise than I have described, and no motion or even tremor of the table, although our hands were upon it.

You know Miss N.'s size and probable weight, and can judge of the force and exertion required to lift her and her chair on to the exact centre of a large pillar-table, as well as the great surplus of force required to do it almost instantaneously and noiselessly, in the dark, and without pressure on the side of the table which would have tilted it up. Will any of the known laws of nature account for this? (Wallace, 1906).

Miss Nichol also produced the standard fare of raps, table tilting, levitation, and musical sounds. Her most remarkable feat was to produce fresh-cut flowers *(apports)* during a winter seance. At this seance were produced "15 chrysanthemums, 6 variegated anemones, 4 tulips, 5 orange berried solanums, 6 ferns, of two sorts, 1 Auricula sinensis, with 9 flowers— 37 stalks in all." Wallace argued that the freshness and coldness of the flowers precluded the possibility that any member of the seance had brought them into the room. Over an hour had passed in a warm room prior to the "materialization" (Kottler, 1974). This production of flowers, along with fruit as well, was repeated in many further seances. Wallace claimed that particular flowers were often produced by request. "A friend of Dr. Alfred Wallace asked for a sun-flower, and one six feet high fell on the table, having a large mass of earth about its roots" (quoted in Fodor, 1974).

By 1867, Wallace was sure of the reality of the phenomena and was leaning toward an explanation of them on spiritualistic grounds. Certainly by 1870 Wallace was a confirmed spiritualist, and much to Darwin's dismay, was led by his new belief to retract his previous belief that natural selection was sufficient to account for the evolution of humans from animals. Wallace was willing to allow human physical attributes to have so evolved, but he argued that human moral, intellectual, and conscious qualities had to be the product of an intelligent designer (Kottler, 1974).

William Crookes

Wallace was a great naturalist and observer, but he was not an experimenter. According to his biographer, "there is no evidence that Wallace ever made an experiment in biology" (George, 1964). A critic who finds the accounts of Hare and Wallace hard to swallow might be tempted to dismiss their evidential value on the grounds of Hare's old age and Wallace's lack of experience as an experimenter. Neither criticism, however, can be applied to the next great scientist to investigate mediums and endorse the reality of their claims. This man was the brilliant chemist and physicist, William Crookes, who was later knighted for his many contributions to science—the discovery of thallium, the invention of the radiometer and the Crookes tube (which made the electric light bulb possible), the investigation of radiation effects, and many others.

When Crookes began attending seances with Mrs. Marshall (the same medium who had helped to convert Wallace) and J. J. Morse in 1869, he was thirty-seven years of age. In July 1870, he announced his plans to conduct a scientific inquiry into the claims of mediums. He wrote, "I prefer to enter upon the inquiry with no preconceived notions whatever as to what can or cannot be, but with all my senses alert and ready to convey information to the brain; believing, as I do, that we have by no means exhausted all human knowledge or fathomed the depths of all physical forces" (quoted in Medhurst, 1972). According to Fodor (1974), "the Press received the announcement with jubilation. It was taken for granted that Spiritualism would be shown a clear and simple humbug. Foregone conclusions have never met with more bitter disappointment." Although most of the scientific community assumed that he was undertaking the investigation as a skeptic, his biographer tells us, "But it is certain, at all events, that when in July 1870 Crookes, at the request, it is said, of a London daily paper, announced his intention of 'investigating spiritualism, so-called,' he was already much inclined towards spiritualism. What he really intended to do was to furnish, if possible, a rigid scientific proof of the objectivity and genuineness of the 'physical phenomena of spiritualism,' so as to convert the scientific world at large and open a new era of human advancement" (Fournier d'Albe, 1924).

Indeed, a careful reading of Crookes's 1870 announcement (which is reprinted in full in Medhurst, 1972) leaves no doubt that he was fully convinced of the reality of the physical phenomena of spiritualism. "That certain physical phenomena, such as the movement of material substances, and the production of sounds resembling electric discharges, occur under circumstances in which they cannot be explained by any physical law at present known, is a fact of which I am as certain as I am of the most elementary fact in chemistry. My whole scientific education had been one long lesson in exactness of observation, and I wish it to be distinctly understood that this firm conviction is the result of most careful investigation." Crookes's goal, then, was not to verify the phenomena, which he felt he had abundantly done in several seances he had attended before making this announcement, but to provide an explanation for them. He goes on to say: "But I cannot, at present, hazard even the most vague hypothesis as to the cause of the phenomena. Hitherto I have seen nothing to convince me of the truth of the 'spiritual' theory. In such an inquiry the intellect demands that the spiritual proof must be absolutely incapable of being explained away; it must be so strikingly and convincingly true that we cannot, dare not deny it."

Crookes was able to conduct several seances with the celebrated medium Daniel Dunglas Home. Home is probably the most colorful and enigmatic psychic in the history of modern spiritualism (for accounts of Home, see Burton, 1974; Dingwall, 1962a; Fodor, 1974; Podmore, 1963). In one session, which took place in the evening of May 31, 1871 at Crookes's house, Home held an accordion (which had been purchased for the occasion by Crookes) by one end so that the end with the keys hung down towards the floor. The accordion was placed in a special cage under the table that just allowed Home's hand to be inserted to hold the accordion. Home's other hand was visible above the table. The individuals sitting on either side of Home could see his hand as well as the accordion in the wire cage. "Very soon the accordion was seen by those on each side to be moving about in a somewhat curious manner, but no sound was heard." After putting the accordion down, Home picked it up again. This time several notes were heard. Crookes's assistant looked under the table and said he saw the accordion expanding and contracting, but Home's hand was quite still.

Experiments such as this one, Crookes believed, "appear conclusively to establish the existence of a new force, in some unknown manner connected with the human organisation, which for convenience may be called Psychic Force." As a result of three years of seances with mediums such as Home and Kate Fox, Crookes classified the phenomena he felt the evidence had established as follows:

1. The movement of heavy bodies with contact, but without mechanical exertion.
2. The phenomena of percussive and allied sounds.
3. The alteration of weight of bodies.
4. Movements of heavy substances when at a distance from the medium.
5. The rising of tables and chairs off the ground, without contact with any person.
6. The levitation of human beings.
7. Movement of various small articles without contact with any person.
8. Luminous appearances.
9. The appearance of hands, either self-luminous or visible by ordinary light.
10. Direct writing.
11. Phantom forms and faces.
12. Special instances which seem to point to the agency of exterior intelligence.
13. Miscellaneous occurrences of a complex character (Medhurst, 1972).

The most bizarre reports of psychic phenomena are those made by Crookes on his seances with Florence Cook. These sessions took place over a five-month period beginning in December 1873. Florence had just been "exposed" by a Mr. Volckmann, who seized the materialized spirit form known as "Katie King" and discovered that he was holding, instead, the medium Florence Cook in costume. Florence, at that time, was being financially supported by a wealthy benefactor named Charles Blackburn. Blackburn, who had attended the fateful exposure, appeared to be about to cut off his support for Miss Cook. Under these circumstances, Florence appealed to Crookes to help her convince Blackburn that she was, in fact, a genuine medium. Just why Crookes entered into such an arrangement is not clear (for accounts, see Fournier d'Albe, 1924; Hall, 1963a).

A typical performance would proceed as follows: Florence Cook, the medium, would enter a cabinet and go into a trance. The cabinet was usually a curtained-off section of the room in which the sitters were located. After a while a white-robed, turbaned female would emerge from the cabinet claiming to be the materialized spirit "Katie King." Some skeptics thought the resemblance between Katie King and Florence Cook was rather striking. Crookes admitted that there was some resemblance, but believed there were crucial differences. He observed that Katie was six inches taller than Florence; the skin of Katie's neck was smooth, while Florence had a large blister in the same place; Katie's ears were unpierced, while Florence wore earrings; Katie's complexion was very fair, but Florence's was very dark; and they had different mannerisms (Medhurst, 1972).

The real proof that Katie King and Florence Cook were not one and the same person, however, would be to observe both simultaneously. This Crookes claimed he was privileged to do on at least two occasions (Medhurst, 1972).

J. C. F. Zoellner

As we will discuss later, the British scientific establishment did not bestow any gratitude upon Crookes for his discoveries with respect to Psychic Force. But one admirer of Crookes's work in this area was Professor Johann Carl Friedrich Zoellner, professor of physical astronomy at the University of Leipzig. In fact, Zoellner dedicated the third volume of his *Scientific Treatises*, which was entitled *Transcendental Physics*, to William Crookes. The dedication, written in 1879, is worth quoting in part:

> With the feeling of sincere gratitude, and recognition of your immortal deserts in the foundation of a new science, I dedicate to you, highly-honored colleague, this Third Volume of my Scientific Treatises. By a strange

conjunction our scientific endeavors have met upon the same field of light, and of a new class of physical phenomena which proclaim to astonished mankind, with assurance no longer doubtful, the existence of another material and intelligent world. As two solitary wanderers on high mountains joyfully greet one another at their encounter, when passing storm and clouds veil the summit to which they aspire, so I rejoice to have met you, undismayed champion, upon this new province of science. To you, also, ingratitude and scorn have been abundantly dealt out by the blind representatives of modern science, and by the multitude befooled through their erroneous teaching. May you be consoled by the consciousness that the undying splendor with which the names of a Newton and a Faraday have illustrated the history of the English people can be obscured by nothing, not even by the political decline of this great nation: even so will your name survive in the history of culture, adding a new ornament to those with which the English nation has endowed the human race. Your courage, your admirable acuteness in experiment, and your incomparable perseverance, will raise for you a memorial in the hearts of grateful posterity, as indestructible as the marble of the statues at Westminister. Accept, then, this work, as a token of thanks and sympathy poured out to you from an honest German heart. If ever the ideal of a general peace on this earth shall be realized, this will assuredly be the result not of political speeches and agitations, in whch human vanity always demands its tribute, but of the bond of extended knowledge and advancing information, for which we have to thank such heroes of true science as Copernicus, Galileo, Kepler, Newton, Faraday, Wilhelm Weber, and yourself" (Zoellner, 1976).

In the first volume of his *Scientific Treatises,* Zoellner had developed his theory of four-dimensional space. This was not the same sort of theory that Einstein later conceived, in which the fourth dimension was time. Zoellner, following Gauss and Kant, was seriously speculating on what sorts of phenomena might be possible if there were a fourth spatial dimension. At the end of the first volume, which was finished in August 1877, when Zoellner was forty-three years old, he speculated that some so-called spiritualistic phenomena might have a naturalistic interpretation if one postulated a four-dimensional space.

Although Zoellner stated that he followed the spiritualistic literature, he had not himself witnessed any of the phenomena at that time. But on November 15, 1877, the American medium Henry Slade arrived in Leipzig, where he had been invited by two of Zoellner's friends. Zoellner met Slade that evening at the invitation of his friends. Slade made an immediately favorable impression on Zoellner. Zoellner asked Slade if he had ever tried to influence a magnetic needle. To Zoellner's pleasant surprise, Slade said he was willing to accompany Zoellner to his house that very evening and try the experiment.

Zoellner described this first "experiment" with Slade as follows:

Arrived at my dwelling, my friend asked whether I had a compass at hand. I brought a celestial globe in the stand of which a compass was fixed, and placed it on the table. At our request Slade moved his hand horizontally across the closely-fitted glass cover of the magnet case. The needle remained immovable, and I concluded from this that Slade had no magnet concealed beneath his skin. On a second trial, which was made immediately afterwards, in the manner stated, the needle was violently agitated in a way which could only be the result of strong magnetic power.

This observation decided my position towards Slade. I had here to do with a fact which confirmed the observation of Fechner, and was, therefore, worthy of further investigation (Zoellner, 1976).

These further investigations were carried out in a series of seances with Henry Slade in Leipzig during November and December 1877 and during Slade's second visit to Leipzig in May 1878. They form the empirical basis of the third volume of Zoellner's *Scientific Treatises.* Because of the phenomena Slade was able to produce under Zoellner's conditions, the professor felt he had conclusive evidence to support his theory of four-dimensional space. One of the most convincing demonstrations is described by Zoellner as follows:

I have already in the above-cited treatise [Volume One] discussed some physical phenomena, which must be possible for such four-dimensional beings, provided that under certain circumstances they are enabled to produce effects in the real material world that would be visible, *i.e.,* conceivable to us three-dimensional beings. As one of these effects, I discussed at some length the knotting of a single endless cord. If a single cord has its ends tied together and sealed, an intelligent being, having the power voluntarily to produce on this cord four-dimensional bendings and movements, must be able, *without* loosening the seal, to tie one or more knots in this endless cord.

Now, this experiment has been successfully made within the space of a few minutes in Leipzig, on the 17th of December, 1877, at 11 o'clock A.M., in the presence of Mr. Henry Slade, the American. The accompanying engraving [Plate I] shows the strong cord with the four knots in it, as well as the position of my hands, to which Mr. Slade's left hand and that of another gentleman were joined. While the seal always remained in our sight on the table, the unknotted cord was firmly pressed by my two thumbs against the table's surface, and the remainder of the cord hung down in my lap. I had desired the tying of only *one* knot, yet the *four* knots—minutely represented on the drawing—were formed, after a few minutes, in the cord. . . . During the seance, as previously stated, I constantly kept the seal—remaining unaltered—before me on the table. Mr. Slade's hands remained *all the time* in sight; with the left he often touched his forehead, complaining of painful sensations.

Zoellner witnessed many other miracles in Slade's presence. Furniture and other objects moved. A small table disappeared and then reappeared above their heads and came crashing down upon them. Coins were myster-iously transported from within a sealed box to the outside without breaking the seals. Two wooden rings somehow became encircled around a table leg in such a way that it suggested penetration of matter. An impression of a naked foot was unaccountably produced on sooted paper. A bed screen split apart with explosive force.

The most frequent phenomenon witnessed by Zoellner and his col-leagues was Slade's specialty, the production of writing on slates under conditions that seemingly precluded human agency. This, more than any-thing else, convinced Zoellner not only that there was a fourth dimenion to which Slade had access, but also that this fourth-dimensional world was peopled by intelligences of a higher order. And these intelligences were the authors of the messages appearing on Slade's slates.

The End of an Era

Hare, Wallace, Crookes, and Zoellner are just four of the major scientific figures who endorsed mediums and psychical phenomena during the second half of the nineteenth century. It was the work of these eminent investiga-tors that set the stage for founding of the Society for Psychical Research in London in 1882 and began the field of inquiry known then as psychical research and currently as parapsychology. In the last two decades of the nineteenth century and the first two decades of the twentieth, other prom-inent scientists followed the lead of these four pioneers and lent their reputations to the sponsoring of alleged psychics and mediums. The roll call includes two Nobel Prize winners (Charles Richet and Lord Rayleigh), as well as such eminent figures as Cesar Lombroso, Camille Flammarion, Sir William Barrett, Sir Oliver Lodge, William James, Thomas Edison, Giovanni Schiaparelli, and Hans Driesch.

Probably no other scientist endorsed as many mediums as Alfred Russel Wallace. The psychic, on the other hand, who seems to hold the record for converting the most scientists to a belief in psychical phenomena was the volatile and controversial medium, Eusapia Palladino. (For accounts of Palladino's long and stormy career, see Dingwall, 1962b; Fodor, 1974; Gauld, 1968.) Among the scientists who endorsed the reality of her phenomena were Cesar Lombroso, Charles Richet, Giovanni Schiaparelli, Sir Oliver Lodge, Camille Flammarion, Giovanni Ermacora, Enrico Morrelli, and Lord Rayleigh. Eusapia's career spanned the long period from the 1870s until her last seances in 1910. She produced the various phenomena so familiar to spiritualists—moving objects, raps, materialization of limbs, cold breezes, levitation, and so forth. By the time of her death in 1918, the age of the great physical mediums seemed to have gone by. She seemed to be the last of the mediums able to produce physical phenomena. Psychical research became instead the search for telepathy and clairvoyance.

But today, one hundred years after Crookes announced his program to investigate the possibility of a Psychic Force, we seem to be witnessing a return to the involvement of scientists with physical or telekinetic types of psychic phenomena. The psychiatrist Jules Eisenbud endorsed the ability of Ted Serios to project pictures mentally onto Polaroid film. The physicists Russell Targ and Harold Puthoff have vouched for the abilities of psychics such as Ingo Swann and Harold Price to describe a geographical location with which they have no physical contact—even to scan mentally the surfaces of Jupiter and Mercury. And the Israeli psychic, Uri Geller, has persuaded Targ, Puthoff, and countless other scientists that he possesses a variety of psychic abilities—ranging from telepathy and clairvoyance to the ability to bend metal with his mind.

Contemporary Reactions

The cases I have reviewed each involve an accomplished scientist who investigated one or more alleged psychics and who, as result, publicly endorsed the reality of the claimed paranormal phenomena. Many details of the circumstances under which the scientist and the alleged psychic interacted differ from case to case, but I will focus upon the common elements. In each case the scientist involved was an accepted and respected member of the scientific establishment, who had made important theoretical and empirical contributions to his field. This is as true of the scientists who endorse the claims of psychics today as it was of the scientists of the last century. In the cases we are discussing, we cannot simply write off the claims on the grounds that the scientist involved was generally incompetent.

Each scientist paid a penalty for his championing of an unorthodoxy. The scientific community bitterly, and often unfairly, attacked both the offending scientist and his claims. With respect to Hare's claims we are told that "reaction was quick to set in against its influence. The professors of Harvard University passed a resolution denouncing him and his 'insane adherence to a gigantic humbug.' He was howled down by the American Association for the Advancement of Science when in Washington in 1854 he tried to address them on the subject of Spiritualism. Finally he paid for his convictions by resigning from his chair" (Fodor, 1974).

Wallace first acquainted his scientific friends with his interest in spiritualism when he sent them his pamphlet, *The Scientific Aspect of the Supernatural,* written in 1866 (George, 1964). "His friends were astonished that he should be taking spiritualism so seriously. Lewes, having convinced himself of the trickery of one medium, would not discuss it. Tyndall, who had already rebuked Thackeray for his public advocacy of spiritualism, took a later opportunity to rebuke Wallace. 'I see the usual keen powers of your mind displayed in the treatment of this question. But mental power may show itself, whether the material be facts or fictions. It is not a lack of logic that I see in your book, but a willingness that I deplore to accept data which are unworthy of your attention.' " Darwin was upset. Huxley, who was a good friend of Wallace's, was vehemently opposed to spiritualism. He wrote, "The only good that I can see in the demonstration of the truth of 'spiritualism' is to furnish additional argument against suicide. Better live a crossing-sweeper than die and be made to talk twaddle by a 'medium' hired at a guinea a seance."

Wallace tried in vain to induce his scientific friends—men such as Darwin, Huxley, Tyndall, Lewes, and Carpenter—to sit in on seances with him and judge for themselves. He did get Tyndall and Carpenter each to attend one session at his house. But either nothing occurred or the scientist in question refused to participate according to Wallace's plans. Kottler (1974) gives a detailed account of Wallace's missionary efforts and his complete failure to persuade any of his distinguished colleagues to evaluate the evidence at first hand.

George sums up the case of Wallace's venture into spiritualism as follows: "Wallace's spiritualism, regarded by his scientific friends with astonished tolerance, was less humanely respected by the scientific world in general, and it resulted in long-lasting damage to his reputation as a biologist. It is suggested that it is the reason why Wallace's scientific contributions are neglected among the works of the great nineteenth-century biologists."

Crookes likewise felt the wrath of the scientific community (Fodor, 1974; Fournier d'Albe, 1924; Gauld, 1968; Medhurst, 1972; Podmore, 1963). Zoellner was subjected to "persecution, contempt, and ridicule from the scientific community" (Fodor, 1974; see also *Preliminary Report . . . , 1920;* Richmond, 1890; Zoellner, 1976). The many scientists who endorsed the reality of Eusapia Palladino's manifestations were considered as dupes and the victims of their own strong desires to believe (Dingwall, 1962b; Fodor, 1974; Gauld, 1968; Jastrow, 1935; Podmore, 1963; Rawcliffe, 1959). Targ and Puthoff, two of the scientists who have investigated and endorsed some of Uri Geller's paranormal powers, have documented in a chapter on "The Loyal Opposition" many of what they feel are the unfair, unethical, and irrational charges hurled against their investigations by incredulous scientists and other critics (Targ and Puthoff, 1977; see Wilhelm, 1976, for further descriptions of extremist critiques against the supporters of Uri Geller's powers).

Although I am skeptical regarding the claims made for Uri Geller and the great "psychics" of the past, and although I am included among the members of the "Loyal Opposition," by Targ and Puthoff, I have to agree that much of the critical reaction against scientists who have investigated alleged psychics has been grossly unfair. Much of the response of the scientific community has simply been silence. Many of the establishment scientists simply ignored Hare, Wallace, Crookes, and the others when they talked or wrote about their psychical research. Some, like Huxley, simply refused when offered the opportunity by Wallace and others to come see the phenomena for themselves. More serious were charges, implied or overt, that the scientists involved were mentally deranged, incompetent, deluded by their religious sentiments, or simply lying. Hare and Crookes, among others, were refused permission to talk or write about their findings before scientific audiences. Sadly, many of the scientist-critics engaging in such attacks were completely unaware of what the offending scientist had actually witnessed, written, or claimed.

Counterreactions

Inevitably, the psychic researchers became defensive under such attacks. They counterattacked by accusing their scientific colleagues of behaving in an unscientific manner, of making misstatements, of misrepresenting what was observed and claimed, of using *ad hominem* arguments, and of being unwilling to accept facts that did not fit in with their preconceptions. Hare, although he was treated very badly by scientific colleagues who had previously given him almost every honor, showed some tolerance for the bitter attacks because he, too, had been highly skeptical before he investigated for himself.

In his *Experimental Investigation,* Hare reproduced the letter he wrote to the *Philadelphia Inquirer* in 1853, which supported Faraday in attributing table turning to unconscious movements on the part of the sitters. He says, in relation to this letter:

> I trust I shall not be considered as self-complacent, when I allege it to be an exemplification of *wise ignorance,* which is about equivalent to folly. The wisest man who speaks in ignorance, speaks foolishly to the ears of those who perceive his ignorance. The great mass of men of science appear in this light to spiritualists when they argue against Spiritualism. Men who are only *nominally* Know Nothings have proved a formidable party in politics; unfortunately, Spiritualism has, in its most active opponents, *real* Know Nothings, who will not admit any fact of a spiritual origin, unless such as they have been educated to believe. In that case, many have powers of intellectual deglutition rivalling those of the anaconda in the physical way (Hare, 1855).

Wallace was naturally disappointed in his failure to induce many of his skeptical scientific colleagues to come witness the seance phenomena for themselves. But he was even more dismayed when some of these same colleagues later wrote debunking articles in which they asserted that the mediums would not subject themselves to true scientific observations. He accused these critics of outright falsehoods. But Wallace had been somewhat prepared for what to expect by his earlier experiences with mesmerism. As a result of his own experiments with mesmerism, "I also satisfied myself that almost universal opposition and misrepresentations of the medical profession were founded upon a combination of ignorance and prejudice" (Wallace, 1906).

Wallace quotes with approval from a letter to him by the eminent mathematician, Augustus de Morgan (who had become converted to belief in spiritualism by the American medium, Mrs. Hayden, in 1853). The letter was to acknowledge receipt of Wallace's pamphlet on spiritualism, written in 1866. De Morgan wrote:

> I am much obliged to you for your little work, which is well adapted to excite inquiry. But I doubt whether inquiry by *men of science* would lead to any result. There is much reason to think that the state of mind of the inquirer has something—be it internal or external—to do with the power of the phenomena to manifest themselves. This I take to be one of the phenomena—to be associated with the rest in inquiry into cause. It may be a consequence of action of incredulous feeling on the nervous system of the recipient; or it may be that the volition—say the spirit, if you like—finds difficulty in communicating with a repellent organization; or, maybe, is offended. Be it which it may, there is the fact.
>
> Now the man of science comes to the subject in utter incredulity of the phenomena, and a wish to justify it. I think it very possible that the phenomena may be withheld. In some cases this has happened, as I have heard from good sources.
>
> I have had students—a couple of dozen in my life—whose effort always was *not to see it*. As I, their informing spirit, was under contract to make them see it if I could—which the *spirits* we are speaking of are *not*—I generally succeeded in convincing them. In their minds I have studied—with power of experiment arranged by myself—the character of the man of science. . . . But I doubt if the man of science of our day can persuade himself of a possibility of his fifth attempt destroying the effect of the failure of the first four.

Wallace comments as follows about this letter: "This seems to me to exhibit the scientific frame of mind, as manifested by Tyndall, Lewes, and W. B. Carpenter, with great perspicuity" (Wallace, 1906).

We can find similar sentiments about dogmatism and unwillingness on the part of incredulous colleagues to face facts that upset their worldview expressed by Crookes, Richet, Zoellner, and the scientists of our day who have been investigating psychics such as Ted Serios, Ingo Swann, and Uri Geller.

De Morgan's letter brings up two different issues with respect to convincing skeptics about the reality of psychic phenomena. One is the assertion that, even in the face of overwhelming evidence, skeptics' motivation to preserve their existing worldview will not allow them to acknowledge the "facts." The second, which raises special problems for psychical research, is that a negative or disbelieving attitude may actually prevent the phenomena from occurring. This raises the question of the privileged status of paranormal evidence. Psychic phenomena—so the claim is made—can occur only in presence of observers who are favorably disposed towards them.

Polarization of Attitudes

Probably the most unfortunate consequence of the bitter opposition to the paranormal claims of some scientists is that it results in a polarization of attitudes. The psychical researchers feel that their colleagues react dogmatically. They believe they are not receiving a fair hearing. Indeed, they feel that they are not listened to at all. As a result, they quickly learn not to discuss their paranormal observations and research with skeptics. Hare, rebuffed in trying to discuss his ideas before the scientific establishment, banded together with like-minded men and kept his future discussions and investigations within this circle of individuals who were already favorably disposed to believe. Wallace, too, finally gave up his attempts to interest his skeptical colleagues and confined his future discussions of spiritual phenomena to a circle of friends such as Crookes, Barrett, and others who believed as he did. Crookes, after three stormy years of trying to gain a hearing before his scientific critics, put aside his psychical investigations and returned to more orthodox pursuits. He did not abandon his beliefs or interest in spiritualism, but he confined his future intercourse in this area to those who would give him a friendly hearing.

This polarization is unfortunate for both sides. On the one hand, it creates a situation of selective exposure. Those already disposed to believe end up talking only with those who also are favorably inclined. Cases that are favorable are discussed more than are negative ones, so beliefs are reinforced. Thus, a positive feedback mechanism is set in operation. This selective exposure works equally upon the critics, who tend to interact with one another and discuss the negative cases and the possibilities of fraud and error.

A most unfortunate feature of this polarization is that the martyred scientists tend to ignore the truly substantive critiques of their findings and claims. This is because the criticism comes from the "enemy camp" or the "loyal opposition," which has already been convicted, in the judgment of the psychical researchers, of misrepresentation, irrelevant arguments, dogmatism, and irrationality.

On the other hand, the critics, having successfully driven their unorthodox colleagues into the ghetto of psychical believers, feel they have solved the threat to rational science by banishing the claims and the claimants. As a result, they no longer have to face up to the challenge of how previously accredited scientists, employing what they believe are the strict procedures and precautions of their calling, can come to believe they have uncovered proof of phenomena that violate fundamental principles of current science. At the very least, facing up to this challenge might lead critics to learn important lessons that could prevent falling into such mistakes, if mistakes they be, in the future. At best, accepting the challenge to account for how such successful scientists can go so far astray, might teach critics new and important things about the nature of science and human cognition.

Problems and Challenges

Many scientists who have endorsed paranormal phenomena—men such as Hare, Wallace, Crookes, Zoellner, the scientists who endorsed Palladino, and many of those who endorse the claims of Uri Geller—would have been accepted and honored by their respective scientific communities on the basis of their contributions to orthodox science. They are controversial and inspire the wrath of establishment scientists only because, in addition to making discoveries within the accepted bounds, they also looked at phenomena outside these bounds and believed that they had obtained evidence to support the reality of these paranormal happenings.

The critics say that they are mistaken, that they have been duped or somehow self-deluded. The believers feel that they have been treated unfairly, that their arguments have been misrepresented, and that their data and arguments have not been taken seriously.

Two challenges emerge from this dilemma. One is a challenge to the believers to recognize the internal problems of their claims. The other is to skeptics to face the problem of explaining—if the believers are wrong— just how they are wrong and what factors in scientific method and/or human cognition allowed them to become persuaded by a false proposition.

The scientists whose cases we have considered face the same problems as psychical researchers in general. They were attacked because of their conclusions regardless of the grounds for these conclusions. (Some critics equate belief in the paranormal with irrationality.) Their sanity was impugned, their competence questioned, and their integrity challenged by critics who had not looked at their data or tried to repeat their observations.

Without question these inquirers into the unorthodox were and are victims of prejudice. But despite this unfairness, there are also good reasons for orthodox scientists to be skeptical of the claims of their unorthodox colleagues. Some of these reasons, it is true, do not form the basis of many of the criticisms. But the reasons, I believe, are sufficient to justify withholding any attention to the claims for the paranormal on the part of orthodox science. One of the reasons is that there are grounds, in retrospect, to doubt the assertions of these eminent, but unorthodox, scientists. But the most important reason is the elusive and erratic nature of the phenomena—if there be such. The psychic researchers must somehow catch and tame their quarry before they can place a legitimate claim upon the time of their fellow scientists.

Reasons for Withholding Support

The unbiased reader who tries to evaluate the claims made by Hare, Wallace, Crookes, Zoellner, Richet, Targ, Puthoff, and others will find it difficult to dismiss them on obvious grounds of experimental naivete, gross deception, or other forms of blundering. All these investigators claim knowledge of obvious ways that deception might occur. They spell out a variety of precautions and experimental controls that they undertook. It is not easy, on the basis of the descriptions we are given, to suggest normal or conjuring bases for much of the phenomena. In some cases, it is true, we can imagine on the basis of current knowledge how a given effect might have been accomplished by trickery on the part of the psychic or unconscious muscular movement on the part of the experimenter or the subject. But it is probably useless to try to spin out plausible ways in which the seemingly paranormal events might have been accomplished. And in my opinion, this is unnecessary.

With the exception of Daniel Dunglas Home, the evidence is quite convincing that the psychics who provided the major phenomena actually cheated on at least some occasions. Herne and Williams, who performed effectively for Crookes, were exposed many times. These two mediums trained Florence Cook, who provided the most dramatic phenomena for Crookes in the form of full-form materializations. Florence herself was exposed convincingly both before and after her successful seances with Crookes. Wallace endorsed a whole host of mediums who were subsequently exposed as fraudulent; he continued to support many of these mediums even after they had been exposed. In fact, Wallace testified on their behalf in many court cases. He believed that he had never met a medium who was fraudulent. Wallace even went so far as to claim that S. J. Davey, who openly conducted his seances as conjuring feats, was a medium who for some reason was pretending to be a trickster. (For accounts of mediums endorsed by Crookes and Wallace and subsequently exposed, see Edmunds, 1962; Fodor, 1974; Fournier d'Albe, 1924; Gauld, 1968; George, 1964; Hall, 1963a; Hall, 1963b; Kottler, 1974; Podmore, 1963).

Zoellner's whole case rests on the feats of Henry Slade. Yet Slade was exposed many times both before and after his seances with the Leipzig professor (Fodor, 1974; Podmore, 1963; *Preliminary Report . . . ,* 1920). The circumstantial evidence that Geller cheats is overwhelming (see, *e.g.,* Gardner, 1977; Hyman, 1976; Hyman, 1977; Marks and Kammann, 1977; Randi, 1975; Wilhelm, 1976). The case of Palladino is the best example of blatant fraud side-by-side with vehement claims of authenticity by leading scientists (Dingwall, 1962b: Fodor, 1974; Gauld, 1968; Jastrow, 1935; Podmore, 1963; Rawcliffe, 1959). Palladino was caught several times in outright trickery. She freely admitted that, given the chance, she would cheat. At other times, investigators who were clearly aware of her tendency to exploit every opportunity to cheat (she even allegedly cheated at games) were sure that she produced unquestionably psychic phenomena because, in their opinion, they had blocked off all her opportunities for cheating.

Palladino brings to the fore one of the frustrating paradoxes of psychical research. Most critics would assume that once it is established that a given psychic cheats, the phenomena generated in other circumstances by that same individual become suspect. But this is not the case. It has become an accepted part of the belief system of psychical researchers that just because a psychic cheats under some circumstances does not mean that he or she cheats under others. In the case of Palladino, for example, who worked while entranced, her defenders asserted that her cheating was not wilful; she had no control over her impulses while entranced, they explained, and sometimes came under the control of evil influences. Indeed, most of Palladino's supporters, including many of those now living, blame the experimenters for her trickery. When experimenters were negative and out to catch her, and when they were somewhat lax on their controls, then Eusapia would be induced to cheat. Dingwall, who supports this position, criticized the Cambridge University researchers for letting Palladino free her hand from control over and over again during their seances with her.

> Mrs. Sidgwick was unable to understand why the Cambridge group was blamed for allowing Eusapia repeatedly to do this. She did not apparently realize that by permitting it they were actually inviting Eusapia to produce fraudulent phenomena and lessening their own chance of observing any that might not depend on such manoeuvres. Eusapia thought they were dupes and treated them as such, and I cannot help feeling sometimes that

they got what they deserved, although it may have been true that for some unexplained reason Eusapia refused to them what she granted to others (Dingwall, 1962b).

This tendency to blame the experimenter for the faults and defects of the psychic still survives. Targ and Puthoff give their version of a visit I made to Stanford Research Institute in December 1972 (Targ and Puthoff, 1977). They say that they suggested that we (the three members of the visiting committee) "conduct some experiments" of our own with Geller. "They [the committee] then spent an engaging couple of hours with Geller in which they observed the informal coffee-table type of demonstration that Uri favors. They tried a number of their own, and from our standpoint largely uncontolled, experiments. . . . Hyman and Lawrence were not impressed by the results obtained in their experiments, however, which were not as controlled as Van de Castle's, and left feeling that Geller was probably simply a clever magician; not an altogether unreasonable conclusion given what they saw and the informal manner in which they chose to interact with Geller." In other words, the fact that Geller employed trickery to create the illusion of telepathy and psychic metal bending was the fault of Lawrence and myself, according to Targ and Puthoff. But when *they* are in charge of the observations Geller, in their view, does not cheat but settles down and employs his psychic powers.

Many past and current psychic investigators take it for granted that gifted psychics might resort to cheating at times. This is because they do not have voluntary control over their powers and are highly motivated to please the experimenters so as to continue getting attention and other rewards. Also, over time, the power disappears altogether, and the psychics then resort to trickery to compensate for this loss.

Apparently, all of the investigators discussed in this paper subscribed to this position. So when a favorite psychic was exposed they felt it was unjust to assume that the psychic was also cheating when they were experimenting with him or her. Such an accusation was taken as an insult to the scientist's credentials as an investigator.

Nevertheless, it is unrealistic for psychic investigators to expect the rest of the scientific community to accept as genuine phenomena that defy normal explanation and that are produced by a so-called psychic who has been proven to cheat on at least some occasions.

Related to this matter of cheating are some other issues that raise questions about scientist's competence to conduct a controlled study and accurately report the results with a gifted psychic. Wallace, as already noted, endorsed all manner of mediums, including many who were exposed again and again. Moreover, he attributed psychic abilities to performances such as that of S. J. Davey, who openly acknowledged that he used trickery as the sole means of accomplishing his effects. In the case of Zoellner's investigations of Slade, not only do we know that Slade was exposed before and after his sessions with Zoellner, but also there is ample reason to raise questions about the adequacy of the investigation. Carrington (1907), Podmore (1963), and Mrs. Sidgwick (1886–87) are among a number of critics who have uncovered flaws and loopholes in Zoellner's sittings with Slade. In addition, the Seybert Commission (*Preliminary report . . . ,*1920) sent one of its members to Germany to interview Zoellner's witnesses— Professors Scheibner, Weber, Fechner, and Wundt. (Zoellner himself was already dead.) Fechner and Scheibner apparently had defective eyesight at the time of the investigations; none of the witnesses had had experience with conjuring; and Wundt expressed the opinion that conditions had been poorly controlled, and that Slade could easily have gotten away with trickery.

Crookes's investigation of Florence Cook has become the center of a heated controversy since the publication of Trevor Hall's *The Spiritualists* in 1963. (For reactions to this book, see Edmunds, 1962; Edmunds, 1972; Gauld, 1968; Hall, 1963b.) Hall amasses an array of evidence, some of it recently having come to light, to argue that Crookes was having an affair with Florence Cook and had to endorse the reality of Cook's materializations in order to keep the affair private. Regardless of how one decides the case for this assertion, there is no question that Hall has unearthed much material that throws strong suspicions on Crookes's handling of this investigation.

But even more damaging to Crookes's case, in my opinion, is the recently revealed correspondence between Crookes and Daniel Home with respect to the medium Mary Showers (Hall, 1963b). Home asked Crookes to explain the defamatory accusations that had come to him involving Crookes with the young Mary. Crookes admitted that because of the stories being circulated in the latter half of 1875 about his association with Mary Showers, he, Crookes, was "getting the reputation of a Don Juan." Crookes tried to explain how the scandal arose in a series of letters to Home that he asked be kept in confidence. "According to Crookes he had obtained a complete confession from Mary Showers in her own handwriting that her phenomena were wholly dependent upon trickery and the occasional use of an accomplice. Crookes said, however, that he had undertaken not to reveal the fact that Mary was fraudulent, even to her own mother, because of 'the very great injury which the cause of truth would suffer if so impudent a fraud were to be publicly exposed.' "

We need not explore further Crookes's explanations and Hall's reconstructions of what really happened. What is important is that this admission of a willingness to suppress the fact that Mary Showers was completely fraudulent as a medium raises serious questions about the authenticity of

Crookes's other investigations. For example, Mary Showers had partic-
ipated in a joint materialization seance in conjunction with Florence Cook.
Obviously this presumably must implicate Florence in fraud even though
Crookes always maintained that Florence was strictly genuine.

The Problem of Repeatability

The question of fraud or some form of self-deception can always be raised
with respect to any experiment involving humans. Hare, Wallace, Crookes,
Zoellner, Targ, Puthoff, and other scientists whom we have been discussing were quite vehement in insisting that their experiments were fraud-
proof and carefully contrived to eliminate all other forms of deception.
Often critics try to point out ways that the psychic could have tricked
the experimenter or to show how the experimenter's unconscious biases
might have led him or her to falsely report or interpret what happened.
In reply, psychical researchers defend themselves by pointing out how, in
fact, they not only were aware of the possibilities for such deception but
also took obvious steps to preclude them. The references to cases discussed
in this paper are full of such debates. Hansel's critique of the best cases
in parapsychology depends not upon his ability to prove that deception
did in fact take place, but rather on the demonstration that cheating *could*
have occurred under the existing protocols (Hansel, 1966).

  Both sides of the debate, it seems to me, are badly off course. Both
the critics and the defenders in this ongoing argument assume that there
are such things as crucial or decisive experiments. Critics claim that if they
can find flaws in the key or best experiments in parapsychology, they have
destroyed the entire case for parapsychology. Defenders assert that if they
can show that the critiques do not apply to their crucial experiment, then
they have established the reality of the paranormal phenomenon.

  It takes only a slight acquaintance with the history of science to realize
the illogic of this continuing debate. In just about any other area of systematic science, a single experiment or a series of experiments that seemingly
demonstrates some effect or relationship has no force if subsequent investigators in independent laboratories cannot reliably obtain this same effect
or relationship. It does not matter if we cannot retrospectively find loopholes
or flaws in the original experiments. We do not have a candidate for a
scientific phenomenon if we cannot specify some sufficient conditions for
observing the effect. A few examples in the history of science would be
mitogenetic radiation, the "patchwork mouse" affair, N-rays, the Davis-
Barnes Effect, and the Allison Effect.

  Admittedly, this is somewhat of an oversimplification. As Gardner
Murphy (1971) points out, repetition is not the only hallmark of science.

In astronomy and archaeology, for example, unique events do play a key role. But such events make sense against a background of systematic laws. Murphy makes it clear, however, that for a new discovery to become part of science, it has to have both rational consistency within the accepted framework and repeatability under specifiable conditions. And if the discovery is weak on one of these criteria it must be doubly strong on the other. The problem with the claims for paranormal phenomena, as Murphy makes clear, is that they are weak on both of these criteria. Since, by their very nature, the claims are inconsistent with the accepted framework, the need for reliable, reproducible, and robust phenomena in this area is especially critical. Until this need is met, psychical research cannot realistically claim to be an important concern either to the rest of science or to human affairs in general.

Although some parapsychologists see this criticism as a pseudo-issue or claim that they do, in fact, have repeatable experiments (see Rogo, 1975), many serious psychical researchers recognize the problem of repeatability as the fundamental reason why parapsychology still lacks general recognition within the scientific community. In this regard, the claims of the scientists we have been discussing and those of psychical research as a whole face the same difficulties.

Apologists for the lack of repeatable experiments have argued that they are dealing with a unique kind of phenomenon that must be judged by rules other than those applied to more common scientific phenomena. Excuses made for nonrepeatability of an experiment in paranormal phenomena include claims of skeptical attitudes on the part of the onlookers or fatigue and boredom on the part of the psychic (Ransom, 1971). We have already seen a beginning of this excuse in the letter written to Wallace by de Morgan.

It is difficult to know how to respond to the statements about optimal conditions made by Wallace, Crookes, Zoellner, Targ, Puthoff, and many other investigators who have dealt with gifted psychics. Certainly, it makes sense to try to put the medium or subject at ease, to treat him or her, as far as possible, as a human being, and to provide a fair opportunity to demonstrate his or her claims. Unfortunately, many of the conditions that are proposed as necessary for the phenomena to succeed appear to be just those that are needed for deception to occur. And it seems that the list of such conditions was generated by attempts to rationalize failures to obtain results. Thus, by trial and error, experimenters generate a list of conditions conducive to bringing about occurrences of the paranormal phenomena. If the alleged psychic is, in fact, a swindler, such a list becomes a recipe for the conditions that must obtain before the faker can safely get away with his or her tricks. Having had a background as a professional magician and mentalist, I have always been struck by the fact that the optimal conditions for the occurrence of psychic phenomena within a given setting seem to coincide with just those conditions I would require in order to pull off my deceptions.

An example of a modern version of such a list of conditions is an article orginially published in *Nature,* April 10, 1975, and reprinted in Panati (1976) (Hasted, Bohm, Bastin, & O'Regan, 1975). The first three authors are distinguished physicists at the University of London who have conducted experiments with Uri Geller and believe that they have obtained proof that the Israeli psychic can supernormally bend metal, deform crystals, and activate a Geiger counter. I will selectively quote from the article, which emphasizes their ideas about how to experiment with psychics, to illustrate the sorts of problems involved. They begin:

> We have come to realize that in certain ways the traditional ideal of the completely impersonal approach of the natural sciences to experimentation will not be adequate in this domain. . . . This does not mean, of course, that it is not possible to establish facts on which we can count securely. Rather, it means that we have to be sensitive and observant, to discover what is a right approach, which will properly allow for the subjective element and yet permit us to draw reliable inferences.
>
> One of the first things that reveals itself as one observes is that psychokinetic phenomena cannot in general be produced unless *all* who participate are in a relaxed state. . . . The entire process goes most easily when all those present actively want things to work well. In addition, matters seem to be greatly facilitated when the experimental arrangement is aesthetically or imaginatively appealing to the person with apparent psychokinetic powers.

Already we are in trouble. A "relaxed state" is incompatible with alert and focused observation. It plays into the hands of a highly active and unpredictable performer such as Geller. But, in the present context, this set of conditions supplies a ready alibi for failures to repeat a phenomenon even for the same observers. We cannot measure or observe whether "all those present actively want things to work well," and sometimes we find that on occasions when an experiment with Geller fails we can retrospectively discover that someone present did not want it to happen. And, later in the article, the authors tell about trying out some experimental arrangements "that are beyond any reasonable possibility of trickery." Geller could not succeed with these arrangements, and the authors attribute this failure to the fact that such arrangements were aesthetically unappealing to him. A critic, of course, would point to the inability to employ trickery as a more reasonable explanation of the failure.

These same scientists remark that

we have found also that it is generally difficult to produce a predetermined set of phenomena. Although this may sometimes be done, what happens is often surprising and unexpected. We have observed that the attempt to concentrate strongly in order to obtain a desired result (*e.g.,* the bending of a piece of metal) tends to interfere with the relaxed state of mind needed to produce such phenomena. It appears that what is actually done is mainly an unconscious function of the mind, and that once the intention to do something has been firmly established, the conscious functions of the mind, insofar as they have bearing on the goal, tend to become more of a hindrance than a help. Indeed, we have sometimes found it useful at this stage to talk of, or think about, something not closely related to what is happening, so as to decrease the tendency to excessive conscious concentration on the intended aim of the experiment.

This last condition constitutes a startling admission. It is quite similar to comments made by Zoellner when remarkable things would happen in Slade's presence, but ones that were unexpected, while the planned results never came off. The experimenters are saying, in effect, they do not have repeatable phenomena. They cannot decide in advance to investigate a certain event (such as the bending of a spoon) and then witness the event. Instead, they must keep their minds occupied with other things and then something they were not looking for—such as a spoon bending, or a watch starting to run, or a crystal deforming—might occur. If nothing happens, of course, it could be that one or more of them consciously thought of some possible phenomena or because someone was not relaxed. The authors do not try to reconcile the conflicting need to want a certain happening with the necessity of not consciously intending it to happen.

Two basic rules of every conjuring manual are: (1) never announce ahead of time what you intend to do; and (2) never repeat the same trick on the same occasion. The goal of both rules is to prevent the onlookers ahead of time from knowing where to focus their attention. If the spectators do not know what to expect, they cannot anticipate precisely what features of the situation to attend to, and they thus become much easier to deceive. Another bonus—as illustrated by the extensive experiments of Hodgson (1887, 1892) and Davey (1887)—is that the spectators' recapitulation of what did happen will typically omit or distort essential details in such a way that it is impossible to account for the happening on normal grounds.

Ironically, the condition of not concentrating on what is about to happen creates just those circumstances for deception that the conjuror works so hard to achieve. Only in this case the deceiver does not have to create the necessary misdirection; instead, the experimenters go out of their way to put themselves in just that psychological frame of mind that makes them most vulnerable to trickery. The authors of this report recognize that they are laying themselves open to deception. But they feel that this may be a worthwhile risk if necessary to encourage genuine psychic phenomena.

As I read what these scientists and other psychical researchers have to say about the difficulties they encounter in pursuing the paranormal, I cannot help feeling that they are trying to have their cake and eat it too. On the one hand, these scientists—and psychical researchers in general—continually lament that they have to be much more rigorous in their application of scientific procedures than do scientists in more mundane areas because their methods are constantly being attacked and challenged (see, *e.g.,* Rogo, 1975). They claim to meet higher standards in their conduct of research than are met in other areas of science. But, at the same time, there is a strong element of special pleading. In fact, they cannot meet the usual standards of controlled experimentation because their quarry is too elusive, unpredictable, and sensitive to emotional states of both the experimenter and the subject. They cannot constrain the alleged psychic too drastically because this might convey a sense of distrust; they cannot exhibit the phenomena when skeptics are present because negative attitudes inhibit the phenomena; and they cannot employ many obvious controls because these make the situation too "unnatural" for the proper functioning of the psychic's powers.

Some parapsychologists, however, realize that the elusiveness and unpredictability of their phenomena are a problem they must overcome before they can expect to gain the ear of establishment science. Beloff (1976) puts the matter this way: "Positive results still largely depend on having the right subject, and a good card guesser is no less of a rarity than a good medium in the bad old days of psychical research. Independent corroboration is still the exception rather than the rule, and it is now beginning to look as if we need not only the right subject but even the right experimenter. . . . I think that one thing we have got to recognize is that our field is so much more erratic, anarchic and basically subversive than we like to admit when we are engaged in one of our public-relations exercises." Johnson (1975) echoes the same thoughts and adds that parapsychologists must both achieve repeatable results and show that the results matter before they have a right to demand attention from the rest of the scientific community.

> I must confess that I have some difficulties in understanding the logic of some parapsychologists when they proclaim the standpoint, that findings within our field have wide-ranging consequences for science in general, and especially for our world picture. . . . I believe that we should not make extravagant and, as I see it, unwarranted claims about the wide-ranging consequences of our scattered, undigested, indeed rather 'soft' facts, if we

can speak at all about facts within our field. I firmly believe that wide-ranging interpretations based on such scanty data tend to give us, and with some justification, a bad reputation among our colleagues within the more established fields of science.

Similar sentiments are also conveyed by James (1960) and Murphy (1971).

The claims of the eminent scientists we have discussed and psychical researchers in general have no import for regular scientific pursuits unless and until they can show us how it matters. Obviously it cannot matter until, at the very least, the parapsychologists capture and tame their quarry. They have to be able to spell out sufficient conditions for observing the phenomena. It will not do to point to the few experiments that have been repeated successfully, such as the sheep-goat or the ganzfeld studies (Rogo, 1975). It is true that these studies have been repeated on some occasions with positive results, but just as often they have been attempted and failed. The point is that no one knows what conditions lead to success and which result in failure. Worse, no one knows how to put together conditions that will give a reasonable chance of success. Antony Flew, a serious and sympathetic student of parapsychology, put the matter in these words: "If scientifically-minded people view the evidence of psychical research with suspicion because nothing is repeatable, they are quite right. The whole object of the scientific exercise is to discover true laws, and theories which explain the truth of these laws. If the alleged phenomena are not repeatable at all, they clearly cannot be fitted into any laws, even if they do occur. The things previously said about historical method are reasons for doubting in the present state of the evidence whether paranormal phenomena have occurred at all" (Flew, 1975).

The Problem of Disconfirmation

Before leaving the challenges that face psychic researchers, I should briefly mention the vexing issue of disconfirmation. What in fact would constitute a disconfirmation of the findings by Hare, Wallace, Crookes, Targ, and others? Perhaps nothing would. If Slade was caught cheating and confessed both before and after his sittings with Zoellner, this does not mean he was cheating when Zoellner was observing him. Eusapia Palladino cheated whenever she was given the opportunity, according to both her critics and her staunchest supporters. But this does not invalidate the results obtained at those sessions when she was not caught cheating. Even our preceding discussion of fraud could be treated by believers as being no grounds for disconfirming previously successful results.

Similar remarks can be made about blank, or unsuccessful, sessions.

Indeed, sometimes blank sessions are treated as *confirming* the reality of preceding phenomena. On a recent radio broadcast dedicated to a discussion of Uri Geller, Dr. Thelma Moss of the University of California–Los Angeles indicated that at first she was skeptical of the genuineness of Geller's powers because when she saw him on the Merv Griffin television show everything he attempted seemed to work. This made her suspicious because, in her experience, legitimate psychics cannot produce their effects at will. But everything was set right when she later watched Geller on the Johnny Carson show where he failed to produce any effects. This failure convinced her of the genuineness of Geller's powers because, as she pointed out, if he were a trickster he certainly would have made sure to produce effects on the prestigious Carson show.

As already pointed out, all of the conditions that have been listed as desirable for psychic phenomena can be called upon to account for why a replication failed. Interestingly enough, no combination of these conditions is sufficient to guarantee successful results, but can always account for failures. Indeed parapsychology is unique in that failure to replicate earlier successes never calls into question the previous successes. It merely illustrates the tendency of initially powerful psychic abilities to decline with time—and study.

The Challenge to Critics

One conclusion that can be drawn from the preceding discussion is that, while it is unjust to denounce a scientist who makes paranormal claims unless one has seriously and fairly evaluated the claims, there is quite a bit of justification for ignoring the claims. The justification resides in such problems as the nonrepeatability of the phenomena, the privileged status of the observations (in that only special individuals are capable of witnessing them), the fact that many psychics who provide the data are later caught cheating, and the detection of flaws in the original investigations (often retrospectively).

But, in my opinion, it would be a serious mistake for orthodox science to draw this conclusion. We should *not* ignore such claims. At worst, by banning such claims from further consideration, we fail to learn lessons about why the claims were made in the first place and thereby make it likely that many good scientists will fall into similar traps in the future. At best, by looking at such claims seriously we may learn many important things about the nature of science, the functioning of human cognition, and the nature of deception.

Why should we attend to the claims of Hare, Crookes, Wallace, Richet, and others? If for no other reason, it is sufficient that these are among our most eminent and important contributors to orthodox science. Each showed himself to be a master in his chosen area of physics, chemistry, physiology, biology, or other branch of science. Each showed beyond dispute that whatever "science" means within his specialty, he knew how to "do science" successfully. Crookes and Zoellner forcefully pointed out the inconsistency of accepting and honoring their contributions to physics and astronomy, respectively, while withholding from them the label "scientific" when they ventured into controversial areas. Both men believed they were behaving according to the same rules and principles that they employed in their orthodox pursuits when they investigated the claims of the mediums. "If we are being unscientific," these men and their fellow psychical researchers seem to be saying, "show us in what way we have departed from the rules so that we can mend our ways."

This is indeed a good question. If these men have gone astray, how can we account for it? The most obvious explanation is some form of mental aberration. Hare was seventy-two, at the end of his career, when he became involved with spiritualism. Perhaps he had become senile. But such a charge cannot be leveled at Wallace, Crookes, and most of the others who were young—at the beginning or in the middle of their careers—when they became involved with alleged psychics. Some other form of mental abnormality? Temporary derangement? But this will not do. Crookes and Wallace, for example, continued to make important contributions to their orthodox specialties at the same time, and after, they felt they had obtained solid grounds for affirming the reality of psychical phenomena.

If mental abnormality is to be the explanation, what sort of a defect enables victims to function successfully when they tackle orthodox problems and leads them astray when they deal with unorthodox matters? Perhaps the defect lies in the individual's scientific training in such a way that it leads to success within the relevant field but to disaster when the individual tries to apply the same procedures outside the specialty?

Crookes, Barrett, Targ, Puthoff, Bohm, and many other psychic investigators are, or were, accomplished physicists. One might want to conclude that training in physics is insufficient to prepare an individual for investigating the claims of a psychic. But Hare was a chemist; Zoellner, an astronomer; Lombroso, a psychiatrist; Richet, a physiologist; and James, a psychologist. Does training in any of these fields leave one equally ill-prepared to investigate psychic phenomena?

It may well be that training in any particular branch of science does not enable one automatically to function well in another branch, especially in a branch as far removed from the others as psychical research. But, this does not answer the question of why such training does not help in the new field. More important, it does not help us to understand how scientists become so thoroughly persuaded by their investigations that they have demonstrated the reality of psychic phenomena. I do not think we are in a position as yet to answer the question. But we can at least recognize why the question poses an important challenge to critics.

I believe that we can reap important benefits by keeping the claims of Hare, Wallace, and Crookes constantly before us. We do not have to agree that they have isolated paranormal phenomena. But we should recognize that *something* is going on and that there are important lessons to be learned from trying to understand just what it is. Almost certainly, whatever is taking place cannot be attributed to a mental defect, mendacity, or some other gross aberration on the part of erring scientists. If the scientists have erred—and in believing that they have erred I concur with the majority of critics—I believe that the error must reflect some inherent vulnerabilities in our current scientific practices, our educational system, and our cognitive processes.

If we could understand what is going on, one immediate benefit would be the possibility of preventing such errors in the future. But the more interesting aspect of the challenge is that an understanding of what enables accomplished scientists to fall into such traps promises to teach us much about the social and psychological aspects of scientific inquiry, about the nature and limits of scientific skills within certain branches, about cognitive processes in general, and about the nature of deception.

One myth that should immediately be debunked as a result of such an investigation is that of the existence of a generalized scientific method that can be applied to any problem whatsoever. Even a cursory examination of the history of science and contemporary practices suggests that training and skills in one branch of inquiry do not transfer to other branches of inquiry. Even within one branch, training and experience within a given subspecialty may leave individuals helpless to operate effectively within another subspecialty of the same discipline.

Another myth that should just as quickly be dispelled is the belief that, through sheer will and attention to details, one can produce a "scientific investigation" of a "psychic." Scientific disciplines cannot be created simply by applying a set of abstract principles called the scientific method to a given phenomenon. A serious mistake made by Hare, Wallace, Crookes, Zoellner, and the rest was the belief that by applying their specialized skills and trying to institute plausible controls they would achieve a "scientific" experiment upon the claims of a psychic. Critics also seem to accept this assumption, because they chastise psychical researchers for not having conducted a "scientifically controlled" study. The scientist-turned-parapsychologist tries to rebut such charges by pointing to the experimental controls and claiming that he or she did indeed conduct a scientific experiment. Zoellner and Crookes, among others, insisted that their standing as accredited scientific investigators in orthodox fields should certify that they knew how to conduct scientific investigations.

But both sides miss the point and show woeful ignorance of the nature of science. There is no such thing as a "scientific study" in isolation from a larger context. In any accepted area of scientific inquiry, there is a history of initial investigations, a shakedown period during which previously unsuspected artifacts and flaws are discovered and corrected, and a gradual discovery of what sorts of variables have to be controlled and which can be ignored. This takes time, and often several embarrassments, before the area settles down to more or less accepted ways of studying the phenomena in question. Along with this goes much standardization of concepts, observational and recording instruments, measuring scales and units, and much else. A common jargon develops that has precision mainly because it is employed by a small and highly specialized community of investigators who share a common context of experience, history, and training. Within this community, when someone writes up an experiment, others can quickly judge if it was well-controlled and competently conducted and can know pretty well what did and did not occur on the basis of the report alone.

Contrast this with the problem of investigating the claims of psychics. There is no well-developed and standardized set of procedures for investigating psychics in general, let alone the peculiar claims of a Henry Slade or Uri Geller. There is no history of trial-and-error procedures to develop standardized tools that are relevant to investigating this psychic. There are no standardized observational tools, variables, tests, recording instruments, measures, paradigms, or control procedures. There is no specialized jargon and no community of shared training and experience to give precision to concepts and terminology. There is no lore, developed through painful experience over time, about what variables must be controlled, which have to be taken into account, and which can be safely ignored. Under these circumstances, the claim that someone has conducted a "scientifically controlled investigation" becomes nothing but a vague metaphor for a sort of claim that could have meaning only within a well-developed discipline of science.

Presumably many other myths could also be flushed out and banished. By such a process we would close in on the really important and relevant issues in the controversies generated by these unorthodoxies committed by previously conforming scientists.

The False Dichotomy

Partially as a result of the pioneering work done by Hare, Wallace, Crookes, and Zoellner, the Society for Psychical Research was founded in London in 1882. In his presidential address to the first general meeting, Henry Sidgwick began with the question, "Why form a Society for Psychical Research at this time?" One reason, he suggested, was to amass "sufficient scientific proof of thought-reading, clairvoyance, or the phenomena called Spiritualistic." He elaborated,

> What I mean by *sufficient evidence* is evidence that will convince the scientific world, and for that we obviously require a good deal more than we have so far obtained. . . . Thirty years ago it was thought that want of scientific culture was an adequate explanation of the vulgar belief in mesmerism and table-turning. Then, as one man of scientific repute after another came forward with the results of individual investigation, there was quite ludicrous ingenuity exercised in finding reasons for discrediting his scientific culture. He was said to be an amateur, not a professional; or a specialist without adequate generality of view and training; or a mere discoverer not acquainted with the strict methods of experimental research; or he was not a Fellow of the Royal Society, or if he was it was by an unfortunate accident. Or again, national distrust came in. . . . But we can no longer be told off-hand that all the marvels recorded by Mr. Crookes, Professor Zoellner, and others, are easy conjuring tricks, because we have the incontrovertible testimony of conjurers to the contrary. They may be conjuring tricks, but they are at any rate tricks that conjurers cannot find out (Sidgwick, 1882).

It is just five years shy of a century since Sidgwick gave this address. Despite uninterrupted work by the Society for Psychical Research and other such organizations since that time, nothing much really seems to have changed. By Sidgwick's definition, *sufficient proof* has still not been amassed. The scientific community still does not accept the claims—although there may be more tolerance now than one hundred years ago. And it is still true that if a scientist ventures forth from the safety of mundane pursuits to endorse the claims of a psychic, the same techniques are still employed to discredit him or her.

Sidgwick finished up his address in a defiant tone: "We must drive the objector into the position of being forced either to admit the phenomena as inexplicable, at least by him, or to accuse the investigators either of lying or cheating or of a blindness or forgetfulness incompatible with any intellectual condition except absolute idiocy."

Here we have a clear statement of the false dichotomy that has unwittingly been presupposed by both sides of the dispute. In different words, Hare, Crookes, Zoellner, and contemporary scientists have echoed the same sort of defiance. Each side feels compelled either to accept the purported claims as true or to accuse the claimant of being a liar or an idiot. The critics, in fact, often assume that if scientists are vouching for paranormal phenomena, they must, in fact, be either lying or mentally incompetent. Advocates, on the other hand, tend to assume that if critics reject their claims, this is tantamount to calling them liars or incompetent.

In this paper I have tried to urge that this is a false and destructive dichotomy. A scientist can be competent, honest, sincere, and sane—and still be badly mistaken. This is especially so in such a difficult area as psychical research. The reason, I suspect, why more scientists do not blunder in such gross ways as Crookes, Zoellner, and the others is simply because they have wisely avoided becoming entangled with psychics. From everything that I have observed, I am reasonably certain that many of the scientists who are vocal critics of physicists who have endorsed Uri Geller would be completely baffled by Geller if they ventured to employ their own "expertise" to investigate his claims. Geller, like many other confidence men, is more than a match for most scientists. Scientific competence, no matter how good, does not enable one to deal with alleged psychics who are trying to "beat the system."

The tragedy of the dichotomy in its present form is that it keeps us from realizing just how vulnerable scientific and other ways of knowing really are. By getting rid of this false dichotomy and looking at the matter not as an issue of individual defects but of the limitations and vulnerabilities of specific types of expertise, we can learn much about ourselves and how to better employ our cognitive skills. The issue, in other words, is to learn when to trust our own cognitions and the testimonies of others and when not to trust them. A careful study of the interactions between psychics and scientists suggests that we still do not know when to be trusting or distrustful.

References

Asimov, I. 1976. *Asimov's Biographical Encyclopedia of Science and Technology.* New York: Equinox.

Beloff, J. 1976. "The Study of the Paranormal as an Educative Experience." In B. Shapin & L. Coly (eds.) *Education in parapsychology.* New York: Parapsychology Foundation. Pp. 16–29.

Burton, J. 1974. *Heyday of a Wizard: Daniel Home, the Medium.* New York: Warner.

Carpenter, W. B. 1877. "The Radiometer and Its Lessons." *The Nineteenth Century,* 1, 242–56.

Carrington, H. 1907. *The Physical Phenomena of Spiritualism: Fraudulent and Genuine.* Boston: H. B. Turner.

Davey, S. J. 1887. "The Possibilities of Mal-observation and Lapse of Memory from a Practical Point of View: Experimental Investigation." *Proceedings of the Society for Psychical Research* 4, 405–95.

Dingwall, E. J. 1962a. *Some Human Oddities: Studies in the Queer, the Uncanny and the Fanatical.* New Hyde Park, N. Y.: University Books.

—— 1962b. *Very Peculiar People: Portrait Studies in the Queer, the Abnormal, and the Uncanny.* New Hyde Park, N. Y.: University Books.

Edmunds, S. 1962. "Cooking the Evidence?" *Tomorrow* 10, 35–44.

—— 1972. *ESP: Extrasensory Perception.* North Hollywood, Calif.: Wilshire Book Co.

Faraday, M. 1853. "Experimental Investigation of Table Turning." *Athenaeum* (July), 801–3.

Flew, A. 1975. "Laws, Miracles and Repeatability." *New Humanist* 91 (November), 175–76.

Fodor, N. 1974. *An Encyclopedia of Psychic Science.* Secaucus, N. J.: The Citadel Press.

Fournier d'Albe, E. E. 1924. *The Life of Sir William Crookes.* New York: D. Appleton & Co.

Gardner, M. 1977. "Geller, Gulls, and Nitinol." *The Humanist* 37 (May/June), 25–32.

Gauld, A. 1968. *The Founders of Psychical Research.* New York: Schocken.

George, W. 1964. *Biologist Philosopher: A Study of the Life and Writings of Alfred Russel Wallace.* London: Abelard-Schuman.

Hall, T. H. 1963a. *The Spiritualists: The Story of Florence Cook and William Crookes.* New York: Garrett Publications.

—— 1963b. "Florence Cook and William Crookes: A Footnote to an Enquiry." *Tomorrow* (Autumn), 11, 341–59.

Hansel, C. E. M. 1966. *ESP: A Scientific Evaluation.* New York: Scribner's.

Hare, R. 1855. *Experimental Investigation of the Spirit Manifestations, Demonstrating the Existence of Spirits and Their Communion with Mortals: Doctrine of the Spirit World Respecting Heaven, Hell, Morality, and God. Also, the Influence of Scripture on the Morals of Christians.* New York: Partridge & Brittan.

Hasted, J. B., D. Bohm, E. W. Bastin, & B. O'Regan. 1976. "Experiments on Psychokinetic Phenomena." In C. Panati (ed.). *The Geller Papers.* Boston: Houghton Mifflin. Pp. 183–96.

Hodgson, R. 1887. "The Possibilities of Mal-observation and Lapse of Memory from a Practical Point of View: Introduction." *Proceedings of the Society for Psychical Research* 4, 381–404.

Hyman, R. 1976. "Review of *The Geller Papers.*" *The Zetetic* 1 (Fall/Winter), 73–80.

—— 1977. "Psychics and Scientists: *Mind-reach* and Remote Viewing." *The Humanist* 37 (May/June), 16–20.

James, W. 1960. *William James on Psychical Research.* New York: Viking.

Jastrow, J. 1935. *Wish and Wisdom: Episodes in the Vagaries of Belief.* New York: D. Appleton-Century.

Johnson, M. 1976. "Parapsychology and Education." In B. Shapin & L. Coly (Eds.). *Education in Parapsychology.* New York: Parapsychology Foundation. Pp. 130–51.

Kottler, M. J. 1974. "Alfred Russel Wallace, the Origin of Man, and Spiritualism." *Isis* 65, 145–92.

Marchant, J. 1916. *Alfred Russel Wallace: Letters and Reminiscences.* New York: Harper & Row.

Marks, D., & R. Kammann. 1977. "The Nonpsychic Powers of Uri Geller." *The Zetetic* 1 (Spring/Summer), 9–17.

Medhurst, R. G. (ed.). 1972. *Crookes and the Spirit World: A Collection of Writings by or Concerning the Work of Sir William Crookes, O.M., F.R.S.* New York: Taplinger.

Murphy, G. 1971. "The Problem of Repeatability in Psychical Research." *Journal of the American Society for Psychical Research* 65, 3–16.

Panati, C. (ed.). 1976. *The Geller Papers: Scientific Observations on the Paranormal Powers of Uri Geller.* Boston: Houghton Mifflin.

Podmore, F. 1902. *Modern Spiritualism.* London: Methuen. 2 vols. Rpt. 1963. *Mediums of the 19th Century.* New Hyde Park, N.Y.: University Books.

Preliminary Report of the Commission Appointed by the University of Pennsylvania to Investigate Modern Spiritualism in Accordance with the Request of the Late Henry Seybert. 1920. Philadelphia: J. B. Lippincott.

Randi, James. 1975. *The Magic of Uri Geller.* New York: Ballantine.

Ranson, C. 1971. "Recent Criticisms of Parapsychology: A Review." *Journal of the American Society for Psychical Research* 65, 289–307.

Rawcliffe, D. H. 1959. *Illusions and Delusions of the Supernatural and the Occult.* New York: Dover.

Richmond, A. B. 1890. *What I Saw at Cassadaga Lake: A Review of the Seybert Commissioners' Report.* Boston: Colby & Rich. (3rd edn.).

Rogo, D. S. 1975. *Parapsychology: A Century of Inquiry.* New York: Dell.

Sidgwick, H. 1882–1883. Presidential Address. *Proceedings of the Society for Psychical Research* 1, 7–12.

Sidgwick, Mrs. H. 1886–87. "Results of a Personal Investigation into the Physical Phenomena of Spiritualism with Some Critical Remarks on the Evidence for Genuineness of Such Phenomena." *Proceedings of the Society for Psychical Research* 4, 45–74.

Targ, R., & H. Puthoff. 1977. *Mind-reach: Scientists Look at Psychic Ability.* New York: Delacorte.

Wallace, A. R. 1906. *My Life: A Record of Events and Opinions.* Vol. II. New York: Dodd, Mead, & Co.

Wilhelm, J. L. 1976. *The Search for Superman.* New York: Pocket Books.

Zoellner, J. C. F. 1976. *Transcendental Physics.* New York: Arno Press. (Rpt.).

Physicists and Psychical Research:
Perils and Pitfalls*

Up until 125 years ago, miracles and so-called supernatural phenomena were investigated, if at all, by religious authorities. Scientists concentrated on only those types of phenomena that promised to have a mundane explanation. But a variety of circumstances—involving changes in religious concepts, the increasing success of science and its accompanying naturalism, and the quest by many scholars for a conception of humankind that was constrained neither by the dogmas of religious fundamentalism nor the materialism of positivistic science—induced many eminent scientists to employ their investigative skills in an attempt to demonstrate that supernatural forces exist.

Another factor was the rise of modern spiritualism, beginning with the alleged spirit rappings produced by the Fox sisters in 1848. Unlike other religions, spiritualism was unique in offering material proof to back up its claims. Many spiritualists saw their movement as being completely compatible with the scientific spirit and actively encouraged scientists to test the claims of mediums.

I will not deal here with these social, religious, and cultural factors. But we should keep them in mind as we examine the interaction between alleged psychics and scientists. They will help to account for the bitterness of the controversies that arise when a scientist endorses the claims of a psychic.

Michael Faraday, one of the greatest physical scientists of all time, was the first major scientist to take time out from his regular investigations

---

*Presented at Symposium on Physics and Parapsychology, Annual Meeting of the American Physical Society, New York, January 30, 1979.

to examine claims for a supernatural force. One of the spinoffs of the founding of modern spiritualism in 1848 was the practice of table turning. A small group of sitters would arrange themselves around a table with their hands resting upon its top. After an interval of time and after entreaties by the sitters, the table would rise up on one leg and rap one or more times. Sometimes the table would turn in circles or begin moving across the room. The accepted belief was that the table's antics were caused by a spirit and that this spirit would also answer questions by tapping in code.

By the early 1850s, this practice had become so widespread that Faraday was induced to investigate it. He found individuals for whom this phenomenon would occur within his laboratory and whom he considered to be "very honorable." In 1853 he published the conclusions of his investigation. No electrical force was involved. Only a mechanical force applied by the sitter's hands was involved. The sitter did not deliberately make the table move. Instead, because of strong expectations, the sitter's muscles involuntarily pushed the table in such a way that the sitter was deluded into believing that the table was moving of its own accord.

Faraday's findings were a setback for the spiritualist movement. But the setback was temporary. Robert Hare, professor emeritus of chemistry at the University of Pennsylvania, in response to a query wrote a letter to the *Philadelphia Inquirer* in July 1853. His letter, based upon Faraday's findings, denounced table turning as superstition and self-delusion. A Dr. Comstock invited Hare to attend one of his circles to test the phenomenon for himself. In the spirit of fair play, Hare accepted the challenge. The result was astonishing. Hare became convinced that the table turning could not be explained according to Faraday's account or, for that matter, by any naturalistic means.

Hare began a systematic study of spiritualistic phenomena. When he began these investigations at age seventy-two, he described himself as a nonreligious skeptic. Not only did his findings convert him into a deeply religious believer in spiritualistic phenomena, but before he died at age seventy-seven, he himself claimed mediumistic powers and said that he was receiving messages from Ben Franklin, George Washington, and Jesus Christ. In 1855 he published a book on his findings with the bizarre title: *Experimental Investigation of the Spirit Manifestations, Demonstrating the Existence of Spirits and Their Communion with Mortals: Doctrine of the Spirit World Respecting Heaven, Hell, Morality, and God. Also, the Influence of Scripture on the Morals of Christians.*

Until his belated conversion to the cause of spiritualism, Hare had been one of the most respected men of American science. But when he tried to defend spiritualism at the meetings of the American Association for the Advancement of Science in Washington, D.C., in 1854, he was howled down by his colleagues. And the Harvard University faculty passed a resolution condemning Hare's "insane adherence to a gigantic humbug."

Hare's scientific colleagues could easily dismiss his support of supernatural phenomena as due to the eccentricities of old age. But the charge of senility cannot be leveled against later scientists who also endorsed the claims of alleged psychics. Some ten years after Hare's death in 1858, both Alfred Russel Wallace—cofounder with Darwin of the theory of evolution by natural selection—and William Crookes, who was later knighted for his contributions to physics and chemistry, independently began investigating psychic phenomena. Like Hare, Wallace became convinced when he had personal experience with table turning.

In July 1870, William Crookes, who was then thirty-eight years of age but already recognized as an outstanding chemist and physicist, announced his intention to investigate scientifically the claims of spiritualistic mediums. Both the press and the scientific establishment welcomed this announcement. They thought Crookes, with his scientific credentials, was just the man to dispose of this humbug once and for all. But this reaction was the result of not reading Crookes's announcement very carefully. Crookes had already been attending seances for some time before his announcement and was convinced of the reality of the phenomena. His intention was not to debunk but to provide a solid scientific basis for the phenomena, which involved, he was convinced, a new force—one he called *Psychic Force*.

Crookes's first systematic experiments were conducted with the famous medium Daniel D. Home. But his investigations of the controversial medium Florence Cook gained the most attention and were the focus of his most bitter disputes. Crookes carried out his studies of Cook over a five-month period beginning in December 1873. In a typical session, Cook would retire to a curtained-off cabinet and presumably enter a mediumistic trance. After a while the fully materialized form of a spirit, claiming to be one "Katie King," would emerge from the cabinet and chat with the onlookers. Crookes was allowed to walk hand in hand with "Katie" and even, upon one occasion, to embrace her.

Some witnesses to these seances remarked how much "Katie King" resembled Florence Cook. Crookes admitted some resemblance but pointed out many physical differences that he argued were sufficient to establish separate identities for the medium and the spirit. Finally, in one dramatic seance, Crookes claimed simultaneously to observe both Florence and "Katie" together in good light. For the believers, at any rate, this observation established the reality of the "Katie King" materialization beyond any doubt.

Not long after Crookes experienced his dramatic encounter with "Katie King," Professor J. C. F. Zoellner, of the University of Leipzig in Germany, published the third and final volume of his *Scientific Treatises, Transcen-*

dental Physics. This volume, which was dedicated to Crookes, immediately stirred up heated controversy and made Zoellner the focus of bitter attacks by many of his academic colleagues.

Zoellner was professor of physical astronomy at Leipzig and, among other things, one of the world's foremost experts on comets. In August 1877, when he was forty-three, he had published the first volume, in which he developed his theory of a fourth dimension. If we had access to a fourth spatial dimension, he speculated, this might provide a naturalistic explanation of many so-called spiritualistic phenomena. Three months later Zoellner was introduced by friends to the American spiritualistic medium Henry Slade, who had stopped over in Leipzig on his way to St. Petersburg. During their conversation Slade indicated that he could accomplish many phenomena such as causing a compass needle to rotate psychically.

That very night Zoellner took Slade to his home to test this claim. Sure enough, Slade caused the compass needle to move without the apparent use of any known force. Zoellner later wrote, "This observation decided my position towards Slade." Zoellner held a series of seances with Slade in November 1877 and again in May 1878. During these sessions, Zoellner claimed that Slade was able to produce psychically such phenomena as raps, levitation of furniture, breaking of furniture, tying knots in an endless loop of cord, and causing writing to appear on the surfaces of slates that were sealed from physical access.

Zoellner describes the results of these seances in his third volume. He uses the phenomena produced by Slade as evidence for his theory of the fourth dimension.

Psychical research became an institutionalized area for investigation largely through the efforts of another scientist, William F. Barrett (later Sir William), professor of experimental physics at the Royal College of Science in Dublin. Barrett began his investigations into paranormal phenomena in 1874 when he was twenty-nine years old. In 1876 his paper, "Some Phenomena Associated with Abnormal Conditions of the Mind," was rejected by the Biological Committee of the British Association for the Advancement of Science. But he was able to read the paper before the Anthropology Subsection when Alfred Wallace, who was the chairman, cast the deciding vote. During the discussion that followed, Barrett urged the formation of a special committee to study psychic phenomena. But, despite support from Wallace and Crookes, nothing was done about it at this time.

Barrett's initial interests were in mesmerism and thought transference. He was heavily influenced by the very popular Victorian pastime called "the willing game." An individual would leave the room while the remaining persons would decide upon an object. When the individual returned he or she would try to guess the object by picking up clues from onlookers. Barrett believed that the successes in such games were often inexplicable in terms of cues obtained through normal sensory channels.

In 1881 Barrett received a newspaper clipping in the mail from the Reverend Andrew Macreight Creery. The clipping described telepathic feats performed by his three daughters and a servant girl. Barrett visited the Creerys at Easter, 1881, and was very much impressed with what he witnessed. Typical of what he witnessed was the following demonstration. One of the daughters was chosen as the "thought reader" and stood outside the door. An object was decided upon and written down on a piece of paper, which was handed around to all the individuals in the room. The "thought reader" returned to the room and stood facing the others. After an interval she would name an object. During this visit eleven objects were guessed correctly on the first trial out of twenty-nine tests.

In a letter to *Nature* (July 7, 1881), Barrett referred to the investigation of the Creery sisters in this manner: "This case is historically of importance, for it led to the first clear evidence of thought transference in the normal state of the percipient." And as Trevor Hall aserts in *The Strange Case of Edmund Gurney* (London: Duckworth, 1964), this case also resulted in the founding of the Society for Psychical Research. Encouraged by the results with the Creery sisters, Barrett called a meeting in January 1882 at the offices of the British National Association of Spiritualists. The meeting resulted in the founding of the society later that same year. Thus, psychical research was launched as an institutionalized activity. While on a visit to the United States in 1885, Barrett was also instrumental in the founding of the American Society for Psychical Research. Both societies are still active and publish journals and proceedings.

The second half of the nineteenth century saw many prominent scientists in England, on the Continent, and in the United States risk their reputations by investigating and endorsing the reality of various psychical phenomena. Such activity continued up to and through World War I, but seems to have become dormant during the period between World Wars I and II. However, the second half of the twentieth century seems to be the occasion for another upsurge in psychic investigations by prominent scientists that may parallel what took place during the Victorian era.

As just one example, the alleged psychic Uri Geller has attracted both the interest and endorsements of several prominent physicists throughout the world.

Many questions come to mind as we review these cases from the past as well as those of our own times. One of the most obvious questions is: Was there or is there any substance to the claims for paranormal phenomena put forth by these established scientists? If yes, why did they make no impression upon the rest of the scientific establishment (other than to call down the wrath of some their colleagues)? Why were the claims rejected out of hand by the majority of the establishment?

If no, then how can we account for the stubborn and often impassioned defense of their claims by these deviant scientists? As pointed out, Hare might have been senile, but most of the scientists I have mentioned, as well as many others, were at the peak of their scientific prowess and still were doing acceptable science at the time they also investigated and endorsed the claims of psychics.

And why have the rejections by the establishment involved so much hostility and often a refusal to listen to the deviant scientist's evidence?

Does the possibility that all these claims were mistaken indicate serious defects or limitations on scientific methodology and training?

How can a neutral outsider evaluate the competing claims between those scientists who are proponents and those who are opponents of claims of the paranormal?

I chose these cases for illustration because, so far as I can tell, the alleged psychics in each one almost certainly resorted to trickery and deception in at least some portions of their careers. Florence Cook was clearly exposed in cheating both before and after she came under the scrutiny of William Crookes. Henry Slade was caught in flagrant cheating many times both before and after his sessions with Zoellner. The Creery sisters were not only caught employing a code but confessed to cheating, at least on some occasions, in the experiments with Barrett. And by now the circumstantial evidence appears overwhelming that Geller employs trickery and deception to accomplish many, if not all, of his feats.

So far as I can tell, the situation is similar with just about every alleged psychic who has been investigated and endorsed at one time or another by scientists. This list of psychics would include Eusapia Palladino, Ted Serios, and others.

The scientists who have endorsed such alleged psychics and their supporters respond in a variety of ways to evidence that indicates that their favorite superstars have employed deception. One is to deny the evidence and insist that the so-called psychic is the victim of a frame-up or biased testimony. Another is to admit that the superstar, in order to keep in the limelight, has to resort to trickery on those occasions when the elusive powers fail. The current position of many parapsychologists with respect to Uri Geller, for example, is to hedge their bets. A typical reaction is to admit that Geller may cheat on many occasions, but that they as scientists are responsible for his actions only when the superstar was under their scrutiny.

One reason why the controversy over the claims put forth to support the paranormal feats of these superstars is so bitter is because of the false dichotomy implied by both the defenders and critics. Scientists defending their evidence for paranormal phenomena place their reputations on the line. They tend to insist that their competence in an accepted field of science guarantees the integrity and reliability of the observations they have made on the superstar. They view challenges to their claims as accusations that they have behaved in a glaringly stupid manner or are deliberately falsifying the facts. The critics also tend implicitly to accept this dichotomy—either the scientists actually witnessed paranormal events, or they were grossly negligent in their role as scientific observers. The critics further implicitly assume that if they, the skeptics, had been the observers the presumed deception would never have succeeded.

I have written at length elsewhere (Hyman, R., "Scientists and Psychics," in G. Abell and B. Singer [eds.]., *Science and the Paranormal,* New York: Scribner's, 1981) about why this dichotomy, assumed to be the case by both sides, is false. I have little doubt that if critics were observing Uri Geller in the same circumstances as did the believing scientists, they, too, would be baffled. Nothing in the training of a physicist—or in the training for any other scientific specialty for that matter—prepares one for coping with the deceptions of a Slade or Geller.

The mistake made by both sides of the controversy is to assume that a properly trained scientist, when acting competently, ought to have little trouble in setting up tests that will discriminate truly paranormal events from ones that have a naturalistic basis. Almost without exception, the scientists we have discussed defended their paranormal claims on the basis of their acknowledged competencies in their accepted scientific specialties. Crookes, for example, argued eloquently that his colleagues accepted for publication, and even praised, his work when it was on topics in chemistry and physics. But they refused to publish or take seriously his work on supernormal phenomena. Yet, he insisted, he was still acting with the same scientific competence and standards that he employed in his more mundane pursuits. Therefore his colleagues were being bigoted and unscientific in refusing to accept the latter type of work.

But no matter how competent and successful an individual is within his or her chosen area of scientific expertise, work in a new area is not automatically "scientific" no matter how strongly the scientist desires it to be so. An individual cannot simply decree that he or she will be "scientific" in this new area and automatically make it so. This is not the place to become involved with the complicated matters about what science is and is not—issues that occupy historians and philosophers of science. But as a minimal set of properties, we can say that the scientific enterprise is a *shared* venture; it is *cumulative;* and it is *focused* on problems within a delimited conceptual framework. Individuals working within the same field of inquiry share many common features—similar training; agreed-upon vocabulary; general consensus of the ways to gather data; agreement about what can be ignored and what needs to be controlled; standardized ways of analyzing the data and reporting it, and so forth.

So when Zoellner moves from his specialty of physical astronomy to the study of spiritualistic phenomena, he goes from a highly structured and well-developed field of inquiry into a completely unstructured realm with no standardized procedures, paradigms, or concepts. In doing astronomical studies he is accountable to assistants, students, colleagues, and journal editors—all of whom share similar backgrounds, technical vocabularies, standards, and frameworks. This shared context provides a variety of checks and balances. At every stage of the inquiry there are clear-cut criteria to inform scientists when they are on firm ground and when they had better recheck or pull back. When Zoellner insists that he has performed a scientific study on some astronomical problem, his colleagues know exactly what he means—they know from his training, his previous accomplishments, and from the shared paradigms and ground rules that prevail within that specialized area of astronomy.

But when Zoellner, the accomplished astronomer, experiments upon Henry Slade, he leaves behind all these safeguards, shared contexts, and check and balances. His training, skills, and expertise are with respect to the tightly knit and highly structured divisions of astronomy within which he has made his reputation. Even if he moved to another highly structured area of science, he would be out of his element until he mastered the new vocabulary, ground rules, paradigms, and conceptual frameworks that characterize the new area. The situation is much worse when the scientist jumps into the business of testing the claims of alleged psychics.

Although scientists have been testing the claims of alleged psychics for over 125 years, there does not exist anything even approximating a structured framework and discipline for conducting such investigations. There is no shared community of vocabulary, procedures, ground rules, safeguards, or agreed-upon controls. Each investigation is *ad hoc* and involves employing unstandardized tasks and procedures uniquely tailored to the peculiar claims of each psychic. No matter how vehemently Hare, Crookes, or one of the other scientists in our account insist that they are being just as "scientific" in this new type of investigation as in their regular specialties, the claim is meaningless.

For a number of other reasons that I have documented elsewhere (Hyman, in Abell and Singer, 1981), the scientific status of such investigations can be discounted. Not a single investigation of an alleged psychic by a scientist, for example, has met minimal standards that social scientists have demonstrated are required for trustworthy observation. Neither the tasks, the observers, the observational procedures, nor the recording procedures have been pretested, standardized, or validated. When looked at from a scientific viewpoint, the situation with respect to tests of psychics is chaotic and incoherent.

Not all psychical research, however, is as chaotic and haphazard as the testing of specific claims of alleged psychics by scientists. As I have already indicated, it was the attempt to test such claims by scientists that eventually resulted in the establishment of psychical research in 1882 as an institutionalized form of inquiry. Ever since, psychical research has included tests of specific claims. But so far as I can see, no advances in bringing coherence or common standards into this endeavor have been achieved over the century and a quarter since Robert Hare rashly plunged into spiritualistic investigations. Each scientist who accepts the challenge seems content to begin from scratch with no reference to past attempts and with strictly *ad hoc* procedures. Imagine how other areas of science might have fared if each investigator employed *ad hoc* methods, ignored the work and procedures employed by predecessors, and reported the results in idiosyncratic formats!

Other areas of psychical research involve the investigation of spontaneous cases and the experimental investigation of unselected subjects on more or less standardized tasks. It is this latter activity that is most closely associated with the term *parapsychology* (although some parapsychologists use the term as the equivalent of psychical research). In contrast to the tests of specific claims of alleged psychics, experimental parapsychology more nearly approximates what I have called a scientific endeavor in that it employs standardized tasks, shared paradigms, accepted principles of controls and double-blind procedures, and standardized procedures for analyzing and reporting data.

Parapsychology as an experimental science in this latter sense dates mainly from the 1930s and is largely due to the pioneering efforts of J. B. Rhine. Rhine's first major work was published in 1934 under the title of *Extra-Sensory Perception*. The book was both widely hailed as a major breakthrough and attacked by skeptics and some psychical researchers as being scientifically inadequate. The experimental controls and the analysis of the data both were subjects of controversy.

One consequence of the controversy is that parapsychologists gradually became more sophisticated in their experimental controls, designs, and data analysis. Indeed, some parapsychologists even make the debatable claim that their standards for experimental and statistical adequacy far exceed those of other areas of inquiry, such as experimental psychology.

Ironically, many established physical scientists who jump into the field of experimental parapsychology take it for granted that they can safely ignore the lessons and safeguards that are now accepted within the field of parapsychology. The work by the physicists at Stanford Research Institute, for example, on Uri Geller and on remote viewing has disregarded many of the standard operating procedures of regular parapsychology. I have talked with some physicists who are now doing work in parapsychology. They tend to take the position that their training in physics is sufficient to guarantee that they will not make mistakes in setting up controlled experiments. Indeed, a few have boasted to me that they have deliberately avoided learning about how regular parapsychologists do their experiments. The implication is that parapsychology has not gotten anywhere following its traditional paths and that it needs the new directions and guidance that only physicists can give it to make it a solid scientific discipline. This may be so, but in the meantime these *paraphysicists,* as they prefer to call themselves, are repeating many of the errors in experimental controls, randomization of targets, uses of statistics, and the like that plagued early experiments in parapsychology.

One obvious contribution that physical scientists have made to the advancement of parapsychology has been in the development of sophisticated random number generators and the automation of both data collection and data analysis. The work of Dr. Helmut Schmidt is one of the most successful examples of this. Another sort of contribution that may also have import is the attempt to reconcile parapsychological phenomena with the latest theoretical conception in quantum and relativity theories. This latter contribution, however, is a bone of contention within the field of parapsychology.

My task as a responsible critic and skeptic of paranormal claims would be relatively simple if I had to deal only with the role of physical scientists in the testing of claims of alleged psychics. As I have already indicated, such tests have resulted in nothing as yet that requires explaining. I think the scientific community can fairly and wisely ignore the claims put forth so far in behalf of the reality of psychic powers attributed to Henry Slade, Florence Cook, Uri Geller, and the other psychic superstars. Despite some assertions to the contrary, none of the claims has been backed with the sort of evidence or replicability that requires an explanation on the part of skeptics. Indeed, I have argued elsewhere (Hyman, in Abell and Singer, 1981) that critics have made a serious mistake in trying to "explain away" the evidence offered on behalf of such psychic claimants. Such attempts imply that there is indeed something in need of explanation. And they shift the burden of proof away from the original claim to the plausibility of the critics' counterproposals. Only when the evidence is backed up with clear indications of having been collected within standardized paradigms using reliable observational procedures and with demonstration that the alleged phenomena can be reliably reproduced for independent observers—only then can we begin to ask established scientific disciplines to take notice.

But my task as a responsible critic is more complicated when I am confronted by the mounting evidence for clairvoyance, precognition, and psychokinesis that is emerging from parapsychological laboratories in ever greater numbers. I think it is fair to say that the standard criticisms that are still leveled against parapsychology by casual critics just cannot be justifiably maintained by anyone who seriously undertakes to examine carefully the reports that are currently available in the several parapsychological journals. These standard criticisms are, to list briefly some of the major categories:

    a. Parapsychological phenomena are *a priori* impossible because they violate some of the basic principles of particle physics.

    b. Methodological inadequacies allow for sensory leakage or other experimental artifacts.

    c. Inappropriate uses of statistics falsely exaggerate significance levels or violate important assumptions.

    d. Various forms of "data massage" involve selective reporting, recording errors, alternative ways of analyzing and grouping the data, and so forth.

    e. Subtle and unwitting biases are introduced by overzealous experimenters, assistants, or subjects.

    f. Deliberate deception is carried out by subjects, assistants, or experimenters.

One criticism is acknowledged by some parapsychologists to have substance—the problem of nonrepeatability of experimental results. Many parapsychologists argue that their important findings have been successfully repeated both by themselves and others. But the replicability that is usually meant is the ability to specify conditions that will always or, at the very least, very often result in successful results. For example, many successful replications of the ganzfeld experiments have been reported. However, several well-known scientists have failed to obtain results with the paradigm even though they have gone out of their way to maximize all the conditions that allegedly are conducive to psi functioning, such as providing experimenters and subjects with the proper attitudes, informal and attractive environments, and so forth.

But even with the very serious problem of replicability, I believe that good grounds exist for taking the claims of parapsychologists very seriously. Most skeptics and critics understandably do not have the patience, motivation, or time to wade carefully through the hundreds of current reports of parapsychological experiments. Indeed, I suspect that even a full-time parapsychologist cannot keep up with all the experimental literature in the field. But when a critic does take the time to examine the literature in depth, he or she invariably concludes that the methodology or statistics cannot be faulted. These critics—such as Price, McBurney, Hansel, and others—typically find that the experimental reports, taken at face value, make an irrefutable case, by current scientific standards, for the existence of the phenomena they call *psi*. They then switch tactics and try to challenge the evidence on the basis of possibilities for deception on the part of the experimenters, the subjects, or both. Such tactics explicitly or implicitly concede that the case for parapsychology has passed muster on ordinary scientific grounds.

My own infrequent attempts to examine seriously the literature and claims in parapsychology have resulted, each time, in my being compelled to acknowledge that something is going on. The case made by the parapsychologists is much stronger and more sophisticated than my fellow skeptics typically acknowledge. The *a priori* arguments against the claims are weakened by the current crisis in philosophy of science about whether one can successfully draw the line between science and pseudoscience. They are also weakened by the debates within theoretical physics about the meaning of certain apparent paradoxes, such as the Einstein-Podolsky-Rosen paradox, coupled with Bell's theorem and Bohm's notions of interconnectedness and hidden variables. The methodological arguments tend to be badly misguided and out of date because many of the current experiments are quite sophisticated—as attested by the work of Schmidt. The statistics tend to be more sophisticated than is alleged. Even the possibilities for fraud are less obvious in the most likely versions because of designs that involve multiple observers and dual recording procedures. And certainly it grows increasingly difficult to explain away hundreds of experimental studies within certain areas of parapsychology as reported in some of the chapters of the recent *Handbook of Parapsychology.* Certainly they cannot be dismissed on the more obvious grounds that are typically put forth by my fellow skeptics.

Yet, the reasons for hesitating to endorse the claims of parapsychology seem to be also quite compelling. First, let me give my own personal reasons for being dubious. Then, I will list more general concerns about the nature of the field and its claims. My first opportunity to examine the literature of parapsychology in depth was in 1957 as a result of being invited by the *Journal of the American Statistical Association* to review S. G. Soal and Frederick Bateman's *Modern Experiments in Telepathy* (the review appeared in the December 1957 issue). In my review I pointed out a number features that, in my opinion, made "the Soal and Bateman argument one of the most formidable in the annals of psychic research." Yet I noted serious flaws in the basic experimental setup, which was rather complicated but still allowed, in my opinion, opportunities for sensory leakage and cueing.

However, I pointed out that Soal and Bateman could ignore my criticism because of the successful long distance series with Mrs. Stewart that would rule out the possibility of sensory leakage of the type I had postulated. I went on to say that "this successful long distance series is indeed fortunate for the argument of Soal and Bateman. It is only because of the outcome of this series, in this reviewer's opinion, that the entire set of 170 sittings becomes plausible evidence for nonsensory communication."

It was only a few years later that I discovered that the long distance series were flawed with serious loopholes, ones that I could not have known about from the book (see Hansel, C. E. M., *ESP: A Scientific Evaluation,* New York: Scribner's, 1966). And my reservations about leakage possibilities now have become academic with the recent revelations that prove that Soal must have tampered with the data to make them come out significant.

On a more recent occasion, I was asked to evaluate a proposal for parapsychological research for a granting agency. I could find no flaws in the proposal as written or in the preceding publications by the applicant; the reported work was quite sophisticated. But I was hesitant and suggested to the granting agency that they send me to the applicant's laboratory where I could watch the applicant doing research firsthand. While I was in the middle of negotiating a possible on-site visit, I was notified that the proposal was being withdrawn because the investigator had confessed to obtaining false significance by manipulating the apparatus.

My point in relating these two personal experiences is that if I had to make judgments on the basis of the available published reports, I would have no other recourse than to admit that the experimental data support the psi hypothesis because it would be difficult, if not impossible, to imagine any other alternative. It was only on the basis of later information—information that could not have been obtained from the published accounts—that it became evident that very plausible alternative explanations—nonparanormal ones—were available and consistent with the results after all.

But beyond these personal experiences there seem to be many good reasons to withhold support for parapsychological claims. I have pointed out that the standard criticisms about methodology, statistics, and inadequate controls are badly misguided in terms of current practices in parapsychology. But this does not mean that the investigators meet the ideals of experimental and statistical perfection in all their work. Any actual experiment has to make several compromises with such ideals, and parapsychological experiments are no exception. While I find the level of sophistication generally far beyond what many critics give the parapsychologists credit for, I still find it rare to come across a given experiment without some serious defect of one sort or another. Typically, I find rather primitive methods of randomization being used in an experiment that is a model of sophistication in terms of other types of controls and data analysis. Or I will encounter a place for possible sensory leakage in an experiment that is otherwise flawless. On the occasions when I have had the opportunity to point out such weaknesses to a parapsychologist, the retort has been that the reported weakness was one that could not plausibly have accounted for the successful results. In one particular case, the parapsychologist acknowledged that he had used an inappropriate method of randomization but charged that my criticism was "irrelevant." Irrelevant or not, it seems that most of the parapsychological research, while sophisticated in many ways, is still not a model of flawless science. Typically the experimenter in this field devotes attention to making some parts of the design highly sophisticated and then trusts his or her own subjective judgment about what other parts can be treated rather casually.

Parapsychologists acknowledge that deception is a serious problem in their field. They have to take steps to ensure that subjects do not cheat, and it is now considered desirable, even if not always built into the experiment, to arrange matters so that a single experimenter could not get away with cheating. As the parapsychologists point out, cheating is not unique to parapsychological research. But it does occur, and some of the experiments that once were considered "classics" of parapsychology have now had to be discarded from the roster of "solid" cases because of subsequent evidence that cheating was involved. Most of these cases were uncovered accidentally under circumstances that might not have occurred. The problem is that it is possible that many other cases of cheating will go undetected because of the lack of such "lucky" accidents.

The most disturbing aspect of the case for parapsychology is the shifting basis for its claims. At any point in time there do seem to be a set of outstanding candidates for the repeatable experiment or the major breakthrough. But at a later time many of these candidates drop from the running because either they are subsequently found to be flawed, or it becomes difficult to replicate them, or suspicions of fraud have been raised. When the Society for Psychical Research (SPR) was founded in 1882, one of its most solid cases for the existence of genuine telepathy was the series of studies done with the Creery sisters. These investigations were no longer employed as part of the case for telepathy after the girls were caught using a code. Another of the ironclad cases for telepathy was the series with Smith and Blackburn. Some years later Blackburn confessed how he and Smith had employed a code to outwit the SPR investigators. Both these cases, which at one time were billed by the SPR as the two most outstanding pieces of evidence for thought transference, were subsequently discarded as evidence.

From the 1940s until the last few years, the Soal-Goldney experiments with Shackleton and Mrs. Stewart were advertised by many parapsychologists as among the best, if not the very best, experimental arguments for psi and precognition. As the result of recent scandalous revelations, these experiments also must now be put on the scrap heap. The same can be said of Walter Levy's series of experiments employing random number generators and completely automated recording of data.

Other outstanding candidates for the convincing experiment have also faded into oblivion with the passage of years. In some cases, although no fraud has been demonstrated, peculiarities have subsequently turned up in the data or in other information that create doubt about their evidential status. And some experimental paradigms, like the cross-correspondences, the sheep-goat experiments, and some others, which at one time seemed to promise to be the hoped-for repeatable experiment have simply not lived up to the initial hopes.

These judgments about the shifting nature of the set of promising candidates are not just my own. At least one major parapsychologist has expressed similar doubts about the replicability of these experiments (Pratt 1978, pp. 127-139).

We find, then, that over the years the psychical researchers have put forth a stock of model experiments that they have offered to skeptics and friends as examples of solid proof for their claims. But the stock keeps changing in content over time. Many of the earlier prize cases no longer form part of the stock. But new ones keep rising up to take the place of the abandoned ones. So the specific evidence keeps changing; only the belief in psi remains constant. And this belief, in the case of most psychic investigators, existed before the quest for scientific proof.

Other reasons exist for hesitation. Some alleged characteristics of the phenomenon known as psi seem to mimic characteristics of what in other areas of science we designate as artifact or error. For example, psi effects tend to be strongest at the initial stages of an investigation or during the early trials of a new paradigm. This tendency for psi effects to fade away after initial successes with each new paradigm has been attributed to the loss of the enthusiasm or novelty that originally accompanies any new approach. But in more mundane areas of science such fading away of promising effects is usually attributed to the elimination of artifacts because of the inevitable improvement of observational techniques and experimental controls once more experience has been gained with a given paradigm. And psi is said to manifest itself only in the presence of subjects and experimenters who have a favorable attitude toward it or who have some other personality characteristics conducive to the effects. Again, in psychological experimentation such experimenter-dependent effects are considered to be artifacts.

In all other areas of scientific inquiry, the imposition of controls to cut down error variance or "noise" usually increases the signal-to-noise ratio. That is, the effects of the phenomenon under study now dominate the experimental data much more clearly than when unwanted error variation was present. Just the opposite seems to characterize psi. As tighter controls are imposed and as error variance is cut down, the signal-to-noise ratio tends to *decrease*—that is, psi tends to disappear as we increase controls to make it stronger!

Psi also has a very disconcerting way of manifesting itself in increasingly different ways. Sometimes it occurs as psi-hitting, other times as psi-missing. Sometimes both psi-hitting and psi-missing alternate such that the overall hit rate is at chance level but the variance of hits is larger than expected. Then there are decline effects of various kinds and durations. And, of course, there are various displacement effects—effects wherein the subjects' guesses seem to match targets other than those they were aiming for.

Today, I would say that the best candidate for the great psi breakthrough is the work of Dr. Helmut Schmidt. Without question, his work on precognition and psychokinesis using his random number generators is the most sophisticated that I have come upon. Not only is much of the target selection and data gathering almost completely automated, but also various controls, precautions, and safeguards have been instituted that are rarely seen in even the most sophisticated parapsychological experiments. These include: setting the total number of trials in advance (for the experiment as a whole, but not for individuals); testing the apparatus for randomness before, during, and after an experimental series; plotting the hits over time to look for any possible local fluctuations in performance (which could indicate temporary biases in the random number generator); running preliminary tests as a basis for predicting the specific outcomes of the main series; and sometimes recording the data in two independent ways as further checks upon unwitting biases in one of the data series.

Yet even here I feel we have to be cautious and show patience. Although Schmidt began his work ten years ago, it is still too new to make a proper judgment. History has shown that it takes fifteen to twenty years before we realize the weaknessess and problems of a new and promising paradigm in parapsychology. In addition, despite all this space-age sophistication, the determined skeptic can find many points to quarrel about in Schmidt's work so far. For one thing, the effects are extremely small—typically only a very few percentage points, or a fraction of a percentage point, above the expected chance level. The high levels of significance are the result of enormous numbers of trials. With such huge numbers of trials, slight biases or slight deviations of the underlying chance model from reality will produce results for reasons other than psi. We do not have much experience in applying our statistical models under conditions of possibly very weak signals and huge numbers of trials. Under normal circumstances we do not have to worry if the underlying assumptions of our chance distribution are literally true. The relatively high signal-to-noise ratio and the moderate number of trials result in a test that is highly robust—that is, a test that responds to true deviations from expected values rather than one that is sensitive to other departures from the underlying distribution.

Also, Schmidt's standard operating procedure places most of the burden for the integrity of his experimental results on the properties of his random number generators. For what are well-intentioned motives, his subjects are given quite a bit of latitude in how they choose to interact with the machine. The experimenter often is not observing the actual behavior of the subject, or is deliberately casual. Schmidt clearly assumes that the subject has no way to bias the machine except through psychic means. Yet, in his first technical report, Schmidt tells us about a fellow physicist who tried to "beat" the machine and succeeded. He managed to achieve a highly significant number of hits above chance without employing psychic powers. As a result of this experience, Schmidt writes that he put new safety features into his generator. But Schmidt does not tell us what his colleague did to beat the machine or what these additional safety features are and how they are supposed to prevent other ways to beat the machine.

Schmidt has actually employed a number of different types of generators in his various studies. This has the virtue of increasing the generality of his findings. But it has the negative feature of cutting down the number of opportunities to understand better the peculiarities and special properties of each machine.

I see an interesting irony in the fact that just as we have reached the point where we are beginning to understand better the strengths and weaknesses of human beings as observers and manipulators of data, we are systematically replacing them with automated systems whose properties and potentialities for bias we do not yet fully understand. We will need to attend closely in the future to the results of extensive tests and checks on these generators to see in which ways, if any, they can be biased and in what ways they can malfunction.

Again, personal experience may have sensitized me to such possibilities. In 1972, I was introduced to a parapsychologist who was eager to show me his portable ESP-testing machine. So far as I can tell, the machine was built upon the same principles as some of Schmidt's machines. When I asked about the properties of the random number generator, I was assured that its output had withstood the most rigorous and extensive tests for randomness. On the very first series, I managed to score a significantly high number of hits. On the second series I did even better. By this time the parapsychologist and his engineer were noticeably excited. But on the third series, the engineer noticed what I was doing and realized what was wrong. He quickly picked up the generator and apologetically remarked that he had to take it back to the laboratory for adjustments. What I had noticed on the first series was that two of the four targets seemed to come on more frequently than the other two. I simply played these.

Schmidt, to his credit, continually monitors the properties of his generators by automatically collecting data from them before, during, and after a test series by running the devices overnight when no humans are around to "bias" the output (although since time and space seem to be irrelevant to psi powers, it is not clear how meaningful such a control really is). But his checks for randomness are still relatively primitive in that he checks only for first- and second-order effects—that is, he looks only at the distribution of the individual targets as well as pairs of targets. But there is mounting evidence that subjects can and do exploit sequential dependencies in target series of a higher order than this. More careful analysis of both the target and the guessing series is required. Furthermore, the tests for randomness are done on blocks of trials that are orders of magnitude larger than those on which subjects are tested. Thus, there could be shorter-term biases in the output that would not be detected by his analyses.

Some "confirmatory" studies employing Schmidt's own generators or ones similar to his generators have been reported by other investigators. This is encouraging as far as it goes, but some well-known parapsychologists have systematically failed to get any significant results at all with such generators. So, at this point in time, we do not know how replicable Schmidt's paradigms will be. Will the initially interesting findings fade away for this paradigm as they have for so many other promising paradigms in the past?

In addition, many of the confirmatory studies strictly do not count as confirmations at all. For example, Eve André reported a study in 1972 as confirmation of Schmidt's experiment on the effects of PK upon electronic equipment. The overall deviation from chance was not significant, whereas the overall deviation in Schmidt's study was significantly negative. But when she broke the data down into morning and afternoon sessions—a breakdown she claims was decided upon in advance—the morning sessions showed a significantly greater number of hits, while the afternoon sessions showed a nonsignificant negative deviation. It seems that André could also have claimed a confirmation for a variety of other possible outcomes, such as nonsignificant outcomes in both the morning and afternoon sessions but with significant deviations of the overall score, or if the total score or the morning score had come out in the negative direction as did Schmidt's.

Again I wish to emphasize that by any standards, Schmidt's experiments are highly sophisticated and represent quite an advance over prior parapsychological research. But even the most sophisticated research can have its faults. And pioneering research such as Schmidt's may contain many unsuspected and novel types of problems that will take a while to thresh out fully. New and sophisticated technology can hold much promise, but it inevitably takes time to debug and fully understand the quirks of any new instrumentation.

So what do I conclude from these observations and remarks? Obviously, I am ambivalent towards the current findings and claims of parapsychology. I find much in it to puzzle me and to challenge my skepticism. I often feel that something must be going on. On the other hand, when I review the history of the field as well as my encounters with it, I find compelling reasons to postpone making any conclusions. The most disturbing aspect is the shifting basis upon which the foundations of parapsychological claims are built. The material of the foundation keeps changing. Many alleged properties of the phenomena of psi are also disturbing in that they resemble properties of things that, in other fields of science, we tend to dismiss as random or systematic error.

Yet I now am willing to admit that something important might be going on, something that may reward the attention of outsiders. But this something may not, in the end, be a new force or power outside what is currently considered permissible within the laws of physics. Instead what is going on may be something that will be of more interest and value to historians and philosophers of science, to methodologists, to sociologists, and to psychologists. Even if it all turns out to be massive fraud or self-delusion, it is important to study because this would have important implications for what could take place in other areas of scientific inquiry.

Pathological Science: Towards a Proper Diagnosis and Remedy*

How would you react to the following situation:

A competent and respected colleague reports to you that he held a seance in his own home. During the course of the seance, one of the sitters asked if the medium could materialize a sunflower. Following this request, a sunflower, six feet high, fell upon the table. Your colleague produces affidavits from witnesses, each of whom is a respected and honorable individual. He insists that both the house and the medium were carefully examined prior to the seance and that all precautions were taken to prevent trickery. Furthermore, he concludes that the only explanation is that the medium somehow had access to a new force, one that he refers to as a "psychic force."

Take a moment to consider what your response might be. Remember that this colleague is one who has earned a reputation as a competent and successful scientist in his chosen field. He is still doing acceptable science within this field. But now he insists that as a result of the seance just described, as well as a number of others which he conducted under carefully controlled conditions, he has obtained many phenomena that cannot be accounted for by currently accepted scientific principles.

Such a situation actually occurred to scientists during the Victorian era in England. Alfred Russel Wallace, the cofounder of the theory of evolution by natural selection, shocked his scientific colleagues in 1869 when

*Paper presented at the Annual Meeting of the American Association for the Advancement of Science, San Francisco. Section 17: History and Philosophy of Science. Program: Science and Pseudoscience, January 4, 1980. Reprinted from *Zetetic Scholar* 6 (1980), 31–39. Reprinted by permission.

he made public his conversion to spiritualism. Up until that time, his scientific colleagues had taken it for granted that he shared the same materialistic and naturalistic outlook that they had. In addition to shocked disbelief, Wallace's colleagues responded in a number of confused ways—with embarrassment, with attempts to ignore it, with open hostility, with attacks on his character, with refusals to listen to his arguments or view his evidence, with misrepresentations of his claims, and with a variety of other reactions that could hardly be called rational, dispassionate or scientific.

Pathological Science

Wallace's bizarre claim and the confused reaction of his scientific colleagues is a good illustration of what I am calling *pathological science*. I have borrowed this term from a talk that Irving Langmuir, late Nobel Laureate, gave at the General Electric Company back in December 1953 (Langmuir, 1968). Langmuir defined pathological science as "the science of things that aren't so." His examples dealt mainly with claims of mysterious radiations or forces such as N-rays, mitogenetic radiation, and the like. I would add to his examples such cases as Martian canals, the nonexisting planet Vulcan, Gall's faculties, as well as Wallace's "psychic force." I would also broaden his definition to include cases in which scientists have wrongly insisted something *wasn't* so. For example, meteorites, the impossibility of heavier-than-air flying machines, Semmelweiss's childbed fever, and many cases of missed discoveries. We should also include cases of data massage, unconscious plagiarism, deliberate cheating, and a variety of mixed cases.

The distinctive characteristics of these examples, as I see them, are the following:

> (1) A scientist of acknowledged competence and accomplishments (2) surprises his colleagues by claiming the existence of a phenomenon or relationship that is considered to be bizarre or even impossible by currently accepted principles. (3) The scientific establishment either ignores or attacks with hostility this bizarre claim. (4) The deviant scientist, along with a few deviant supporters, sticks resolutely to his or her guns in the face of attacks and indifference. (5) The bizarre claim is considered to be discredited in the eyes of the scientific community. (6) The claim is banished from further consideration in scientific literature, textbooks, and education.

The Problem Posed by Pathological Science

Wallace's scientific colleagues, for the most part, could not believe that a six-foot sunflower could be materialized out of thin air by a psychic force. I suspect that most of you cannot believe this either. But this posed a problem for Wallace's friends and colleagues who respected him as an honest and outstanding scientist. They could not accuse him of being an incompetent scientist, nor of being dishonest.

How should scientists respond to such a bizarre claim from one of their own trusted and distinguished members? Whatever the answer, one would like to say that the response should be consistent with rationality, objectivity, fair play, integrity—in short, with accepted scientific principles. Unfortunately, scientists are not trained or given models about how to behave under such circumstances. The reactions, understandably if regrettably, are typically confused, ambivalent, erratic, and emotional. The reaction in these cases of pathological science appears to be more one of panic than of considered critical analysis.

If there is truly "pathology" in these cases, the pathology seems to be exhibited as much in the reaction of the scientific community as in the claims of the offending scientist. The gut reaction of the scientific orthodoxy is to discredit the offending claim by any means possible—*ad hominem* attacks, censorship, innuendo, misrepresentation, etc. This panic reaction usually does succeed in discrediting the bizarre claim. It becomes completely cut off from the main body of scientific lore and future generations of scientists have little opportunity to become exposed to and possibly contaminated by it. But the manner of the discrediting and the results, I will argue, have consequences for the future of science that may not be worth the price.

The Reaction to Wallace's Claims

As I have already indicated, the response by the scientific community to Wallace's psychic claims was confused, erratic, inconsistent, and often emotional. Some, like Darwin, merely tried to avoid any public reference to the matter. Others dismissed it out of hand without actually trying to account for the specific evidence and arguments put forth by Wallace. The most dedicated critic—one who seemed to act as the "hit man" for the rest of the scientific community—was the physiologist William B. Carpenter. His basic position can be summarized in his own words:

> I have no other "theory" to support, than that of the constancy of the well-ascertained Laws of Nature; and my contention is, that where apparent departures from them take place through Human instrumentality, we are justified in assuming in the first instance either *fraudulent* description or unintentional *self*-deception, or both combined,—until the absence of either shall have been proved by every conceivable test that the sagacity of skeptical experts can devise (Carpenter, 1877).

In addition to assuming fraud or self-deception, Carpenter also attacked claims on the grounds that the scientist making the claim was incompetent and had earned his reputation by being specialized in one narrow field of science.

Carpenter saw the psychic and spiritualistic claims as part of an "epidemic delusion" and saw his mission in these terms: "I have no other motive than a desire to do what I can to save from this new form of Epidemic Delusion some who are in danger of being smitten by its poison, and to afford to such as desire to keep themselves clear from it, a justification for their 'common sense' rejection of testimony pressed upon them by friends whose honesty they would not for a moment call into question" (Carpenter, 1877).

Thus, Carpenter had no hopes of saving those such as Wallace and Crookes who were already "smitten by its poison." Instead, he was crusading to save those not yet contaminated. This might account for why Carpenter did not feel it necessary to look closely at the exact nature of the evidence and claims put forth by Wallace and Crookes. His task was to attack the epidemic by any means available. He was not concerned with the specific arguments and evidence being put forth. Rather, he wanted to make sure that those who might be tempted to listen, would not. His job was to frighten them away from temptation by any means possible.

And it is just in this sort of reaction that I see a serious problem for the continued viability of science.

The Negative Consequences of Inappropriate Reactions

It may be both understandable and almost inevitable that the reactions of the scientific critics to heretical hypotheses are emotional, irrational, and irrelevant to the specific arguments put forth. But whatever the reasons for such reactions, I believe that they have negative consequences for the conduct of science. The sorts of tactics employed by the establishment's "hit men" against the offending claims—blocking access to regular communication outlets, *ad hominem* attacks, misrepresentation of claims, dismissal on *a priori* grounds—do succeed in a way. They serve to "discredit" the deviant hypothesis, and once it is so tainted, then the establishment scientists feel relieved and ignore it.

But "discrediting" is not the same as disproving. As it turns out, often only through hindsight, most of the discredited hypotheses deserved their fate. And perhaps the militant crusaders such as Carpenter can take comfort in the fact that their emotional and often irrational put-downs of pathological sciences saved both contemporary and future generations of scientists from becoming smitten by the poison of wrongheaded heresies.

But the nature of the discrediting and some of its aftermaths may actually foster the very "evils" the crusaders were hoping to banish from science. Let me briefly elaborate upon this point.

First, let us consider the effect of the discrediting procedure upon the proponents of the "pathological" claim. Biographers and historians have written about how his defense of embarrassing causes harmed Wallace's subsequent fame. The main effect during his lifetime, however, was a forced compartmentalization of Wallace's orthodox biology and his unorthodox psychical inquiries into separate worlds. His scientific colleagues continued to accept and respect his orthodox contributions while they simultaneously tried to ignore his unorthodoxies. As a result, Wallace had to live in two separate worlds. When he did "regular" biology, he could talk, correspond, and publish within the world of established science. When he talked or wrote about his investigations of mediums, he could do so only in an entirely different world of individuals who were outcasts or nonentities with respect to the scientific establishments.

The same was even more strikingly so for Wallace's contemporary, William Crookes. Crookes tried to conduct laboratory research on psychic phenomena produced by mediums. He not only was bitterly attacked for this, but all his attempts to get his work read at scientific meetings or published in scientific journals were ruthlessly blocked. He finally gave up trying to get a hearing for these unorthodox views among his scientific colleagues and published his findings in spiritualist magazines. At the same time, however, he continued his purely orthodox chemical and physical experiments, which were not only completely accepted by the scientific establishment, but eventually won for him just about all the honors possible for a scientist of his period, including knighthood (Palfreman, 1976).

This enforced compartmentalization, in fact, seems to be true for most of the other cases of pathological science.

Consider what this compartmentalization accomplishes. It isolates deviant scientists and their claims from further debate and interaction with orthodox science. They are restricted in their further consideration of their position to discussions and exchanges with individuals who already believe in and support their claims. In addition, most of these individuals have neither the training nor aptitude for rigorous scientific evaluation. Thus, deviant scientists have no further incentive to refine, improve, or correct loopholes in their position. This further entrenches them in their belief that their initial claims were correct.

But even when deviant scientists were in the process of being discredited by establishment spokesmen, the ineptness and irrelevancies of the criticism further strengthened them in their belief. For the proponents and their few supporters within the scientific establishment could see that the criticisms were based on misrepresentations, irrelevancies, character assassination, and plausibility arguments, and failed to deal with the actual substance and specific arguments put forth. Such inept criticism, far from forcing the deviant scientists to reexamine their evidence and arguments, strengthened them in their belief that they were being treated unjustly and unscientifically. It further strengthened them in their conviction that they must be right.

But such inept discrediting procedures, in my opinion, have an even worse impact upon the conduct of science itself. By discrediting the offending hypothesis, the critics succeed in getting further consideration of it banned within the scientific community. This, indeed, might have the intended effect of saving the uncommitted scientists from becoming contaminated. But at what cost?

By banishing the failures of otherwise accomplished scientists, we prevent the learning of any lessons from them. Future scientists not only do not learn why and how such failures occurred, they do not even learn that they *did* occur. If they read about Wallace at all it is in connection with the theory of natural selection or Wallace's line. They do not read about his defense of psychic phenomena or phrenology, or his attacks on vaccination. If they come across discussions of Sir William Crookes, it is in connection with his discovery of thallium, his work with the cathode ray tube, and his invention of the radiometer. They are kept ignorant of his claims to have discovered a psychic force that enabled the medium Home to float or that allowed Florence Cook to materialize full-bodied spirits out of thin air. Similarly, they do not read about Newton's commitment to alchemical pursuits or Sir Oliver Lodge's studies of survival, and so forth.

Is it any wonder, then, that several scientists today endorse as genuine psychic feats the conjuring antics of Uri Geller? Or that others claim scientific evidence for the ability of certain individuals to project thoughts upon camera film? Or that still other competent scientists argue that we can cure cancer with large doses of vitamins?

If we keep future generations of scientists ignorant of the follies of some of their most accomplished ancestors, how can we hope to prevent repetitions of these very same follies? How can we learn lessons from examples that are banished from further consideration?

When I talk about cases of pathological science such as that of Wallace, I often get two related responses from scientists in the audience. One is that Wallace's situation occurred one hundred years ago. But it could not happen today, because we know more today and science has become more sophisticated. The other response is to the effect that Wallace or whatever example I happen to be using is a special case and that most scientists could not become trapped into such an error. Both these responses seem to me to illustrate beautifully what Zimbardo and his coauthors call "the illusion of personal invulnerability" (Zimbardo *et al.,* 1977). Both are a way of saying it cannot happen to me.

In fact, it not only can happen today, but appears to be happening with increasing frequency. Paradoxically, this very attitude that it cannot happen to "us" or to "me" contributes to the vulnerability of scientists to such pathologies. And the fact that the discrediting procedure keeps scientists unaware of the many failures by otherwise recognized scientists further contributes to this illusion of scientific and personal invulnerability. Scientists, as part of their education, hear only about the success of their great predecessors. The illusion is enhanced that science is much more a series of successes than is actually the case. By banishing the many and outstanding failures to a skeleton closet, both the scientists and the laymen become victims of the myth of scientific invulnerability and continue along a path of false security.

Another counterproductive aspect of this discrediting procedure is that sometimes otherwise promising students of science do go back and check upon the circumstances of the supposed debunking of a bizarre claim. They sometimes become antiscientific or cynical about the objectivity and rationality of science when they see how the establishment has reacted in putting down a heresy.

I could list other counterproductive consequences of the typical reaction of the scientific establishment to suspected heresies among their ranks. But I probably have suggested enough at least to raise questions in your mind about the advisability of continuing to condone such tactics just because they seem to be effective in keeping us from having to cope with uncomfortable embarrassments.

The Benefits of a More Appropriate Response

At this point, let me recapitulate my main points to forestall any misunderstandings that might arise. Maybe I can do this best by putting my message into a more positive format.

First, I want to make it clear that I am not defending unorthodoxy as such. Nor do I believe that most claims of pathological science deserve serious consideration in themselves. I do not believe, for example, that Wallace's claims about a psychic force have any chance of being true.

Second, I fully appreciate that it is very difficult and demanding to develop an effective and rational response to such bizarre hypotheses. I myself know how demanding and difficult this can be from my experiences in trying to be a responsible critic of parapsychological research.

Nevertheless, I strongly urge the scientific community to bring the pathologies out of the closet and to work openly towards developing a more appropriate and rational response. The fact that such pathologies have occurred and continue to occur should be taken as a sign that all is not well. At the very least, there are germs that can potentially contaminate much that will be done under the name of Science. The very fact that these pathologies are committed by otherwise competent scientists means that the response to them should be sober and scientific.

We need to keep the great failures as well as the great successes constantly before us—not just as reminders of our own vulnerability, but as the first step towards comparing and contrasting them in the hopes of finding out just what, if anything, led the very same scientists, such as Wallace, to recognized success in one instance and ignominious failure in another. At the very least, we can hope that such a step will prevent us from repeating identical mistakes in the future. At best, it might help us discover what it is about scientific thinking and procedures that leads to success and what it is that can produce failure. Or, as some historians and philosophers of science seem to be implying, it may teach us that any system for discovering truth has built-in limitations.

Furthermore, by insisting upon proper criticism and fair play in any critiques of heretical claims, we may move closer to a proper diagnosis of what actually went wrong. We focus on the claims and the evidence, and this forces the deviant scientist to respond with further replications, refinements, and controls. At the same time, it forces the critic not only to show that the proponent is wrong, but in what ways he or she went wrong. This could lead to better understanding about how trained scientists can be trapped into defending false systems.

If "pathologies" do exist in the sense that some of our best scientists defend bizarre positions, then like all sicknesses, they are a symptom of something. Something is wrong and requires remedy. We cannot discover what is wrong by bad diagnoses—by failing to acknowledge the disease exists, by preventing others from learning about it, or by isolating the disease from the main body of science. Good science requires good and effective criticism. Bad and irrational criticism, even when the object is bizarre or outrageous, benefits no one. In the short run it "discredits" the object of the attack; in the long run, however, it "discredits" science itself.

References

Carpenter, W. B. *Mesmerism, Spiritualism, & C.* New York: D. Appleton & Co., 1877.
George, W. *Biologist Philosopher: A Study of the Life and Writings of Alfred Russel Wallace.* London: Abelard-Schuman, 1964.
Langmuir, I. *Pathological Science.* Schenectady, N.Y.: General Electric Technical Information Series, No. 68-C-035 (April, 1968).
Palfreman, J. "William Crookes: Spiritualism and Science." *Ethics in Science and Medicine* 3 (1976), 211–27.

Wallace, A. R. *On Miracles and Modern Spiritualism: Three Essays.* London: James Burns, 1875.

Zimbardo, P. G., E. B. Ebbesen, & C. Maslach, *Influencing Attitudes and Changing Behavior.* (Second edition). Reading, Mass.: Addison-Wesley, 1977.

Commentaries on Hyman's "Pathological Science"*

Comments by Joseph Agassi

I find it hard to respond to Dr. Truzzi's kind invitation to comment on Ray Hyman's "pathological science" since I do not share so many of his background assumptions. I am in great sympathy with his proposal to keep an open mind about the paranormal, yet find his effort wasted on trite examples. But let me try.

It has been reported that a leading philosopher of science responded with alarm at the reported success of Rhine regarding parapsychology. If these reports were true—they are false, it turns out—then, he feared, his whole philosophy would collapse. It is amazing to me that this should be possible. Certainly, if the Rhine experiments were judged bona fide, or if flying dragons were as real as elephants and castles, then our view would need adjustments, since today we exclude them. It is clear that if clairvoyance were bona fide, this would call for a very radical change of our opinions about time and causation, no less than if Fred Hoyle were successful at obtaining signals from some future inhabitants of our own planet. Yet, somehow, we have to agree, it is good to have an idea of what is empirically impossible and to be ready to change one's mind when scientifically observing the allegedly impossible.

Certainly Hyman is right in advocating this, and certainly there are examples where the allegedly impossible was first denounced as hoax and then admitted as scientifically attested fact; at least one example is the midnight sun, and another is mesmerism. No doubt hypnosis is mesmerism sans some claims about its causes, its magnetism or what-have-you. No doubt, Mesmer unknowingly meddled in hysteria without knowing what he was doing. Nevertheless, it may be convincingly argued, were Mesmer's contemporaries more open-minded, the recognition of hypnotism could have come sooner.

It is a misfortune, however, that Hyman confuses this with bona fide

---

*Reprinted from *Zetetic Scholar* 6 (1980), 39–65. Reprinted by permission.

errors, whether a nonexistent planet claimed by a scientist to exist, or a similar nonexistent chemical element or radiation, etc. These bona fide errors do not at all resemble factual reports which are presumably impossible: when two people's opinions as to what is possible or impossible clash, there may be room for honest debate. Yet factual claims are a major weapon in a debate, and if they are ineffective perhaps it is better to give up the debate and write the opponent off as a mere dogmatist. The question, then, is, what are the conditions under which we must recognize and accept observation reports and thereby reject hypotheses which contradict them?

There is a traditional view of the matter, officially endorsed by the Royal Society of London from its very start and since then taken as a matter of course by the whole scientific community. It is first stated in Robert Boyle's *Certain Physiological Essays* of 1661, second essay, on the unsuccessful experiment. Boyle proposes this attitude and explains it at great length. He says that when an experiment is unrepeatable we need not call the one who has reported it a liar, but we should also not accept his report as true: we must suspend judgment until we can repeat the experiment. He gives two examples, one of a blind man who can sense color by his fingertips and one about white gold from Madagascar. Though he is suspicious of both, especially since the blind man senses, it is reported, black more strongly than white, he suspends judgment. White gold, we know, does exist; it is doubtless platinum. The blind man was used by Jonathan Swift in Gulliver's journey to Laputa. Since then the story has repeated itself a few times. I myself remember having read in a newspaper a few years ago that the blind man with the magic fingertips has reappeared, in Russia this time.

Boyle's proposal is no clear solution to the problem. It is, no doubt, always possible that an experiment is repeated two or three times, yet turns out to be unrepeatable. And vice versa. And there are examples for that from the annals of science. Yet, if an experiment was repeated, we do declare it repeatable. Are astronomical data repeatable and in what sense? Are psychoanalytic observations repeatable and in which sense? Surely phobia and conversion hysteria are, yet each case is observed as individual and as markedly different. Also, of course, many repeatable observations were mistakenly reported, including reports of discoveries of unknown elements in the sun (helium is the known example since it is, for all we know, the one truly observed in the solar spectra). Even when an experiment is repeatable, it is repeatable under specific conditions, some of which we know since we can vary them, some of which we do not know. This is a known fact, and Isaac Asimov based his novel *The Currents of Space* on it.

Are any paranormal experiments repeatable? Not to my knowledge. The fact that Rhine's experiments were faked is unimportant: were they repeatable his assistant's hand would not matter, and as they are not they do not matter either.

This raises the question, why do we insist on repeatability? The answer is given by Karl Popper: science equals testability equals repeatability. We want to be able to test the test, to refute the refuting observation. Suppose a refuting observation is repeatable. Do we have to endorse it and give up our theories? Karl Popper says, yes, or else the game is foul. I say, no, we may have a good excuse for rejecting an observation. But then the excuse has to be given and discussed. If it cannot be given, at the very least we must recognize this as a defect and explain why we tolerate it.

Suppose some paranormal evidence were indeed repeatable. To take Hyman's example, suppose every medium in a trance could produce a sunflower out of thin air upon request. This would be an enormous boon for people who frequent mediums, since they could always verify that the medium is (deep enough) in a trance by requesting that a sunflower be produced out of thin air. Will this convince me? I honestly do not know. Perhaps, following Michael Faraday, I would inquire why no medium opens a sunflower seed oil factory. If the answer be interesting, I would pursue it and I cannot now say with what impact. But I am exasperated by the fact that mediums claim to know such utter trivialities as details from my own past, rather than details of, say, Agamemnon's childhood, or of Elijah the prophet. My greatest complaint about all claims for the paranormal that I have ever met is that they are very boring.

It may be a matter of taste to decide what is boring. Some people find excitement in watching the wheel turn and decide whether someone standing by it be a millionnaire or a pauper. For my part, I find it a bore even if I would be fascinated and hypnotized to watch the wheel as everyone else does. And perhaps fascination is many people's substitute for interests, and perhaps this is why so many intelligent people are voluntarily using so much of their time on boring sets of data. There is no reason to think this interesting or useful in any way.

All paranormal discussions leave open important questions. Astrologers seldom ask, how could my moment of birth be so crucial to my career, how could the distant stars affect it? They do not ask, is extrasensory perception the communication of information with no channel or with a hitherto unknown one (as radio waves were but a century ago)? Necromancy practitioners and ghost seekers have no idea how the dead behave, what mentality they possess, etc. And, to my way of thinking, the study of the general psychology of ghosts is much more advisable a way to detect them than the study of rotating doorknobs and squeaky door hinges. The study of the paranormal is all too often an escape from thinking. Hence, the invitation to be open-minded about the paranormal often leads those who accept it to much frustration. Can this impasse be broken?

I do not mean my question rhetorically. The great W. B. Cannon, the inventor of homeostasis and author of *The Wisdom of the Body,* has claimed to have observed voodoo death, *i.e.,* murder by a magic spell. His observation was ignored until it was explained by a body reaction to chemicals produced by fear and by despair and after these chemicals were reported to have killed a laboratory rat. This story shows how unwilling we are to accept reports of paranormal facts until their paranormality is explained away. For my part I find the dogmatic hostility to the paranormal no less boring than what thus far goes under the banner of the paranormal.

Comments by Stephen Braude

I am in substantial agreement with Hyman about how scientists ought to respond to the radical or unorthodox proposals and hypotheses of their colleagues. And I agree that scientists often disgrace themselves and damage their profession through the manner in which they attack apparently heretical claims. But ironically, Hyman's paper appears simply to be a non-hysterical example of the sort of practice it purports to condemn.

Hyman first describes proponents of radical or unorthodox hypotheses as "deviant" scientists whose claims are ineptly or irrelevantly attacked by the scientific establishment. And as he discusses the undesirable impact of such procedures upon the scientific community, the reader is led to believe that Hyman wants to be a spokesman for a rational and fair assessment of such unorthodox claims. But then a sudden and revealing shift occurs in Hyman's dialectic. He begins by referring to the class of unorthodox or radical proposals as "failures" and "follies," even though he acknowledged earlier that pathological science sometimes attacks hypotheses that are later vindicated and incorporated into the body of accepted scientific knowledge. Moreover, this choice of words is not merely an isolated verbal slip. The remainder of the paper strongly supports the conclusion that Hyman (despite his apparently self-serving protestations to the contrary) is really an ally of those whose critical practices he decries.

I'll return to this last point shortly. But first I remark that there are no grounds, as far as I can see, for condemning the studies of D. D. Home as "failures," or Wallace's investigation of psychic forces as "ignominious failures." For example, Hyman's apparent assurance that the case is closed, so to speak, on Home flies in the face of the considered judgment of many competent people who have studied this material closely and thought about it (and associated issues concerning the acceptability of spontaneous case material in parapsychology) very carefully. It seems to me that, under the circumstances, a defender of *non*pathological science ought to be more agnostic, or at least open about the fact that others in the scientific community do not regard the Home case as closed.

I have a similar reaction to Hyman's indictment and cavalier dismissal of all studies of psychic photography as "follies." I am confident that Hyman realizes that many people have studied this material carefully (I suspect more carefully than he), and do not regard the case as closed on psychic photography either. In fact, I have studied this portion of the parapsychological literature rather closely recently, and in my view the shabby treatment of Jule Eisenbud's studies of Ted Serios would make an ideal example of the dishonest and intellectually cowardly criticism that Hyman thinks can only harm the scientific community. Again, it seems to me that the position Hyman ought to take—the one consistent with his objection to pathological science—is to ackowledge that such cases are still controversial, no matter what his own intuitions about such alleged phenomena might be. If Hyman were not a victim of the sort of pathology he describes, I would think he would not select currently debatable cases as examples of failures and follies in science.

Anyway, returning to the subtleties of Hyman's dialectic later in the paper, consider the force of the analogy from medicine he uses in his final paragraph. Hyman refers to the scientific defense of bizarre positions as "sicknesses," something requiring remedy. Apparently, Hyman has forgotten that he earlier admitted that in the history of science, some radical proposals, no matter how maligned they may have been at one time, later become incorporated into the body of science. It would appear that Hyman regards the "objective" study of radical proposals as merely a way of cleaning the scientific house by a respectable method. But he sees it as housecleaning nevertheless. (Analogously, I suppose, one might argue that it is better to remove a derelict from one's doorstep by asking him nicely to leave, rather than by kicking him bodily into the street. And of course, construed this way, what is at issue is the best way to get rid of something *undesirable*.) Hyman apparently does not see the scientific enterprise as one whose method permits not only the close scrutiny of radical proposals, but also their eventual acceptance if they pass the test of such scrutiny. A disease, after all, is something that *must* be destroyed. A radical proposal, however, may prove to be revolutionary and salutary.

Another telling feature of Hyman's discussion is his decision to call what should neutrally be designated as *radical, alternative,* or *unorthodox* positions as "bizarre." Some, of course, are. But to use this term throughout the paper to refer to the entire class of radical proposals is already prejudicial.

It seems to me, then, that Hyman does not really advocate the impartial, open-minded assessment of radical scientific claims, and that he is specifically unwilling to entertain seriously the radical proposals of parapsychology. His paper is only a plea to banish them in a way that preserves the surface integrity of the scientific community. To use the overworked terminology of Thomas Kuhn, Hyman's paper would seem to be a manifesto in defense of current normal science, and in fact appears to display a deep lack of confidence in the scientific method. And as a result, Hyman's description of pathological science turns out to be rather shallow, ignoring a very important kind of symptom of the pathology. It strikes me as significant and revealing that Hyman fails to observe (both in print and in practice) an important truth. The pathological response to radical scientific claims need not be manifest either in the shrill indictments or the supercilious disregard of those claims and their advocates. It may, instead, be expressed perniciously under the guise of objectivity and fair play. Like Brutus, perhaps, Hyman professes one set of attitudes and beliefs, and betrays another. One's dagger may be brandished openly or concealed under one's cloak. Real malevolence may be served either way.

Comments by Harold I. Brown

Thank you for the opportunity to comment on Hyman's excellent paper. I have two comments to offer.

1. If the notion of "pathological science" is to be of any use it must be defined much more narrowly than "the science of things that aren't so," or the defense of "false systems." Hyman recognizes that we must include cases of mistaken denials by scientists under this rubric, and that there will turn out to be much more pathological science than is usually recognized, but he does not make clear just how much of science will be pathological on this definition. Strictly speaking, idealizations such as the ideal gas laws and approximations such as that objects near the surface of the earth fall with constant velocity, are false. Similarly, much of the classical mechanics that still forms the basis of our physics courses is, from the point of view of relativity and quantum mechanics, strictly false. In contemporary physics there are a number of unsettled debates: there are competing gravitational theories and new disagreement over the exact value of the Hubble constant and the processes by which the sun produces its energy, about the existence of quarks, about the distance of quasars and the source of their energy, etc.; in each of these cases only one of the extant views could turn out to be true, and they may well all be false. The *normal course of science* requires the discussion and testing of many theses which are eventually rejected as false, and a definition which makes most science pathological is not very illuminating. If there is a useful distinction to be drawn between pathological and nonpathological science,

it must distinguish between those false views which are scientifically respectable and those which are not.

2. There is an assumption that many advocates of extrasensory perception, psychic forces, etc., share with their most vehement critics—*i.e.*, that if such phenomena exist, then, at the very least, there are phenomena that cannot be investigated in scientific terms, and perhaps the entire scientific approach to understanding the world around us is misconceived. There is no reason for accepting this assumption. Of course, if such phenomena do exist, then contemporary science will have to be supplemented, perhaps revised, but, as I have already indicated, this is happening regularly as a part of normal scientific research. Where the supposed challenge to science lies is in the claim that these phenomena are "supernatural" and thus not open to a scientific account. There is, however, no more basis for believing this to be true in the case of these putative phenomena than there was in the past for assuming that meteorites or dreams have a supernatural origin. Rather, if psychic phenomena and such do exist, then we have every reason to believe that they will be open to study by the usual processes of observation and theory construction.

Comments by Mario Bunge

I suppose that the thrust of Hyman's paper can be summarized thus. First, once in a while reputable scientists come up with unorthodox views that do not resist a careful rational or empirical analysis. Second, this suggests that there must be something wrong with the way we educate scientists. Third, the way such unorthodoxies are usually treated by the scientific community is often unscientific and always counterproductive.

I agree with all three theses, but I disagree with Hyman's claim that there is such a thing as *pathological science*. The very notion of pathological science seems to me to be just as self-contradictory as the notions of atheistic religion (or religous atheism), irrational logic, and illiterate literature. The examples of "pathological science" mentioned by Hyman, such as the hypotheses of psychic forces and of Martian canals, suggest that he has fused two essentially different categories under the single name "pathological science"—namely, pseudoscience and false science, or pseudoscientific beliefs on the one hand and scientific statements that have been proved false on the other.

This distinction is necessary, because science does not have the monopoly of truth. (The telephone directory of New York and even the Sears catalogue contains more true statements than all of the social sciences put together.) While science pursues truth, it is not characterized by truth, but rather by corrigibility. At any given time every science is full of falsities as well as of hypotheses that cannot be tested at the time. But science is self-correcting: far from regarding their hypotheses and data as dogmas, scientists put them to the test and, if the statements fail the tests, they attempt to replace them with truer hypotheses or data. Not so pseudoscience, which is a body of fixed beliefs rather than a field of research. What was "pathological," or rather contrary to the "spirit of science," was not Gall's hypothesis that mental functions are discharged by special subsystems of the brain, but the tenacity with which phrenologists clung to this hypothesis in the absence of experimental evidence. (Incidentally, contemporary physiological psychologists have independently revived Gall's general hypothesis; not, however, his particular cerebral map of the brain. Thus phrenology may be said to have had a grain of truth even though it was practiced in a typically pseudoscientific fashion.)

In science dissent and controversy are normal and healthy. In pseudoscience they are punishable heresy. (Remember how Freud treated Jung, Adler, and other dissenters?) In science controversy can be settled, at least in the long run, by observation, calculation, or rational argument. In pseudoscience controversy is either hushed up or dissolved by resorting to authority or even force.

To be sure, there is occasional data doctoring and deliberate cheating or stealing in the scientific community. But the former is eventually found out. (Remember the frauds committed by Sir Cyril Burt?) And malpractice can be exposed and punished. But such breaches of the *ethos* of science do not deserve to be put together with honest errors, such as errors of measurement or calculation, or mistakes, or the proposing of erroneous hypotheses. Let us keep the distinction between a mistake and a lie. There is nothing pathological about making mistakes; rather, what would be abnormal is hitting on the truth every time. Nor is it necessarily pathological to commit forgery under the guise of science: it is simply to indulge in a *non*scientific activity.

I submit, then, that: (a) no field of scientific research is free from error, but (b) in every such field one can discover errors and correct them; (c) dissent is of the essence of the scientific process, and the occasional pressure to suppress it in the name of the orthodoxy of the day is even more injurious to science than all the forms of pseudoscience put together; and (d) what is wrong with pseudoscience is not that it is wrong, but that it clings tenaciously to its tenets and does not make the slightest attempt to find any laws, or to harmonize its hypotheses with the bulk of science. In short, *there is no pathological science:* there are instead false scientific ideas, some dishonest researchers, and nonscientific belief systems parading as scientific. There is also, among scientists as well as laymen, a remarkable ignorance about the philosophical underpinnings of science and such general concepts as hypothesis, rule, theory, evidence, and inference: such ignorance *is* pathological.

So much for diagnosis. As for treatment, I would propose that every science student should be exposed to one course in each of these fields: logic, philosophy and methodology of science, and history of science (if possible his own). But not *any* logic: modern, *i.e.,* mathematical logic rather than Aristotelian logic. And not *any* philosophy of science: only one done by someone who knows what he is talking about through having engaged himself in scientific research, rather than someone who has never come near it or has become disenchanted with it. And not *any* history of science either, but one that, as Hyman demands, tells us about "the great failures as well as the great successes"; one teaching us that doing science is not hoarding truths but searching for more accurate and deeper truths as well as for more reliable research methods.

Of these three remedies the second is the most difficult to procure. Indeed most philosophers have had no experience of scientific research, and they have been exposed mostly to nonscientific philosophies that place either authority or sophistry higher than agreement with mathematics and the science of the day. Therefore it may be best for scientists to try their hand at building a philosophy of science that at least agrees with their own research experience. Still, they should not ignore professional philosophers in the process: they ought to engage in dialogue with them. There are at least two ways students can derive benefit from such cross-disciplinary discussions. One is by inviting them to participate in group discussions. Another is by organizing faculty courses on the philosophy of science (or of psychology, or social science, or any other field of scientific research). Who knows: a new philosophy of science, one relevant to live science, may be born from some such attempts.

Comments by Roger Cooter

To accept Hyman's paper as merely a joke intended to solicit replies, is to miss the fact that it is a well-conceived caricature of uncritical academic thinking. As belied by the unscholarly dogmatism of "a *proper* diagnosis and remedy," this surely is one of those clever end-of-the-session papers designed gently to mock the political and social naivete of science's practitioners, historians, and philosophers. With a few good strokes and well-sustained tongue-in-cheek, Hyman has skillfully written himself into a Dickensian script: the mixture of Smilesean values, pneumatic pumps, phrenology, and chemistry that the Uncommercial Traveller encountered in the Dullborough Mechanics' Institute in the early nineteenth century is updated by Hyman to the American Association for the Advancement of Science at its annual meeting in, appropriately, San Francisco.

If Hyman did not intend his paper as a caricature, then there would indeed be cause to worry about his critical poverty and about how a "learned" audience could have been duped. The possibility that a part of Hyman's audience might have missed the joke and taken this junk propaganda seriously is a frightening thought, and on that account his paper merits comment.

By "junk propaganda" I refer of course to the paper's obvious manipulative tactics rather than to its contents per se. To anyone who has studied science from a critical social perspective, the contents of Hyman's paper will not appear as problematic, for the issue of the "truth" or "falsehood" of the paranormal is irrelevant. After more than a decade of sociological inquiry into scientific knowledge and practice, no one doubts that "scientific truth" is, as Sir James Fraser said of truth, "merely the hypothesis which is found to work best" in any given socioeconomic and cultural context. Thus from a social perspective what would be interesting about Hyman's paper (if it were straight) would not be the matter of the "scientific truth" that he hopes will be advanced through the creation of a scientific community receptive to the (ill-named) "pathological science," but rather, the way in which, by failing to question the cultural specificity of modern scientific truth, Hyman legitimates its superiority. In part this legitimation is overt, through the lauding of orthodox science and its practitioners as rational, responsible, and rigorous and dedicated to refining, improving, and correcting through a process of debate and interaction out of which supposedly issues the wonderful one and only "objective reality." More interesting, however, is the way the wisdom of modern science is covertly celebrated by the diversionary tactic of appealing to the scientific community for open-mindedness: On the face of it, Hyman seems to be suggesting the illegitimacy of the demarcation between science and "pseudoscience." But in fact nothing is further from his mind; he accepts that there is "true" and "false" science and requests only that orthodox science (which is otherwise irreproachable) give some consideration to "deviant" sciences before wholly or partially rejecting them. In retaining the dichotomy between true and false knowledge, Hyman reveals himself as locked within what Harry Collins calls a "sociology of error," which claims to "explain" false science only by reference to orthodox science, and by that process reinforces belief in the latter's supposed value-neutral veracity. Hyman is also, of course, feigning ignorance of the fact that modern science mediates only a partial view of reality—one that treats the world as a set of interacting facts in which human essences are separated out in the dichotomies of fact/value, science/ scientism, science/ideology, science/pseudoscience, science/society—and is further pretending (?) to have no idea that this positivist "thingifying" view of reality was historically created (largely in the seventeenth century when constitutive with the "scientific revolution" was the reification of labor through the ascendance of a bourgeois capitalist class). The way in which this ignorance of the history and philosophy of science leads to the reproduction of uncritical support for the dominant ideological mode of scientific thought is nicely illustrated in Hyman's acceptance of Langmuir's term *pathological science,* meaning "the science of *things* that aren't."

Mostly Hyman accomplishes his celebration of science's reifying (capitalist-constituted) ideology through an empty-headed (naive liberal) desire to have others share his open-mindedness. But in the failure to mention Wallace's commitment to socialism must be seen a *deliberate* attempt to underwrite the orthodox scientific audience's unquestioned and self-righteous belief in the superiority of their way of viewing the world. Wallace's socialism is as well-known as his interests in phrenology, antivaccination, spiritualism, and the transmutation of species, and the failure to mention it is as gross as the failure decried by Hyman of considering Wallace's contribution to evolutionary theory without considering Wallace's phrenology and spiritualism. Anyone uncritically steeped in scientific rationalism, attempting to treat Wallace's beliefs without treating the political and social outlook that gave those beliefs a delicate coherence, naturally comes to the mistaken conclusion that Wallace's mind was fragmented into orthodox and unorthodox scientific compartments. (Does Hyman interpret all sincerely religious scientists in a similarly unreal way?) Obviously, he has no idea of the glass house he lives in, nor has he ever been warned about the danger of throwing stones.

Hyman's pastiche makes crystal clear what is really vital in considering "pathological" in relation to "orthodox" science. By focusing on the bogus question of the "costs" of the orthodox scientific community's rejection of the "pathological" and thus revealing to us the sorts of metaphors that come easiest to the kind of mind being caricatured, Hyman succeeds in making us aware of the question begged: what are the human consequences of this point of view being taken seriously? The paper leaves little doubt that the answer must be the extension of orthodox science's philosophical hegemony—the "metrication," as it were, of spiritualist and other deviant "extra-scientific" activities. Hyman nicely illustrates the classic liberal tactic of gelding what threatens to upset orthodoxy by enfranchising it into the dominant preordained scheme of things. With paranormal deviancy *already within* the academy, Hyman offers the means by which the orthodox scientific community can both save face and further assert its authority and dominance: the orthodox scientific community has only to admit that it has let its "traditional" open-mindedness slip. Therewith one can begin the historical rerun of the cultural imperialism of orthodox science. But there is an interesting historical difference: whereas (as Everett

Mendelsohn has revealed) the second generation in the Scientific Revolution in the seventeenth century discarded alchemy, astrology, and the like in order to erase awareness of the social and ideological construction of their natural knowledge and thus enhance their authority on the basis of an image of heavenly descended pure truth, the modern inheritors of that subjective (so-called "objective") knowledge must now take back the deviant discards in order to retain the image of the objectivity in their pursuits.

The naivete that Hyman projects in his paper should also serve among spiritualists and other lay practitioners of "pathological" sciences to instill awareness of the social and ideological interests that lie beyond what they might otherwise take simply as sincere scientific curiosity in their knowledge and activities. (Hyman, or Hyman's persona, they will see, is the "nice guy" in history to whom Mannheim alerted us: his goods are all the more worthy of critical inspection for their being offered innocently as face-value commodities.) Spiritualists ought now to be conscious of what is so self-evident as to be often forgotten: that in attempting to recover the inner spirit of man they mediate and practice the antithesis of the worldly reifying materialism of modern rationalist science. It is no coincidence that the widespread interest in spiritualism of Wallace's mid- and late-Victorian generations occurred at that moment in history when the central contradiction of industrial capitalist "progress" was revealed most nakedly—*i.e.,* man's dehumanized alienation from man as a result of the ruthless exploitation of labor conceived of as a mere commodity. Though spiritualism was for the most part an unconscious and individualistic response to people's soul destruction under advanced capitalism, in its attempt to restore to people something of their human essence, it can be seen as an untheoretical non-materialist complement to the socialist project. Although spiritualism has never been concerned with rearranging social structures and relations, it nevertheless offers, as socialism does, a means of fighting against the socio-economically constituted corset mediated by the scientific productions of the Newtons, Carpenters, and Darwins.

Insofar as Hyman's paper alerts us to all of this through its blatant disregard of history and unawareness of science as a social and cultural product, it performs a useful heuristic service. Much more could of course be said about the built-in absurdities of the attempt "to bring the pathologies out of the closet," but all else is largely contingent upon the two interconnected points raised here: (1) that the plea for orthodox science to be open-minded about the claims of "false science" deflects attention from the social and ideological constituents of modern science that are harbored in the imagined dichotomy and thus *pari passu* strengthens faith in the illusion of modern science's objectivity, and (2) that behind the plea for open-mindedness is the attempt to bring deviant scientific activity within the hegemony of orthodox science and hence extend the hegemony whilst castrating heterodox science of its actual and potential value to mediate alternative social and human interests and meanings.

For so cleverly caricaturing all of this, Hyman deserves to be commended.

Comments by Allen G. Debus

Ray Hyman is quite right in asserting that the history of science has traditionally perpetuated the myth of the constant advance of "real" science—and that abnormal science (if judged from our present viewpoint) has not been examined with the care that it deserves. However, this situation has been changing in the past two decades. There has been an increasing interest in the alchemical studies of Isaac Newton, the mystical views of Johannes Kepler, and even the meaning of natural magic in the thought of Francis Bacon. And in addition to the mechanical philosophy, we now have some understanding of Hermetic and Paracelsian influences on the development of the Scientific Revolution. In short, there is a new picture of the rise of modern science—one in which nonmodern elements play an essential role.

However, one should contrast the free interplay of the "occult" and the "scientific" in the period of the Renaissance with the period after the mid-seventeenth century. The development of scientific societies after 1660 made possible the emergence of a scientific establishment having the power to admit to their ranks those with similar beliefs and to exclude those with whom they disagreed. And the simultaneous publication of the first scientific journals ensured the dominance of the mechanical philosophy. These developments have affected the scientific enterprise since that time. The views of Wallace and Crookes on spiritualism might well have been tolerated had they flourished in 1600. Such would not have been the case a century later.

There is little doubt that if the historian of science hopes to understand Wallace and Crookes he must study their thought *in toto*. That is, he must study both their "occult" and their "scientific" views. That is the only way in which we will be able to comprehend the key figures in the development of the sciences. To this extent I am in complete agreement with Hyman. However, I do not think it is practical to extend this method to the present. Most of the proponents of "deviant" scientific views today are to be found among the occultists. Perhaps we could begin by turning to some concepts held by otherwise renowned scientists that are condemned by their colleagues, but if we do, we would soon find ourselves deluged with a flood of cranks demanding that the same attention be paid to their own pet theories. One need only recall that Michael Faraday devoted himself to the exposure of spiritualism in the closing years of his life only to give up the task as hopeless. Today there are astronomers who regularly seek to expose astrology, while the American Association for the Advancement of Science recently devoted one session to an examination of the claims of Velikovsky. Little is to be expected from such efforts since these people thrive on the attention paid to them—even when such attention is negative. Commenting on the statement against astrology signed by 186 leading scientists several years ago, Vivienne Killinsworth rightly noted that "the spectacle of the Scientific Establishment bashing astrology is only likely to increase astrology's underground appeal. The comment of one of the prime movers behind the [scientists'] statements, to the effect that he makes it a practice to denounce astrology every five years, can only give heart to his opponents."

I would conclude then that if we are interested in the development of modern science we must endeavor to place the work of earlier savants in their proper context. We must not define such work only in terms of the present. Hyman is absolutely correct in calling for a study of the total work of Wallace and Crookes. But to recommend an examination of all "pathological" science today would open doors to occultists as it did in the nineteenth century. I doubt whether an open dialogue would develop— only charges and countercharges by those who cannot really understand each other.

Comments by Gerald L. Eberlein

The "pathological science" situation is no peculiar situation, but rather a phase of aparadigmatic science or antiparadigmatic science. The scientist or the scientific community concerned with the controversial topic does not yet have a theory or, better, a research program (Lakatos), a paradigm, or more precisely, a disciplinary matrix (Kuhn). In the language of the structuralist or nonstatement view (Sneed, Stegmüller) no theory core exists, nor could the researcher/scientific community afford the intended applications of a theory core. As Kuhn, Stegmüller, and others have shown, this shortcoming has been blamed on the researchers as personal incompetence in the situation, "science in crisis." In my opinion this applies even more so if the aparadigmatic phase of the discipline under formation is evasive or even hostile toward the meta-paradigm of predominating normal science.

References

J. D. Sneed, *The Logical Structure of Mathematical Physics.* Dordrecht, 1971.

J. D. Sneed, W. Stegmüller, T. S. Kuhn, and C. Ulises Moulines, *Symposium on Theory Change of the Fifth International Congress of Logic, Methodology and Philosophy of Science* (London, Ontario, 27 August–2 September, 1975), *Erkenntnis,* 10 (1976).

W. Stegmüller, *The Structuralist View of Theories.* New York, 1979.

Comments by Paul Feyerabend

The first and, to my mind, most fitting reply to Ray Hyman's conundrum is: who cares? If scientists cannot get on with each other, then this is *their* problem. There is no reason why anyone else should get into the act, or be interested in its ramifications.

The reply assumes that science is an association of people sharing certain interests and beliefs, that it is a kind of *club.* A club has every right to insist on criteria for membership and to expel those who do not conform to the criteria. The work of the members occasionally pleases outsiders and may even be supported by them (use of clairvoyants by the police). This does not mean that the interests and the beliefs of the club members are the only interests and beliefs that count and that internal conflicts about them concern everyone. It only means that *some* people *sometimes* like the products (the ideas, the procedures, the gadgets) the club has to offer.

Today only few people regard science as a club in this sense. The attitude is rather that scientific procedures and the results that emerge from them are parts of the *right way.* Science is therefore taught in schools as providing the only kind of knowledge that counts; the judgment of scientists and of quasi-scientific organizations such as the American Medical Association plays a major role in public affairs; scientific activities are supported by tax money, just as the Roman Catholic hierarchy was once supported by the tithe—as a matter of course. Science is a *church*—and salvation is not possible outside of it. Small wonder that domestic quarrels of scientists tend to become a public malaise.

Regarding science as a church has a variety of consequences, none of them desirable.

A person engaged in a difficult project has only finite resources (time, money, brains, patience) at his disposal. He cannot possibly consider and argue against every idea and procedure that differs from his own. Still, he has to make a choice. Naturally, he will choose ideas and procedures he likes, is familiar with, and can defend to a certain extent. If he belongs to a club—say, the club of high energy physicists—then the shared assumptions of the club will provide further boundary conditions for his choice. Whatever the basis—the choice will contain a large *subjective component,* which reflects his inability to examine and to close all alternative routes. Presenting his case in an honest and straightforward way the researcher will therefore say: "This is my research program and this is the method I have chosen to check, defend, and perhaps to improve it. I am aware that there are many alternatives; I have studied some of them, I have heard about others, I know there are many more I have never heard about and may never encounter. I can give you some reasons for my choice. The reasons are neither conclusive nor complete. As a matter of fact, they hardly count in face of all the problems and objections that still remain. I can also tell you why I have not chosen the alternatives known to me— but even here you will notice that my reasons are quite thin in places; I just didn't have the time and patience to work out all the details. The rest I simply disregard not because they are obviously wrong, or can be shown to be wrong, but because I had to make a choice, and this is the choice I and my friends at the club find most attractive. I hope you will like what we have come up with—but I quite understand if you disagree and prefer some other approach. After all, your ideas and presuppositions may be very different from mine and those of the club." It is clear that such an attitude cannot possibly lead to the problems raised by Hyman.

It is equally clear that most scientists and almost all philosophers of science not only do not practice this kind of honesty, but explicitly discourage it. Blinded by the myth of the Right Way they feel constrained to give "objective" reasons for their choice: the excluded alternatives—*all* excluded alternatives—were not just omitted, they did not deserve being considered. Of course, the task cannot be carried out. Most alternatives are unknown to the scientists in the field in question, and many are above the heads of the average practitioners (it would take a nuclear physicist years to understand even the elements of Aristotle; and the average training in acupuncture and the associated philosophy takes from ten to twenty years). What scientists do in such circumstances is the following: they interpret the discomfort they feel in the presence of unusual ideas as a clear perception of the worthlessness of the ideas and so transform their own personal or group idiosyncrasies into "objective" criteria of excellence. This "objectiviza-tion of the subjective" explains the simplistic and downright infantile character of arguments against "bizarre" deviations. (Example: the *Humanist's* encyclical against astrology, signed by almost 200 scientists, 18 Nobel prizewinners among them. It is a monument of conceited illiteracy. And note how easily W. B. Carpenter, whom Hyman quotes, turns a questionable metaphysical principle into a condition of honesty and scientific good sense.) The similarity to the arguments some less gifted theologians raised against the motion of the earth is astounding, but not at all surprising: the predicament of the "objectivization of the subjective" is shared by all churches.

However, there is no reason why the sciences should be dragged into this predicament. True, scientists now play a role that is in many respects similar to the role bishops and cardinals played not too long ago—but that cannot prevent us from cutting them down to size. True, science has been quite successful in *some* areas—but this does not mean that it should be imposed on *everything* and be regarded as the one and only measure of knowledge and even of humanity. Scientists invented an atom bomb; put a few wrapped-up bodies on a dried-out stone, the moon; found the structure of DNA; improved chemical warfare—but this does not mean that they and nobody else will be able to cure cancer, restore man's harmony with nature, or make a contribution to our spiritual lives. Besides, it is difficult to judge success without the help of alternatives. Scientific medicine is often praised for the tremendous contributions it made to our lives— but how would it fare in a competition with traditional Chinese medicine that explores not only those few areas where Western medicine is obviously ahead (surgery, for example) but the *entire* domain of sickness and health? *We do not know,* because we have no control groups (groups treated by Chinese medicine only). And we have no control groups because scientists have turned unchecked principles of their activity into conditions of sound medicine and so prevented the practice of alternative forms of medicine (*cf.* the remark on W. B. Carpenter made earlier): the church aspect of scientific enterprises very cleverly prevents us from checking their efficiency. We must also realize that success always means success *with respect to certain values:* for a mystic who can face God in all His splendor the moon shots are a monumental exercise in futility. Result: there is not the slightest reason to turn the local ideas and principles of special enterprises, such as scientific medicine or elementary particle physics, into standards of rationality, and there exist weighty objections against this procedure.

Now in a *free society* all values and all traditions have equal rights. Traditions different from science must be given equal access to tax money, public instruction, and public decision making—no matter what other traditions think about them. If the Roman Church is separated from the State, then the Church of Science must also be separated from the State. If the Church of Science receives public funds, then the Roman Church must receive public funds, too. Giving all traditions equal rights in this sense also means an increased ability to judge the products of every one of them (*cf.* my brief remarks about the use of control groups in medicine): the church aspect of science conflicts both with the right of people to live as they see fit and with their right to judge the institutions they support and whose products they use. Science in a free society is therefore one church, one club, one private association among many, very much like an overgrown local theater group, or a sock factory, or a flat-earth society. It will be encouraged and financed, and its products will be used as long as it performs in accordance with wishes of the buyers. Financial support will be withdrawn as soon as the citizens prefer other products (support for scientific cancer research will be drastically reduced as soon as the citizens decide to give acupuncture a chance). Internal quarrels among scientists, however, are of no greater interest than the quarrels, within auto factories, about the shape of next year's cars. They are bothersome for practical reasons (delay in the production of new cars)—they have no deeper significance.

Comment by Antony Flew

The clues we need are in Hume's *Inquiry concerning Human Understanding*. He begins Section X by distinguishing the merely marvelous from the authentically miraculous, notwithstanding that he can on his own principles have no means of so doing (Flew 1961). Ray Hyman by contrast starts from an imaginary example. A colleague reports that, in a scrupulously supervised seance in his home, the medium materialized a sunflower. This sensational alleged performance is then described, very weakly, as "phenomena that cannot be accounted for by currently accepted principles." But, we should remind ourselves, phenomena satisfying that description come ten a penny: it must apply to everything in every new field still without the scope of present theories.

It is only with his second bite at the cherry, in treating the actual case of Alfred Russel Wallace on spiritualism, that Hyman begins to speak of a "phenomenon or relationship that is considered to be bizarre or even impossible by currently accepted scientific principles." Nevertheless, although he is here holding the critical clue in his hands, Hyman does not recognize it as such. The crux is that the rejectors, whether rightly or wrongly, believe that they possess overwhelmingly good reason for dismissing the alleged phenomena. This they do: not merely as unaccountable by currently accepted scientific principles, or unmanageably bizarre and marvelous; but also, much more reasonably, as just plumb impossible. They appeal, or at any rate they should appeal, to nomological propositions which are contantly tested and—it would appear—never found wanting in the daily living of scientists, technologists, and plain men. In particular perhaps, they appeal to some "basic limiting principles" seeming somehow prior to and more fundamental than even the oldest and best established of named laws of nature. (See on this, for instance, Broad 1978.)

But, you may say, is it not always conceivable that, for once, and at last, the outsider is right; that this alleged phenomenon does genuinely occur; and that it is now high time for everyone to shake up their fossilized old notions of what is and is not, as a matter of contingent fact, impossible? Yes indeed, it is conceivable; as the Humean ought to be the first to admit. Did not the good David himself labor to destroy "that implicit faith and security, which is the bane of all reasoning and free inquiry" (p. 26)? Yes, but, but, but. The heretical claims being considered here are all singular, and in the past tense: on such and such an occasion the medium said this, and then that sunflower materialized out of nothing; and so on, and so on, and on. So, in assessing the evidence for the truth of every such singular historical claim, we have to appeal to all which we know about what is probable or improbable, possible or impossible. For how else can the critical historian proceed? Yet in that appeal to the essential criteria of critical history the case for the miraculous collapses. At the very most, it can return a noncommittal and typically Scottish verdict: "Not proven."

If we are really to be required to shake up our notions of what is possible and impossible, then we need to be confronted: not with a singular past-tense proposition, which it is now too late to put to any direct test; but with an open general hypothetical, which can in principle be tested and retested at any time and in any place. We need, to put it less philosophically, a repeatable phenomenon. It would also help if the supposedly impossible could be naturalized by the excogitation of a fresh theory simultaneously explaining both these recalcitrant occurrences and a whole lot else of undisputed authenticity.

References

C. D. Broad, "The Relevance of Psychical Research to Phliosophy," in *Philosophy*, XXIV (1949), reprinted in J. Ludwig (Ed.), *Philosophy and Parapsychology* (Buffalo, N.Y.: Prometheus, 1978), pp. 43–63.

A. G. N. Flew, *Hume's Philosophy of Belief* (New York: Humanities, 1961), chap. 8.

———, "Parapsychology: Science or Pseudo-Science?," *Pacific Philosophical Quarterly*, I (1980).

D. Hume, *Enquiries concerning Human Understanding and concerning the Principles of Morals*, ed. L.A. Selby-Bigge and rev. P. H. Nidditch (Oxford: Clarendon, 1975).

Comments by J. N. Hattiangadi

Hyman's call for "fair criticism" is indeed a valuable reminder that even views we find outrageous deserve a fair hearing. There is evidence in the history of science, moreover, that "pathological" science had a great part to play in the development of what we today interpret as "healthy." Luigi Galvani, for instance, illustrated his idea of a special electricity of life by making a frog's leg twitch—after it had been amputated—by inserting lead and zinc pins into it. This is a science of "things that aren't so." But Volta, who thought otherwise, argued that it is not the frog's leg, but the metals which give rise to electricity. He constructed a stack of alternating sheets of metal separated by a dilute acid. This is a great scientific discovery, *even though Volta was doing "unhealthy" science, too!* For we now know that the metal electrodes in a voltaic cell get their charge from the *solution* in the middle, not from the metal. Two "pathologies," it seems, led to a "healthy" result.

But this doesn't mean that every bizarre idea must be followed up and fairly criticized. That advice is impossible to follow, because we have limited time and resources to examine every wild idea that comes up before us. Sometimes what appears "pathological" is nevertheless valuable. A faithful history of science is a history of some "pathological" science that nevertheless had valuable consequences. But only *some* "pathologies" played a part, and most were useless, in the past and today. A scientist's choice of what to study, to attack, to defend, or to research cannot depend on the sense of what is right and what is not. Science is always teaching us about new, undreamt-of possibilities, and so scientists must always be open-minded. Nevertheless, scientists must choose. How?

By and large, the question of what to consider for study and what to ignore does not depend on whether a point of view is plausible or not. Very few great scientific theories have initial plausibility. They *seem* at first to be about things "that aren't so." They are nevertheless given serious attention, because *they are solutions to difficult relevant problems of the science in question.* Every science at any time has some central problems around which research is conducted. Some of these are technological problems, some problems of applied science, and some of a purely abstract variety. It is this focus of scientific interest which determines what to study and what to ignore.

What is scientific and what is not is therefore different from age to age—there is no eternal demarcation of scientifically "healthy" from "pathological" science. At any given time, however, there are irrelevant speculations, and relevant ones. Only the relevant ones deserve consideration. Relevance in science is relevance to its own set of important problems.

The general analysis of how ideas are relevant to the state of a science is a large question, beyond the scope of this comment.[1] It is clear intuitively, however, that Wallace's "psychic force" would not solve any problem of nineteenth-century biology—or psychology.

There was a time in the history of science when it was believed that the Scientific Revolution (from Copernicus to Newton) produced the true and final laws of motion. Science, on this account, was the *establishment,* once and for all, of the truth. The scientist could hope to do this only if he or she abstained from believing corrupt nonscientific speculation. When scientists held this view of science, they were always embarrassed by and hostile to other scientists who held peculiar views. These views would naturally seem to "discredit" science.

Today we learn from Darwin's revolution in biology, Einstein's in physics, and the ferment in new subjects like biophysics, sociology, and economics, that though scientific laws are the very best, they are not necessarily the true and final ones. We do not need to feel embarrassed by a piece of "pathological" science. If it is relevant to our problems, we should give it the criticism it deserves—after all, it may lead to great results (*pace* Galvani and Volta). If it is irrelevant, we ignore it. There is no evidence that idiosyncratic views of any scientist have ever damaged the development of scientific knowledge. But the scientist cannot spend all his time attacking superstitions, or even criticizing them fairly.

Reference

1. *Cf.* J. N. Hattiangadi, "The Structure of Problems," Parts I & II, *Philosophy of the Social Sciences,* 8 (4) (December 1978), and 9 (1) (March 1979).

Comments by Seymour H. Mauskopf

I experienced a strange oscillation of sentiment, from hearty agreement to intense objection, in reading Hyman's paper. I think that my reaction was a reflection of a contradiction, or at least ambivalence, internal to the paper, which I would state as follows: Hyman calls for a "more appropriate and rational" response from the scientific community to deviant or "pathological" scientific claims than the usual crude, ill-supported *ad hominem* accusations and innuendos. But he does so not in the interest of really open-minded discussion of unsettling assertions but rather the more effectively to lay them to rest: to disarm the recalcitrant deviant, to show him the error of his folly, and to admonish the naive who might be similarly tempted to go astray. Whatever else "more appropriate and rational" might mean, the phrase, as used in this context, clearly means "prejudged" response.

Hyman would enlist the services of Clio in his proposed program, and it is to his uses of the history of science that I shall devote the bulk of my remarks. His proposal is, *prima facie,* something with which I can only concur: that the total activities of past scientists be taken into account and not just the achievements which get recounted in the introductions to scientific textbooks. In particular, he would have brought to light those activities of some past scientists which have been forgotten or suppressed because of their disreputable aura: Newton's alchemy and A. R. Wallace's interest in spiritualism, to cite two of his examples. But as a historian of science, I take vigorous exception to his purpose in unearthing this material, which is to teach contemporary scientists lessons from "the follies of some of their most accomplished ancestors . . . to prevent repetitions of these same follies." His "pathological" metaphor is clearly a considered one here: like anaerobic bacteria in a dank sewer, the pseudoscientific heresies of the past will continue to fester down the dark corridors of time unless brought into the light and air by diligent scholars.

My own aim as historian of science is quite different, even if at first glance it might seem to share similarities with Hyman's. In dealing with scientists (and science) of the past, I try to delineate the scientific outlooks and systems of belief as comprehensively as possible and to avoid, as far as possible, obtruding my own presuppositions into my analysis and understanding. If, for example, Aristotle believed in the perfection of circular motion (as did Copernicus and Galileo, for that matter), he must have had good reason within his system of scientific thought, and it behooves me to try to understand this belief rather than to condemn it out of hand as a wrong-headed aberration. By extension, the same applies to Newton and alchemy, and to Wallace and spiritualism.

I give Hyman credit for calling for an end to achievement-oriented assessment of past science and scientists, but it seems to me that his scheme leads to the same result; indeed would even reinforce it since positive achievements of scientists are now to be set in relief against their more "pathological" interests. ("We need to keep the great failures as well as the great successes constantly before us.") And how does one assess what was "pathological" if not in terms of presentist presuppositions? What other criteria, after all, could possibly define "the science of things that weren't so"? The game is given away by Hyman's list of scientific pathologies; why, for instance, denial of meteorites before 1800 should be considered "pathological" while mid-nineteenth-century denial of the existence of a planet within Mercury's orbit be deemed "scientific" utterly escapes me unless "scientific" is to be defined according to the criteria of what we happen to believe to be true today. But if this is how we are to judge the creditability of past scientific activity, then the history of science becomes a futile exercise indeed. More honest, in my opinion, simply to go on to chronicle past scientific achievements à la "textbook" history of science.

Moreover, Hyman's dichotomy between healthy and pathological science leads him to distort somewhat the historical context of his principal exemplar, A. R. Wallace. First of all, Hyman seems to imply (or to assume?) that Wallace was (or must have been?) a bifurcated individual with two unrelated interests, one scientific and the other pathological. Even if it be granted that, concerning the reception of his ideas, there "was a forced compartmentalization of Wallace's orthodox biology and his unorthodox psychical inquiries into separate worlds," this compartmentalization by no means applied to Wallace's own scientific thought, as Malcolm Jay Kottler has recently shown.[1] Wallace's psychical beliefs have to be taken into account to understand fully his ideas on evolution. This is hardly what I expect Hyman has in mind in having Wallace's spiritualistic interests dredged up.

Secondly, Hyman's characterization of Wallace's psychical audience as a "world of individuals who were outcasts or nonentities with respect to the scientific establishment" shows ignorance of the intellectual distinction of the leadership of the Society for Psychical Research, for instance, which included both outstanding scientists and others like Henry Sidgwick who certainly held the esteem of the scientific and academic communities. This is not to deny that the spiritualist-psychical research movements encompassed (and still do) socially, professionally, and intellectually diverse sets of people, but Hyman's oversimplification can only appear tenable to those who must assume what they wish to see proven.

Beyond my professional objections as a historian of science to Hyman's scheme, I fail to see how it furthers the cause of science today. Hyman seems to be most exercised over parapsychological claims (along with therapeutic claims for ascorbic acid). But what is so terrible about a scientifically trained person taking an interest in these claims? Why must he be insulated ideologically from them? And finally, to play devil's advocate: While I do applaud Hyman's call for a fuller and more equitable response to "pathologies," I would query why the scientific community should bother to invest more of its resources to answer pathological claims if it has indeed prejudged them as such to begin with? Such investment could only be worthwhile in the expectation that reasoned, careful consideration of such claims might yield concrete scientific advance. But I presume that Hyman himself has no such expectation; elsewise he would not have placed these claims under the rubric of "pathologies."

If parapsychology indeed be a "pathology" (though how we are to know except in hindsight of future knowledge escapes me), then better to conserve scientific resources and continue the traditional indifference and inattention of the greater part of the scientific community. But, of course, if there should prove to be something to parapsychological claims, then Hyman's scheme would be worse than useless; it would be pernicious. And he himself might well face the prospect of being dubbed "pathological" by a future policeman of scientific thought, much as he has stigmatized the opponents of meteors of two centuries ago.

Reference

1. Malcolm Jay Kottler, "Alfred Russel Wallace, the Origin of Man, and Spiritualism, " *Isis, 65* (1974), 145–192.

Comments by Andy Pickering

In his paper, Ray Hyman defends two propositions concerning anomalous observation reports in science.[1] The first is that "good science requires good and effective criticism," and that therefore unusual claims should not be denied access to the scientific community simply because they are unusual. Rather, they should be as widely discussed as possible, in order to facilitate constructive criticism. This proposition I entirely agree with, and I will not discuss it further. However, there is a second proposition—or, better, presumption—which permeates Hyman's argument, and with which I wish to take issue. This presumption, which I believe to be false, is crystallized in the following quotation: "If 'pathologies' do exist in the sense that some of our best scientists defend bizarre positions, then like all sicknesses, they are a symptom of something. Something is wrong and requires remedy."

That this argument is false can be shown through counterexamples. Bizarre positions often prove to be justified. For instance, it is well known that there were many reported sightings of stones falling from the sky— i.e., meteorites—before this bizarre idea was clasped to the bosom of scientific orthodoxy.[2] A second, possibly less well-known, example, which I will discuss, concerns the first observation of parity violation, which was made in the 1920s, although the existence of parity violation did not become established until the 1950s. One could extend the list of "prediscoveries" indefinitely and, since the bizarre positions of the prediscoverers have since become part of present-day reality, one would surely not wish to say that their defense of those positions was a symptom of any sickness.

Now, how does the observation of stones falling from the sky differ from Alfred Russel Wallace's reports of the materialization of six-foot sunflowers and the like, and from Langmuir's "pathological science" in general? In nothing more, I would suggest, than that meteorites are now accepted belief while psychic phenomena, and so on, are not. It is noteworthy, in this respect, that throughout his paper Hyman repeatedly commits the very sin against which he is preaching, by denying the validity of claims such as Wallace's without a shred of argument. Thus, in order to decide what a reasonable response to bizarre claims should be, one has to ask whether, in general terms, one can understand (a) what enables one to perceive a claim as bizarre, and (b) how it is that bizarre claims sometimes achieve normality. Both of these questions, I suggest, are readily answered if one recognizes the role of scientific theory: it is in terms of some accepted theory that one distinguishes between bizarre and normal phenomena, and it is change in accepted theory which mediates the transformation between anomaly and orthodoxy.

To illustrate what I mean by this, let me refer very briefly to the history of parity violation.[3] In the late 1920s a group of experimental physicists at New York University reported the existence of an asymmetry in the double-scattering of electrons. The precise meaning of these technical terms is not important here; what is important is that the asymmetry could find no interpretation in the physical theories of the day. Thus, in the specific theoretical context of the late 1920s, the report of the asymmetry was seen to be bizarre, and it was eventually dismissed, even by the experimenters themselves, as due to some unidentifiable defect in the experimental procedures. For almost thirty years this experiment suffered the fate of Wallace's sunflower. Then, in the 1950s anomalous results started to appear in experimental elementary particle physics, and, at the brilliant suggestion of theorists T. D. Lee and C. N. Yang (for which they shared a Nobel Prize), these results were recognized as manifestations of parity violation. In the context of this dramatic theoretical development it became readily apparent that there was no reason to believe that the work of the New York experimenters was defective, and that, in fact, they had been observing a straightforward consequence of parity violation. The theoretical work of Lee and Yang had transformed their incongruous observations into a commonplace.

What, then, are we to learn from episodes such as this? Firstly, that what counts as an anomalous observation and what is run of the mill is a function of the contingent theoretical context in which the observations are made. Secondly, that the transformation of anomaly is also a contingent matter: not every anomaly can expect to find its Lee and Yang, and there is no way to legislate for such transformations in advance. If at some particular time no such conciliatory hypothesis has been forthcoming in respect of a given anomaly, that cannot be construed as evidence that such a hypothesis will never appear. It is, of course, possible to recommend further experimental investigation of the anomaly itself and of the techniques involved in its initial production, but the idea that such investigations can be conclusive is never, in principle, true, and seldom if ever in practice.[4] For just one illustration of this, let me return to my previous example. When physicists set out to explore the existence of the reported asymmetry in electron double-scattering, they noted that the original experiments had been done with a rather low-powered source of electrons, and, in order to see any novel effect more clearly, a more powerful source was used in subsequent experiments. No effect was found, making the original report appear to be highly implausible. The change of sources was unfortunate, one can say in retrospect, because the original experiments used electrons emitted in the weak decay of a radioactive substance, while the "replications" used a beam derived from thermionic emission from a hot wire. The improvement was actually a step backwards, since we now recognize that parity violation occurs only in the weak interactions which lead to the emission of electrons from radioactive substances, and not in processes such as thermionic emission. Since the weak interactions were not distinguished as an independent force at the time, the recognition of this would have required an even greater shift in the theoretical context than that of parity violation alone.

The conclusion of this discussion, then, is that anomaly is simply a function of the contingent theoretical milieu within which phenomena are reported. It is clear that scientists should not seek to obliterate anomalous reports from their consciousness, and the constructive response to such reports is to investigate the possibility of mutual reconciliation through theory;[5] but, beyond this, it seems misguided and misleading to ask, as Hyman does, for one specifically rational method for the diagnosis and remedy of pathology. Anomalies are constituted by their context, not by any intrinsic, peculiarly "pathological," attributes. A corollary which follows from this is that one of the most pathological features of the contemporary scene, which stands sorely in need of explanation, is the concept of "pathological science." But that is another problem.

Notes

1. R. Hyman, "Pathological Science: Towards a Proper Diagnosis and Remedy," *Zetetic Scholar*, 6 (1980), 31–38.
2. See Ron Westrum, "Science and Social Intelligence about Anomalies: The Case of Meteorites," *Social Studies of Science*, 8 (1978), 461–493.
3. For good extended accounts of this episode, see "Discovery of Parity Violation in Weak Interactions," in B. Maglich, ed., *Adventures in Experimental Physics* (Princeton: World Science Education) 3 (1973), 93–162; and A. Franklin, "The Discovery and Nondiscovery of Parity Nonconservation," *Studies in History and Philosophy of Science*, 10 (1979), 201–257.
4. For work which argues the point of principle and illustrates its working out in practice, see, for example, my "The Hunting of the Quark: The Experimental Method in Science," *Isis* (forthcoming), and references therein.
5. For case studies and analysis of the relevant processes of transformation in scientific theory, see my *op. cit.*, and "The Role of Interests in High-Energy Physics: The Choice Between Charm and Colour," in R. D. Whitley (ed.), *Sociology of the Sciences Yearbook*, Vol. 5 (Dordrecht and Boston: Reidel, 1981).

Comments by Theodore Rockwell

Ray Hyman offers a fresh approach to the important question: How should scientists react to an outrageous scientific claim? I agree with nearly everything he says, except for his most basic, unstated premise. I think he reaches the right answer for the wrong reason.

He describes some of the greatest minds in the history of science— Newton, Lodge, Crookes, Wallace—devoting major efforts to investigations which led them to believe in the possibility of psychic phenomena. He admits these conclusions have never been rationally examined by the scientific majority. (He does *not* note that their conclusions are remarkably consistent with each other.) And then he jumps to the unexamined position that these great men's findings were "follies." He gives no indication that they might have something.

He describes Lodge being listened to with respect concerning his discovery of thallium, his work with cathode ray tubes, and his invention of the radiometer. Yet, he notes, this same great mind is ignored when he talks of his work on psychic phenomena. Having never even suggested— let alone demonstrated—any basis for concluding Lodge and the others were wrong about psychic phenomena, Hyman then chides present-day scientists who are similarly intrigued by such phenomena, and argues that they must also be foolish. He has rationally analyzed every aspect except the crucial one: Might these men, and many others, be wholly or even partially right?

I have no quarrel with Hyman's recommendation. He asks scientists to act like scientists when faced with a scientific claim. He argues that to do otherwise damages science. I agree. But I disagree that the task is particularly "difficult and demanding." First, we have to clear away some distracting debris. We are talking about science, not horoscope columns, card tricks or fortune tellers. Some critics insist on mixing these, and this is inexcusable. Criticism is part of the scientific process, and I agree with Hyman that such criticism is pseudoscience or pathological science. If some people prefer horoscopes to crossword puzzles or fortune tellers to football games, it is no business of scientists to interfere.

But, we are talking here about experimental or theoretical papers in the classical mold, unorthodox only in the subject under investigation. The rules for handling such papers are well understood. First, they require peer review. This implies review by persons personally competent in the field, although an occasional scientist from a related field may be used in addition. Second, it requires that the reviews and the responses to the authors be fully professional. No shortcomings in the paper under review can excuse nonprofessional or uncivil work by reviewers, editors, or program sponsors.

If papers do not meet well-understood scientific standards, it should be an easy matter to state specifically and clearly wherein this occurs.

I find it disgraceful that *Science* has never run a serious research paper on psychic phenomena, yet it devotes space to improperly reviewed and sweeping denunciations of the field, derogatory comments by itinerant magicians, and side-of-the-mouth editorial jibes.

So I agree with Hyman: Let's treat these claims in a straightforward, scientific manner. This includes the right of most scientists to remain indifferent. But the work should go through the regular process. Bad papers should be rejected for clearly stated and valid reasons. Good ones should be published. Criticism, evaluation, and attempted replication should follow the usual course (which does *not* include public demonstrations before magicians). I expect this would lead to one or two major articles a year in *Science,* a couple of research notes, a news item or two, and an occasional letter and a book review. This would probably take less effort and no more space than *Science's* present antipsychic campaign.

Evaluating such work under normal scientific procedure also includes sincere attempts to replicate. In normal science, one does not suppress the original research and then rush hasty failures-to-replicate into print. Failure to replicate is easy—anyone can do it. Randi makes a living at it. All it means is that the original conditions have not been duplicated. The real scientist tries to understand what conditions are critical to achieving the reported phenomenon. To assume that every unusual event has been produced by fraud is a cop-out. The claim that psychical research is peculiarly vulnerable to fraud is overworked. The record of fraud and failure to predict results is equally bad in many accepted fields of research, *e.g.,* cancer and hypnosis.

So, let us proceed to use the scientific method. If Hyman is right, we may learn why so many brilliant scientists each made the same foolish mistake. But nature has a way of surprising those who too confidently try to predict her ways, and we may learn something quite different, and considerably more important.

Comments by Paul Thagard

Ray Hyman's discussion of pathological science is a valuable contribution to what might be called the "political philosophy of science." In judging how to deal with disciplines such as astrology, parapsychology, and Velikovskian cosmology we face both methodological questions of validation of scientific theories and political questions of appropriate practical reaction to those disciplines which are judged methodologically inadequate. Hyman argues that even obviously bizarre and outrageous science (or pseudoscience) should be subject to the best sort of scientific criticism. To exclude pathological science by means of sketchy, dogmatic dismissal is to lose the opportunity to have science learn from its mistakes.

I have much sympathy with Hyman's liberalism, and agree that such fields as parapsychology and astrology should receive less peremptory criticism than they have generally received. After all, they could turn out to have some validity. If we are not to violate C. S. Peirce's injunction not to block inquiry, then it seems necessary to give careful attention even to theories which, because they conflict with accepted theories or lack verification, are judged to be pathological.

However, Peirce's liberal principle of not blocking inquiry may, in the case of pathological science, come into conflict with another of Peirce's principles: the economy of research. Peirce stressed that a leading consideration in deciding what hypotheses to investigate is economy—of money, time, thought, and energy. Our intellectual resources are limited with respect to all these factors, so it becomes a legitimate methodological question whether the careful investigation of pathological science is worth the effort. No general answer is possible: we will have to decide in each case whether systematic investigation of a claim judged to be without scientific merit is worth the expenditure of time and energy subtracted from other pursuits. We have at least to allow the possibility that for reasons of economy a merely superficial dismissal of a discipline is in order.

There is another reason why in some cases Hyman's liberalism may be unwarranted. This is the social cost of rubbish. Fields like astrology have some fairly serious investigators, but, independently, they have a social impact which goes far beyond their minimal scientific content. For deplorable social reasons, people embrace astrology as a guide to life, with personally and socially undesirable results. It thus becomes a social question how best to combat irrationalism. Polemics may well be more socially effective than detailed criticism.

Reply to the Commentators on "Pathological Science"*

When I first read the comments on my paper, "Pathological Science," I was both puzzled and astonished. The various commentators seemed to be reacting to propositions and arguments that I had not made. I even considered the possibility that Marcello Truzzi had mistakenly sent them someone else's paper.

After further consideration, I decided that the fault for what I considered to be incorrect readings of my paper may lie, at least in part, with myself. I tried to scrutinize my paper with as much objectivity as I could muster (even though at least some of the commentators seem to believe that such objectivity cannot be achieved and may be a capitalist myth). Sure enough, I found that I could read my paper in ways that at least partially justified some of the interpretations.

When I was preparing my paper, I was trying to accomplish something different from what I eventually chose to do. I changed my objective almost at the last moment prior to the delivery of the talk at the meeting of the American Association for the Advancement of Science. The actual paper still retains some of the matter that was relevant to the initial objective. The paper is awkward and ambiguous at various points because of this failure completely to eliminate traces of the original paper.

Originally I was going to examine what Langmuir and others have labeled *pathological science.* Philosophers of science have so far failed to find any consistent criteria for distinguishing such rejected science from more acceptable science. The verifiability criterion, the falsifiability test, and various contemporary proposals to solve this "demarcation" problem all fail because they either include many obvious cases of bad science or exclude many accepted instances of good science. As a cognitive psychologist, I have tried to reconstruct the thought processes that underlie many of the "pathological" claims to compare them with those underlying the "healthy" claims. In most cases I cannot find any difference. And so I was going to argue that there was no "pathology," in fact, involved. The same sort of thought processes that lead some scientists to make claims that Langmuir calls "pathological" are just those that have led the very same scientists to make claims, on other occasions, that have found acceptance within the scientific community.

---

*Reprinted from *Zetetic Scholar,* 1980, 113–21. Reprinted by permission.

But I dropped this initial plan for a number of reasons. I felt that it might be too complex to develop in a half-hour talk before a general audience of scientists. Also, I had already written about this matter in other forums. And a new idea occurred to me that I felt would be simpler to get across and would be relevant to the symposium in which my talk was scheduled (on Science and Pseudoscience).

Langmuir's definition of "pathological science" as "the science of things that are not so" is colorful but useless. Much acceptable science falls under this categorization. In addition, controversies arise in science with respect to other sorts of cases, such as missed discoveries, competing interpretations of things that are so, etc. Although Langmuir's definition is not helpful, his cases do stand out as deviant in another sense. They all involve attempts by the scientific community to reject them out of hand—to prevent by any means their entry into the regular channels for scientific evaluation and argumentation.

My first suggestion was that if there is anything "pathological" about such cases, the pathology was not to be found by looking into either the truth value of the claims or the manner in which they were justified. Rather the "pathology" was in the scientific community's reaction to such claims—a reaction that was entirely out of keeping with the scientists' own image of rational, fair, and dispassionate dealing with claims. My second suggestion was that such extreme reactions in trying to discredit the radical claims of otherwise credentialed scientists has a number of consequences for the conduct of the more orthodox science. And these consequences, in turn, might foster the very "evils" that the guardians of scientific purity feel they are trying to expunge.

It is within this context that I will try to respond to the various comments. For convenience, I will organize my replies under a number of general headings.

1. *What was I trying to accomplish?* At least seven of the commentators deal, in one way or another, with my intentions. I am depicted as urging upon my readers an open-mindedness and fair-handedness in dealing with deviant claims of fellow scientists. A few of the commentators see such a plea as an unrealistic ideal. Both Feyerabend and Hattiangadi point out that a scientist operates at any given time with limited resources. It would be self-defeating if scientists tried to give equal attention to every claim competing for their attention. Feyerabend censures contemporary scientists, not because they limit themselves to investigating only some of an indefinitely large set of possibilities, but rather because they pretend that they have actually dealt with all the reasonable ones.

I fully agree that it would be foolish for the scientific community to try to give "equal time" to all claims put before it. Probably the success of the scientific enterprise has come about from the enforced limitations within an area of inquiry to only certain kinds of problems handled within a narrow disciplinary matrix. In this way the ramifications of a certain paradigm become thoroughly exploited before ultimately being abandoned for a new paradigm.

Unlike many of the commentators, I did not consider my talk as a plea for open-mindedness in science. For one thing, I restricted myself to those seemingly radical claims made by scientists who had already established themselves in some orthodox branch of inquiry. I had nothing to say about the much more numerous claims made by individuals outside the scientific community. And for another thing, I was not urging that all radical claims by accomplished scientists be given a hearing within the scientific forum.

What I did want to urge was that if the scientific community did take it upon itself to challenge such radical claims, that it do so according to those standards of fair play and criticism that it employs in dealing with less radical claims. My concern was that the discrediting procedure for some radical claims was obviously carried out in ways that violated those canons of rationality and objectivity that the scientific community typically endorses. The consequences of such a nonrational discrediting process could be negative both for the deviant scientist as well as for the scientific community itself.

One sort of negative consequence that some of the commentators brought up was the possibility that the radical claim was actually justified and might contain important truth content. While obviously a possibility, my paper was not concerned with that consequence as such. I was more concerned to explore the cases of nonrational discrediting to see what lessons they might contain for scientists, historians of science, philosophers of science, sociologists of knowledge, and cognitive psychologists. One effect of the discrediting process makes it very difficult to extract lessons from such cases. The discrediting usually succeeds in banning from further consideration, at least in regular forums of education and scientific studies, the "discredited" claim. We learn about the successful "orthodox" achievements of Kepler, Newton, Wallace, Crookes, Richet, Lodge, Flammarion, James, and other scientific greats who also put forth radical and paranormal claims. But we do not hear about their "failures" (as defined by the scientific community). Or, if we do hear about them, we do so only in passing and with insufficient detail to judge whether the deviant claims differed in cognitively important ways from the accepted ones.

It may be true, as Allen Debus points out, that the situation with respect to the rejected claims of scientists is changing. During the past twenty years, historians have taken interest in the mysticism of Kepler, the alchemy of Newton, the astrology of Bacon, and the psychic interests of Wallace. These studies have been helpful in revising our ideas about how scientists' various interests and beliefs interact with their orthodox scientific work and theorizing. But these pioneering investigations are still exceptions to the rule and have as yet had little general impact upon scientific and general education. And they are handicapped by the fact that the discrediting process kept these deviant interests of the scientists from being given a full airing during their lifetimes. Newton's alchemical notebooks, for example, were kept in code, and it takes great ingenuity and speculative hindsight to gain insights into what role they played in his mechanical and optical studies.

Because I do not view my purpose as advocating a general open-mindedness, I am not sure how to reply to critics such as Rockwell— who welcomes my appeal to open-mindedness but disagrees with my reasons—or Braude, Cooter, and Mauskopf who, each in his own way, accuse me of hypocrisy. Nor does it help matters when the commentators do not make it clear if they consider my "manipulative tactics" to be the result of a conscious decision on my part or an unconscious bias that reveals itself. Presumably these critics diagnose my "true" intentions on the basis of my choice of words and examples, so I will now deal with those matters.

2. *My choice of terms and referents.* The majority of the commentators question my use of the term *pathological science*—both because of its connotations and because the distinction it implies does not exist. First, let me deal with the problem of reference. Is there in fact a distinction between two sorts of science, such as that made by Langmuir? Here we get into the murky area of the so-called "demarcation" problem. I have no doubt that Langmuir's definition fails completely to separate two sorts of science. As far as I can tell, philosophers and historians of science have still not succeeded in finding a consistent way to discriminate pseudoscience from science, pathological science from science, or indeed any sort of systematic inquiry from science. It has been easy to generate obvious counterexamples to any criterion that has been suggested so far.

However, the fact that we cannot draw a clear boundary between "good" and "bad" science does not mean that the distinction is either meaningless or useless. At the extremes, I think we can point to cases of relatively good science and bad science. And although conceptual, logical, and epistemological matters are involved, I feel that the matter is ultimately an empirical one. Can we find distinctive features that will enable us to classify consistently those cases we agree are good science as "good science"?

I handled this matter very clumsily in my paper. And many of the readers thought I was endorsing, or merely expanding upon, Langmuir's characterization of pathological science. What I intended to do, however, was to abandon Langmuir's approach and simply identify my cases by the six indicants that I listed as "the distinctive characteristics of these examples." These indicants were:

> (1) A scientist of acknowledged competence and accomplishments (2) surprises his colleagues by claiming the existence of a phenomenon or relationship that is considered to be bizarre or even impossible by currently accepted principles. (3) The scientific establishment either ignores or attacks with hostility this bizarre claim. (4) The deviant scientist, along with a few deviant supporters, sticks resolutely to his or her guns in the face of attacks and indifference. (5) The bizarre claim is considered to be discredited in the eyes of the scientific community. (6) The claim is banished from further consideration in scientific literature, textbooks, and education.

I now realize that my attempt to isolate a category of cases for further consideration needs elaboration. I do not claim that such cases can be consistently isolated from regular scientific studies on the basis of truth content, justifiability, or logic. What I do claim is that such cases do exist. We cannot decide, at least as of now, in advance that a particular claim put forth by a scientist will become one of these cases. This is because my indicants depend upon *how the scientific community perceives and reacts to the claim.* Some claims, even ones that are anomalous and controversial, are accepted as legitimate problems for debate and evaluation within the accepted scientific forum. Others are rejected out of hand. They are not allowed further consideration within the regular forum. It is not the claim as such that I labeled "pathological," but the manner in which the scientific community responds to and disposes of it.

Even with this latter characterization, I admit that the term *pathological* is premature. We do not yet know if the nonrational discrediting process that I have described is simply a dramatic and more extreme form of the normal way that scientists actually operate or whether it represents a qualitative break with normal scientific practice.

Again I want to emphasize that it is the scientific community that distinguishes between two kinds of science. One kind is allowed to be conducted within the normal forum. The other kind, the one I called "pathological," is denied access to this forum without due process. This raises a number of interesting questions. What is it that scientists are responding to when they treat a claim by a colleague as "pathological"? The fact that neither scientists nor philosophers have succeeded in articulating consistent criteria for such a distinction does not mean that there are none. Presumably the scientific community is reacting to something. And one issue for future research is to see if we can isolate what that something may be.

My distinction has also been called into question because of the labels

I employed. By employing *pathological science,* I am accused of falling into "a 'sociology of error,' which claims to 'explain' false science only by reference to orthodox science, and by that process [I reinforce] belief in the latter's supposed value-neutral veracity." Within Cooter's ideology, this neutrality of science is a myth created to justify capitalism. I also give away my "true" motives, according to my critics, by my use of terms such as *bizarre, follies,* and *failures.*

Much of this sort of objection, I take it, is the sort of posturing that establishes one as a bona fide neo-Marxist. Within certain contexts and among a certain domain of readers such attacks upon my latent motives and my witting (or unwitting) espousal of the capitalist party line on the objectivity and rationality of science makes sense and arouses the appropriate sort of emotions. But for those readers, like myself, who are not thoroughly immersed in this ideological way of slicing up the world, it is more confusing than enlightening. Even if I had the ability and inclination to respond in kind to such attacks upon my latent motives and alleged ideological blinders, I do not think it would clarify matters to do so.

However, let me say this much about my use of such terms. They certainly are not value-free. In employing them I was thinking of how the scientific community perceives and characterizes the radical claims. In this context, the claims are *bizarre, follies,* and *failures.* Again, it is perhaps an awkwardness of my paper that I did not make clear that the terms I was employing were chosen to reflect the scientific community's attitudes to such claims rather than the actual truth value or justifiability.

3. *My attitude towards anomalous and paranormal claims.* Some of the commentators take me to task for prejudging the validity of the paranormal claims that I discuss. Rockwell finds me inconsistent when I admit that Wallace's and other such claims were never rationally examined and then jump to the "unexamined position" that the findings were "follies." Braude, Cooter, and Mauskopf make similar accusations. And this becomes part of the basis for accusing me of hypocrisy. I seem to be advocating impartial and fair evaluation of deviant claims. But, in reality, say these critics, I merely want a less emotional way of disposing of these embarrassments.

Even though Wallace's claim that a sunflower was materialized by means of psychic force was never rationally examined by the scientific community, I did say that I did not believe his claim. I also labeled such claims as "failures." But I do not see any inconsistencies in this position. Braude, for example, remarks that "there are no grounds, as far as I can see, for condemning the studies of D. D. Home as 'failures,' or Wallace's investigation of psychic forces as 'ignominious failures.' For example, Hyman's apparent assurance that the case is closed, so to speak, on Home flies in the face of the considered judgment of many competent people who have studied this material closely and thought about it . . . very carefully."

Although I did not refer to Home in my paper, I would have also been willing to cite Crookes's studies of Home's psychic powers as "failures." It is true that no one who has studied the reports of seances by Home or Crookes's accounts of his tests on this medium has come up with plausible ways he could have cheated or produced the alleged results by normal means. But the word *failure* is appropriate because these accounts did not lead to further research and systematic findings on such phenomena by later investigators. The scientific community refused to be convinced. And the subsequent psychic researchers have repeatedly expressed dismay that most of the feats attributed to Home have never been witnessed with other psychics. Claims such as those made for Home by Crookes and those made for other mediums by Wallace are what Flew properly puts into the category of singular and in the past tense. They have not been repeated; they have led to no lawful relationships; we do not know how much of what was reported depended on singularly unique circumstances that will never recur. The burden of proof is not, as Braude would have it, on those who want to say it was not paranormal. The burden is upon those who do claim it was paranormal. In the sense that psychical researchers have yet to provide repeatable evidence that Home's type of exploits can actually occur, there is no reason, in my opinion, to believe that they did.

At any rate, as I have already indicated, the truth value of the rejected claims is not the point of my paper. Some claims *are* rejected out of hand by the scientific community. And this raises a problem.

4. *My ignoring of the social determination of scientific knowledge.* Cooter is most explicit about my "failing to question the cultural specificity of modern scientific truth." One does not have to be a Marxist to realize the powerful role that social forces play in the determination of scientific practice and theory. I do not know an important historian or philosopher of science who does not acknowledge this fact. However, the exact nature of this role, for many of us, is still an open question, one that has to be settled empirically rather than by appeal to Marxist or other dogma. Nor is it clear that social determination precludes rationality and objectivity. This too is still open for many serious scholars.

Cooter raises the matter in a way that I feel is irrelevant to the point of my talk. Whether science can be rational, objective, or value-free in any sense, or in any degree, is currently a hotly debated problem. But it is only tangentially related to the fact that scientists do in fact respond to some claims by colleagues by the discrediting process I characterized. The scientific community, in its own eyes, does believe that it deals with matters in a rational and value-free manner. This belief, as Cooter claims, may be badly misguided. But that does not change the fact that it is widely accepted. On some occasions—those I have labeled as *pathological science*—the scientific community seems willing to abandon even the pretense of rationality and refuse some claims the right of a fair hearing. And it is this that raises a number of interesting questions for philosophy, history, sociology, and psychology. Cooter writes as if the answers to such questions are already known and given to him by means of his neo-Marxist faith. Those of us who prefer to find the answers by empirical investigation are accused of "unscholarly dogmatism" and of peddling "junk propaganda."

5. *The forced compartmentalization of Wallace's orthodox biology and his unorthodox psychical inquiries into separate worlds.* Cooter takes me to task for coming "to the mistaken conclusion that Wallace's mind was fragmented into orthodox and unorthodox scientific compartments." And Mauskopf accuses me of distorting the historical context of Wallace's commitments by implying "that Wallace was (or must have been?) a bifurcated individual with two unrelated interests, one scientific and the other pathological." I can only assume that both of these gentlemen were so caught up in the fun and games of showing how ignorant I was of both the history and sociology of science that they failed to appreciate fully what I was saying.

In the first place I said nothing about Wallace's mind being divided; nor did I indicate that he was a split personality. In the second place, what I did say about forced compartmentalization describes an objective fact that neither Cooter nor Mauskopf can deny. In the case of Crookes, Wallace, and other scientists whose claims were discredited in the manner I was describing, the outstanding feature was that they were denied the regular scientific channels for arguing their claims. Wallace may very well have been of one mind and quite internally consistent in his views, which encompassed spiritualism, socialism, antivaccination attitudes, phrenology, and a limited version of natural selection.

But scientific cognition is not simply a function of an individual mind operating in isolation. And it is here that both Cooter and Mauskopf seem to be the ones who are seemingly denying the powerful role of sociocultural factors in scientific knowing. What one knows and how one thinks about it, especially in science, are heavily influenced by the interchange with colleagues, students, rivals, and predecessors in the scientific marketplace. The paradigms, disciplinary matrices, and other contexts that Kuhn and others try to characterize are quite real and potent. Even scientists who work alone in their laboratories are heavily influenced by their internalized versions of these disciplinary matrices. Their formulating of hypotheses; design of research; use of instruments; choice of variables and measures; manner of graphing, analyzing, and summarizing the data; and

mode of presenting it are decisively colored by the anticipated and actual reactions of colleagues, referees, editors, and the like.

When Wallace wrote articles on new plants and species, on natural
selection, and on the geographical distribution of species, he did so within
the context of the existing scientific forum. He got reactions from other
scientific colleagues. They provided new data and arguments, which ampli-
fied, challenged, or supported his views. And he knew what he had to do
to refine, change, or defend his ideas within the context of this arena. But
Wallace was completely denied such a forum for his ideas on psychic matters. He was forced to discuss such ideas in an entirely different forum—
one that had different standards of proof, was already tolerant of such ideas,
was less standardized in both the presentation and justification of claims,
and was of quite a different makeup and much less homogeneous than
the scientific forum. Inevitably, the feedback and critiques he received and
types of responses he had to make in this second forum were quite different
in stringency, shared assumptions, and other disciplinary features from the
scientific forum within which he explicated his less radical ideas.

Everything that I know about cognitive psychology indicates that the
ideas developed within these two very different forums, despite the fact
that they originated within the same mind, would become organized separately in memory and would behave quite differently. And, yes, in an
important sense, it could very well result in a form of dissociation or split
within the mind of the individual who harbors both sets of beliefs.

To me this possibility may contain important clues about how to tackle
some of the problems about rationality, objectivity, and commitment in
science. I would have liked to have seen Cooter's and Mauskopf's thoughts
on this matter if they had fully considered its implications.

I have not tried to answer each specific comment, but I appreciate
the time and thought that each commentator devoted to the task. They
found much more in what I originally thought was a simple talk than
I imagined possible. Even when the comments were caustic and unflat-
tering, they stimulated interesting thoughts and forced me to reconsider
what I was trying to accomplish. Many of the commentators were obviously using my remarks as an excuse to ride their own hobby-horses. But
there is nothing wrong in that. I think most of the commentators mis-
read both my intent and my message; but, as I indicated, I believe I am
at least partially to blame for these varied readings. I originally thought
I could get away with making a simple point in an uncomplicated way.
But if my talk revealed naivete on my part, it was with respect to this
idea that I could isolate and talk about a simple idea in this very complicated matter about what constitutes good and bad science.

Further Comments on Schmidt's PK Experiments*

C. E. M. Hansel begins his provocative "Critical Analysis of H. Schmidt's PK Experiments" by quoting me. As part of a talk to the American Physical Society (APS), I said, "By almost any standard Schmidt's work is the most challenging ever to confront critics. . . . His approach makes many of the earlier criticisms of parapsychological research obsolete." In seeming contrast, Hansel quotes his own assessment that Schmidt's work is far from watertight and that he "may have been a careless experimenter." That assessment was made in his recent book *ESP and Parapsychology: A Critical Reevaluation.* The implication is that Hansel and I disagree in our judgment of this work.

Surprisingly, both Hansel and I agree about the bottom line. We both conclude that Schmidt's experiments with random number generators do not provide an adequate case for the existence of psi (PK, ESP, etc.). So in this very fundamental sense we are in the same camp. Neither of us believes that a scientific case has been made for the existence of psi.

However, we differ in what is probably an even more fundamental attitude toward such work. We differ both on how we *justify* our skepticism and on how we *proclaim* it to the world. I try to justify my position in terms of how well the evidence fulfills explicit standards of reliability and coherence. Hansel builds his case almost entirely upon the possibility of trickery having taken place during the research process. These two modes of argument are quite different, as I will try to make clear. Furthermore, I try to present my arguments in such a way that they can be constructive and possibly help researchers to get close to the truth. Hansel puts himself

Skeptical Inquirer 5 (3) (Spring 1981), 34–41.

into an adversary role—one that obviously invites hostile responses from the parapsychologists. Another way to draw this distinction is in terms of the objectives of our critiques. Are we skeptically viewing the work of the parapsychologists with the hope of discovering what is truly going on? Or are we engaged in a struggle in which one of the sides must emerge victorious and the other must be vanquished?

Before I continue with my elaboration of these points, I should point out that Hansel and I are not responding to the same set of experiments. For some unexplained reason, Hansel confines his critique to the first two years of Schmidt's program. He cites no work conducted by Schmidt or others with random number generators after 1971. Yet Schmidt and other parapsychologists have been publishing such work right up to the present. So my evaluation of Schmidt's work is based on experiments conducted by him and others over a ten-year period. The fact that other experimenters have claimed varying degrees of success with machines of the Schmidt type, for example, changes the import of some of Hansel's criticisms.

Kendrick Frazier's summary of both Schmidt's and my talks at the APS symposium on physics and parapsychology (New York, January 30, 1979) is excellent, and I urge those who are interested in the basic points made to read that account in the Summer 1979 issue of the *Skeptical Inquirer*. Schmidt and I were allowed forty-five minutes each for our presentations, and, as Frazier indicates, the written account of my talk covers twenty-eight typewritten pages. Frazier fully summarizes my general criticisms of parapsychological work, including that of Schmidt. But he obviously could not fully detail my specific critique of Schmidt's work. As I will point out, this detailed critique includes some of the points made by Hansel. In addition, it mentions others.

Hansel was not the only reader of Frazier's summary to focus upon the good things I said about Schmidt's work. Many reporters and readers also picked this up as the apparent theme of my talk. And Hansel is not alone in treating my position as in seeming contrast to his own. Theodore Rockwell, in his review of Hansel's book in a recent issue of the *Parapsychological Review*, juxtaposes our two assessments in such a way as to maximize the apparent divergence in our views. Neither Hansel nor Rockwell seems to realize that my talk was a rebuttal to Schmidt's claims. I was on the panel to represent the skeptical viewpoint, and the thrust of my remarks was to warn the physicists to take Schmidt's and other parapsychologists' claims with a grain of salt.

In the course of carrying out this task I also pointed out those grounds for listening to the parapsychologists, and I tried to make it clear that current work in parapsychology cannot be dismissed by the stock criticisms that were generated during Rhine's early work. Instead, the work of Schmidt and his contemporaries has to be evaluated on different and more sophisticated grounds. For example, criticisms that were relevant to the hand shuffling of cards, to sensory leakage, to mistakes in the hand recording of scores, and to the misuse of standard statistical tests no longer apply—at least not in the same way.

So one proper context within which to interpret my statement about Schmidt's work making "many of the earlier criticisms of parapsychological research obsolete" is that it employs a new technology and a new level of sophistication regarding randomization of targets, recording the data, sensory leakage, and sources of experimenter bias. This does not by any means make it beyond criticism. In fact, I supplied a number of specific criticisms.

The other context is in terms of the overall objectives of my contribution to the symposium. Schmidt, a quantum physicist, talked about his own research and theories on psychokinesis. My task was to react responsibly and skeptically to Schmidt's presentation. I did this by first placing this specific research into the larger context of physicists working in psychical research. I reviewed 125 years of involvement in such research by physicists. Among other lessons that emerged from this historical survey was the important one that training in physics was not highly relevant to investigating claims of psychical powers. Expertise in one field does not necessarily transfer to another—especially one so unstructured and untidy as parapsychology.

Schmidt's particular program introduced some space-age technology and new levels of sophistication in instrumentation, selection, and presentation of targets, in recording the data, and in theory. His reports showed care and attention to certain details that were a step forward. For these reasons I commended what he had accomplished so far. And I felt that his work would not be dismissed out of hand—at least not in terms of the type of objections that have been leveled at more traditional forms of parapsychology.

On the other hand, I pointed out reasons for reserving judgment and being somewhat dubious about the results at this time. Some of these reasons were general in terms of the lessons derived from the overall history of parapsychology. Beginning with the founding of the Society for Psychical Research in 1882, each generation of parapsychologists has put forth its current candidates for the proof of ESP or PK. These candidates were particular experiments or experimental programs that, allegedly, ought to have convinced any rational person who fairly assessed the results. In 1882, for example, the candidates included the telepathy experiments with the Creery sisters and with Smith and Blackburn. Both these candidates were dropped from the pool of evidence when the sisters were later caught and then confessed to fraud and when Blackburn explained how he and Smith had employed a code to outwit the researchers. But they were quickly replaced with other candidates. In the 1940s and 1950s the Soal-Goldney experiments with Shackleton and Mrs. Stewart were the centerpieces of the candidate pool. Partly as a result of Hansel's suspicions, these experiments eventually left the pool. Today the pool features the ganzfeld experiments, remote viewing, and Schmidt-type of research.

What this history revealed is that the parapsychologists at any time have a pool of candidates for the iron-clad, repeatable experiment to put before the critics. The problem is that the members of this pool keep shifting in and out. Yesterday it was sheep-goats, Levy's experiments with implanted electrodes, and dream telepathy. Today these experiments are hardly mentioned by proponents and are rarely carried out. By analogy, then, we have to be cautious in taking too seriously the current contenders. Experience shows that the most promising research programs in parapsychology will most likely be passé within a generation or two.

But I also pointed out more specific reasons for hesitating to accept Schmidt's results. Some of these reasons overlap with those Hansel has given. Schmidt places complete reliance on his machine to protect the integrity of the experiment. The subjects, for the most part, are unsupervised and unobserved. The assumption is that instrumentation can replace old-fashioned controls in human experimentation. This assumption is unacceptable for a variety of reasons. An obvious one is that, no matter how sophisticated and automated a random number generator may be, we still must learn its properties by a lot of experience and testing. Rarely does any new device behave fully according to its theoretical or expected specifications. It takes time to discover the biases and peculiar properties of the new gadget. And this difficulty seems to increase, rather than decrease, with the sophistication and complexity of the device.

Ironically, Schmidt keeps changing the design and components of his random number generator from experiment to experiment. This has the desirable property of achieving generality among devices—*if* one could show consistency of results. But, at the same time, it prevents us from gathering the cumulative experience with one particular generator to fully understand its peculiarities and to properly "debug" it.

Neither Hansel nor I was fully satisfied with the control trials employed by Schmidt. Schmidt allows the machine to run during periods when subjects are not trying to influence its output, and he makes sure to run it on such control series before, during, and after the experimental series. In principle this is highly commendable. If the machine has any long-term, or even temporary, trends away from equality of outputs this sort of control might catch it. But Schmidt does not conduct these control series systematically, and Hansel's suggestion is important. Hansel feels that control and experimental runs should be conducted in pairs and that which particular run will be a control or an experiment should be decided by a randomization procedure. The experimenter monitoring the generator should be kept blind as to whether the run is a control or not.

Hansel probably sees this control as another constraint upon trickery. But I see it as a necessary control against possible short-run biases in the generator output. Schmidt's subjects try to affect the generator output only for runs that last for relatively short bursts. The control runs, however, cover extended intervals that are many orders of magnitude in length compared with experimental runs. If the generator has short-run biases, these could easily fail to be detected by the sort of tests that Schmidt applies to the control runs.

I could continue listing further possible weaknesses in Schmidt's experiments. These weaknesses are of two kinds. There are general weaknesses that one would point out as flaws in any experiment involving human subjects and information transfer. The fact that subjects are neither systematically observed nor treated in a uniform way, for example, would be such a weakness. Other weaknesses would be specific to this particular sort of paradigm and its objectives. For example, the fact that Schmidt's tests for randomicity only test dependencies once removed and not beyond is such a weakness.

Of course no single experiment can conceivably control or systematically deal with every relevant variable. Indeed, the point of doing research is to discover those conditions and variables that *are* relevant. When we point to a procedure or the omission of a procedure as a "flaw" in the design, we are making an informed judgment. We are saying that such a procedure or precaution was both reasonable and feasible under the given conditions. Further, we are stating our belief that a competent investigator would have taken the matter under consideration.

Pointing to some flaws, for example, is equivalent to suggesting alternative reasons for the outcome. If Schmidt had not frequently tested his generator for bias, then pointing out this oversight would be equivalent to strongly suggesting that the alleged PK results were simply the result of a systematic bias in the machine. But, of course, Schmidt did conduct such tests. Both Hansel and I consider the way he carried them out to be a weakness in the studies. But this latter type of weakness, while an obvious departure from the ideal, does not automatically provide an alternative explanation for how Schmidt obtained his results.

Hansel, as a critic, feels called upon to provide alternative explanations for the results. He restricts his search for alternatives completely to deliberate trickery on the part of the experimenter, the subject, or an outsider. His position is that, if he can conjure up a scenario in which trickery *could* have produced the results, then the resulting experiment cannot provide evidence for psi.

The parapsychologists, of course, see Hansel's position for what it is—a dogmatism that is immune to falsification. There is no such thing as an experiment immune to trickery. Even if one assembles all the world's magicians and scientists and puts them to the task of designing a fraud-proof experiment, it cannot be done. I could always insist that, of the infinite number of variables not explicitly taken into account in this "fraud proof" design, many of them—ones still unknown to us—could leave loopholes for a form of trickery we have not yet discovered. In practice, it would be impossible even to take into consideration all the known variables that could allow some form of deception.

I think it is possible and rational for skeptics to avoid committing themselves to this false dichotomy—that the results must be either paranormal or fraudulent. There are other alternatives, many of which we have yet to learn about, but I do not think it necessary or wise to feel that we must always provide an alternative explanation for alleged paranormal claims.

Applying these considerations to Schmidt's work, I think the wise course is to wait. The work is in its preliminary stages. The generators have been neither standardized nor debugged. The research paradigm is still fluid and far from scientific. The results are provocative but far from lawful, systematic, or independently replicable. We have no need to try to explain or account for any of this now. Only when the parapsychologists settle upon a standardized paradigm, tidy up the procedures, demonstrate that the results follow certain laws under specified conditions, and that these results can be duplicated in independent laboratories, will we have something that needs "explaining." Of course by the time circumstances reach such an orderly stage there may very well be nothing left to explain. So far, in my opinion, this has been the normal course of events in things parapsychological.

The drawback of my position is that it counsels patience. We might never know, by following my advice, just what did account for Schmidt's data. But the alternative, which is to insist on settling the matter now, leads to the inevitable shrill claims, on the one side, that here is proof of psi and, on the other side, that cheating must be going on.

One more aspect of Hansel's approach bothers me. Each experiment, he says, must stand on its own feet. (Such a demand, unnfortunately, is at odds with every contemporary history and philosophy of science account that I have read.) In "analyzing an experiment it is wise *initially* to adopt the assumption that ESP (or in this case PK) is impossible and then see how the result could have arisen through already established processes." If Hansel had worded this somewhat differently, I think I could agree.

If he had said, for example, that it is wise to assume that the initial odds in favor of psi are exceedingly low, I could not take exception; for Bayesian and other models of rational behavior still allow for some change in these odds as a result of new empirical data. But, if we start with the initial assumption that the odds in favor are zero, then no amount of empirical evidence can change our position.

Notice that a feature of such models of rational judgment hinges crucially upon how we conceptualize the outcome. Hansel's critique reads as if he had restricted the outcome to just two possibilities—psi or fraud. But even these two possibilities may not be simple or mutually exclusive, and they certainly far from exhaust all the possibilities. The category "psi," even among parapsychologists, covers a number of existential possibilities. Some talk about a category of phenomena that are independent of any physical laws now known or conceivable. Others see new types of phenomena and forces that were hitherto unknown but entirely compatible with modern physics. We even find some parapsychologists arguing that, when properly understood, psi phenomena result from the operation of already known forces, such as extremely low frequency waves. And fraud ranges from deliberate, conscious cheating to vicious psychological aberrations and self-delusions. But in between these complex alternatives is a vast array of other alternatives involving the operation of statistics of rare events, subtle subject-experimenter-environment interactions, improper but nondeliberate manipulation of data, and many, many other possibilities. Among these alternatives could very well be new sorts of biases or ways for experiments to go wrong that we don't know about. In my own field of experimental psychology we still are uncovering novel ways in which experiments can be biased. There is certainly no reason to suspect that all known ways that experiments in parapsychology can go wrong have been discovered.

In short, I see no need to rush matters. I agree with Hansel that the data so far produced by parapsychologists do not justify the claims for the existence of something called "psi." But I see no need to buttress such a conclusion by creating scenarios in which trickery could have occurred. Why try to account for something that does not yet need accounting for?

C. E. M. Hansel Replies*

Ray Hyman, discussing my article "A Critical Analysis of H. Schmidt's PK Experiments," takes the opportunity to criticize my general approach to parapsychology. For this purpose he isolates statements made in my article in which I made reference to a fuller discussion given in my book.[1] These are as follows:

1. *Each experiment must stand on its own feet.* This Hyman states to be "at odds with every contemporary history and history of science account that I have read."

My statement arose when considering telepathy experiments in which conditions have been changed from one sitting to another. Originally it was in the form: "Each experiment must be considered solely on its own merits. A weakness cannot be excused because it was absent in a second experiment, which may have its own weakness; if it has not, the first experiment should be ignored and conclusions obtained only from the second."[2]

The same statement applies to experiments in general. If it had been ignored we would still be considering Rhine's early card-guessing experiments.

2. *In analyzing an experiment it is wise initially to adopt the assumption that ESP (or in this case PK) is impossible and then see how the result could have arisen through already established processes.*

Hyman would have preferred me to write "it is wise to assume that the initial odds in favor of psi are exceedingly low."

What I originally wrote here was: "The basic problem of parapsychology is relatively simple. . . . Either it is possible for at least some people to communicate by extrasensory perception or else ESP does not and cannot exist because the underlying processes necessary for its occurrence do not exist."[2]

I was not concerned with the odds in favor of the one or the other possibility eventually emerging as correct, nor even with the particular beliefs of the reader in this respect, but with considering the two mutually exclusive possibilities.

My statement arose after considering the attitude we adopt when seeing a conjurer saw a woman in half on the stage. I concluded: "Thus, in analyzing an experiment that purports to prove ESP, it is wise to adopt initially the assumption that ESP is impossible, just as it is assumed that the conjurer cannot saw the same girl in half twice each evening. . . . If

---

*Hansel's reply appeared in *Skeptical Inquirer* 6 (3) (Spring 1982), 76–78.

analysis shows that this assumption is untenable then the possibility of ESP has to be accepted."[3]

In my later account,[4] I extended this discussion, in view of the manner in which my original statement had been misquoted and misunderstood in the intervening years. Hyman has ignored this discussion.

Hyman writes: "He restricts his reason for alternatives completely to deliberate trickery on the part of the experimenter, the subject, or an outsider." But in my article I referred to my fuller discussion of Schmidt's experiments in which I did not mention the possibility of trickery.[5] The aim in the article was to indicate the possibility of trickery in view of the statements made at the meeting of the American Physical Society. I wished to indicate that in addition to numerous other weaknesses even the "space-age technology" employed by Schmidt was not sufficient to eliminate the possibility of conjuring tricks being employed by the subjects had they wished to employ them. I then indicated the possible ways in which a trick might have been employed by the subjects or the experimenter or some other persons. This was hardly restrictive.

What I wished to convey was that Schmidt's "particular program"— far from introducing "new levels of sophistication in instrumentation, selection, in recording the data, and in theory," as stated by Hyman—fell miserably short of the program employed by the VERITAC team of investigators in 1963 and, in some respects, short of the work at Duke University carried out in the late thirties.

Hyman writes that "only when the parapsychologists settle upon a standardized paradigm" and show "the results can be duplicated in independent laboratories, will we have something that needs explaining." This is so if we assume PK to exist; but 100 years of research have failed to achieve this state of affairs. If quantum processes cannot be affected by human beings so as to produce a particular desired—or not desired—end result in a display of lights, and if Schmidt's PK experiment employed space-age technology to ensure that frequent errors did not arise when counting the numbers of outputs, then I suggest that something does need explaining.

In my 1965 survey of parapsychology experiments I isolated for particular scrutiny those regarded by parapsychologists as "conclusive." These were experiments in which stringent safeguards were claimed to have been taken against experimental error and in which the antichance odds obtained were such that it was clear that something had happened to bring about the observed result. For my 1980 account, no such experiments appeared to have arisen during the intervening years. The PK experiment carried out by Schmidt came nearest, however, since over a period of ten days two subjects consistently scored high or low, giving antichance odds of 10 million to one. The most likely cause of this result, as discussed in my book, was the fact that there were several unsatisfactory features in the methods employed that could lead to experimental error. But an essential consideration in any experiment—as stated by J. B. Rhine himself[6]—is that it should not be possible for the subject to cheat. In my article I attempted to show that it may have been possible for the subjects, the experimenter, or some outside person to have brought about the result by employing a trick. If that is so, whether the result was in fact due to trickery or not, no further discussion of the experiment is required. But if this experiment is to be advanced as providing evidence for PK, and if it is to be proclaimed in the manner of Hyman as making "many of the earlier criticisms of parapsychological research obsolete," then it is necessary to examine it further in order to account for the findings.

Hyman writes: "The parapsychologists, of course, see Hansel's position for what it is—a dogmatism that is immune to falsification. There is no such thing as an experiment immune from trickery."

Whatever parapsychologists' or Hyman's interpretation or misinterpretation of my view may be, I would agree. There is no experiment immune from trickery on the part of the investigators. This applies to any experiment in science. But as the result of an experimental demonstration of a phenomenon is confirmed—and very seldom rejected—by an increasing number of independent investigators, the likelihood of the result being an artifact becomes increasingly remote. Failure to confirm, on the other hand, makes it increasingly likely that the phenomenon is bogus.

Over the past hundred years a large number of experiments and procedures have been reported by parapsychologists, not one of which has afforded a reliable demonstration of any supposed paranormal process. Not one of these experiments can stand on its own feet, but Hyman appears to assume that this large number of unreliable experiments taken en masse can provide evidence for the supposed process. Rather, it may be argued that this repeated failure to provide a reliable demonstration indicates that the supposed processes are nonexistent.

Hyman writes that he tries to justify his position "in terms of how well the evidence fulfills explicit standards of reliability and coherence" and that he tries to present his arguments "in such a way that they can be constructive and possibly help researchers to get closer to the truth." What is the truth about Schmidt's PK experiment? Were the two subjects, K. G. and R. R., affecting a random number generator or the emission of electrons from a radioactive source? Or was Schmidt incapable of accurately recording the result of his tests and checking the readings with a printout? Neither of these possibilities may apply. Is it not then constructive, and likely to assist researchers to get closer to the truth, to indicate how the subjects, the experimenter, or other persons might conceivably have rigged the experiment? The truth is only likely to emerge if all these possibilities are made apparent and closely examined.

Notes

1. C. E. M. Hansel, *ESP and Parapsychology: A Critical Re-evaluation.* Prometheus Books, Buffalo, N.Y., 1980.
2. C. E. M. Hansel, *ESP: A Scientific Evaluation.* Scribner's, New York, 1966.
3. See Note 1.
4. See Note 1.
5. See Note 1.
6. J. B. Rhine and J. G. Pratt, *Parapsychology: Frontier Science of the Mind.* Charles C. Thomas, Springfield, Ill., 1957.

Reviews

The Geller Papers: Scientific Observations on the Paranormal Powers of Uri Geller. Ed. **Charles Panati. Houghton Mifflin, Boston, 1976. 327 pp.***

Charles Panati has assembled 23 contributions by several scientists, four magicians, and a photographer that constitute, presumably, the best possible case for the reality of Uri Geller's supernatural powers. In addition to making these papers available, Panati has attempted to integrate and interpret their import by means of a preface, a long introduction, and an epilogue. In his preface he anticipates the various responses.

> Geller-advocates who read this collection of firsthand observations may feel confirmed in their present opinion of him. His critics will dissect these papers and will find large loopholes and countless faults with the experiments and descriptions they contain, for all of the evidence presented here is certainly not of equal quality. There is, nevertheless, a considerable amount of new and impressive information—from responsible scientists and professional magicians alike. Their observations taken as a whole are hard to dismiss on the grounds of simple fraud or mass delusion.

Panati asks that "the thoughtful reader . . . give these reports a careful review before drawing final conclusions on the phenomena associated with Uri Geller." Let's assume that our "thoughtful reader" is imbued with the rationalistic and naturalistic viewpoints that take it for granted that all phenomena, both animate and inanimate, obey the fundamental laws of natural science as we currently understand them. Certainly his or her first perusal of this book is bound to be unsettling. The reader will discover

---

*This review was published in *The Zetetic* 1(1) (Fall/Winter 1976), 73–80.

that scientists, many of them with impressive credentials, report that they have observed Uri Geller "deform solid steel rods without touching them, cause part of an exotic crystal to vanish from within a sealed container, alter the memory of a rare metal alloy, erase information from computer tapes, set Geiger counters ticking with only his thoughts, and read the thoughts of others while he is sealed in a room that blocks out all types of radio waves."

But perhaps scientists are no match for a clever illusionist? Our thoughtful reader might protest that it takes a deceiver to catch a deceiver. But even this loophole is seemingly blocked. Artur Zorka, a professional magician, placed his own fork into Uri's outstretched hand. "His fingers curled around it, and in moments, without the fork's leaving my sight for even an instant, it literally exploded, sending fragments of the handle across the room." Danish conjuror Leo Leslie took a nickel-plated, enameled key that Uri had just lightly stroked. Leslie writes that "while I sat looking at the key the enamel suddenly started to crack, and a second later strips of the nickel plating curled up like small banana peels, while the key actually started to bend in my hand." Both Zorka and Leslie claim that they have no explanation for how Uri accomplished these feats.

The thoughtful reader, it is easy to imagine, may find these observations disturbing, to say the least. But Panati has urged a "careful review," and any argument for a proposition—especially one so revolutionary in import—claiming scientific status requires careful scrutiny. Such careful scrutiny, it turns out, produces results that I am sure were not those intended by Panati. The careful scrutiny yields disturbing feelings. But these disturbing feelings are no longer the ones associated with the possibility that Uri is able to bend the laws of nature. Rather, they derive from the possibility that Geller is able to bend the judgments of otherwise competent scientists.

The first inkling that something is not as it seems comes from a simple classification of the types of reports on Uri's accomplishments. Of the 23 contributions we find 18 separate observational accounts or "studies" of Geller. Many of these studies were carried out under conditions that both Panati and their authors admit were informal, uncontrolled, or otherwise badly flawed from a scientific viewpoint. In fact, of the 18 separate studies, 10 can be so classified. Therefore, even by the editor's standards, over half of the evidence has no scientific status.

What about the 8 remaining candidates for scientific respectability? Our careful scrutiny again raises serious doubts. The prime candidate for scientific respectability is obviously the paper by Harold Puthoff and Russell Targ, "Information Transmission Under Conditions of Sensory Shielding," which was published in *Nature* on 18 October 1974. This is the only study in the entire collection that has made it through the usual scientific procedure of peer review and ultimate publication in an accredited scientific journal. What Panati and many others seem to overlook is that the paper was not published in *Nature* because of its scientific qualities but in spite of the lack of such qualities. An editorial that accompanied the paper when first published, and which Panati includes here, makes it clear that the editors and the referees judged the study to be weak and inadequate to a point that ordinarily "could be grounds for rejection of the paper." The editorial lists five reasons for printing the paper—none of them having anything to do with its scientific merits—"despite its shortcomings." If it had been a paper on a less controversial subject and one which had not been accompanied by such publicity and widespread rumors, it clearly would not have been accepted for publication.

The strongest of the remaining seven candidates for scientific status would seem to be Eldon Byrd's "Uri Geller's Influence on the Metal Alloy Nitinol." Byrd is an engineer at the Naval Surface Weapons Center in Maryland. He is also a psychologist who has published papers on the alleged ability of plants to telepathically sense harmful intent toward themselves. Nitinol is an alloy of nickel and titanium which has "a physical memory for the shape in which it is formed at the time of manufacture." Byrd reports that on three separate occasions Uri was able to produce a kink or bend in pieces of nitinol wire that resulted in permanent change in the wire's memory. One of the occasions took place at what is called the Isis Center (and not at the Naval Surface Weapons Center, as Panati mistakenly reports), a now-defunct parapsychological organization. As Byrd points out, the claim to "control" in these experiments rests not on careful observation or recording of Uri's behavior, nor on any search of or other constraints placed upon him, but rather on the assumed properties of the testing material. Byrd's case for natural powers on Uri's part depends on two assumptions: (1) that at the time he tested Uri "nitinol was generally not available to the public" and (2) that to effect the sort of change produced by Uri normally requires that one heat the wire to 900 degrees Fahrenheit. Both these assumptions, it now turns out, are questionable. Charles Kalish experimented with nitinol in 1972 (a year before the first experiment with Uri) and developed a magic trick based on its use; the trick was actually marketed by an English magic company. And, separately, the memory of nitinol can be changed by strong mechanical pressures without high temperatures. (Both of these pieces of information come from Martin Gardner.) Here, as with the other papers in this collection, review by peers and appropriate experts would have helped.

The case for the remaining six claimants to some sort of control of the observations and conditions is even weaker. Wilbur Franklin's two reports on metal fractures, for example, depend on observations made at Stanford

Research Institute. The physicists at SRI, however, explicitly admit that these observations of metal bending were made under conditions that could not exclude trickery. The reports by John Taylor, Albert Ducrocq, and the scientists at Birkbeck College, University of London, all suffer from insufficient details and records of Uri's behavior during the alleged psychokinetic happenings. Like Byrd, these scientists seem to believe that they can compensate for inadequate controls and recording of Uri's behavior by scientific analyses of the deformed or altered materials he leaves behind.

The final contribution that claims some sort of control is that of magician Artur Zorka. Zorka writes that he and another magician, Abb Dickson, "were able to meet with Uri Geller privately for a personal interview and some *controlled* experiments. I italicize controlled because the type of control put on by a magician is different from that of any other investigator. It is a control designed by those who are trained for a profession in the art of deception, to prevent fraud." It is difficult for me, who also once worked as a professional magician and mentalist, to know what Zorka is talking about. Neither magicians nor mentalists have ever devised any standard set of procedures either to prevent fraud or to evaluate psychic powers. At any rate it is clear that, whatever Zorka means by "control," he did not obtain observations on Uri Geller by any means that would approximate scientific controls—objective recording, constraints on Uri's behavior and so on. Moreover, I have talked with two different individuals who have interviewed Abb Dickson about his observation of what took place and, if my informants are correct, Dickson's account differs enough from Zorka's on several key matters to place an entirely different light on the evidence.

So the first careful scrutiny suggests that not one of these reports constitutes "hard" evidence, in the scientific sense, for the reality of Geller's powers. This conclusion comes from considering the papers in isolation from one another. The situation becomes worse when we try to integrate them. The most extensive series of observations of Uri Geller took place at Stanford Research Institute (SRI) in late 1972 and in the summer of 1973. In all, Uri put in several weeks of performance at SRI, whereas his appearances at other laboratories amounted to one or two visits of a few hours. Indeed, the time that he put in at all the other laboratories and observational settings combined probably does not add up to the amount of time he spent at SRI alone. Yet, in his attempt to provide us with an overview of the case of Uri Geller, Panati seems to overlook completely the astounding fact that, despite all their dedicated efforts, the SRI researchers were unable to come up with any evidence to justify the claim that Uri can bend metal or perform other psychokinetic phenomena by paranormal means. They are willing to grant Uri's paranormal powers only in the realm of perceptual phenomena—telepathy and clairvoyance.

What makes this startling is that the reports from all the other laboratories emphasize Uri's psychokinetic powers. As already mentioned, Franklin's contribution, with its elaborate theoretical analysis, entirely depends on the genuineness of the metal deformation he observed at SRI—a genuineness that the SRI researchers are unwilling to acknowledge.

In his Introduction, which he acknowledges serves as a general review for the layman who might otherwise get bogged down in the technicalities of the individual reports, Panati fails to point out other inconsistencies in his case for Geller. For example, he supplies the text of the SRI film on Uri, which describes the experiments on divining for an object hidden in one of a number of cans, influencing a scale, moving the hands of a compass, and affecting a magnetometer. But he does not discuss the interesting fact that when the SRI physicists came to the point of presenting their case to their scientific colleagues they omitted these experiments from their report. Nor does he or any of his contributors adequately define or discuss the elusive concept of "control" that some of them insist applies to their observations. In the context of these papers it becomes a vague term only remotely related to its usage in specific scientific contexts. For the physical scientists it seems to indicate a fine-grained analysis of the physical properties of objects that have been deformed by Uri. Sometimes it seems to be used in the sense of, "I took adequate precautions to rule out fraud, trickery, or other artifacts." Just what these precautions in fact were and precisely what forms of possible trickery were ruled out is never spelled out. All the studies commit the cardinal sin of failing to report adequately the conditions under which Uri performed and exactly what he did and did not do before, during, and immediately after a supposedly paranormal occurrence. Indeed it is usually unclear both what sort of records were made during the "experiments" and when the record was finally written out. No checks for reliability of observation are mentioned. In a footnote to William E. Cox's contribution we are told that his account was written down two days after the event!

Up to this point my comments have been based on an internal analysis of what Panati has included in his book. The case for Uri Geller becomes even more suspect when we consider what Panati has left out. I would guess that it will be difficult for Panati's "thoughtful reader" to find a clear and unambiguous statement of Panati's criteria for including the paper. My initial impression from the dust jacket and preface was that Panati implies, if he does not actually claim, that the book covers all the scientific evidence on Uri Geller. In his preface, in fact, Panati writes that, "The book is written—through papers, reports, diary entries, and letters—by the scientists and professionals who, in various ways, have scrutinized Geller's talents, and feel that Geller is an individual who deserves further scientific attention." It was not until I read further into the book and noted what Panati wrote in his introductions to separate papers that I finally understood what he meant by the preceding quotation. For example, in the introduction to Thomas P. Coohill's report, Panati candidly admits: "The tests reported in the following pages were not executed with the rigor essential for a scientic investigation. They are presented here as anecdotes because Dr. Coohill, a respected scientist, believes that the events he and his colleagues witnessed that day—and two days after Geller's visit—were paranormal in nature." Or, again, in his introduction to the contribution by Lawrence Fried, Panati tells us: "Because of the impromptu nature of the 'thought photography' session between Lawrence Fried and Uri Geller, the following report cannot be taken as positive proof of the occurrence of a paranormal event. . . . Fried recounts all of these things in his brief report, which is included in this book because of Fried's unimpeachable professionalism and expertise with a camera."

In other words, Panati is telling us that for an author to contribute to his book the following must be true: (1) the person must have had a first-hand experience with Uri Geller, (2) he or she must have status as an accredited scientist or professional; and (3) he or she must have been persuaded of the reality of Uri's powers. This possibly explains the striking failure to even mention Yael Joel's revealing report, "Uri Through the Lens Cap," which appeared in the June 1974 issue of *Popular Photography* and was later reprinted in Martin Ebon's collection, *The Amazing Uri Geller.* Yael Joel can also be characterized by his "unimpeachable professionalism and expertise with a camera." And, like Lawrence Fried, he too was dumbfounded and had no answers when he discovered Uri's features on the negative in a roll of film that had been snapped with the camera lens covered. It was only when the print was made, and because the camera Uri used happened to have a "fish eye" lens, that Joel caught on to what must have happened and was able to reconstruct the events that enabled Uri to pull off his swindle. But Joel, unlike Fried, does not qualify for even a mention in Panati's case for Uri. This is because Joel ended up by not being persuaded of Uri's paranormal powers.

Panati's emphasis on the case *for* Uri Geller explains why he omits even mentioning the first-hand reports of scientists and professionals who were not persuaded of Geller's authenticity. These include psychologists such as David Marks, Richard Kammann, George Lawrence, Charles Rebert, and myself, among others. They include magicians such as Charlie Reynolds, James Randi, and myself (I am also an experienced magician). Some of the most interesting cases are those involving individuals who at first were persuaded by Geller's performance but who later became disenchanted through reconstruction of the original incident or new information. Among these are medical doctor Andrew Weil and physicists Jack Sarfatti, J. Hanlon, and J. W. Juritz. (Hanlon is mentioned only in connection with his suggestion that Uri might have had a miniature receiver implanted in his tooth. His more plausible criticisms of the Geller evidence are not even mentioned.)

Such omissions are regrettable for many reasons. An attempt seriously to come to grips with questions raised by the observers who have not been persuaded of, or who have changed their minds about, Uri's powers would have lent more credibility to Panati's book as well as enabling the reader to put much of what is presented into a better perspective. For example, Jack Sarfatti was a witness at two of the four sessions with Uri Geller reported in the contribution by John Hasted *et al.* from Birkbeck College, University of London. In a report to *Science News* (20 July 1974) Sarfatti concluded: "My personal professional judgment as a Ph.D. physicist is that Geller demonstrated genuine psycho-energetic ability at Birkbeck, which is beyond the doubt of any reasonable man, under relatively well controlled and repeatable experimental conditions." Over a year later Sarfatti wrote to *Science News* (6 December 1975): "On the basis of further experience in the art of conjuring I wish to publicly retract my endorsement of Uri Geller's psychoenergetic authenticity. . . . I have witnessed The Amazing Randi fracture metal and move the hands of a watch in a way that is indistinguishable from my observation of Geller's 'psychokinetic' demonstrations. Also, I am advised of Randi's demonstration of causing bursts in a Geiger counter and of deflecting a compass needle as reported in a letter from Kings College, University of London." Certainly this information from one of the scientific witnesses is part of the total picture that a "thoughtful reader" ought to have in trying to assess the reports from Birkbeck and Kings College which are included in Panati's book.

The letter to *Nature* on spoon-bending experiments with six children by Dr. Pamplin and Mr. Collins of Bath University (4 September 1975) would certainly help to put Taylor's experiments with children and the Geller effect (*i.e.*, the ability of viewers of and listeners to a Geller performance to get their broken watches to run and to bend metal) in a new light. Presumably their experiment is not mentioned because they were able to catch each child on videotape in flagrant acts of cheating when the mini-Geller thought the observer was not watching. And the paper by Richard Kammann and David Marks (read at the November 1975 meeting of the Psychonomic Society and subsequently given widespread coverage in the media) takes away much of the apparent mystery in the long paper by E. Alan Price on "The Uri Geller Effect." By ignoring this rapidly accumulating series of reports of firsthand observations that seemingly bring Geller's effects back into the realm of normality, Panati has seriously deprived his "thoughtful reader" of the opportunity to reach a balanced conclusion based on the total body of evidence.

Unfortunately Panati misleads his reader not only by what he has left out but also by some of the things he actually says. For example, he strongly hints in the preface and again in the epilogue that "respected scientific journals do not publish the results of well-conducted psychical investigations" because of prejudice against the area of parapsychology. The implication is that many of the papers in this book were rejected for publication on such grounds. I find this misleading on two grounds. It implies that many of these papers meet standards of scientific acceptability when, in fact, not one of them does. And, second, as I have already mentioned, the one paper that did get published made it because the editors leaned over backward and ignored their conventional standards just because they wanted to publish the best case for Uri Geller.

Nor do I think Panati helps the "thoughtful reader" by telling him or her in the preface that, in investigating Geller, "to prevent fraud the scientists have searched Geller for metals that might be hidden under his fingernails and magnets sewn to his clothing, x-rayed his teeth for evidence of minute electronic devices, bound his hands, blindfolded his eyes, all but stripped him naked." Such a statement does little to dispel the impression that Panati has produced a public relations piece of puffery rather than a serious attempt to evaluate the case for Uri Geller. Other than one or two indications that Uri was probed with a magnetometer and a Geiger counter, the cases presented in this book are notable for the lack of any mention of serious attempts to search Geller or to place him under any such constraints as are suggested by the statement.

What, in the final analysis, does this collection of arguments for the paranormal powers of Uri Geller really demonstrate? As I indicated, a first reading might be highly persuasive and unsettling. But the book and its arguments fall apart the more closely we examine them. We see that even the subtitle misrepresents the situation. Instead of "Scientific Observations on the Paranormal Powers of Uri Geller" it should read, "Nonscientific Observations That Have Persuaded Some Scientists of Geller's Paranormal Powers." But the book does more than fail to make its case. When we realize that Panati has assembled the best possible scientific case for Geller's powers, we see something that I am sure Panati did not intend. We discover that after almost four years of "cooperating" with scientists in 17 different laboratories in 8 different countries, not one systematic and repeatable series of observations to document those powers has been obtained. Indeed, in the one laboratory that has had by far the most opportunity to study Geller at first hand, it was impossible to gain any scientific evidence to support his metal-bending and psychokinetic powers. What Panati's book does, then, is demonstrate that scientists are wasting their time in trying to build a case for paranormal forces on the basis of "tests" of Uri Geller. It is Geller, not the scientists, who ultimately "controls" the conditions under which he will operate. In describing their "approach to experimentation" with Uri Geller the scientists at Birkbeck College inadvertently reveal the reasons that Geller will either always have his way or will not cooperate with the investigators (see pages 190–96). The one predictable thing about Uri Geller is that, despite promises to the contrary, he will never try to produce his phenomena under conditions that would meet scientific standards of control.

But it would be wrong, in my judgment, to quickly forget about Uri Geller just because the attempt to construct a scientific case for his paranormal powers has failed miserably. This is not the first time that scientists have become involved in a battle of wits with an alleged psychic. Indeed, almost since the beginning of modern science, we can find cases in which outstanding scientists were apparently outwitted by clever tricksters. In the last century alone we have cases like Zoellner and Slade, Crookes and Florence Cook, Lombroso and Palladino, Alfred Russel Wallace and a host of spiritualistic mediums. And, just as in the present case, magicians also came into the picture to maintain that they alone were capable of separating truth from trickery. And, just as in the present situation, there were magicians who were, at least in the first instance, completely baffled by the alleged psychic (e.g., Harry Kellar was originally baffled by Eglinton and John Nevil Maskelyne was completely taken in by Henry Slade).

This raises a host of issues about scientists, magicians, and the qualifications necessary to detect fraud. This is not the place to discuss these issues. But the case of Uri Geller gives us a golden opportunity to examine these issues and see what lessons can be derived from them. If we simply let the Uri Geller Affair fade into oblivion without extracting from it the lessons it has to teach us about the limitations of scientific competence, then we are merely setting ourselves up for a repeat of it in the near future.

Mind-Reach. Russell Targ and Harold Puthoff. New York: Delacorte, 1977.*

The dust jacket of *Mind-Reach* informs us that "this book is a lucid and fascinating record of historic experiments—historic because they put the

---

*This review appeared under the title "Psychics and Scientists: 'Mind-Reach' and Remote Viewing," *The Humanist* (May–June 1977), 16–20.

seal of 'hard' physical science upon evidence that *some degree of psychic ability is universal*—a phenomenon straight out of science fiction that actually happened, and can be made to happen again in any laboratory! The scientists even offer a 'recipe' for developing your own ESP 'information channel.' "

The two scientists in question are Russell Targ and Harold Puthoff, both laser physicists at the prestigious Stanford Research Institute. As scientists, their credentials are impeccable. Targ has important patents to his credit in the laser field. Puthoff, a Stanford Ph.D., in addition to having laser patents has coauthored a textbook in quantum physics. Although Margaret Mead, in the introduction to the book, writes that the evidence put forth does "not appear to be the work of true believers who set out to use science to validate passionately held beliefs," neither author is a novice in psychical research.

Targ's interest in psychic phenomena goes back some twenty years. Prior to the time covered by this book, he had done work with an ESP teaching machine and, he told me, he had investigated the famed psychic Peter Hurkos. Targ also claims to be an amateur magician, who not only has practiced conjuring but also is aware of the standard methods of deception. Puthoff, who has made it to the level of a Class III Operational Thetan in the Church of Scientology, had previously obtained funding to study the Backster Effect—the alleged ability of plants to sense by extrasensory means the thoughts of humans.

The research described in this book began in 1972 when both Targ and Puthoff came to the Stanford Research Institute. The major portion of their work involves *remote viewing,* a term they use to refer to phenomena that cover "a range of subjective experience variously referred to in the literature as astral projection (occult); simple clairvoyance, traveling clairvoyance, or out-of-body experience (parapsychological); exteriorization or disassociation (psychological); or autoscopy (medical)." Remote viewing occurs when a subject is able to describe a target site even though he or she has no sensory basis for doing so. This can come about, according to the authors, by giving the subject the longitude and latitude of any place on the globe, or by sending a team of observers to a randomly selected site that is unknown to the subject.

In addition, the book contains research into other psychic phenomena. Studies are reported with an electronic random generator (ESP teaching machine); with attempts to influence magnetometers, compasses, and other instruments remotely; with Uri Geller's attempts at psychically bending metal, dematerializing objects, seeing the face of a hidden die, and duplicating drawings from which he was shielded.

The authors present us with both "hard" and "soft" evidence. The "hard" evidence consists of outcomes that pass their strict criteria for having occurred under "rigorous" and "controlled" scientific conditions. If they cannot figure out any way that the results could have been produced by trickery, instrument artifact, inadvertent cueing, or by accident, then they pass the test. "Soft" evidence is all the rest of the occurrences that intrigue the authors but that, for one reason or another, cannot pass the test on all the criteria.

Let's look first at what the authors claim as "hard" evidence. They state that "the primary achievement of this research has been the demonstration of high-quality 'remote viewing': the ability of experienced and inexperienced volunteers to view, by means of mental processes, remote geographical or technical targets, such as roads, buildings, and laboratory apparatus." This remote viewing ability, they claim, is unaffected by distance or the type of shielding provided by a Faraday cage. It can also occur precognitively—that is, the subject can correctly describe the target site *before* the target team has randomly selected and visited it. They further claim that this sort of psychic ability seems to be predominantly a function of the right hemisphere of the brain, because accuracy is more in terms of geometric shapes and patterns than in interpretation and also because EEG activity seems to indicate this. They also claim that anyone can do this. They have succeeded with both experienced and inexperienced subjects. Indeed, they claim that no subject has failed to show the ability.

They also claim "hard" evidence for at least some subjects showing success on the electronic random generator. In the case of Uri Geller, they claim scientific evidence for paranormal perceptual abilities in divining the uppermost face of a die in a closed box and in duplicating drawings made under conditions that precluded sensory contact.

The book is replete with accounts of striking and seemingly persuasive phenomena that the authors admit occurred under conditions that do not meet the standards for "hard" evidence. Geller was seemingly able to affect the magnetometer, affect a scale under a bell jar, move a television picture in various directions, cause a compass needle to move, dematerialize part of a camera, and trigger off a number of "coincidences." The last chapter deals with anecdotes involving prophetic dreams, psychic cats, sympathetic magic, and exploring outer space via remote viewing.

What are we to make of all this? What is it that makes this work "historic"? Certainly it is not the fact that physicists are investigating and apparently finding evidence for psychic phenomena. In spite of implications to the contrary on the dust jacket and in Margaret Mead's introduction (she claims that one advantage of these experiments is that "they come out of physics, popularly believed to be the hardest of the hard sciences"), physicists have a history going back over a hundred years of investigating and endorsing psychic phenomena. In the nineteenth century there were such big names as Crookes, Lodge, Barrett, and Zoellner. Other well-known scientists who plunged into psychical research were Alfred Russel Wallace, Robert Hare, Charles Richet, and Claude Flammarion. Nor is it the general approach of Targ and Puthoff, which treats the subject as a full-fledged collaborator rather than a guinea pig. All of the previously mentioned scientists also went out of their way to make the investigative conditions "safe" and sympathetic for the alleged psychics.

What is new, if it stands up to further scrutiny, is the unprecedented consistency of the findings. They simply have no failure in their remote viewing experiments. Experienced and inexperienced subjects succeed. Even skeptical visitors succeed when put through the protocols. (The authors slip into another meaning of "succeed" in this latter case. "Success" in the regular experiments is measured by the agreement of reports with actual target sites as obtained by a neutral judge; "success" in the case of the visitors is measured by subjective judgment that a given description does seem to match, in part, the given site.)

If Targ and Puthoff have actually hit upon a formula for getting results with all subjects, and if these results can be replicated in independent laboratories as they claim, then indeed their work represents a major breakthrough in psychical research. Up to now, this field of endeavor has been plagued by inconsistencies, hidden pitfalls, and nonrepeatability. It has caused its most dedicated workers nothing but frustration. Here is what William James had to say in his last article on psychical research in 1909 (*William James on Psychical Research,* ed. by G. Murphy and R. O. Ballou, New York: Viking, 1969).

> For twenty-five years I have been in touch with the literature of psychical research, and have had acquaintance with numerous "researchers." I have also spent a good many hours . . . in witnessing (or trying to witness) phenomena. Yet I am theoretically no "further" than I was at the beginning; and I confess that at times I have been tempted to believe that the Creator has eternally intended this department of nature to remain *baffling,* to prompt our curiosities and hopes and suspicions all in equal measure so that, although ghosts and clairvoyances, and raps and messages from spirits, are always seeming to exist and can never be fully explained away, they also can never be susceptible of full corroboration.

Some sixty-six years after William James penned these words, the philosopher Antony Flew, after twenty years in psychical research, in an article in the November 1975 *New Humanist,* had this to say:

> It seemed to me that the situation in this misbegotten area could be summed up by saying that there was too much evidence for one just to dismiss it as all a lot of nonsense, and enough to require that one should maintain

a continuing interest in the field, even if a distant interest. On the other hand, it seemed to me then that, though there was too much for one just to reject the whole business out of hand as a lot of superstition, nevertheless there was no such thing as a reliably repeatable phenomenon in the area, and there was really almost nothing positive that you could point to with assurance; there were some bits of negative work you could point to with assurance, but that was all. The depressing thing about the subsequent twenty-two years is that, though people have gone on working in this area—perhaps more has been done in the last twenty-two years than in any comparable period before—it still seems to me that the general evidential situation is just the same.

We do not know yet whether Targ and Puthoff will be making similar laments at some future date.

Meanwhile, however, they have already encountered the inevitable frustrations that confront every researcher in this field. They have become the target for attacks from what they call the "Loyal Opposition." The specific members of the Loyal Opposition that they deal with are The Amazing Randi, Martin Gardner, Joe Hanlon, George Lawrence, and myself. In a chapter entitled "The Loyal Opposition—What Are They Loyal To?" Targ and Puthoff deal with their critics in an interesting manner.

The authors imply that they are aware that resistance to new and radical ideas plays a positive role in the development of science. But they have obviously been stung at the personal level. They describe what from their viewpoint constitutes a series of unethical and malicious misrepresentations of their work by the Loyal Opposition. And I am indicted for a breach of ethics in allegedly "leaking" information about my confidential visit to SRI to *Time* magazine.

Obviously, Targ and Puthoff are puzzled by what they take as fanatic and unfair criticism. So they try to account for it. "At first, we spun paranoid theories with Cold War overtones. Perhaps there really was a developing ESP gap, as implied by the Ostrander-Schroeder book *Psychic Discoveries Behind the Iron Curtain.* Perhaps United States efforts in the study of the paranormal were the target of a deliberate program of disinformation, with the press the unwitting accomplice." After planting this suggestion of a communist conspiracy, the authors dismiss it on the grounds that "the deep-rooted distrust of the apparent paranormal functioning precedes the Cold War struggle by at least a century."

Instead, they graciously grant their critics good faith. The difficulty lies in the fact that the Loyal Opposition consists of individuals who cannot face up to the possibility that their world views may be wrong. Targ and Puthoff supply a psychological analysis of how the Loyal Opposition employs ever more extreme defenses to protect themselves from having to admit evidence that challenges the premises of their world view. They also point out that precognition and other psychic phenomena are compatible with current notions in quantum physics. This means, in their logic, that the burden of proof now lies with the critic who wants to deny such phenomena.

All this is unfortunate. By dismissing their critics as misguided fanatics, Targ and Puthoff miss the legitimate reasons for suspecting their work. If they were not so blinded by the search for psychological blocks in their opposition, the authors might better see how they have supplied the critics with much of their ammunition. My own criticisms of their work cannot be simply dismissed as another case of someone who cannot tolerate challenges to his world view. As far back as December 1957, I committed to print my opinion that if ESP were proved to be a reality it would not provide a serious threat to science or other accepted views (in a review of *Experiments in Telepathy,* by S. G. Soal and F. Bateman, in the *Journal of the American Statistical Association*); and in his recent book, *The Search for Superman,* John Wilhelm writes of my position: "He has a personal belief structure that seemingly would suffer least if psychic phenomena became accepted as a scientific reality." I want to make this clear to emphasize that there are grounds other than dogmatic fanaticism to raise serious questions about the credibility of the evidence that Targ and Puthoff have offered us.

In challenging the validity of their findings, I also want to emphasize that I am not necessarily claiming that they are more vulnerable to error than other scientists plunging into this tricky area. But they are vulnerable. And what seems to be a serious problem is their unwillingness or inability to admit that they are vulnerable. Neither expertise in laser physics nor training in conjuring nor sincere desire to make their experiments error-free and fraud-proof suffices to immunize them from mistakes, misinterpretations, and deception. Indeed, their very insistence that they are free from such defects may actually enhance their vulnerability.

In a given specialty like laser physics, one which has a well-developed history and accepted standards of instrumentation, measurement, experimental paradigms, and other agreed-upon procedures, a scientist's colleagues know what is meant when he or she states that data were gathered under controlled and rigorous conditions. But when the same scientist transfers his or her efforts to a new field, especially one in which scientific development is in its initial stages, it no longer is obvious what constitutes an adequately "controlled" experiment. Even in standard areas of science it takes a long shake-down period before a new problem or phenomenon can be safely studied without fear of generating artifacts or overlooking important sources of variance. In the area of psychical research, especially in such uncharted areas as dealing with a flamboyant psychic who claims to bend metals or in remote viewing, we have no accepted and standardized procedures, no specialized instrumentation, no agreed-upon dimensions and units, no well-developed paradigms, and no accumulation of experience to inform us unambiguously of what sources of error most need attention.

In a visit to SRI on December 8, 1972, I saw little to increase my confidence in the authors' ability to conduct psychic investigations. Targ and Puthoff, on more than one occasion, have insisted that what I witnessed that day was irrelevant for evaluating their research on Uri Geller. In this book, they insist that I have only myself to blame if what I saw was uncontrolled and unscientific. It was my fault that I let Uri get away with what they call his standard coffee-table demonstrations. All this baffles me greatly. As far as I knew, I was part of a visiting team to ascertain if Targ and Puthoff had sufficient evidence and an adequate case to justify the Advanced Research Projects Agency funding their research on Uri Geller. Under the circumstances, I assumed that they would present to us the best case possible for Uri's powers and their competence to harness them. Just what did Targ and Puthoff have to gain by sitting back and letting Uri devote an entire day and their resources to a display of useless parlor tricks? Did they think that what they regarded as unscientific entertainments would nevertheless be sufficient to convince us to recommend financial support?

But this is not the place to go into differences about the visit. The point I want to make is how the authors and I differ on what is a "controlled" experiment. Targ and Puthoff say that the only controlled experiment that occurred during our visit to SRI was the one in which Uri Geller apparently duplicated a drawing that Robert Van de Castle had earlier sealed in an envelope. Here is what I observed, based upon the detailed notes I made at the time it occurred.

Van de Castle had brought a picture with him that he wanted Uri to duplicate by psychic means. When Uri learned that the picture had been clipped from a magazine, he was hesitant. He said that it would be better if it were something that Van de Castle had drawn himself. Van de Castle offered to draw a version of the picture from memory. Uri reluctantly agreed. Uri did not feel confident, but said he would give it a try. Van de Castle sealed his drawing in one opaque envelope and the magazine picture in another. Each was marked outside to identify it. Uri sent everyone out of the room except George Lawrence and myself. He had George place his hands on each envelope. Uri tried to get an impression. But nothing, he said, came through. He asked George to retain the envelopes and he would try later, maybe at lunch or after.

After lunch, while all alone with George, Uri tried again. Again nothing happened. Then Uri decided to try with Van de Castle, who, of course, knew what the drawings were. They went alone into a room. After a half-hour, Uri and Van de Castle emerged. They were obviously flushed with victory—they announced success, or at least partial success. The envelopes had been opened before they emerged! Van de Castle explained this obvious breach of protocol on the grounds that Uri was impatient to know how well he had done. So Van de Castle and Uri opened the envelopes immediately to check out the drawings. It was not clear which one of them had opened the envelopes.

We asked what had taken place during the half-hour in the room. We were told that Van de Castle asked Uri how he could be of help. Uri suggested that Van de Castle keep his eyes closed and keep his hands over his eyes to better visualize what he wanted to project. Van de Castle claimed that during this long time with his eyes closed he had control of the envelopes. This meant, as elicited by further questioning, that Van de Castle had his elbow upon the envelope with his drawing in it. He freely admitted at that point, and again later, that the second envelope could have been out of his possession. As someone pointed out, Uri's drawing was a better match to the magazine picture than to Van de Castle's drawing. Targ commented that this was a perfect experiment.

This, then, is the experiment that Targ and Puthoff claim was done under controlled conditions. From my viewpoint, this fails at being a controlled experiment on a number of grounds: (1) Uri was alone with just one man and the envelopes for a half-hour; (2) Van de Castle had his eyes shut during this entire period; (3) Van de Castle was sure only that he had control of one envelope; (4) the envelopes had been opened prior to their emerging from the room (thereby destroying any evidence of possible tampering); (5) Uri's drawing was a better match to the picture that was in the envelope that Van de Castle admitted could have been out of his possession. This is just one example of why we cannot be satisfied by the simple declaration that the conditions were "controlled."

It is unfortunate that Uri Geller happened to Targ and Puthoff. Ironically, one of the reasons they give for not allowing me to see their regular experiments with Uri is that at that time they suspected that Uri might have been sent to test their competence. They hinted that I might have collaborated with Uri to trick them and then use this successful deception to discredit them as psychic investigators. Whether he was sent to SRI for this purpose or not, Targ and Puthoff will have a hard time convincing even some believers that Geller did not swindle them. They themselves, in trying to show how knowledgeable they are about magicians' tricks, describe how Uri, as soon as he arrived at SRI, pulled the driving-blindfold trick on them. Knowing full well that Uri was willing to trick them, they went ahead with their research program, fully confident that they could separate out the trickery from the real thing. More cautious investigators would have either immediately sent Uri back to his sponsor or treated all subsequent miracles with suspicion.

Because of the Geller affair, perhaps, the remote viewing experiments become even more suspect than otherwise. In a sense, they are too good. Without question they are several orders of magnitude superior as experiments than the one reported with Uri Geller. The protocols are described in much more detail, and we are given rather detailed descriptions of precautions taken against deception, inadvertent cueing, editing, and selection of cases. And the ultimate criterion of success is based upon a sophisticated statistical procedure.

So what is wrong? Without being on the scene it is hard to say, but there are some disturbing aspects. The authors go into great detail about how the subject generates his description, how the target site is selected, and how the team is sent to it. They describe the judging procedure, but in much less detail. In fact, it is just in this detail that problems arise. The statistics and judging procedure assume independence of descriptions for each target site. But this is obviously violated by the experimental procedure. Immediately after the subject generates his description, he is taken to the target site to be given feedback on how well he has done. Although the reason for doing this may be understandable, it makes his next description no longer independent of the first target site. To give one example of how this might generate false hits, assume that the first site is a municipal swimming pool. The next day the subject will probably avoid describing features that obviously belong to a swimming pool. If the second site, say, is a marina, the subject, in the third protocol, would avoid describing things that obviously belong to a swimming pool or a marina, and so on. Such a situation, in principle, could suffice to give a judge sufficient information to make perfect matches at each site from the descriptions. We, of course, do not know if, in fact, such an artifact did actually produce their results. But the very fact that the assumption of independence was violated destroys the validity of their statistical computations. In future experiments, they will have to find a way to ensure independence (such as using only one target per subject and having the judge match a set of descriptions generated by different subjects).

Possibly just as serious is the lack of any description of precautions to ensure post-description security. After each description, the subject and the team of investigators all go to the target site and openly discuss how well the description fits the site. Good, or apparently good, descriptions will become topics of animated discussion. What precautions were taken to make sure that none of this gossip trickled back to potential judges? Similar comments could be made about security of the protocols, recording judges' ratings, randomizing protocols to give to judges, the order in which judges visit sites, and so on.

The authors make the strong claim that everyone whom they have run through their protocol has succeeded to "satisfaction." This is certainly not completely the case. I have talked with two individuals who went through this procedure who were definitely not convinced that they had succeeded beyond simple chance matching. And I know someone who has talked with another individual who also felt it did not work for him. Targ and Puthoff further claim that the remote viewing experiment has been successfully replicated in several independent laboratories. But they mention only one other study by name of investigators and laboratory. In a footnote, they mention the study and say it consisted of a lengthy series. In a report put out by these authors, the "lengthy series" consists of eight trials, two of which they admit were defective. I know of one attempt to faithfully replicate the remote viewing experiment as they described it in an article published in the Institute of Electrical and Electronics Engineers' journal; the results were completely negative.

All this suggests that the authors may not yet have found the magic formula for the repeatable ESP experiment. The history of the field is against them. And enough questions can be raised about their current work to raise doubts, at least for members of the Loyal Opposition. But, as always, time will tell. And if it turns out that they are correct after all, then I am ready to resign my membership in the Loyal Opposition.

Part Three

Psychic Phenomena

Introduction

The papers in Parts III and IV vary more in coverage than those in the preceding parts. One benefit is that they thus overlap less with each other. The first paper in this section and the review of *Dowsing: The Psi Connection* deal with water witching or dowsing. This topic was the focus of a national survey conducted by the Harvard anthropologist Evon Z. Vogt and myself in the 1950s. We also wrote a book, *Water Witching U.S.A.* (second edition, 1979), which covers just about every aspect of the subject. However, the paper and review included here capture our main conclusions quite well.

After we conducted our survey in the 1950s and after the first edition of our book appeared in 1959, the American Society of Dowsers was formed. My colleague Vogt conducted a survey of the membership of the society and discovered that the typical member did not resemble the rural diviners who provided the material for our book. Instead, the typical member of the society comes from an urban environment and obviously has no need to find underground water. These new dowsers, whom Vogt appropriately labels *urban dowsers,* come from an occult background and use the divining rod as another tool for regulating their lives. They use the rod for making decisions about what to eat, which parts of the environment may be unhealthy because of noxious radiation, and other divinatory purposes.

A few summers ago I attended the annual meeting of the American Society of Dowsers in Danville, Vermont. Those who attended, indeed, differed from our typical rural diviners. The typical American water witch is a pragmatic person who has little interest in occult matters. They use the rod because they believe it "works." The urban dowser is part of the New Age movement and looks upon dowsing as another tool for psychic and spiritual development.

Dowsing is important because it probably has been more extensively scientifically tested than any other occult practice. The accumulated evidence makes a consistent story. Whenever the test is conducted according to controlled scientific standards, the diviner performs no better than chance.

Despite this complete lack of scientific support, the act of divining creates strong and compelling beliefs in both practitioners and onlookers. Many individuals, including scientists and some of my academic colleagues, who otherwise profess skepticism of all occult matters, report events they have experienced or witnessed that they believe support the validity of divining. These believers are not swayed by my recital of the accumulated scientific evidence against the claims of diviners. Nor are they persuaded by my attempts to show why their particular evidence fails to meet scientific criteria.

Such compelling belief in the face of hard scientific evidence to the contrary may provide important clues about the nature of belief. The next section deals more directly with this issue.

The experiment on which Jim McClenon and I collaborated ("A Remote Viewing Experiment Conducted by a Skeptic and a Believer") also has much to say about belief. By any acceptable scientific standard, our joint experiment failed to provide any evidence for psi. McClenon, in one sense, is willing to admit this. Yet, in another sense, he is willing to claim that his little experiment conducted "on the side" *did* demonstrate psi. As a sociologist of knowledge, McClenon believes that our different positions on this matter can somehow be rationalized on the basis of the fact that we are "embedded in two different paradigms."

In a way, of course, McClenon is correct. But in a more basic way, I think he is wrong. He knows as well as I that our experiment does not justify any conclusions about psi. However, he would prefer to believe otherwise. The danger in his position, as I see it, is that he seems to believe that the believer's position on this matter is just as rational and sound as the skeptic's position. As a matter of hard fact, we both know what the true odds are for this situation; we also know what the weight of the evidence is. It is not different for him and me—it is the same. What *is* different is that he is willing to discard or ignore this evidence when it does not come out in his favor.

I would recommend my review of the *Encyclopedia of Occultism and Parapsychology* because of my attempts to formulate the rules by which a mind such as McClenon's, for example, might be operating. If skeptics and believers are ever going to conduct a constructive dialogue, then we must understand the underlying premises of each other's actions and beliefs.

Water Witching: Magical Ritual in Contemporary United States*

(with Evon Z. Vogt)

For the past half hour Judd Potter has been pacing slowly back and forth over Mark Bond's pasture, a forked peach branch in his hands. Gripping one fork in each hand so tightly that the veins stand out, his head bent forward, his eyes focused on the juncture of the forks, Judd Potter acts like a man in a trance.

Suddenly the branch begins to quiver and dance as though it were alive. As Judd takes a few more steps, the branch is pulled downward toward the ground so powerfully that the bark peels off in his hands. Judd's tense body relaxes and for the first time since beginning the ritual, he looks at Mark Bond, who has been anxiously following behind. "This is the spot," he says. "Sink your well here and you'll get all the water you need."

Judd Potter has just performed the ancient rite of water witching—also known by a variety of other names such as "water divining," "dowsing," "smelling," "witch wriggling"—and his divining rod, the forked peach branch, has shown by its dance where Bond should drill for water.

Until this moment, Bond has regarded the practice of water witching with extreme skepticism. An up-to-date farmer, graduate of an agricultural college, he knew there was no scientific basis for water witching and that scientists view the practice as a relic of the superstitious past. But there had been a severe drought; his well had gone dry and his attempts to

Psychology Today (vol. 1, Nov. 1967), 35–42. Reprinted with permission from *Psychology Today* magazine © 1967 (Pt. Partners, Ltd.).

drill a new one had produced only dry holes. The county agricultural extension agent, when asked for advice, had nothing better to offer than "Keep trying. Good luck." So in desperation Bond had turned to a neighboring farmer, Judd Potter, an old-timer with a reputation for having successfully witched hundreds of wells. With no other alternative at hand, it seemed sensible to give Potter a chance to see what he could do.

And to Mark Bond's delight and astonishment, when he drilled at the spot where the peach limb had danced and quivered, he found water in abundance. Bond's skepticism was converted into ardent belief in the power of the divining rod, and no wonder.

Mark Bond's plight was of course by no means unique. And neither was his solution. Under similar circumstances, farmers throughout the United States turn today, as they did in the past, to water witches.

Even if water witching were not a fascinating subject for research in its own right, it would be worth studying if only because of its widespread continuing popularity in an advanced technological society, and because it has always been controversial. Ever since the practice began, more than four hundred years ago, authorities of church, government, and science have consistently opposed it. Nevertheless, the drama enacted in Mark Bond's pasture may be witnessed in every state in America.

It was the paradoxical persistence of this outcast art within a scientifically and technologically oriented culture that originally aroused our interest in water witching—the fact that today's farmers, who employ the latest findings to help them in selecting seed and fertilizers, and in fighting plant diseases, nevertheless bypass scientific help and turn to ancient divining practices when they seek underground water. We thought that a closer look at water witching might tell us something about the perseverance of nonscientific beliefs within our culture, as an example of a more general phenomenon— the way people try to cope with uncertain and unpredictable environments. The study of water witching might give us clues about why people, under stress and anxiety, turn to unorthodox and pseudoscientific practices in general.

Water Witching and Magic

Many aspects of water witching indicate that its role in our society is similar to that of magical ritual in primitive societies. Water witching, like magic, has an immediate practical aim; like magic, it is carried out only by those who have "the gift"; it is performed according to an unchanging ritual; it is accompanied by a mythology (about the distribution of underground water); and its mythology supplies ready rationales for apparent failures.

The study of water witching as a form of magical ritual also offers the opportunity to evaluate a widely accepted but seldom tested anthropological theory about the function of magic. As stated by the anthropologist Bronislaw Malinowski, this theory holds that "man resorts to magic only where chance and circumstances are not fully controlled by knowledge." Malinowski believed that people resort to magic when two factors are present in a situation: when there is a gap in knowledge concerning the outcome of an important event in nature, and when an individual must nevertheless act.

In a famous example, Malinowski described the fishing practices of the natives of the Trobriand Archipelago. The villagers living on the inner lagoon could easily and reliably obtain fish by poisoning the waters. Those living on the open coast, however, could obtain fish only under conditions that were hazardous and highly unreliable. "It is most significant," Malinowski wrote, "that in the lagoon fishing, where man can rely completely upon his knowledge and skill, magic does not exist, while in the open-sea fishing, full of danger and uncertainty, there is extensive magical ritual to secure safety and good results."

If Malinowski's theory about the function of magic applies to water witching, we should expect to find a correlation between the prevalence of water witching and the degree of uncertainty and risk that accompanies the locating of underground water. From this we can derive a hypothesis and counter-hypothesis to test Malinowski's theory: We would expect to find that witching is common wherever the outcome of well digging is highly uncertain; on the other hand, we would *not* expect water witching to be practiced where groundwater conditions and geological knowledge make the outcome highly predictable.

We therefore carried out a large-scale study whose primary objective was to gather information that would confirm or contradict the hypothesis. As by-products of our study, however, we uncovered considerable information about the characteristics of water witches, the types of instruments used, and the folklore that supports the practice in the United States.

The Study

We needed to obtain two major sets of data: information on the groundwater problems in a representative sample of rural counties throughout the United States, and on the prevalence of witching in these counties. Our first task, that of obtaining a representative sample of counties, was carried out as follows: On the basis of our survey of the 3017 counties in the United States (as of 1956), we divided them into two strata, one of which included all counties in which 50 percent of the population was classified as urban. The other stratum, consisting of rural counties, was subdivided into 10 smaller strata, based on groundwater regions as classified according to the system devised by Harold Thomas of the U. S. Geological Survey. This gave us a total of 11 strata. From the one large urban stratum, and from each of the 10 rural strata, we drew a random sample of counties, giving us a total of 500 counties.

We mailed a questionnaire to the county agricultural extension agent in each of the 500 counties of our sample. The questionnaire contained 26 queries relating to problems of finding groundwater, and to the practice of water witching. In our covering letter we defined a water witch or dowser as one who: (1) uses or has used a forked stick, wire, or pendulum to locate underground water and (2) as a result of whose activity a well has been dug or drilled on the site indicated.

Our conclusions are based on the 360 usable responses we received, and on the additional information (from census reports and other sources) about precipitation, groundwater conditions, and population characteristics for each of these counties.

The Extent of Witching in the United States

We used two indices of witching activity: (1) the proportion of wells that are witched, and (2) the proportion of diviners in the population. Of the two, the first index is probably the more direct measure of witching activity, but unfortunately it is harder to obtain and is probably less reliable, for many agents were reluctant to estimate the number of wells that had been witched, and when they did, they indicated that they were not confident of their figures. In our sample, this index ranged all the way from none to 100 percent of wells dug—the latter in a county in southern Neveda.

On the other hand, most of the agents seemed to be reasonably sure that they knew the number of diviners in their counties. Our index of witches was based on the number of reported witches per 100,000 population. In our sample, the index ranged from none to 643, the highest concentration occurring in southwestern Kansas. Since we found that the two indices were very highly correlated with each other, we used the ratio of witches-to-population as our index of witching activity.

If we extrapolate this ratio to the United States as a whole, it appears that there are approximately 18 witches per 100,000 population, or a total of 25,000 water witches in the country. A further breakdown reveals that there are about 35 witches per 100,000 population in predominantly rural areas and only eight witches per 100,000 in urban areas. Of course, these figures are only approximate. Nevertheless, our estimates are sufficiently precise to assure us that the practice of water witching is carried out by a significant portion of the population as a whole, and by a rather large segment of the rural population.

Groundwater Problems and Witching

We used several indices of the general difficulty and uncertainty of obtaining groundwater: (1) the type of groundwater region in which the county was located; (2) responses of the county agents as to average depth, range of depth, adequacy of the water supply, and the cost of well drilling; and (3) a "problem score" for each county, based on the agent's estimate of the probability of getting a dry hole, of obtaining sufficient rate of flow, of getting water of poor quality, and having to pay too much, drill too deeply, or drill in an undesirable location.

The percentage of witches is highest in the three groundwater regions where groundwater problems are most severe, and is lowest in the three regions where there is an ample supply of underground water. When we analyzed our data for each county within a groundwater region, we found that the same tendency held good: not only is water witching most likely to be practiced where water is difficult to find, but the greater the problems involved in finding good underground water, the greater the ratio of diviners to population.

The findings confirmed our original hypothesis, and they are consistent with the theory that magic serves an important function, and with the view that witching is a ritual that reduces anxiety in the same way that magic does in nonliterate societies.

A European Import

As mentioned above, one by-product of our study was a much better picture of water witching as it is currently practiced in rural America.

On the basis of the evidence available to us, we conclude that water witching is a European practice that was brought to this country, probably in the seventeenth century, by settlers from Germany and England, especially those from the mining districts of Cornwall. The French and Italians may also have brought it with them, for we now find it among all the European immigrant groups who settled in rural areas, as well as among Negroes who presumably borrowed it from white settlers in the South.

Like almost every other aspect of water witching, its history, too, is controversial. Many claim that the practice goes back 7,000 years, and cite the Biblical story in which Moses strikes the rock with his rod and water gushes forth. Indeed, we have been told by several American diviners that Moses was the first water witch. Scythians, Persians, Greeks, and

Romans used rods for divination, and Mediterranean idols bearing forked rods have been found, but there is no evidence that these rods were used for divining water, particularly since in the detailed directions for finding water given by many ancient naturalists such as Pliny, there is no mention of anything akin to the divining rod.

The first unambiguous account of water witching occurs in *De Re Metallica,* an account of German mining by Georgius Agricola, published in 1556. His description of the ritual might equally well be used to describe the ritual as currently practiced in America. Water witching is unknown among indigenous populations elsewhere in the world; it seems safe to conclude that we are dealing with a European culture pattern that originated in Germany, spread to the rest of Europe, and thence to other regions as Europeans established colonies and spread their culture to other parts of the world.

The variations from standard practice to be found in America, usually involving the shape of the rod or the material used, are all of European origin, and are described in the earliest accounts. Even "long distance" witching above a map as practiced by the famous American diviner, Henry Gross, is a European importation. The only distinctively American contribution is the term, "water witching." In England it is called "dowsing"; in Latin countries, "divining," and in Germany, "wishing" or "striking." In more than 78 percent of the counties in our sample, the term "water witching" is predominant, while "dowsing" is current only in the New England states, New York, and Pennsylvania. The quasi-scientific terms that are widely used in Europe—"radiesthesia," "dryptesthesia," or "rhabdomancy"— are apparently unknown to the American farmer.

Tools of the Trade

From Agricola's time in the sixteenth century until today, the diviner's trademark has been the forked twig or branch. Our data reveal that the forked twig is still by far the most frequently used instrument of American diviners. But even in Agricola's time there were variations. Instead of hazel, ash, or pitch-pine twig, the rod might be of iron or steel; indeed it appears that any rod-like object, forked or not, can serve; walking sticks, surgical scissors, a stalk of grass, and even a German sausage have been pressed into service as divining rods.

We encounter this same diversity in contemporary American practice. Although reports from early colonial days tell us that the witch-hazel twig was the most popular form of rod (indeed, some writers believe that the American term, "witching," originated with the use of the witch-hazel), only two counties in our sample reported hazel of any kind as being commonly used for a divining rod. By far the single most popular tree from which rods are obtained in this country is the peach tree; second in popularity is willow; less popular varieties are cherry, apple (mostly in New England), elm, and in the deep South, persimmon trees. Other trees mentioned only once or twice are hickory, plum, pear, elder, birch, and maple. One informant told us that when nothing else is handy, he has found that poison oak will do!

In arid regions where trees are scarce, wire is used—baling wire, barbed wire from the nearest fence, and coat hangers—or metal tools such as welding rods, tire irons, crow bars, steel files, or pliers. But almost anything will serve in the never-ending quest for water. Our respondents listed horse whips, shovels, pitchforks, and such commercial gadgets as a pair of swiveling rods; the latter is used by the water department of a large New England city to trace leaks in the water mains.

An alternative to the conventional wood or metal rod is the magic pendulum which has a far longer recorded history than has the divining rod. The ancient Romans studied the gyrations of a weight suspended on a thread from their fingers to discover who would win a forthcoming battle or succeed the current emperor. The pendulum was assimilated to water divining, more often to supplement than to replace the information from the forked twig. Today, the American diviner asks the pendulum to tell him how deep he will have to drill before he strikes water. Almost anything can be used as the pendulum: a set of keys suspended from a Bible, a watch attached to a chain or a string, a spool suspended on strands of thread, a penny attached to a wire, or a bottle filled with quicksilver or water suspended on a string.

Who Are the Witches?

The folklore of water witching suggest that witches are born, not made. The most frequently recurring statements contain the belief that the "power" is inherited—"from father to son or daughter," "from mother to daughter," "to one person in a family," or even "to the seventh son of a seventh son." A related belief is that only certain people can be witches; "if you have the gift, you can do it."

Many of our informants assured us that only men have the power. In the Ozarks, for example, this belief is associated with sexual virility. "A feller has got to be a whole man," one old gentlemen said, "if he aims to take up witch wrigglin'." But although it is true that the vast majority of witches are men, women diviners are by no means uncommon. Of the counties in our sample in which there were diviners, as many as 42 percent reported that at least one of the diviners is a woman.

Our data indicate that age has little to do with the "power," although about 78 percent of the counties with diviners report that at least one is more than 65 years old, but only 2 percent reported any knowledge of diviners under the age of 15. As far as we can tell, however, the rod works just as well for children as it does for adults. It is likely that most witches are adult males simply because the opportunity and the need to practice divining is presented much more frequently to this segment of the population.

Among academic skeptics, water witching is apt to be dismissed as being practiced only by the uneducated, and at first sight our data seemed to bear this out, for in about 66 percent of the counties with diviners it was reported that the average diviner has only a grade-school education or less. But the exceptions are impressive. As many as 30 percent of the counties in our sample reported that the average diviner has a high-school education, and no fewer than 3 percent reported diviners who had received a college education. When we consider that the need for witching occurs mainly in rural areas, and that rural areas as a whole have lower educational levels, it is evident that the witch, by and large, is as well educated as the average person in the community. We know personally many highly educated men, including some with M.D.'s and Ph.D.'s, who both believe in and practice water witching.

Our data on the religious and ethnic background of diviners show that the majority are Protestant; only half as many are Catholic. The most common ethnic designation is "Old American," followed by German, Scandinavian, Negro, and American Indian, in that order. When we compared this information with published census data on the counties in which the diviners practice, we found that the ethnic composition of the water witches almost exactly parallels that of the surrounding population.

In the overwhelming majority of cases, witching is not practiced as a livelihood. Of the approximately 25,000 witches in the United States, probably only a handful try to make a full-time living from divining; for the typical diviner, witching is an avocation—a use of his gift to help a neighbor in need. True, he may charge a certain amount for his services, but it is likely to be a token fee, typically about $25.

"It Does Move"

We might expect that a practice with so long a history as witching would be accompanied by an elaborate folklore containing "explanations" of how it works, and rationalizations to account for failures. And indeed such a folklore does exist, mostly borrowed from Europe. But while the European folklore is rich and its theories elaborate, much of it has been shed by the practical-minded American.

If we ask an American diviner to explain why the rod moves, he shrugs his shoulders and says, "I don't know, it just does." If we press him further or seek out other diviners we do get rationales, ranging from supernatural interpretations (for example, that they derive their power from Moses) to quasi-scientific interpretations (for example, that the muscles of the diviner are affected by electromagnetic disturbances). An instance of this type of explanation was reported to us by a Harvard colleague. He was observing a diviner in action in northern New Hampshire. The diviner walked back and forth over a patch of land until the rod dipped straight down. The diviner then took one additional long step and said, "Dig here." Our colleague said to the diviner, "I understand what you are trying to do with this procedure, but why did you take that one extra step after the rod dipped?" The diviner replied, "Oh, I was just correctin' for the hypotenuse!"

To explain exactly how and why the rod moves in the diviner's hands would involve a complicated discussion of physics and psychophysics and of the kind of rod used and the way it is gripped. Here we will confine our discussion to the forked twig, held in the standard, palms-up grip—by far the most common mode of witching.

If you grip the forked twig—palms upward, one fork in each hand, the forks pointing forward at an angle of 45 degrees, hands compressed toward each other—you can cause the rod to move by any of four very slight changes of grip.

First, because the rod is so taut, an imperceptible easing of your grip will cause the rod to rotate in your hands.

Second, a slight rotation of your wrists toward each other will cause the rod to dip; rotating them outward will cause the rod to move upward. Depending upon how much the rod is compressed by the initial grip, a very slight rotation of the wrists can impart a considerable "kick" to the rod.

The third and fourth ways to produce movement consist of pulling your hands slightly apart or pushing them slightly together. Either movement creates greater tension in the rod than in the force of the grip. By so upsetting the balance, the rod, acting like a coiled spring, may straighten out with such force that the bark literally comes off in your hands.

In each case the movement occurs because forces and stresses in the rod become greater than the force by which the diviner grips the rod.

So far as we can tell, not one of the diviners with whom we are acquainted consciously makes the rod move. The same mechanical principles hold, however, whether or not the diviner is aware that he or she has changed his or her grip. From his point of view, the rod moves of its own accord. Indeed, so convincing is this experience, the diviner will swear the rod was moved by some outside force, and may insist that he was actually trying to keep it from moving. Such involuntary movements imparted to inanimate objects have tempted people throughout history to attribute these effects to supernatural forces. Belief in the Ouija board, the magic pendulum, table tipping, and in a variety of other bizarre manifestations testifies to this. These phenomena were explained more than one hundred years ago by William Carpenter, who coined the term *ideo-motor action* to cover all manifestations of behavior that are independent of conscious volition. He observed that "ideas may become the sources of muscular movement, independently either of volitions or of emotions." Carpenter was particularly referring to situations in which the ideas are suggested to the individual, or are the result of expectant attention, as in hypnosis or in the use of the Ouija board and the divining rod.

William James, the American psychologist, accepted Carpenter's concept of ideo-motor action not as a curious phenomenon, but as an important explanatory principle of all behavior, "simply the normal process stripped of disguise." According to James, the natural course of every idea is to manifest itself in overt action: "Wherever a movement *unhesitatingly and immediately* follows upon the idea of it, we have ideo-motor action. We are then aware of nothing between the conception and the execution. All sorts of neuro-muscular processes come between, of course, but we know absolutely nothing of them. We think the act, and it is done; and that is all that introspection tells us of the matter."

An attempt to apply this principle to water witching in terms of contemporary psychology would involve us in too much technical detail, but perhaps we can convey some idea by presenting a composite picture, pieced together from actual accounts, of an individual's first attempt at water witching.

Let us return to the beginning of this article where we encountered Judd Potter in the act of witching a well. Among the onlookers is Jim Brown. Jim has heard of witching, of course, but he has never tried it. As Jim watches Judd, we can assume that his intense concentration on Judd's movements is accompanied by very minute contractions in his forearms which correspond, on a smaller scale, to Judd's own muscular contractions. Perhaps Jim's neck muscles and general musculature are tense as he leans forward awaiting the outcome of the diviner's effort. Already the idea has been implanted. Suddenly, dramatically, the rod points downward.

Judd looks up and notices Jim's incredulous expression. He walks over to Jim, hands him the rod, and says, "Here, why don't you try it?" He assures Jim that the rod will work for him, too. Our knowledge of ideo-motor action and suggestibility tells us that Judd's suggestion to Jim again produces minute contractions in Jim's forearm muscles. This time, we would guess that the action potentials in the arms are even greater than the first time. Witnessing Judd's performance has enhanced Jim's susceptibility to the direct suggestion.

Jim grasps the rod in imitation of Judd. We see the same tense arms, the same trance-like concentration upon the rod, and we note that Jim becomes oblivious to the onlookers as his attention is completely focused upon the anticipated movement of the rod.

This heightened concentration and the increased tension in his muscles will facilitate the later muscular response; an impulse that under ordinary circumstances would not lead to overt muscular response, might then easily trigger a reaction in Jim's tense muscles. Furthermore, the heightened and prolonged tension is reducing the muscular feedback from his arms and hands; he is not aware that his muscles are "ready."

Now Jim is nearing the site where Judd's rod had dipped. His image of the rod's movements is intensified in the face of his expectation that it will move. The contractions in his forearms spread to adjoining muscle fibers; the minute contractions begin rallying together. Suddenly—in a great wave of unison—they produce a much larger muscular contraction. With an almost imperceptible spasm, his hands come closer together and his wrists turn slightly inward, upsetting the delicate balance of forces existing between his grip and the tensions in the rod. The rod suddenly springs downward with such force that the bark peels off, painfully scratching Jim's hands.

All at once Jim is aware that the rod has dipped—seemingly of its own accord—over the same spot where it had dipped for Judd. At first he is at a loss for words. Then he is overcome with a desire to explain to the onlookers that he did not make the rod move; that indeed, he was conscious only of an attempt to hold back. He points to the peeled bark and his injured hands as proof. Jim has now entered the ranks of water diviners.

"But Does It Work?"

The seemingly automatic, self-propelled motion of the rod is one of the many mysteries surrounding the ritual of water witching. When people ask of witching, "Does it work?" they often mean, "Does the rod move of its own accord?" But equally often they mean: "Are the rod's movements connected with the actual presence of underground water?" Is there something special about witching that makes it a better-than-chance method for finding water?

As you might guess, the evidence is sparse, of varied quality, and highly controversial. Most of it, especially that favorable to the case for divining, is drawn from anecdotes and case histories. Some, however, is derived from field tests that have been deliberately arranged to evaluate the diviner's claims. And although a field test provides better evidence than a case history, in that descriptions of what takes place are more objective, the results are usually inconclusive because there is seldom a baseline against which to evaluate the diviner's performance. In other words, a field test cannot be assessed scientifically unless we know what someone other than the diviner might have accomplished under the same conditions.

The only evidence that can properly be called scientific has been obtained from a handful of laboratory and field experiments that did provide an objective baseline. An excellent example is an experiment performed in Maine under the auspices of the American Society for Psychical Research. It is especially relevant since it was conducted by persons who were sympathetic or at least open-minded about the possibility that the claims of the diviners might be valid.

Twenty-seven diviners (22 men, 4 women, and 1 adolescent girl) were tested separately on a field chosen to be free of surface clues to water. Each used his or her own mode of witching to select the "best" spot for drilling a well, and was asked to estimate the depth at which water would be found, as well as the amount. Each was subjected to a second test, this time blindfolded to eliminate any visual clues.

As a control, the experimenters systematically selected 16 sites that convered the area in a representative manner. A geologist and an engineer were asked to estimate the depth and amount of water to be found at each of these sites. After the diviners had picked the "best" locations, test wells were sunk at each, and at the 16 sites assessed by the experts, and the depth and amount of water were measured. The experts did a good job of estimating the depth at the 16 specific points, but did poorly at estimating the amount. The diviners, on the other hand, failed completely to estimate either the depth or the amount of water at the locations they had selected.

The experimenters reported that "not one of our diviners could for a moment be mistaken for an 'expert' . . . we saw nothing to challenge the prevailing view that we are dealing with unconscious muscular activity, or what Frederic Myers called 'motor automatism.' "

There is no need to cite the results of other investigations; indeed, we know of no acceptable laboratory experiment that supports the claims of believers. Both believers and skeptics agree that the most favorable evidence for diviners' claims is to be found in anecdotes and retrospective accounts, and that as we move closer and closer to the controlled experiment and the laboratory, there is less and less evidence that diviners possess any power to detect water.

But this is as far as the agreement goes. The skeptic, of course, inter-

16

prets this as evidence against the validity of witching; it cannot be justified on the basis of scientific standards. The believer, on the other hand, attributes the failure to the inadequacies of the scientific approach, claiming that the witch produces "when it counts"—in his or her home environment, unhampered by the artificialities of scientific control and unhindered by skepticism.

The Diviner's Defense

These counterarguments are less a "rationale for failure," essential to the mythology of any magical ritual, than they are a "rationale for belief" that tends to avoid the problem of scientific confirmation. The following are representative of the arguments we encountered.

The "test of time" argument. Solco Tromp, who attempted to justify water witching in terms of physical theory, wrote: "Nonetheless, undeterred by public ridicule, persistent generations of dowsers have upheld their belief for at least 7,000 years, almost as long as civilization itself has existed. This should suggest even to the most critical scientist that there may be some possibility of truth in the stories of diviners." Even if we overlook the fact that Tromp has added 6,500 years to the known history of divining, longevity seems to be a poor substitute for scientific confirmation. This argument would call upon us to acknowledge the validity of such ancient practices as astrology, palmistry, and other forms of divination that still survive.

The "core of truth" argument. Almost as frequently offered, and usually coupled with the first, is the proposition that even if individual cases for witching cannot be scientifically confirmed, taken together they must contain "a core of truth." That is, large numbers of positive outcomes, no matter how weak each one, must add up to something. This recalls an old Chinese saying, "If a thousand people say a foolish thing, it is still a foolish thing."

The "testimonial" argument. When we refuse to accept the first two arguments, the defense can be relied upon to offer the testimonials of famous people. In a 1962 article in *True* magazine, for example, Dan Mannix quotes the assertion of a Frenchman that divining "has also been endorsed by five Nobel Prize winners." Although the five are not named, we know that Charles Richet, a French Nobel laureate, was an outspoken believer in witching. But we do not usually settle questions of scientific truth by a roll call. Even if we did, however, water witching would undoubtedly lose. For every prestigious figure who has endorsed it, there are a sizeable number of equally prestigious persons who have denounced it.

The "it would be a good thing for mankind" argument. "O.K.! So maybe the evidence at the moment is not scientific but by opposing water witching you may be impeding the development of something that might help mankind" is a typical introduction to this argument. Thus the novelist, Kenneth Roberts, responded to critics of his book on the divining prowess of Henry Gross: "When, in *Henry Gross and His Dowsing Rod,* they [scientists who reject water witching] were brought face to face with the evidence of a clearly defined Seventh Sense, and were shown to be so closed-minded that they would sacrifice the welfare of the human race rather than admit they might just possibly be wrong, they grew almost incoherent in their furious contradictions."

In reply scientists can only reiterate that they do not decide truth and falsity on the basis of desirability. Almost every major scientific boner—and there have been many—can be traced to a zealous desire to see the world as we think it should be rather than as it actually is.

The "artificiality of the scientific conditions" argument. Many of the arguments amount to a plea for special dispensation from the requirement that judgment be based on ordinary scientific standards. One version asserts that the diviner cannot perform well under scientific scrutiny because the controlled, laboratory-like conditions are artificial. Another version argues that the witching "powers" are so sensitive and delicate that they are adversely affected by the skeptical atmosphere characteristic of experimental inquiry. Tromp claims that "it is often the subconscious wish of many research workers to obtain a negative result." But the essence of scientific inquiry is doubt and questioning. Scientists cannot give their seal of approval to a phenomenon that is said to exist only when they are not looking!

We could list many variants of these arguments. They add up to an impregnable wall of defenses in which neither rational argument nor negative evidence can make a dent. This passionate clinging to conviction recalls the story of the psychiatric patient who believes that he is dead. The psychiatrist employs all the logic and psychological persuasiveness at her command to convince the patient that he is alive. But to no avail. Suddenly, the psychiatrist has an inspiration. "Tell me, do dead people bleed?" she asks. The patient carefully considers the question, then answers, "No, dead people do not bleed." The psychiatrist pricks the patient's finger with a needle. Blood oozes out. "Well, now what do you have to say for yourself?" the psychiatrist asks. The patient thoughtfully considers his bleeding finger for several moments and then says, "Well, by golly! I guess dead people do bleed after all!"

Witching and the Question of Rational Behavior

When we conclude that water witching is a form of magic, we are tempted to conclude, also, that its use is a form of irrational behavior. This temptation should be resisted, for ritualistic and magical behavior is not necessarily irrational. Indeed, it can be argued that under some circumstances the resort to the diviner can be defended as a rational choice among available alternatives.

As current research and theory on choice-behavior and decision making demonstrate, there is no universally accepted definition of rational behavior. Most models of rational decision making, however, assume that the individual chooses the alternative that maximizes expected utility—or more colloquially, "gives the best run for the money."

There are other models that prescribe somewhat different principles for choosing between alternatives. But for each of them it is easy to imagine circumstances in which the rational decision would be to call on the water witch, even though the decision maker strongly doubts the validity of the practice. In general, such circumstances would involve the following: very inadequate scientific information about where to drill; the fact that, within limits, the diviner is not apt to create too much hardship by locating the well at an inconvenient site; and where there is some basis, no matter how slight, for believing that calling on a diviner may somewhat increase the chances of finding water.

When farmers need to find water as quickly as possible, they are likely to look for the most immediately accessible solution to the problem, even if it is of questionable validity, rather than search for a more valid solution that involves long delay and great effort.

Moreover, the valid, rational solutions offered by science—in the person of the geologist—are vague and nonspecific as compared with the clarity and authority emanating from the diviner. The geologists can only supply generalized information about the possibility of striking water; they qualify their judgment; they cannot guarantee success; and they leave to the farmer the task of pinpointing the actual spot at which to drill. But the rod's message is decisive and unambiguous. It says, "Dig here." And the diviner goes about his or her task with the certitude of blind faith.

It must be kept in mind, as well, that witching is most prevalent in areas where water is most difficult to find, where expert advice is unavailable, or where, because of unusual geological factors, the advice is inadequate. The farmer turns to the diviner because whether or not witching is invalid, the witch's judgment cannot be worse than the farmer's own. It is, under the circumstances, as rational a decision as any for there is nothing to lose. As an Iowa respondent wrote, "Not too many have faith in witching, but use it in the absence of any other method of locating water." And as another respondent in Nebraska put it, "Farmers drilling an irrigation well feel that the $5 to $25 fee is so small compared to the $3,000 to $15,000 investment that they do it even though they aren't sold on it."

Rarely, if ever, is the choice between witching *or* science. Often the choice must be made between witching or no help at all. Most frequently, though, the choice is to use the best expert advice *plus* witching. Like magical ritual in primitive societies, witching is practiced mainly in circumstances where current scientific and rational procedures are of no avail.

Thus, although water witching may be a type of magic, recourse to it is not only understandable, but is defensible from a psychological standpoint. Because the decision to drill a well is highly important and calls for immediate action, it may be *psychologically* rational to choose an immediately available solution that provides specific guidance, reduces ambiguity, supplies emotional reassurance, and permits decisive action in a situation of anxiety and stress.

From the point of view of the individual who has to make a choice, there can be no rational rule for selection among alternatives if there is no empirically or scientifically valid information upon which to base a decision. Magic is not always a substitute for or an alternative to science; as Malinowski said, it may be "the outgrowth of a clear recognition that science has its limits and that a human mind and human skill are at times impotent."

Occult Healing*

Major C. L. Cooper-Hunt, M.A., Ps.D., Ms.D., D.D., Ph.D., M.S.F., practices "medical radiesthesia." According to his book, *Radiesthetic Analysis,*

> Radiesthesia, or the faculty of radio-perception, is a term describing the power of detecting the vibrations, or waves of force, which emanate from all manifested nature, including the four great kingdoms, or fields, of minerals, plants, animals and humans—yes, and why not the further fields of force beyond our own particular label of consciousness, i.e., the angelic, celestial and divine. . . . In order to detect and measure these inner forces various implements have been employed from the hazel-twig and the pendulum to the latest highly sensitive apparatus evolved by such enthusiastic workers as Abrams, Drown and de la Warr.[1]

In his "great crusade against the inroad of disease both physical and mental," Major Cooper-Hunt has accumulated a "growing pile of testimonial letters extending for over ten years of practice from the so-called 'incurables' testifying to definite alleviation and in a multitude of cases to permanent cure."

Let me cite one of his simpler cases. The patient had acute insomnia that had not yielded to various types of remedies. Using a pendulum to test her "polarity," Cooper-Hunt and his wife discovered that the patient was sleeping with her head in the wrong direction. "Radiesthetic examination indicated a different alignment and the patient [was] advised to try it out," the Cooper-Hunts reported. "Her subsequent report was complete harmony and sound sleep."

Miss F. practices "regression therapy." She believes that most illnesses

*In S. Barrett (ed.), *The Health Robbers: How to Protect Your Money and Your Life,* 2nd ed. (Philadelphia: George F. Stickley, 1980), 26–34. Reprinted by permission.

and emotional problems result from patterns and traumas experienced in "previous lives." One of her patients, she told my psychology class, suffered from severe lower abdominal pains for which medical doctors could find neither cause nor cure. When "regressed" to a previous existence, the patient showed signs of intense pain and complained that a dagger had been thrust into his lower abdomen. At Miss F.'s suggestion, the patient went through the motions of "removing" the dagger. The pain was immediately relieved, and according to Miss F., it has never returned.

Another of her cases is that of a California physician who suffered from overwhelming guilt. In six of his previous lives, it turned out, the doctor had been the innocent victim of false accusations and punishments. This indicated to Miss F. that in some still earlier life the doctor had done something wrong for which he was still punishing himself. With further probing, Miss F. discovered that the doctor, as "one of the major scientists on Atlantis," had made a scientific decision that had contributed to the island's destruction. His subsequent feelings of guilt were based on the assumption that he had been completely responsible for the disaster. Miss F. convinced him that he had punished himself enough and that he alone was not responsible. Indeed, she had another patient who, in a previous life, had also contributed to the destruction of Atlantis! Needless to say, these revelations lifted the burden of guilt from the doctor's shoulders and enabled him to resume living with increased effectiveness.

In *The Psychic Healing Book,* Amy Wallace and Bill Henkin report the following case:

> Martha, a 22-year-old woman, had scarred Fallopian tubes and was supposedly sterile. Doctors told her she would never have another child. After several healings, she returned to one of these doctors, who discovered that the scar tissue had disappeared.

Using methods that the authors feel can be taught to most people, Ms. Wallace claims to have helped to at least "partial recovery," cases of hemophilia, multiple sclerosis, cancer, arthritis, and spinal disorders.

Mary Coddington, in her book *In Search of the Healing Energy,* cites a dramatic case of instant healing. At a beach party, a slightly intoxicated man missed his step as he emerged from an automobile that had parked near the edge of the beach. "As he fell, there was the characteristic snapping sound of breaking bones. Inspection showed a compound fracture of the left leg just above the ankle." An old woman, a practitioner of Hawaiian *(huna)* magic, pressed the man's bones together and recited a healing prayer. After a while, she said: "The healing is finished. Stand up. You can walk." The injured man stood up and walked. His leg was apparently completely healed.

Characteristics of Occult Healing

The above cases all involve use of a supposed force or technique that is unrecognized by orthodox medical science. You have undoubtedly heard about other cases. At first glance, healers who use "black boxes" or other secret machines may seem very different from those who rely upon divine or psychic forces. But in practice, many spiritual healers talk about mysterious energies employed by gadgeteers; and operators of gadgets often refer to psychic aspects of their own procedures. For the sake of discussion, let us group all of them under the heading of *occult healers.*

The word *occult* means hidden, secret, or mysterious. Some cases of occult healing are said to be the result of a psychic power or other supernatural force. Other cases are attributed to a force or energy that is natural but as yet unrecognized by science. Some psychics claim to possess hidden or supernatural powers without specifying their source. Others attribute the source of their power to a Supreme Being, to spirit guides (who may or may not be surviving souls of dead persons), to previous incarnations, to intelligent beings from other "planes" or worlds, or to similar esoteric possibilities. Many healers are eclectic, eagerly embracing all theories and claims, even contradictory ones. The common denominator of all occult practitioners is that they do not produce scientifically acceptable proof of their results—their evidence is *testimonial.*

So what? Is there anything wrong with using reports from satisfied customers as evidence that a method works? Isn't the goal of medical treatment to make people better? If patients believe themselves to be better, shouldn't their reports be accepted as evidence in favor of a treatment? Is there a better way to evaluate a treatment than trying it yourself? Is not the proof of the pudding in its eating?

Life would certainly be simpler if medical treatments could be tested as easily as puddings. But healing is far more complicated than cooking. If a woman sleeps better after being advised to change her position, should we accept this as evidence that a pendulum can determine "polarity"? If two patients improve after undergoing intense emotional experiences with Miss F., does this argue for the reality of "previous existences"? If scar tissue disappears after a patient consults a psychic healer, does this prove that psychic forces did the job? It should be obvious that.in each of these cases, nonoccult factors may be responsible for any improvement.

Instant healing of a compound fracture, if it took place as described above, would provide powerful evidence in favor of *huna.* But how can we be sure that a fracture occurred? No doctor was present and no x-ray films were obtained. We are told that a man fell down while getting out of a car and that someone heard a noise that was interpreted as the breaking of bones. We are told that "inspection" showed a compound fracture, but whether a qualified observer was present is not specified in the account. Worse yet, can we be sure that the entire story is not fabricated?

Dr. Louis Rose, in his book *Faith Healing*, tells how he tried for 18 years to find evidence of healing that could be attributed to a spiritual or supernatural power. Enlisting the cooperation of Harry Edwards and other British proponents, Rose collected 95 cases of reported cures. He found that in 58 of them, medical records were unavailable. In 22 others, available records disagreed with the reported events. The rest of the cases were ambiguous in other ways.

My own experience in tracking down cases has been similar. Adequate records of diagnosis and outcome are either unavailable or contradict the reported accounts.

Dr. William Nolen, a surgeon from Minnesota, spent two years watching faith healers at work and examined some of their patients. He concluded that no patients with organic disease had been helped.

"But It Works"

Despite the lack of "scientific" evidence, it would be a mistake to dismiss occult healing as unworthy of serious investigation. Huge numbers of people believe that occult practices work. Every system—whether based on the position of the stars, the swing of a pendulum, the fall of cards or dice, the accidents of nature, the intuitions of a psychic—claims its quota of satisfied customers. If nothing else, it behooves us to examine the nature and significance of such beliefs.

It is not difficult to understand how people can be misled into thinking that an illness has been healed by an unorthodox method. Most ailments are self-limiting. When spontaneous recovery occurs in conjunction with occult healing, patients often credit the occultist. Some illnesses respond favorably to suggestion and other psychological factors. The positive and confident attitude of the healer may actually relieve symptoms, especially those related to tension. In addition, since people do not like to think of themselves as doing foolish things, those who consult occult healers are strongly motivated to believe and act as though they have been helped. To scientists who insist upon objective evidence, random sampling, controlled experiments and the like, believers respond that "people should be treated as individuals, not statistics." Rather than question the nature of their own beliefs, those who "know" that occult practices work see science as too dogmatic.

The Fallacy of Personal Validation

Much research has been done to explore how people form their beliefs about occult matters. In 1948, the psychologist Bertram Forer administered a personality test to the 39 students in one of his courses. One week later, he gave each student a typed personality sketch with his or her name on it—supposedly the "results" of the tests. Unknown to the students, however, each one actually received an identical list of 13 statements that Forer had copied from an astrology book:

1. You have a great need for other people to like and admire you.
2. You have a tendency to be critical of yourself.
3. You have a great deal of unused capacity which you have not turned to your advantage.
4. While you have some personality weaknesses, you are generally able to compensate for them.
5. Your sexual adjustment has presented problems for you.
6. Disciplined and self-controlled outside, you tend to be worrisome and insecure inside.
7. At times you have serious doubts as to whether you have made the right decision or done the right thing.
8. You prefer a certain amount of change and variety and become dissatisfied when hemmed in by restrictions and limitations.
9. You pride yourself as an independent thinker and do not accept others' statements without satisfactory proof.
10. You have found it unwise to be too frank in revealing yourself to others.
11. At times you are extroverted, affable, sociable, while at other times you are introverted, wary, reserved.
12. Some of your aspirations tend to be pretty unrealistic.
13. Security is one of your major goals in life.

After reading the sketch, students were asked to rate how well it revealed their basic personality characteristics. On a scale of 0 (poor) to 5 (perfect), 34 out of 39 rated it 4 or better; and 16 of these rated it as perfect! Many other investigators have confirmed and added to these findings. It turns out to be surprisingly easy to get people to accept a fake personality sketch as a unique description of their personalities.

Cold Reading

If a fake sketch can convince people, think how much more effective a presentation can be if its information is actually tailored to the client. This tailoring is part of a technique known as *cold reading*. In this situation, a "reader" (of palms, tea leaves, a crystal ball, tarot cards, or whatever) who encounters a client for the first time ("cold") is able to persuade him or her that the reading captures the essence of the client's personality and problems.

The reader may begin by making general and universal statements such as those in the preceding sketch. Then, using observations of the client as a guide, the reader is gradually able to adapt the reading to the specific attributes and problems of the client. Much useful information about the client can be gained just by observing such things as clothing, hair style, complexion, physique, and manner. More important, as the reading progresses, the client will supply other clues in his or her reactions to specific statements. Sometimes these reactions take the form of spoken approval or denial. More often they are nonverbal cues such as pupil size, breathing rate, posture, facial expressions, and other bodily reactions.

A skilled reader can quickly tell which statements "hit the mark" and develop these further. As this happens, clients will usually be persuaded that the reader, by some uncanny means, has gained insight into their innermost thoughts. Their guard goes down and they actually tell the reader the details of what is bothering them. After a suitable interval, the reader feeds back this information so that the clients are further amazed at how much the reader "knows" about them. Invariably the clients leave without realizing that everything they have been told is simply what they themselves unwittingly revealed to the reader.

A classic illustration of cold reading was described by John Mulholland, a magician who was well known during the 1930s and 1940s. A young lady who visited a character reader was wearing expensive jewelry, a wedding band, and a black dress of cheap material. The observant reader also noted that the woman was wearing shoes that were currently being advertised for people with foot trouble. (Pause for a moment, imagine that you are the reader, and see what you would make with these clues.)

Using just these observations, the reader proceeded to amaze his client with his insights. He assumed that she wanted help, as did most of his female customers, with a love or financial problem. The black dress and wedding band led him to reason that her husband had died recently. The jewelry suggested financial comfort during the marriage, but the cheap dress indicated that her husband's death had left her penniless. The therapeutic shoes signified that she was standing on her feet more than she was used to, suggesting that she was now working to support herself.

The reader's shrewdness led to the following conclusion, which turned out to be correct: The lady had met a man who had proposed to her. She wanted to marry him to end her economic hardship, but she felt guilty about marrying so soon after her husband's death. The reader told her what she had come to hear—that it was all right to marry without further delay.

Another factor in the success of cold reading is what the psychologist Sir Frederic Bartlett called "the effort after meaning." We are constantly searching for the meaning of what we see. We try to make sense out of what people tell us, what they do, and what we ourselves do. Most of the time we succeed, but sometimes we overdo it and assume meanings that were not intended.

Suppose, for example, a reader suggests that you have found it unwise to be too frank in revealing yourself to others (item #10 of Forer's fake sketch). If you trust the reader, you will try to make sense out of this statement by thinking of circumstances in your life that confirm it. You may have recently offended a friend by calling the friend's obsession with astrology foolish. You may have upset your parents by announcing that you just moved in with this friend. So you assume that the reader is referring to these events. The more you want the reading to succeed, the harder you will search your memory for evidence to "verify" the reader's statements.

Even if a client is skeptical or believes that psychic reading is nonsense, the very fact of participation will set up powerful psychological forces that encourage belief. A reporter once checked with me before he visited a well-known psychic. After the visit, he declared it a perfect success. The reading had lasted approximately an hour. During most of that time, the reader had made statements that were either completely wrong or so general that they would fit anyone. However, at one point during the interview, the reporter began to think about trouble he was having with his girlfriend. At this moment, the reader said, "I see that you are having trouble with a relationship." This remark, coming at the very moment he was concerned about his affair, had an impact so powerful that consideration of all the other wrong statements and useless banter was swept aside. The reporter could not be talked out of his conviction that the reading had been a "success."

The client is not the only person who can be taken in by what happens between reader and client. I began reading palms during my teens as a way to supplement my income as a magician and mentalist. When I began, I did not believe in palmistry but I knew that to sell it I had to act as though I did. After a few years I became a firm believer in palmistry because it appeared to work. One day another mentalist whom I respected tactfully suggested that it would make an interesting experiment if I deliberately gave readings opposite to what the palm lines indicated. I tried this out with a few clients. To my surprise and horror, my readings were just as successful! Ever since then I have been interested in the powerful forces that can convince people that something is so when it isn't. It is certainly clear that how people feel about a "treatment" they have experienced is often unrelated to its effectiveness.

Unmet Needs

The apparent success of occult healers suggests that they are appealing to needs that the medical profession should be handling more effectively. And the fact that millions of clients not only consult occult practitioners but also wrongly believe in their claims, implies that our educational system is failing. Today we can go from kindergarten through graduate school without having to take a single course in the sort of logic, scientific methods, and self-understanding that would help protect us from quackery.

Concerned citizens should insist that our educational system prepare us to be better consumers. This would entail providing the intellectual tools necessary to separate sense from nonsense. One set of tools would enable us to recognize what constitutes good scientific evidence for a claim. The other set of tools would help us realize the ways our own thoughts and feelings can mislead us.

Note

1. Albert Abrams, M.D. (1864–1924), considered by the American Medical Association (AMA) to have been the "dean of gadget quacks," made millions of dollars treating patients and leasing his gadgets to others. He claimed that all parts of the body emit electrical impulses of different frequencies that vary with health and disease. Illnesses (as well as age, sex, religion, and location) could be diagnosed by "tuning in" on the patient's blood or handwriting sample with one machine; and diseases could be treated by feeding proper vibrations into the body with another machine. Abrams willed his fortune to the Electronic Medical Foundation, whose subsequent president, Fred J. Hart, founded the National Health Federation. Ruth Drown, a chiropractor who followed in Abrams's footsteps until her death in 1965, claimed that she could help patients even if they were thousands of miles away. Work "based on the Abrams principles" (and now referred to as "radionics") is still being carried out at the Delawarr Laboratories in Oxford, England, founded in 1943 by George and Margaret de la Warr.

A Remote Viewing Experiment Conducted by a Skeptic and a Believer*

(with James McClenon)

Remote viewing is a term used to describe the alleged ability of one individual to "view" (mentally) the images perceived by a second individual who is at a separate (and remote) location. This ability may be considered a form of extrasensory perception since it hypothesizes the experience of a target location without sensory contact. Much controversy surrounds the onto-logical status of this alleged ability.

Various remote viewing experiments conducted by individuals who believe in the reality of psi (for example: Targ and Puthoff, 1977; Dunne and Bisaha, 1979; Schlitz and Gruber, 1980) seem to indicate that this phenomenon exists and requires further exploration. Other experiments conducted by skeptics (for example: Karnes *et al.,* 1980; Marks and Kam-mann, 1980) show no evidence for the remote viewing hypothesis and hint that psychological factors can explain, in part, the misguided belief in psi.

It would seem that the conduct of a jointly supervised, believer-skeptic experiment might shed light on this issue. One researcher (R. H.) is a well-known skeptic regarding claims of the paranormal. The other researcher (J. M.) instigated the experiment in order to play the role of a "believer" as an aspect of a sociological participant observation study of the field of parapsychology. This experiment was designed not merely to test the hypothesis concerning the ontological status of remote viewing, but to uncover the various social-psychological factors that might be associated

*Zetetic Scholar, 12/13 (1987), 21-33. Reprinted by permission.

with its experience. We hoped to gain information about this aspect from the subjective and informal reports of the experimenters and also the subjects. The experiment, as set up, can provide only a formal test of the psi hypothesis.

The Experiment

The experiment described in this paper involves eight remote viewing trials using eight different subjects and was conducted during the spring of 1980 in Eugene, Oregon. The experiment was conducted as a replication of the successful remote viewing experiments of Puthoff and Targ (1976) and Dunne and Bisaha (1979). In addition to using independent judges, we also had subjects judge their own protocols as is done in ganzfeld research (Honorton, 1977). A distinct target pool was developed for each subject in order to avoid methodological problems encountered by previous researchers during the judging process.

Method of Obtaining Subjects

Five "inexperienced" volunteers—*i.e.,* ones having no previous experience regarding remote viewing experiments—were obtained through the placement of a classified ad in the University of Oregon newspaper. Three other "inexperienced" individuals volunteered during informal interaction with one of the researchers (J. M.). Although the subjects were "inexperienced" in remote viewing, only one was naive or inexperienced in occult matters. Parapsychologists might label the other seven as "sheep."

All volunteers were asked if they knew anyone with whom they wished to work in this remote viewing experiment. The experiment requires an "agent" who attempts mentally to "send" an image to the "receiver." All the volunteer "receivers" decided to use the available researcher (J. M.) as the "agent."

Apparatus

One researcher (J. M.) took photos of 64 locations in the Eugene area. The number of photographs taken of each site was based on the researcher's judgment of the complexity and size of the possible target. This was the same photography procedure used by Dunne and Bisaha (1979). Notes were taken on 3 x 5 cards describing the observer's exact location, the visual direction to be faced by the observer, and the objects that were to be observed. The 64 site photographs were arranged into 8 sets of 8 sites. An attempt was made to create 8 pictorially distinct possible targets within each set with regard to architecture, objects within the photographs, general forms, colors, etc. This allowed each set of 8 sites to be assigned to each of the 8 trials. A photocopy was made of the photographs of all the potential target sites.

The potential target sets were numbered from 1 to 8, and each site within each set was numbered from 1 to 8. The entire package was given to a lab technician for the Psychology department, O.B., who was totally unconnected with the rest of the experiment. O.B. assigned a second individual to arrange the target sets randomly and to select a target site within each set in a random manner. The PDP-15 computer within the cognitive laboratory at the University of Oregon was used for this random selection process. O.B. had the photographic material arranged in such a manner that he would remain unaware of the target number until the beginning of the trial run. He was always unaware of the target site.

Procedure

The 8 subjects were tested on different days. The subjects remained with the observer while the remote viewing agent (J. M.) went downstairs to the computer area. Here the agent received the target materials from O.B. These consisted of a 3 x 5 card describing the target site and a photocopy of the target photographs. The selected set of 8 sites was then brought up by O.B. to the observer and subject after the agent had left for the target site. Only the agent, who was on his way to a specific site, knew which site was the target. R. H. was the observer in all the trials.

The subject was allowed a 20-minute relaxation period during which the agent traveled to the target site by bicycle. The subjects were allowed to prepare themselves in whatever manner they wished. Most employed forms of meditative procedure while a few spent the time talking with R. H. After this time period, the subject described aloud into a tape recorder the images that came into his or her mind during the next 15 minutes. Paper and pen were available to make sketches if desired. At the end of the 15-minute time period, the subject was shown the photographs of the 8 sites and requested to rank order them as to their similarity to his or her previously described (and tape recorded) description. The subject remained closeted with the observer during this time period. Following the termination of his 15-minute stay at the target site, the agent returned to the closeted subject and observer. He then notified the subject and observer of the correct site. The subject was then debriefed. The researchers were especially interested in changes that might occur in the subject's belief system regarding psi.

Judging

Two forms of judging were planned. The first series involved having each subject rank order his or her 8 photographs regarding their similarity to his or her 15-minute verbalization. The score achieved by each subject was the rank that the individual assigned to the photograph that was later found to be the target site. These scores are listed in Table 1.

A second series of judging involved other individuals, who were geographically distant from Eugene, Oregon. The transcripts were typed by an individual who was unaware of the target site for each trial (this would prevent bias from intruding into the typist's interpretation of words that might be less than completely clear). Dr. Stanley Krippner, at the Humanistic Psychology Institute (presently the Saybrook Institute) agreed to instigate the "remote judging" for this experiment. Eight envelopes, each containing the 8 site photographs and each containing a typed transcript, were mailed to Krippner's assistant, John Geyl. Geyl located five individuals who were asked to rank order the photographic material for each trial. They used the typed transcript of the subjects' descriptions recorded during the designated 15-minute intervals. The judges' scoring on the target site for each trial was averaged and is listed in Table 1.

Table 1
Remote Viewing Experiment Tests of Significance

Trial Number	Subject's Score	Judges' Score (Average)
1	3	4.0
2	6	6.4
3	2	2.6
4	7	4.2
5	8	5.2
6	6	7.2
7	7	6.0
8	1	2.6
Mean	5.0*	4.8*

*Not significant at .05 level.

Results

Table 1 presents the subjects' and average judges' score for each of the 8 trials (derived from the ranking assigned to the target site). A statistical evaluation of the subjects' total score can be conducted using Table A-1 of Solfvin, Kelly, and Burdick's (1978) article regarding the methods of analysis of preferential-ranking data. This method of analysis, the ordinal weighting scheme, reveals the improbability of achieving any sum of ranks. The smaller the sum of ranks, the more improbable that this score could have occurred by chance.

This method was applied to the average rank for the subjects and each of the judges separately. A regular T-test was applied to the averaged judges' rankings, as well as the combined scores of judges and subjects. None of these tests achieved statistical significance.

Table 1 reveals that the subjects' total score does not demonstrate evidence for the existence of a remote viewing facility. Each of the five judges, taken singly, fails to come up with a significant sum of ranks. The subjects' rankings correlate with the average rankings of the judges approximately 0.74, which is significant at .05 level.

The combined scores of judges and subjects yielded a mean ranking of 4.81 with 95% confidence limits of 3.65 and 5.97. Because the average ranking expected by chance is 4.5, our results are fully consistent with the complete absence of psi in the subjects' target descriptions. (The error term used to construct the confidence units was derived from the repeated-measures analysis of variance on the judges' and subjects' rankings.)

Discussion by J. M.

In order to properly play the role of "believer," I decided to conduct various investigations outside the domain of the remote viewing aspects of this experiment. The hope was that these investigations would shed light on the nature of the psi phenomenon. Believers (among the parapsychological community) are generally more interested in experiments that attempt to be "process" oriented rather than those that are oriented only toward "proving" psi. These additional investigations consisted of (1) attempting to evaluate my personal clairvoyant ability on the day of each trial in order to determine the possibility of a relationship between agent clairvoyance and subject remote viewing (RV) ability and (2) interviewing each subject before and after the subject's trial in order to determine the effect that participation in the experiment might have on each subject.

Previous to taking part as the agent during each trial (and to having any contact with O.B., the randomizer), I attempted to predict the target site number. Each day, while in a meditative state (induced through a method of progressive relaxation), I rank ordered the numbers between 1 and 8 as to my feeling of the probability of each being the target site number. In this manner a prediction series was generated in the exact same format as that which would be later generated by the subject. The possibility of

sensory cueing could not enter into this aspect of the experiment since
O.B. had his target information arranged in such a manner that he remained
ignorant of future target site numbers on each trial day. These predictions
were written each day on a 3 x 5 card that remained in my possession.
O.B. was aware of this aspect of the research before the experiment began,
and R. H. was informed after the completion of trial 2. This separate
clairvoyant test has no bearing on the formal test of the remote viewing
hypothesis.

Table 2
Result of Clairvoyance Experiment

Trial Number	J. M.'s Score
1	6
2	1
3	4
4	1
5	2
6	2
7	2
8	3
Mean	2.6

$p = 0.012$ (one-tailed)

Table 2 presents the results of my clairvoyance experiment. My total
score reveals a level of significance of 0.012 (using the same Solfvin, Kelly,
Burdick [1978] table as was used in the RV aspect of the experiment). This
one-tailed value was selected in order to maintain equivalency with the remote viewing analysis. Some parapsychologists (and also critics) might argue
that, due to the nature of psi, two-tailed tests are always required. In the
case of my clairvoyance experiment, this would yield a p value of 0.024.

There appears to be no relationship between my score each day and
the subject's score. The correlation between my scores and the scores of
the subject is $-.68$. My scores correlate with the average of the judges'
scores $-.53$. Neither correlation is significant at the .05 level (two-tailed).
Since this is an "informal" aspect of the RV experiment, I will include
my discussion of these results within the discussion of changes in belief
among the RV experiment participants.

Interviews with the subjects before and after each trial revealed that some individuals changed their attitude toward psi as a result of participating in the experiment:

Trial 1. S-1 was a former student of R. H. and maintained an open-minded skepticism concerning psi. S-1 seemed to increase his belief in the possibility of the existence of psi after finding that he had ranked the target site in the third position. The subject's description of numerous facets of the target, which were either not prominent in its photograph or outside the borders of the picture, seemed more than coincidental. S-1 claimed a continued open-minded skepticism but "an increased interest in future experiments."

Trial 2. S-2 experienced a situation that might be expected to decrease belief; he reported, "It hasn't altered my belief. I still believe pretty much." S-2 rationalized his apparent failure while talking to J. M. "I was thinking about where you would be instead of letting things just pop in my head."

Trial 3. S-3 experienced a situation (achieving a score of 2) in which her belief might be increased. She reported, "I've always thought this kind of thing could work. I generally believe that this can happen but I'm not totally confident in it. My belief stays about the same."

Trial 4. Although S-4's performance on this test might be expected to reduce her belief in psi (she ranked the target site in the seventh position), her numerous anecdotal stories from personal experience supported her continuing, undiminished belief in psi.

Trial 5. S-5 stated previous to the experiment that he felt that the demonstration of psi was very possible. After his session, he stated that he felt he had great difficulty in clearing his mind of his normal residue of personal thoughts. Following his unsuccessful trial (he achieved the worst possible score, an 8), he stated, "I was a believer before and I still am. Some people are more receptive than others. Just because I didn't get results doesn't change anything. If I see your ad in the newspaper again, I'll help you out by not replying." (S-5 laughs after stating this.) "This one trial doesn't prove anything."

Trial 6. S-6 related various anecdotal evidence of psi in her personal life. Following her unsuccessful attempt to demonstrate psi under experimental conditions (she achieved a score of 6), she reported: "It's depressing. I still know it works; I'm just not that good at it." She then went on to describe several more personal psi experiences that had occurred previously.

Trial 7. S-7 believed in the efficacy of astrology and·was a believer in psi. Her protocol consisted more of a personality reading of the agent (J. M.) than an attempt to describe his location. Her inability to choose accurately the target photograph disturbed her only slightly (she placed the target site in the seventh position). She was convinced of the accuracy of the personality reading. Personal friends of J. M. also believe that she gave an accurate reading.

Trial 8. S-8, a believer, was very extroverted and outgoing. Although she seemed to be a perfect psi subject, both experimenters were aware that it would be impossible at this stage for the remote viewing aspect of the series to demonstrate statistical significance overall. S-8 achieved a direct hit on the target photograph and described numerous similarities between her protocol and the target picture after being informed of her accuracy. R. H.'s notes of the experimental protocol reveal that almost immediately after the tape recording of the session ended, she remarked that she "kept thinking he was at the downtown mall." When one of the target photographs was indeed of the downtown mall, she felt certain that this was the target and she was correct. S-8 stated that her belief in psi increased due to her experience. Her success was an exhilarating experience for her.

R. H. and J. M. remained interested but both recognized that future judges would find it difficult to rank her transcript. Many of her remarks concerned activities and emotions of the agent (later verified), which were of no value to the future judges. Although S-8's comment concerning the Eugene mall appeared in R. H.'s notes, it was not entered into the typed transcript since it did not occur during the 15-minute time period. Later, the judges in San Francisco were apparently unable to note an extreme similarity between the typed transcript and the target site. Their average ranking of this trial was 2.8.

It would seem from these observations that an individual's evaluation of psi performance is dependent on the past experience of the individual and on the person's "frame of reference." S-8 should not be expected to dismiss her own successful experience because others had failed to obtain remote viewing results. Rather, it would be more logical for her (from her personal vantage point) to increase her belief in the methodology that she utilized (belief in God, goodness, etc.). The fact that she had chosen the correct site from a possible set of only eight locations did not diminish her achievement in her mind. She reasoned (probably correctly) that the experimenters could have supplied her with a hundred possible sites. She still would have chosen the correct one. My belief regarding my personal clairvoyance "success" follows a similar pattern. Although the RV results indicate that my belief in the RV methodology should be reduced, my clairvoyance results indicate that my belief in deep relaxation and meditation as a means for eliciting clairvoyance should be increased (at least to a slight degree). These changes in belief might be logical from the vantage point of a "believer" yet less logical for a "skeptic."

This observation regarding belief in psi seems to support vaguely some of the observations noted by Marks and Kammann (1980) regarding the psychology of the psychic. There *does* seem to be a tendency for an individual to pick out aspects of what he or she observes and to use these aspects to reinforce a system of belief that has been developed in the past. At the same time, my observation of the subjects during this RV experiment revealed little that seemed irrational within their comments. Indeed, they manifested few of the irrational aspects that Marks and Kammann (1980) observed, but appeared to be typical college students who happened to believe in psi because of their past experiences.

Rather than argue about the ontological status of psi, it might be more fruitful to consider the means by which an increasing percentage of the population has come to believe in it. Social phenomena, such as *belief in psi*, can be accepted by both believer and skeptic.

At the heart of the psychological aspect of this issue is the question regarding the nature of experiences that induce belief in psi. Some skeptics have presented simplistic analyses that reflect their belief that psi does not occur. For example, Singer and Benassi (1981) seem to attribute belief in psi to "deficiencies of human reasoning" and to "faulty cognitive apparatus." Since personal psi occurred for me under the conditions that I devised, I feel that I might shed light on this issue. While meditating, I evaluated my feelings with regard to the possible target numbers. Sometimes I felt numbers "popping into my head" and found that these numbers frequently were correlated with the actual target numbers. It does not seem to me that either my clairvoyant success or S-8's RV success can be attributed to "faulty cognitive apparatus." The "deficiencies of human reasoning" may be a more valid theory for explaining belief. The tendency to focus attention on memories that coincidentally coincide with "target" objects, states, or events could create the illusion for the experiencing individual that psi has occurred. Consequently, I cannot claim that psi was "proved" by my experience, but I do claim that my belief in psi was increased by it. Various factors explain this phenomenon:

1. The small number of tests of significance (preset as one-tailed tests) that were planned and the high level of significance obtained on the clairvoyance test.
2. The great degree of care exercised by the randomizer, O.B. (who was a skeptic), in order to preclude the possibility of sensory cueing.
3. The emotional experience of feeling the numbers "popping into my head" and the finding that this "popping" process was a successful means of gaining information. This experience was compounded by the fact that during my meditation for trials 6 and 7, I felt a high degree of certainty that one number would be correct but

later in the day decided that it would be "better" to choose another number. In both of these cases, the first choice proved to be correct. At the end of the series, I felt a degree of relief that I had not obtained an extremely high level of statistical significance. Such an event would force many skeptics to accuse me of fraud. With the present level they will probably dismiss this result as a case of selective data analysis (for example, see the discussion of this aspect of the experiment by R. H.).

I would suggest that my personal experience, that of S-8, and, to a lesser degree, S-2, is similar to the spontaneous experiences that seem to be a major source of the high level of belief in psi that exists within the general population (McCready and Greeley, 1976). Some of these experiences are quite powerful. An individual who sees an apparition of a relative and later finds that this relative died at the very moment should not be accused of "deficiencies of human reasoning" or "faulty cognitive apparatus" if he or she increases belief in psi as a result of the experience. R. H. and J. M. may explain to S-8 that her experimental result does not "prove psi is real," since the other subjects were less successful. R. H. may present an analysis to J. M. (using aspects of the data that fail to support the psi hypothesis) showing that statistical significance would not be demonstrated even if his clairvoyance test had been built into the formal experiment. A skeptic might explain to an individual that apparitions are results of "faulty cognitive apparatus" and that to believe that a relationship between such an apparition and the death of a relative is more than coincidental demonstrates "deficiencies of human reasoning." These arguments seem rational to the skeptic, yet from the vantage point of the experiencer, the impact of the experience negates these explanations. Such experiences, although they cannot be granted the evidential quality of results derived from formal tests, still generate belief in the existence of psi. My argument is that such modification of belief should not always be deemed irrational, especially when viewed from the framework of the "believer."

The problem lies in the different assumptions inherent within the believer and skeptical positions. It makes these orientations incommensurate. Believers have difficulty explaining the inability to demonstrate the existence of psi in a consistent manner. They must resort to explanations that involve expectancy and researcher effects (White, 1977). They find it easy to explain why people have spontaneous experiences that lead to belief in psi since they feel psi produces these experiences. Skeptics, on the other hand, have no difficulty explaining the failures within parapsychological experiments. They believe that psi probably does not occur. Their problem lies in devising an explanation as to why so many people have had experiences that lead to belief in psi's existence. Their present theories do not stand up under empirical testing.

In considering the investigation of controversial claims, both skeptics and believers engage in a process of selective observation and interjection. Will our claim of failing to support the RV hypothesis reduce belief in psi among believers? Probably not. Their past experiences have led them to believe that we did not induce the "proper conditions" for psi to occur. In controversial areas, observers tend to ignore or re-evaluate results that do not coincide with their previously formed opinions.

When experiences relevant to an inquiry occur outside the formal experiment format, is it rational to grant them a degree of validity? Of course it is! Yet because of the conditions under which the experience occurred, much of the rhetorical power to persuade others concerning the authenticity of the experience is lost. It is rational to believe one's own experiences, but less rational to grant equal weight to the description of others' experiences. Scientists use their own experiences, which occur both inside the laboratory and out, to evaluate reports of others' experiences, which occur inside the laboratory and out.

A major problem is the question of "rationality" and the extent to which a universal rationality can be assumed. Both believers and skeptics present "rational" arguments, but this "rationality" is derived from the speaker's initial assumptions. Theoretical orientations devised within the "relativistic" sociology of science explain this dilemma:

> It would seem that evidence is so bound up with the sociology or social group which gives rise to it that theories held by members of radically different scientifico-social groups cannot be adequately tested against each other by experiment. It matters not whether the evidence is intended to corroborate, "prove" or refute the theories in question. Similarly, these differences cannot be settled by logical argument (Collins and Pinch, 1982: 184).

This does not mean that science *cannot* resolve issues such as the question regarding psi, but that such resolution will not be brought about by any single series of experiments. Such issues are eventually resolved through the rhetorical and political processes or argumentation that constitute science. If this issue is to be resolved, the question must be reformulated in such a manner that arguments will convince major elements of the scientific audience regarding the validity of the new claim. Parapsychologists might present their "expectancy" or "experimenter effect" theories in such a manner that they can be empirically verified by skeptics. When this is done, such "failures" to replicate the psi hypothesis as occurred in our experiment may be deemed as "successes." Skeptics might devise hypotheses, which can be empirically verified by believers, that explain why such a high percentage of the general population reports experiences that lead to belief in psi. McCready and Greeley (1976) found that 58% of the American public claim to have had an ESP experience, for example. Observations within this present experiment hint that incorrect reasoning cannot account for all experiences that lead to increased belief in the psi hypothesis.

The content of some paranormal experiences has universal aspects that transcend the cultural interpretation (Hufford, 1982). This hints that some portion of the folklore regarding psi (which has been developed both through scientific experimentation and popular experience) is more than likely associated with accurate observations that have been interpreted in a logical manner. It is hoped that the scientific process of argumentation will eventually uncover which aspects of this folklore are valid. This will require individual researchers to transcend the "culture of disbelief" that seems inherent within modern science. Researchers cannot assume that some observations are invalid merely through *a priori* reasoning. Investigators must seek a better knowledge of the experiences lying behind belief in the paranormal and consider the role of these experiences in causing that belief.

Discussion by R. H.

As indicated in J. M.'s discussion, it could be argued that because we employed only 8 trials, our experiment lacked sufficient power to demonstrate psi even if it were operative. However, it is unlikely that psi was operative, but at a low level, in our experiment. If pure chance were operating, the expected average rank would be 4.5. Our eight subjects, in judging their target sites, averaged 5.0, which is just barely below expectation. Furthermore, there was only one direct hit, which is also right at chance level. The five judges who supplied complete data produced an overall average of 4.8, which is reasonably close to the expected 4.5. Furthermore, among the 40 separate scores for the 5 judges, there were five direct hits, which is exactly the number expected by chance.

The only hint that anything like psi was connected with our experiment is the results of J. M.'s separate predictions of target sites. Taken by themselves, they yield a probability of 0.024 of having this degree of departure from the expected value on the assumption of chance. However, they cannot be taken by themselves. In the first place, as J. M. correctly acknowledges, this aspect of the experiment was not part of the original design. As such the probability figure for it is meaningless. What if, after the fact, we found that O.B. as well as each of the subjects also had kept their own secret lists of predictions? Would we also test each of these unplanned sets of scores separately as if each were the hypothesized dependent variable? Obviously, only the tests planned and taken into account in the design of the experiment can have meaning. Even so, we were somewhat careless in specifying in advance which patterns of results would have led us to conclude in favor of psi. We tested the average rankings of the judges and the separate rankings of the subjects separately at the 0.05 level criterion. But what if one of these had come out "significant" and the other had not? What would we be permitted to conclude? And what about the fact that five separate judges produced complete data? Should we test each judge separately or treat them as a composite? We have a number of options, each of which could be convincingly justified after the fact. However, as the options increase, the chances of obtaining a "significant" result according to currently employed criteria goes up greatly.

We are fortunate, in this case, that all 5 judges and the subjects were consistent in providing us data that were nonsignificant no matter which of a number of data analyses we might have tried. I say "fortunate" because if the results had turned out inconsistent in the sense that some judges had provided highly significant scores, or that the subjects had differed from the judges significantly, the two authors might have found themselves sharply divided on what the results indicated about psi.

We see that even with a simple experiment such as ours, the number of options for testing psi are many, and this makes it essential that the exact outcomes that will be taken as evidence for psi be carefully specified in advance of each experiment. My recent readings in the parapsychological literature indicate that this standard is consistently violated. Now, what should we have done if, say, we decided to build J. M.'s target guesses into the original experimental design? One reasonable option would have been to specify that we would restrict ourselves, say, to just three tests of significance: (1) a test on the sum of ranks for the subjects' scores; (2) a test on the sum of ranks (averaged) on the judges' scores; and (3) a test on the sum of ranks for J. M.'s scores. We would also plan to make these tests as two-tailed because it is common practice in the psi literature to test for psi-missing as well as psi-hitting. And, wishing to keep the overall error rate for the experiment no higher than 0.05, we would make each of our 3 tests at the 0.05/3 or 0.0167 level of significance. Having done this, if we obtained the results we actually did, then none of our 3 tests, including J. M.'s results, would have been judged significant.

An important innovation, which I credit to J. M., is the use of a separate target pool for each subject. As he points out, this avoids many serious problems of independence among trials in remote viewing experiments. This is not the place to discuss the many ways such nonindependence in remote viewing experiments cast serious doubts on their statistical findings. I strongly recommend to future researchers in this area that they make every effort to employ this innovation.

I agree with J. M. that the important contribution of our collaboration lies in the informal aspects that deal with the social-psychological consequences of participation in such an experiment both by the experimenters and the subjects. J. M. makes it clear how his own orientation has enabled him to seize upon various outcomes and personal experiences that reinforce his previous tendencies to believe in psi. The interviews with our subjects further illustrate the persistence of prior beliefs regardless of the outcomes of their trials. And, of course, I, the skeptic, found everything in our joint venture to agree with an outcome consistent with chance combined with strong psychological tendencies to discover meaning in every *post hoc* departure from a chance pattern.

Conclusions

A remote viewing experiment was conducted in which subjects judged their own protocols by rank ordering individual target pools. These same protocols were later rejudged by individuals who were geographically distant from the experimental site. In neither case did statistical analysis of the results reveal evidence for the existence of a remote viewing ability. This would indicate that, within the context of this experiment, either the remote viewing ability was not present or that, given only eight trials, it was occurring in such a slight or sporadic manner as to be undetectable.

On the other hand, various individuals increased their belief in psi as a result of this experiment. This indicates the capacity of experimental procedures associated with remote viewing to induce experiences that increase belief in the existence of psi. In that psi is a phenomenon that is accepted by a large percentage of the general population, it is a legitimate scientific endeavor to attempt to gain a greater understanding of the means by which such beliefs come about. Individuals who believe in psi and those who remain skeptical of the reality of this phenomenon can both participate in attempting to uncover the factors that surround these experiences, both in and out of the experimental situation.

References

Collins, H. M., and T. J. Pinch, *Frames of Meaning: The Social Construction of Extraordinary Science,* Boston: Routledge and Kegan Paul, 1982.
Dunne, B. J., and J. Bisaha, "Precognitive Remote Viewing in the Chicago Area: A Replication of the Stanford Experiment," *Journal of Parapsychology,* 43, 1 (Mar.), 1979, 17–30.

Honorton, C., "Psi and Internal Attention States," in *Handbook of Parapsychology* (B. Wolman; ed.), New York: Van Nostrand Reinhold, 1977.

Hufford, David J., *The Terror that Comes in the Night,* Philadelphia: University of Pennsylvania Press, 1982.

Karnes, E. W., Sussman, E., Klusman, P., and L. Turcotte, "Failures to Replicate Remote Viewing Using Psychic Subjects," *Zetetic Scholar,* 1980, No. 6, 66–76.

Marks, David, and Richard Kammann, *The Psychology of the Psychic,* Buffalo, N.Y.: Prometheus Books, 1980.

McCready, William C., and Andrew M. Greeley, *The Ultimate Values of the American Population,* Vol. 23, Sage Library of Social Research, Beverly Hills, Calif.: Sage Publications, 1976.

Puthoff, Harold E., and Russell Targ, "A Perceptual Channel for Information Transfer over Kilometer Distances: Historical Perspective and Recent Research," *Proceedings of the IEEE,* 64, 3 (Mar.), 1976, 329–54..

Schlitz, Marilyn, and Elmer Gruber, "Transcontinental Remote Viewing," *Journal of Parapsychology,* 44, 4 (Dec.), 1980, 305–18.

Singer, Barry, and Victor A. Benassi, "Occult Beliefs," *American Scientist,* 61, 1 (Jan.–Feb.), 1981, 49–55.

Solfvin, G., E. Kelly, and D. Burdick, "Some New Methods of Analysis for Preferential-Ranking Data," *Journal of the American Society for Psychical Research* (April), 1978, 93–109.

Targ, Russell, and Harold Puthoff, *Mind-Reach,* New York: Dell Publishing Co., 1977.

White, Rhea, "The Influence of the Experimenter Motivation, Attitudes and Methods of Handling Subjects in Psi Test Results," in *Handbook of Parapsychology* (B. Wolman, ed.), New York: Van Nostrand Reinhold, 1977.

Reviews

Dowsing: The Psi Connection. **Francis Hitching. Garden City, N.Y.: Anchor Books, 1978. Pp. 306.***

Francis Hitching believes dowsing—the finding of water, minerals, ancient artifacts, and almost anything else with the aid of a divining rod or pendulum—works, is important, and involves forces or aspects of human capacity that are revolutionary when finally recognized by orthodox science. As the coauthor of the only skeptical book on dowsing (Vogt, E. Z., & Hyman, R., *Water Witching U.S.A.,* University of Chicago Press, 1979), I disagree with Hitching's beliefs about its validity. Surprisingly, I find that he and I do agree on many important issues about the topic.

We both agree that the rod or pendulum moves because of involuntary movements by the dowser. And we have no doubts that the trigger for these movements is controlled by the diviner's unconscious expectations (although we disagree about the source of the unconscious knowledge). Both of us assess the evidence for divining in the same way. We find that the data that have been collected according to scientific standards do not support the claims of dowsing. The anecdotal data that fail to live up to scientific standards often do seem to offer striking examples of success.

At this point we part company. Vogt and I, taking into consideration the variety of ways uncontrolled human observation and experience can deceive us, conclude that dowsing's failure to pass scientific muster over a 500-year period, justifies the current indifference by scientists towards its claims. Hitching, firmly convinced of dowsing's omnipotent validity, implies that there must be something wrong with science and scientists.

---

*This review was published in *Zetetic Scholar* 5 (1979), 98–103. Reprinted by permission.

Because he *knows* that dowsing works, he seems to be asking that science grant dowsing a special dispensation from its regular standards. If dowsing cannot succeed by current scientific standards, then let's weaken the standards in such a way that it can succeed!

In many ways this is a good book. In my opinion it is the best book available that is written in behalf of the case of dowsing. Hitching not only writes well, but he has been encyclopedic and thorough in his coverage of all the major questions. It constitutes a complete handbook on the subject. He begins with a characterization of the phenomenon and its many applications. He includes short biographical sketches of a number of master dowsers in England and the United States. The history of the practice is well covered and various contemporary applications in warfare, criminal investigations, and other areas are illustrated.

The middle third of the book deals with an extensive account of attempts to provide an explanation of the phenomenon in terms of known scientific forces. An entire chapter is devoted to magnetism. If some of the experimental claims are to be believed, the human dowser can detect variations in magnitude greater than any known physical detector. It is not made clear how we can check on this if we have no independent way of measuring these minute variations. Another chapter considers the pros and cons of attributing the effects to various portions of the electromagnetic spectrum.

Hitching does a very good job of introducing the layman to the scientific ideas of magnetism and electromagnetic radiation. Even if Hitching is wrong on dowsing, his readers will gain a good scientific introduction to some of the major physical forces. The message from these chapters on physical forces is that humans may be directly sensitive to portions of the electromagnetic continuum and to magnetic fields sufficiently to account for alleged divining successes on site.

The paradox—which Hitching does little to try to resolve—is that, according to his accounts, dowsers can succeed just as well when divining over a map thousands of miles from the site. Such an ability, if real, would make all the accounts based on known scientific forces superfluous. Instead, we would require some sort of a paranormal account. And this is the subject to which Hitching devotes the last third of his book and it is also what gives the book its subtitle, "The Psi Connection." One gets the impression that a small group of dowsers is valiantly trying to demystify the practice by providing evidence to show how physical forces could conceivably account for successes for on-site searches. But other dowsers seek an account in paranormal possibilities and look to psychic phenomena for their explanations.

Hitching reviews many contemporary events in parapsychology such as psychokinesis, remote viewing, and psychic detectives, and he attempts to fit them to current theoretical developments in quantum physics. The implication is that dowsing is a very practical and, in the hands of the master dowsers, a very reliable form of psi.

As an added bonus, or perhaps even as the showpiece of the book, Hitching devotes a chapter and an appendix to a description of his own intercontinental dowsing experiment. He obviously considers his experiment to be a milestone of sorts and characterizes it as "the most thorough and extended test of map-dowsing yet undertaken." Bill Lewis, a British dowser, picked sites from maps of parts of the northeastern and north central United States at which he felt that Hitching would discover ancient megaliths or burial sites. Hitching then visited the United States and checked out the sites against the descriptions given by Lewis. He interprets the results as "conclusive and astonishing." By this, he means that Lewis's locations and descriptions were well beyond what could be expected by chance.

It is clear that a lot of time, effort, and expense went into this experiment. But in spite of Hitching's optimistic pronouncements to the contrary, the results are scientifically meaningless. The tragedy is that given his design the results were foredoomed to be useless even before the data were collected. The elementary precautions that were overlooked in conducting this investigation were many. For one thing, no meaningful attempt was made to take into consideration the knowledge about location of settlements that one can gain from a map (*e.g.,* intersections of rivers would be more likely than places far from water, etc.). The success rate of Lewis depends crucially on the comparison with the control sites. These control sites were selected in such a way as practically to guarantee that they would be less likely to match their targets than would Lewis's choices. We are not told what instructions or motivations guided the selection of these control sites by John Stiles. But it was a serious flaw to present Stiles with the maps with Lewis's locations already marked upon them and then ask him to pick a random control site. For example, if Lewis always placed his choices at reasonable places on the maps, then, in trying to pick a control site in the vicinity of Lewis's choice, but not too close to it, Stiles would inevitably be forced to put most of his choices in nonoptimal locations.

We are not told if Stiles was highly motivated to try to find control sites that would be most likely to contain "megaliths" or if he was simply instructed to pick a site at random (as implied by Hitching's account). We are told, however, that the dowser Lewis has had a long-standing interest in locating such burial sites and is an expert on them. But we are not told if Stiles has any knowledge or expertise in this area. It would seem to be important to compare Lewis's map-dowsing not with a random selection of sites, but with sites chosen from the same maps by experts in this aspect of archaeology.

Hitching tells us that he is aware of the possibility of subjective bias in judging the goodness of fit between the sites and Lewis's and Stiles's descriptions. Yet here as well as in other places in the book Hitching assumes that such awareness is sufficient to protect him and the readers from these biases. It is because such awareness is not adequate that scientists insist upon various safeguards such as double-blind procedures, reliability checks, etc. But no such safeguards were employed.

These and many other weaknesses that I have not described were tragic blunders just because it would have been so easy to have avoided them in the initial planning of the study. I am sure that any Department of Psychology in a British university, just as would be the case in this country, has at least one staff member who teaches research methodology and who would have been only too happy to advise Hitching in advance about the flaws in his intended investigation and to suggest a variety of ways that he could have avoided them. The mistakes that Hitching made are just those that we teach students to avoid in their very first course in research methods.

Where should we place the blame for this ambitious miscarriage of the scientific method? In part, I suspect it has something to do with the way British and American educational systems deal with science. Hitching is obviously intelligent, cultured, and motivated to produce arguments favorable to dowsing that will also be scientifically acceptable. But in several places in his book he betrays a muddled grasp of what scientific methods are and what they are designed to achieve. Let me illustrate with just one example.

In a revealing chapter on "Dowsing versus Science," he cites the book by Vogt and myself as one of "the two enquiries in the United States that have done most damage to official confidence in dowsing." Hitching then mentions our arguments that there are many ways dowsers can deceive themselves into falsely believing they have succeeded. He goes on to say, "But this leads the two authors to the premise that dowsing *never* works, and in support of this they are ruthless in selecting, overwhelmingly, from the individual records of dowsers, cases where dowsing has failed, and ignoring times when they have spectacularly succeeded." In support of this last assertion, Hitching accuses us of ignoring the data on Henry Gross, about whom the late novelist Kenneth Roberts "was meticulous in chronicling his development from traditional water-divining to more advanced techniques of map-dowsing for other substances."

Just in this apparently simple accusation Hitching has confused so many issues, contradicted statements in other parts of his books, and misrepresented the issues in such a way that I hardly know where to begin with a rebuttal. In the first place, Hitching himself has already made it abundantly clear that the *scientific* evidence for dowsing is almost uniformly negative. What he labels as our "ruthless" selection of cases of failure is simply our attempt to survey every known scientific study available. If Hitching knows of scientific studies in favor of dowsing that we have overlooked, he should cite them. In our book we make it very clear that the anecdotal or nonscientific evidence, such as the stories Roberts tells about Gross, do sound impressive, especially to laypeople who do not realize the limitations of such accounts. Our describing a particular failure of Gross in detail was to show that Roberts's absurd claim that Henry Gross was infallible and *never* made wrong diagnoses was easily refuted.

The point that Hitching does not seem to grasp adequately here as well as elsewhere is that scientific procedures in various domains of inquiry were devised to protect us from strong human tendencies towards self-deception. In our book, Vogt and I first document in detail how many of these tendencies operate in observation and testimony and the conduct of inadequately controlled investigations. And then we show how almost all the evidence in favor of dowsing comes from situations in which such tendencies for deception are likely to be operative. When controls are instituted to remove the possibility of such deceptive factors, the findings indicate that the divining rod acts no better than chance.

Given these circumstances, our position is that it is up to the dowsers and their supporters to obtain scientifically acceptable data in favor of dowsing before they can expect scientists to take their claims seriously. Neither Vogt nor I accept the blame for the fact that dowsers have consistently failed to make a scientific case for their craft. And, as I have indicated, Hitching agrees that the dowsers have been unable or unwilling to meet the standards of scientific credibility. In the light of these admissions by Hitching, it seems incoherent for him to blame the skeptics for lack of acceptance of dowsing. Would he want us to ignore the scientific evidence and give our approval to dowsing on nonscientific grounds? This latter suggestion seems to be, in fact, what he is demanding from us.

Although I disagree with some of his implications, I do recommend reading Hitching's book, and especially the chapter "Dowsing versus Science." Much of the writing is clear and the issues well stated. Only in places does he become obviously muddled; other inconsistencies or weaknesses of his arguments come through only after more careful textual analysis. The most important issue that runs through this presentation is the role of personal, subjective experience in establishing the reality or validity of any phenomenon. Hitching clearly believes that such nonscientific, but compelling, experiences should be allowed to outweigh the negative verdict of scientific, but impersonal, evidence—at least on some occasions and for some phenomena. In my opinion, such a view—which he obviously shares with many believers in the occult and paranormal—entirely misses the point of scientific inquiry. If you make special exceptions or dispensations from scientific validation for one's special pet theories and beliefs, then the point of scientific inquiry is lost. Each person can push for special exemptions for his or her own beliefs. Such arguments are frequently put forth on the grounds that there are other ways of "knowing." Such a claim confuses the source of ideas with the justification or testing of them. Scientists, like anyone else, can get their ideas from dreams, inspiration, meditation, logical deduction, accidental occurrences, reading, poetry, or any other source. All these are useful sources of ideas or hypotheses. But to call them alternative ways of "knowing" is to confuse the generation of possible explanations with the evaluation of them by objective testing.

In my opinion the value of this book is that it brings to the fore the real, but often neglected, basis for the differences between believers and skeptics.

Encyclopedia of Occultism and Parapsychology. Ed. Leslie Shepard. Detroit, Mich.: Gale Research Co., 1978. Pp. 1084. 2 vols.*

The subtitle of this encyclopedia—"A Compendium of Information on the Occult Sciences, Magic, Demonology, Superstitions, Spiritism, Mysticism, Metaphysics, Psychical Science, and Parapsychology, with Biographical and Bibliographical Notes and Comprehensive Indexes"—indicates its ambitious range of coverage. States the editor: "The scope of the present work is a very broad one. The word 'occult' has been interpreted in its widest sense of 'hidden, secret, beyond human understanding,' as well as pertaining to magic spells, miracles, and witchcraft. Certain mysteries, such as the Loch Ness Monster, Bigfoot, and Unidentified Flying Objects have a valid inclusion, even if they may someday be identified as elusive but objective entities around which legends and mythologies have grown."

Three individuals have written the more than 4,000 entries. Approximately 3,000 entries have been taken over from the two standard works: Encyclopedia of the Occult by Lewis Spence (1920) and Encyclopedia of Psychic Science by Nandor Fodor (1934). In most instances the items have been taken over unchanged. In a few cases, Shepard has added a paragraph or a bibliography to bring some of the entries up to date. In addition, Shepard has written around 1,000 new entries, as well as provided a complete and useful general index along with nine helpful special indices on such topics as "Animals, Birds, Insects," "Demons," "Gods," "Paranormal Phenomena," "Societies and Organizations," and so on. The special index on "Paranormal Phenomena" is further divided into fifty subcategories, such as "Animal

---

*This review appeared in Skeptical Inquirer 3 (4) (Summer 1979), 51–58.

Magnetism," "Apparitions," "Automatic Writing," "Dowsing," "Extrasensory Perception," "Eyeless Sight," "Haunting," "Healing, Psychic," "Levitation," "Mediums" (more than 220 are indexed), "Multiple Personality," "Poltergeists," "Psychic Photography," "Slate-Writing," and so on.

The handiest standard for comparison is the 24-volume set of *Man, Myth, & Magic: An Illustrated Encyclopedia of the Supernatural,* edited by Richard Cavendish (1970). The Cavendish encyclopedia has three times as many pages but many of these are covered with lavish illustrations (the Shepard volumes have no illustrations). The Cavendish work has more entries, but the Shepard volumes have longer entries that cover special topics in greater depth. Both works have superb general and special indices.

The major difference between the two contemporary encyclopedias is in the authorship of the entries. Cavendish's work contains contributions from more than two hundred experts. This gives the advantage of expertise for each entry. It also results in the inevitable unevenness of such varied authorship. The majority of entries in Shepard's book have been left just as they were written by Spence in 1920 or Fodor in 1934. In many cases, this does not matter greatly because the entries refer to events or persons of the past, but some of the entries would have profited from the addition of material that has emerged since the Spence and Fodor accounts. However, because of the material that Shepard has added and the entries he has written, the *Encyclopedia of Occultism and Parapsychology* benefits from being published eight years later than the Cavendish work. In addition, the Shepard work will be kept contemporary by interedition supplements that come out four times a year (a subscription costs $30 a year).

Shepard's encyclopedia exhibits both the advantages and disadvantages of limited authorship. Both Spence and Fodor produced works of heroic proportions. The range and thoroughness of their scholarship is impressive. I am equally impressed with Shepard's attempt not only to include many of the original entries but also to provide coverage of what has taken place since 1934.

But a single individual cannot have command of the entire range of knowledge relevant to occultism and the supernatural. And this results in inevitable gaps or weaknesses in specific instances. The fact that all three authors share the same biases is both a minus and a plus. It is a minus because a specific bias creates a filter for deciding what is and is not to be included; and it colors the presentation of debatable issues. To be fair, however, I should point out that the three authors, although proponents of the genuineness of many paranormal phenomena, seem to lean over backward to present many of the skeptical arguments. And since their collective biases become readily apparent through reading the entries, the careful reader can take such biases into account when using the encyclopedia.

All three authors included in this work seem to share not only a common set of attitudes and beliefs but also rather similar backgrounds. Lewis Spence (1874–1955) was a journalist and a Scottish scholar of the occult. He was especially concerned with the problem of Atlantis, on which he wrote four books. L. Sprague de Camp described Spence's first book on Atlantis as "the best pro-Atlantis book published to date" (as of around 1950). Although less naive than Ignatius Donnelly's wild speculations, a recent expert on classical studies (E. S. Ramage) has characterized it as "full of misconceptions about chronology, geology, archaeology, and ethnography." Both in his Atlantis books and in his entries in this encyclopedia, Spence shows signs of impatience and hostility toward what he calls the "tape-measure school" of science and pushes for a more "inspirational" approach.

Nandor Fodor (1895–1964), who began as a lawyer in Hungary, became a journalist and then a psychoanalyst. Spence's *Encyclopedia of Occultism,* which came out in 1920, is more heavily oriented toward mythology and folklore than is Fodor's *Encyclopedia of Psychic Science* (1934). The latter work is much more concerned with mediums and spiritualistic phenomena. But both authors share remarkably similar beliefs about the role of fraud, self-deception, and psychological states in the production of allegedly paranormal phenomena.

Other than his contributions to the current encyclopedia, I know of Leslie Shepard only through the forewords he wrote to reprints of Baron von Reichenbach's books on the Odic force. Reichenbach, a nineteenth-century chemist and metallurgist, began in 1850 to publish works that presented his theories and results of experimentation with what he considered to be a new force. This force could only be detected by special individuals whom he termed "sensitives." These sensitives could see colored flames emerging from magnets and they could see auras emitted from individuals. The Odic force could also account for table turning, divining, and many phenomena attributed to animal magnetism. Reichenbach's contemporaries ridiculed his claims and refused to take him seriously. But with the current pop-occultism revival of interest in mysterious forces such as radiesthesia, Kirlian auras, ley lines, and orgone energy, the Odic force has been rediscovered. Shepard is among those who feel that "it is time that Reichenbach had another hearing."

Shepard gives a clear presentation of his views toward his subject matter in his Introduction. He has taken

> much care . . . to present occultism and parapsychology in a way that avoids the sensational presentation so often associated with such topics in modern times. . . . Occultism and parapsychology are still highly controversial subjects and there are varying shades of opinion on all aspects, ranging

from uncritical acceptance to invincible disbelief. . . . It has to be admitted that the occult world has been permeated by deception, fraud and folly, although this does not invalidate much that is genuine and of great cultural and scientific importance. . . . Social responsibility requires the avoidance of a too ready acceptance of the dubious and dishonest as much as a too hasty rejection of the bizarre and paranormal. Because of this, every effort has been made to maintain a realistic presentation that strikes a fair balance between credulity and skepticism.

How does one evaluate such a work? I tried a number of approaches. I have had a reprint of Fodor's *Encyclopedia of Psychic Science* for a number of years and have found it a very useful reference on a number of occasions (paperback reprints are available for less than $10, a very good buy). The Shepard work, containing not only most of Fodor and Spence but additions by Shepard, is even more useful because of the several indices (Fodor has no index). In the few months I have had Shepard on my bookshelf I have found it useful on a number of occasions—in preparing book reviews and in researching talks on psychics and scientists. It is useful for historical material, especially with respect to the heyday of spiritualism during the Victorian era.

I drew a random sample of fifty items to read. Most were highly informative and seemed to be written from a neutral or nonevaluative standpoint. In some cases, such as the entry on Florence Cook, the accusations of fraud are fully described, but the writer tends to dismiss them or to find ways to save the case for at least some genuine paranormal elements. On some phenomena, such as ectoplasm, psychometry, and clairaudience, the entries are written as if there is no question about their reality. The article on Nostradamus is especially credulous and, in this respect, compares unfavorably with the one in Cavendish.

I supplemented this sample with a selection of items that I felt somewhat knowledgeable about. I will briefly indicate some of my reactions. I was surprised to find no separate entry or indexing of Clever Hans. Clever Hans and his owner, Herr von Osten, are briefly alluded to in an article on the Elberfeld Horses, who were the direct successors to Hans. Shepard presents the case for these horses having either human intelligence or mediumistic powers in a credulous manner. Surprisingly, he does not mention Pfungst's classic book on Clever Hans or his systematic investigations that produced a completely normal explanation of the phenomenon. Indeed, in my opinion, Pfungst's book is the classic debunking job of all time.

For Harry Edwards, England's famous faith healer, Shepard reports an 80 percent recovery rate for such illnesses as cancer, tuberculosis, and the like. He vaguely alludes to skepticism on the part of the medical profession but, surprisingly, does not refer to Dr. Louis Rose's important book

Faith Healing, in which he describes working closely with Edwards and failing, after a determined effort of many years, to find one single case of valid faith healing. Kathryn Kuhlman's faith healing is also described by Shepard in a completely credulous manner with no mention of William A. Nolen's careful study of her methods and his inability to find any proof that she can produce results.

On the other hand, Shepard seems skeptical of dianetics and Scientology, cloudbursting, some claims of modern gurus, Castaneda's Don Juan, and the reality of Bridey Murphy. But such skepticism is more than offset by his positive verdicts on the reality of water witching, the Cottingley Fairies, table turning, psychic surgery, Abram's Black Box, Ted Serios's psychic photography, Reich's orgone energy, dermo-optical perception, the Davenport brothers, Jeane Dixon, psychic plants, some of Madame Blavatsky's miracles, and the Raudive voices.

Nevertheless, I find the encyclopedia a useful reference work. Shepard, for the most part, does honor his commitment to present both sides. His biases are out in the open and easy to discount when using the material. I do find some striking omissions on the skeptical side, but I attribute these to the limitations inherent in a work for which a single individual is responsible. Some of these omissions are the following:

1. On water witching, pendulum divination, Ouija boards, and related practices, the encyclopedia presents Chevreul's and Faraday's arguments that these are the result of involuntary muscular movements. But Fodor and Shepard dismiss these arguments as inadequate to account for all the phenomena and attribute paranormal forces to many of the applications. No mention is made of the many scientific studies, all casting doubt on the reality of these phenomena, that are covered in the book by Vogt and myself (*Water Witching U.S.A.*) or of studies made since that time. Nor does Shepard make it clear that no scientific evidence has ever been accumulated for the position he takes.

2. N-rays, Abrams's Box, and related ideas on mysterious radiations are presented without reference to the striking and convincing evidence against their reality (*e.g.,* Wood's famous *Nature* paper on N-rays).

3. The Kirlian aura, acupuncture, and alleged phenomena of psychic plants are all presented in a credulous manner with no reference to many scientific studies that failed to replicate the phenomena or demystified them in terms of very normal science.

4. The entry on Raudive voices, which concludes that "there is impressive evidence that the communications are mainly from dead

individuals" fails to mention the work of Ellis, which indicates that most, if not all, of the phenomena can be attributed to artifact.

5. Arthur Ford's mediumship, and his alleged breaking of Houdini's code through spirit contact, are presented with no reference to damaging revelations in books by Spraggett and Rauscher.

Even when Shepard, or his deceased coauthors, do bring up the damaging material, they often find excuses, sometimes very farfetched, somehow to save the day for paranormality. Here are some examples from my notes:

1. Shepard discusses Abrams and his famous Black Box. He admits that Abrams's approach to diagnosis was unconventional—the patient could send a drop of blood (or even a sample of his handwriting), and this could be the basis of a diagnosis from long distance by use of the Black Box—but argues that he "was no quack." Compare this with James Harvey Young's quotation of Cramp's that Abrams "easily ranked as the dean of twentieth-century charlatans." In his entry on Black Boxes, Shepard admits that the box does not operate reliably but claims that this is because "special sensitivities were involved."

2. In the entry on psychic surgery, Shepard admits that "there is a strong possibility that some 'operations' . . . have been fakes." He concludes, however, "But, as with Spiritualist and related paranormal phenomena, it is possible that the healers and a large proportion of their phenomena are genuine, but that trickery may sometimes be resorted to when natural powers fail."

3. After presenting Fodor's account of Helene Blavatsky, with its summary of the Hodgson report that concluded, "We think that she has achieved a title to permanent remembrance as one of the most accomplished and interesting impostors in history," Shepard adds some paragraphs of his own that state: "The character of this remarkable woman was too complex for instant judgments on whether she was a genuine mystic or a charlatan. In fact, she seemed to manifest genuine paranormal phenomena with the same unconcern as the most childish frauds. She had a great contempt for stupidity, and it is possible that much of her undoubted trickery was performed as a prank, to mock the credulity of foolish followers. . . . That she had genuine occult inspiration and powers cannot be doubted."

4. On Jeane Dixon, Shepard remarks: "Because some of her predictions have not been realized, Mrs. Dixon has been widely disparaged by some critics, who have also taken exception to what they regard as her right-wing bias. However, most sensitives have a certain failure

rate, often based on faulty interpretation of symbols. . . . Mrs. Dixon has had an impressive rate of successful prediction of important world events." Shepard does not document this record. The attempts to tally her predictions and compare them against outcomes, at least the ones I have seen, are impressive mainly for how strikingly wrong she has been.

5. With respect to the medium Eva C., Shepard comments, "Some ambiguous or even fraudulent phenomena [have] often been mingled with genuine mediumship. Mediums in a state of trance do not have conscious control over their actions, and often respond to the desire of sitters for paranormal phenomena by ingenious frauds. Sometimes a strong expectation of fraud will result in fraud."

6. But my nomination for the "Bent-Spoon Award" goes to Shepard's ability to salvage some genuineness for Keely and his notorious motor. Ord-Hume in his book on *Perpetual Motion* opens his chapter on Keely with the following words: "Of all the perpetual motion frauds the story of John W. Keely's carefully planned deception and the manner in which the Keely Motor Company defrauded people of large sums of money rank supreme. As a perpetual motionist, it is difficult to imagine that he ever set out with honourable intent." Apparently such a feat of imagination is not beyond Shepard's abilities. Shepard reports: "After Keely's death . . . startling evidence of fraud was uncovered, and it has since been assumed that all his inventions were fraudulent. The real motive force seems to have been compressed air, concealed in cylinders in a secret basement and conveyed to the apparatus by thin hollow wires. Nonetheless, many individuals even today believe that any fraud may have been merely because of the intense pressure to show practical results, and that there may have been some genuine basis to Keely's life work."

This is just a small sampling of many of the defenses of the reality of paranormal phenomena put forth by Spence, Fodor, and Shepard. Such defenses will surely tend to raise the hackles of many of the readers of this journal. But if such readers can make the proper emotional and intellectual adjustments for these biases, I think they can profit in many ways from careful use of this reference work. As I have indicated, the biases are out in the open. They typically show up when the authors are trying to cope with accusations of fraud, error, or mistaken judgments. To the credit of the authors, they do, for the most part, try to acknowledge the arguments of skeptics. In most of these cases the skeptical reader is alerted to counterarguments and can make his or her own conclusions.

For me, the most valuable benefit of browsing through this encyclopedia was the opportunity to gain insights into the mentality of a type of believer who falls into error because of good intentions. Spence, Fodor, and Shepard represent the type of believer that, in my opinion, we skeptics should take quite seriously and try to understand. These men are not fanatics, cranks, or crackpots. Unlike the more extreme supporters of the occult, such as Arthur Conan Doyle, Alfred Russel Wallace, and the like, they pay careful attention to the critics and accept many of the charges of fraud or error as true.

In their own way, Shepard and his coauthors are trying their best to be scholarly, fair, and balanced. In many ways they are more open-minded and impartial than some of the skeptics and critics. But it is just this commitment to balance and fair play that, in my opinion, traps them into false beliefs. I find it somewhat touching and appealing that these men are so willing to try to accommodate all sides.

The problem comes from trying to balance testimonies from two sides as if they were equal in trustworthiness. In treating all parties fairly, they easily err in giving credence to testimonials that have no place in the court of science. Spence's entry on Evidence reflects this tendency. He complains, "The whole history of science and discovery is a triumph of true testimony, yet it is a strange fact that very little thought is generally given by the very representatives of science to the enormous amount of testimony and experimental observation that has been piled up by spiritualists and psychical researchers in the last eighty years."

Spence wrote that entry in 1920. The sort of "testimony and experimental observation" that he was talking about was just the kind that is useless for scientific purposes—it depended upon unsystematic accounts, untrained and unaided observations, nonstandardized tasks, and phenomena that were generally unrepeatable and inaccessible to skeptical eyes. Shepard seems to sense that adherence to the ground rules of science might never allow paranormal claims to become accepted. In his article on parapsychology he concludes: "It is this separation of parapsychology from life which makes laboratory experiments tedious, lacking in warmth or incentive, whereas the uncritical believer, whether Spiritualist, Christian Scientist or member of a witchcraft or Voodoo cult may generate a powerful emotional drive which produces sensational phenomena or exalted states of consciousness. It may eventually become necessary for certain areas of parapsychology to sacrifice some of their objectivity and discover a philosophical or religious basis for the validation of the paranormal as a functional part of everyday life, as it was in primitive societies."

The dilemma for Spence, Fodor, and Shepard is how to make sense out of the conflicting testimonies of believers and skeptics without impugning the integrity of any of the witnesses. The irresolution is more creative than the simple decision that one of the sides must be wrong. They assume that there must be truth on both sides. Shepard accepts the testimonies of those who claim to have seen Tony Agpaoa faking his "operations." But he also accepts the testimonies of those who claim they saw Tony perform his psychic surgery under conditions that precluded trickery. Fodor apparently accepts some of the testimonies of individuals who claim they saw Henry Slade, the nineteenth-century medium, cheating. But he also accepts the testimonies of Zoellner and others of the genuineness of Slade's effects at other times.

Out of the sincere attempt to give credence to witnesses on both sides, certain scholarly proponents of the reality of paranormal phenomena have developed a belief system that not only handles these seemingly conflicting testimonies but insulates their beliefs from any possible falsification. I think it is important fully to understand this belief system and how it works. It is built up of basic cognitive principles that most of us, in our daily lives, probably employ to protect our cherished beliefs from erosion by the inroads of reality.

What follows is a tentative and incomplete attempt to make explicit the propositions and presuppositions that underlie the sincere and scholarly attempts to justify the paranormal. I hope to achieve a better and more complete characterization of this thought pattern at a later time. What I am presenting here is merely an illustration of what can be extracted from the study of the entries in Shepard's encyclopedia. The system will be presented as a set of numbered propositions:

1. Some apparently supernatural events can be accounted for by natural causes, such as: (a) unconscious muscular acts, (b) perceptual illusions, (c) selective perception, (d) hallucinations, (e) selective memory, (f) dissociation, (g) unconscious deception, (h) coincidence, and (i) deliberate fraud.
2. When such natural causes are duly taken into account, some phenomena still remain that are truly paranormal.
3. These paranormal phenomena may be due to (a) new forms of energy or radiation previously unknown to science, (b) nonphysical causes that are beyond the pale of science, or (c) nonhuman intelligences, such as spirits of the dead or entities from another realm.
4. A sensitive who cheats may do so (a) only as a way to supplement erratic or failing powers, (b) because it is less costly in effort and health than to employ genuine powers, (c) as a way of teasing or poking fun at stupid or incompetent observers, (d) because of possession by, or the influence of, evil or mischievous spirits, (e)

because of suggestions implicitly accepted from a skeptic, or (*f*) as a way of anticipating a truly paranormal occurrence.

5. An observer who honestly believes he or she has witnessed cheating by the sensitive may be making wrong inferences. In Shepard, for example, we learn that the spirit photographer Hope was discredited as a fraud when it was discovered that some of the alleged spirits that appeared in his photographs were of living persons. But a current reinterpretation exonerates Hope in that it is assumed that portraits of living as well as dead persons can be achieved paranormally. Likewise, as reported in Shepard, when a materialized "spirit" was seized by an intrepid witness and found to be the medium in disguise, this was originally considered evidence of fraud. But revised theories of materialization now allow for such occurrences to be perfectly genuine after all!

6. When a witness catches a sensitive in the act of cheating, this often is because (*a*) the witness secretly wanted the sensitive to cheat and indirectly induced the cheating; (*b*) the witness is incompetent and his laxity actually encouraged the sensitive to take the easy road of cheating rather than the difficult path of producing genuine phenomena. (This charge was not only brought out against the scientists who caught Palladino in trickery, but it was also leveled against me because I allowed Uri Geller to employ trickery when I was investigating him. The implication is that if I was a good investigator, Geller would have not had the opportunity to cheat and would have been forced to display his genuine powers.)

7. A magician or critic who demonstrates that he or she can simulate, through trickery, an apparently paranormal feat (*a*) may actually be a renegade psychic who is not employing trickery but merely claiming to be using trickery (such charges were leveled at one time or another in all sincerity against Davey, Houdini, Maskelyne, Randi, and, recently, against myself); (*b*) further emphasizes the reality of the original paranormal event, because one can simulate or counterfeit only that which is real; (*c*) cannot do so under the "same" conditions as those under which the alleged "real" phenomenon occurred (whatever these "same" conditions were, it turns out that the "psychic" also cannot duplicate his or her own feats under these "same" conditions).

8. Because of the nature of paranormal phenomena, strict scientific controls are often inappropriate and self-defeating.

9. Truly paranormal powers and strong tendencies to cheat often occur together within the same individuals. In the case of poltergeists, we are told that the adolescent around whom the phenomena

originally occur eventually learns to imitate the genuine phenomena through trickery.

10. If a sensitive has not been detected in cheating over several demonstrations, then the phenomena must be genuine. Richet stated as a rule that a medium who cheats could get away with it for a maximum of two years.

The Mind Race: Understanding and Using Psychic Abilities. Russell Targ and Keith Harary. New York: Villard Books, 1984.*

Russell Targ is a physicist with patents in optics and laser physics. He also has devoted much of his adult life to research on psychic abilities. In collaboration with Harold Puthoff, in 1972 he originated the experiments on remote viewing at the Stanford Research Institute (now SRI International). He and Puthoff also gained considerable publicity for their experiments with Uri Geller. Targ and Puthoff summarized their earlier work on remote viewing and Uri Geller in their book *Mind-Reach* (1977).

In many respects Targ's new book, *Mind Race: Understanding and Using Psychic Abilities,* coauthored with Keith Harary (1984), is an updated version of the earlier book.

Harary, a psychologist, is well known both as a parapsychologist and as an apparently successful percipient in parapsychological experiments. He and Targ founded Delphi Associates, an organization that sells psychic consulting services to individuals and businesses seeking advice on investments, exploration, or other important decisions.

Although Targ and Harary inform us that both the Soviet and the American defense establishments spend millions of dollars on psychical research, the "race" of the title does not refer to the competition for psychic superiority between the superpowers. Instead, as the authors put it:

> The Mind Race is a race to determine the future of your own consciousness before other forces decide the future for you. We must develop our ability to experience compassion and empathy with our fellow creatures, before we lose contact with our own humanity and exterminate one another over an ideological difference of opinion, or for some similarly foolish reason. The Mind Race is not a race between nations. Though the U.S. and Soviet governments are heavily involved in psi research, we are all in a more vital and personal race to determine whether we will be able to wake up to our deeper potential before we have exhausted the limited time available to us.

---

*This review appeared under the title "Outracing the Evidence: The Muddled 'Mind Race'," *Skeptical Inquirer* 9 (2) (Winter 1984–85), 125–45.

> As a society we are in the process of making wide-ranging decisions about our evolutionary future. This decision is in our hands right now. The quality of future life on this planet will be determined for us by others if we do not choose to participate actively in determining our own destiny. We do not believe that any psychically sensitive human being would choose to live in a future that is dominated by robots, especially if we are to be the robots. We believe that our future must include psychic functioning if we are to achieve our full potential as human beings. We call this requirement the psi imperative (p. 246).

The stakes are high. If Targ and Harary are correct, we have to enter the Mind Race and develop our psychic powers or end up as robots subject to the manipulation of others. But what if we lack psychic abilities? Or, if we have them, how can we develop them? Not to worry. The authors assure us that we all possess such powers. Furthermore, they supply directions for developing them. "It is past time for bringing psi into the open, where everyone can benefit from a realistic awareness of it. We believe it is time for all of us to claim our right to function psychically. You own your own mind. It is important not to give it away, or fail to use it to its full potential. So get going! You have to enter the Mind Race in order to win" (p. 246).

The authors' intentions are clear. They would like each of us to follow their directions and develop our inherent psychic faculties. They imply that some form of world utopia would automatically follow once each of us has heeded their advice.

But, as they see it, obstacles prevent many of us from making this commitment. Gurus, superpsychics, and occultists frighten and mislead many of us by depicting psychic functioning as special, abnormal, or available only to the initiated. The media portray psychic powers as weird, evil, or dangerous. Organized religion views such powers as satanic in origin. And critics—for what the authors assert are ulterior religious and philosophical motives—proudly proclaim that psi does not exist. "To those who refuse to develop their psychic abilities it makes little difference whether the force that manipulates them into repressing their human potential is organized religion, cults, materialistic critics, or the mass media. The end result of such repression is the same no matter where it originates" (pp. 245–46).

Targ and Harary's goals of creating a better world by helping us gain access to our psychic powers assume the truth of a number of propositions. I would list them as follows:

1. Psychic functioning, or psi, is real.
2. The reality of psi has been scientifically established beyond any reasonable doubt.

3. The individual reader can test the reality of psi by personal experience in demonstrations suggested by the authors.
4. Psi is normal. It is a natural human function and does not depend on secret or occult rites, special states of mind, or abnormal circumstances.
5. Psi is universal. It is not a special gift. We all have the potential for psychic functioning.
6. Psi can be developed through simple exercises that help to discriminate valid psychic signals from "mental noise."
7. Psi can be put to practical use in any situation where decisions must be made with inadequate information, such as gambling, investing, finding parking spaces, etc.
8. It is important that we all develop and employ our psychic powers to the fullest.

The most basic claim, of course, is that psi is real. The arguments of the book make sense only if this claim is true. This "totally convincing book" (according to the dust jacket) employs a number of different grounds to convince the reader of the existence of psychic functioning. For the scientific justification they point to the list of 28 "published formal experiments" on remote viewing that they append to the book. Even more compelling, as far as the average reader is concerned, are the authors' accounts of the many impressive qualitative descriptions of targets by viewers and the successful applications of psi to predicting silver futures and the outcome of gambling choices. Readers are also urged to follow the directions and experience their own psychic success.

The Scientific Case for Psi

Let's look first at the scientific case they present. This is supported entirely by the published experiments on remote viewing. The term *remote viewing* was coined by Targ and Puthoff in 1972 as a neutral term to describe the phenomenon they believed they were capturing in their experiments at the Stanford Research Institute. These experiments employed at least three participants. A viewer, or percipient (the psychic), was isolated with an experimenter (the interviewer) in the laboratory. A second experimenter (the out-bound experimenter, or "beacon") then drove to a randomly selected geographical location (the target site) within a 30-minute drive from the laboratory. While the beacon was at the target site, the viewer described his or her impressions of the scene to the interviewer, and often made drawings as well. When the trial was over, the beacon would return to the laboratory and then all the participants would visit the target site to give the viewer feedback about how well the impressions had matched the actual target.

After a series of such trials (usually 7 or 9) had been conducted with a given viewer, the descriptions and drawings made by the viewer for each session were given to a judge, who then visited each site and ranked all the descriptions from best (a low score) to worst (a high score) according to how well each matched the target. If the agreement between the viewer's description and the actual target was simply a matter of guesswork, then, for example, with 9 possible target sites we would expect to find that the average rank of the descriptions would be 5. If the descriptions were actually related to the targets (by psi or some other means) then we would expect the rankings to be lower. In fact, this is what Targ and Harary claim the data from their own and other experiments on remote viewing have shown. In more than half the series the rankings have correlated significantly with the target sites.

Targ and Harary have no doubts that the scientific case for the reality of remote viewing has been established beyond all reasonable doubt. "In an examination of the twenty-eight formal published reports of attempted replications of remote viewing, Hansen, Schlitz, and Tart at the Institute of Parapsychology found that more than half of the papers reported successful outcomes." Part of this report is included as an appendix to the book. Hansen *et al.* compiled reports of remote viewing experiments conducted during the years 1973 through 1982. They concluded: "We have found that more than half (fifteen out of twenty-eight) of the published formal experiments have been successful, where only one in twenty would be expected by chance."

To both the casual and scientifically trained reader the fact that 15 of 28 "published formal experiments have been successful" should seem rather impressive. But a more careful study of the list of experiments suggests that this data base may not be as strong as implied.

The scientific literature in any given field consists of formal experiments published in scientific journals. Only those papers that survive a rigorous screening and revision procedure make it into print. In fact, many scientific journals reject more than half of the papers submitted to them. Rarely does a paper get published as submitted. Manuscripts are sent to two or more referees who are experts in the subject area of the manuscript. These referees advise the editor about whether the paper is of sufficient merit to be a candidate for publication. They also carefully scrutinize the manuscript for inconsistencies, unsupported claims, adequacy of the statistical analyses, unclear arguments, and so on. Typically, before a manuscript finally is accepted for publication, it has gone through several revisions as a result of this refereeing process. Such a screening process is not perfect, and some defective papers do get published. But, for the most part, the process ensures that scientific reports have passed a number of tests.

Only 13, or less than half, of the "published formal experiments" meet the standards of having been published under refereed conditions. The remaining 15 were published under conditions that fall short of scientific acceptability. Some appeared as brief reports or abstracts of papers delivered at Parapsychological Association meetings or some other parapsychological conference. In addition to not having undergone the standard refereeing process, such abstracts present insufficient documentation for scientific evaluation. The same can be said for the other studies that appeared in print only as brief or informal reports in book chapters or letters to the editor.

The scientific case for remote viewing, then, rests upon 13 scientifically reported experiments, 9 of which are classified as "successful." Seven of these experiments were conducted by Targ and Puthoff. The remaining 2 came from two other laboratories. This harvest of 9 "successful" scientifically reported experiments emerging from just three different laboratories over the past 12 years hardly seems to justify the strong impression conveyed by the authors that remote viewing studies have been successfully carried out in large numbers in laboratories all over the world. ("In laboratories across this country, and in many other nations as well, forty-six experimental series have investigated remote viewing. Twenty-three of these investigations have reported successful results and produced statistically significant data, where three would be expected" [p. 5].)

But even 9 "successes" out of 13 tries would not be bad if the successful studies met reasonable standards of adequacy. But all 9 suffer crippling weaknesses. At least 3, and possibly more, are what I would classify as "retrospective experiments"—experiments not explicitly planned in advance but apparently reconstructed from separate trials that were originally conducted simply as demonstrations. According to Kennedy (1979a), remote viewing experiments have employed the wrong statistical test. When Kennedy applied a more appropriate statistical test he found, for example, that only 2 of 6 experiments reported by Puthoff and Targ were significant, whereas they had concluded that 5 were significant. This alone would reduce the total number of successful remote viewing experiments to 6. Of these 6, all but one suffer from a "fatal flaw" that I first pointed out in 1977 (Hyman 1977b), and Kennedy (1979b) independently noted two years later. The one experiment that escapes this "fatal flaw" unfortunately suffers from another serious drawback. I will discuss these flaws later in this article.

Marks and Kammann (1978) raised serious questions about the validity of the findings on the remote viewing experiments with Pat Price (Puthoff and Targ 1976). Marks obtained copies of the five unpublished transcripts from the series with Price. He found a number of clues in the transcripts to target sites without assuming the operation of psi. For example, in one transcript the interviewer mentions the nature reserve that had been the target for the previous day. Such a clue obviously helps the judge by informing him or her that the transcript in question should *not* be matched with the nature reserve. In addition, if the judge has information on the order of the target sites, it enables him or her to identify *uniquely* the transcript with its intended target. Using such clues within the transcripts, Marks successfully matched each description against its intended target without actually visiting any of the sites.

Tart, Puthoff, and Targ (1980) responded to this critique with three rebuttals. Charles Tart, a parapsychologist who had not been involved in the original experiments with Price, reviewed the transcripts and removed "all phrases suggested as potential cues by Marks and Kammann" as well as "any additional phrases for which even the most remote *post hoc* cue argument could be made." The edited series was rejudged by a new and "qualified" judge who was able successfully to match seven of the nine transcripts. The parapsychologists argued that this successful rejudging refuted the "cueing-artifact hypothesis" as it applies to the Price series. Furthermore, they claimed that the hypothesis could not apply to their subsequent successful experiments because the transcripts were carefully edited to avoid such cues. Finally, they argued that the successful replication of their experiment in other laboratories confirms the reality of their psychic interpretation.

There is no need here to discuss the continuation of this controversy (Marks 1981; Puthoff and Targ 1981). Possibly this controversy as well as the critique of the statistical analysis being applied to nonindependent trials has helped to prevent the participants from realizing the full implications of the criticism raised by myself and Kennedy. Neither a more conservative test nor the editing out of obvious cues referring to previous targets can overcome the defect we have pinpointed. Once the viewer and the interviewer have been given feedback about a particular target, then *every* word and phrase in the subsequent descriptions of targets has been tainted. And it is not just the words and phrases that have been included but also those that have been excluded that create the problem.

The problem arises from the fact that the viewer is provided immediate feedback after each session. Say that the target for the first session was the Hoover Tower at Stanford. This will almost certainly influence what both the viewer and the interviewer say during the second and subsequent sessions in the same series. Almost certainly the viewer, during the second session, will not supply an exact description of the Hoover Tower. So, whatever the viewer says during the second session, a judge should find it to be a closer match to the second target site than to the first one. Now, assume that the second target site happened to be the Palo Alto train station. The viewer's descriptions during the third session will avoid describing either the Hoover Tower or the Palo Alto train station. We do not need to hypothesize something as mysterious as psi to predict that a judge should find this third description a better match to the third target site than to either of the first two. As we add sessions, this effect of immediate feedback should continue to make the correlation between the viewer's descriptions and the target sites better and better.

Every experiment that has followed the original SRI protocols with immediate feedback is irrevocably flawed because there is no way of separating out a true psychic signal from the information in the transcripts provided by the fact that the viewer knows the previous target sites. So far as I can tell, only one of the nine "successful" experiments does not contain this fatal error.

This experiment (Schlitz and Gruber 1980) suffers from its own serious problems. Gruber, who was the beacon, also translated the viewer's target descriptions into Italian for the judging process. The translator knew which description went with a given target. With almost an infinite number of choices to be made in translating a description from English to Italian, and with the translator's task of trying to capture in the new language what the viewer "meant," it would seem inevitable that translations by the beacon would match the intended target sites. As just one example, assume that, as a part of her description, the viewer had mentioned "wood." One can translate the English word "wood" into Italian in a number of ways depending upon whether the translator believed the wood in question referred to the trunks of trees, the logs, the finished boards, the wood in furniture, or some other form of wood. If, as in this case, the actual target site was a forest, then it seems reasonable that the translator would be strongly influenced to translate the English description to fit this known feature of the target. Given this blatant violation of controls, skeptics should not be surprised to learn that this experiment yielded the highest degree of significance of any remote viewing experiment.

The foregoing considerations should make it clear that the scientific case for remote viewing rests on very shaky foundations. Further problems could be mentioned. For example, not one of the several skeptics who have seriously attempted to replicate the remote viewing experiment has succeeded. I even know of two cases, neither yet published, in which a skeptic and a parapsychologist collaborated on a remote viewing experiment with negative results.

Many problems involve inadequate documentation. In the early years of science, the ideal of a scientific paper was a report that was sufficiently complete so that any competent reader could both fully evaluate the results and repeat the experiment. The same ideal holds today, but with journal space costly and limited some practical compromises have to be made. Not all the data or complicated details of procedure can be included, but to the extent this is so the scientific community understands that the omitted details and data are publicly available and the authors are obligated, within the constraints of expense and practicality, to make them available to serious readers. A hallmark of scientific research is this public availability of the data for scrutiny by all interested parties.

The problem of public availability of the data is especially critical in the case of remote viewing. The raw data upon which the scientific case is built consist of the protocols or individual descriptions of targets provided by the viewers. It would take up a prohibitive amount of journal space to publish the complete set of transcripts from an experiment that consists of the typical nine or so trials. Without access to the original transcripts, the reader gets to read only those one or two exceptional transcripts selected by the authors. And, for the most part, only excerpts from the chosen transcripts are supplied.

The scientific public would never have been aware of the cues available in the Price transcripts if David Marks, overcoming strong resistance from Targ and Puthoff, had not obtained the original data. Because of the controversy that had arisen about those transcripts, Dr. Christopher Scott, an English mathematician and former parapsychologist, requested that Puthoff and Targ send him copies of the transcripts to signal to the scientific community that, in fact, these data were available for public inspection by responsible and qualified scientists. When his initial written inquiries failed to result in his getting the transcripts, Dr. Scott publicly repeated his request to Targ and Puthoff at the Parapsychological Association meeting in Cambridge, England, in August 1982. Puthoff admitted that Scott was entitled to inspect the transcripts and indicated that he would make them available for this purpose. Dr. Scott happened to be visiting California in the spring of 1983. Since, despite further requests, he still had not received copies of the transcripts, he made a special trip to SRI International to put his request to Puthoff directly. Unfortunately, Puthoff could not meet with Scott because of an illness in his family, but none of his associates would allow Scott to see the transcripts. Scott has persisted in his quest to see the data, but Puthoff and Targ, two years after they promised to make them available, still prevent public scrutiny.

Targ and Harary depict their critics as unreasonable dogmatists. They put all the blame for the failure of their work to gain scientific acceptance upon the religious fanaticism of blind materialists. Tragically, Targ does not realize how much of the blame must be attributed to his own unscientific behavior. By allowing only a small band of select initiates to inspect their raw data, Targ and Puthoff appear more like the leaders of an occult society who jealously guard their secrets rather than scientists who try to make their case in the public arena.

I do not have to develop my psychic powers to anticipate Targ and Harary's next reaction to the preceding critique. They preview their rebuttal, among other places, on pages 174 and 175 of *Mind Race*. Here they describe their reactions upon listening to the critics at the meeting of the Society for Psychical Research and the Parapsychological Association in August 1982:

> One question was repeatedly asked at this centenary conference: What has been accomplished in a hundred years of research? An answer that most of the scientists in the field would support is that as a result of thousands of laboratory experiments, comprising millions of trials, any fair-minded man or woman should be convinced beyond reasonable doubt that psi exists, and might possibly even be important. But many people at the conference did not share that view. Some were critics, and some were psi researchers. . . . It became clear from listening to these critics that any experiment, no matter how carefully carried out, may reveal a flaw in retrospect. There is always something that could have been done better. *This is true in every field of science*—and in recent years there have been many more examples of fraud in medical research than in psi research.
>
> Hearing what the critics have to say, we began to realize that psi may never be accepted into the mainstream of science on the basis of laboratory experimentation alone.

Like many other things the authors have to say, one can find circumstances and contexts in which the foregoing remarks apply. Some critics do fit this description. And not one will deny that after the fact we can always find in any experiment a defect or subtle variable that was overlooked. But the authors have again used an excuse that makes sense in some other context to avoid dealing with legitimate criticism.

The "critics" who gave papers at the 1982 conference were Chris Scott, Susan Blackmore, Piet Hein Hoebens, and myself. Scott is a former parapsychologist who has become a critic, but he is recognized by parapsychologists and others as scrupulously fair. He maintains good relations with psychic researchers and has written extensively for their journals. Susan Blackmore is a practicing parapsychologist. She has become skeptical of many claims in her field as a result of a decade of research in which she has failed to replicate many of the major findings. She remains in the field because she feels parapsychology badly needs friendly and constructive critics. Hoebens is a Dutch journalist who has gained an international reputation as a skeptic who leans over backwards to give the parapsychologists a fair hearing. All of us on the panel had agreed ahead of time that our task was to provide constructive and responsible criticism.

The flaws I have attributed to remote viewing experiments in this article are definitely not flaws that are found retrospectively as new and better experiments emerge. They are the very same flaws I wrote about seven years ago (Hyman 1977b). Kennedy (1979a, 1979b), a parapsychologist, complained about these same flaws along with others. Unfortunately, Targ and Puthoff, in their haste to dismiss any criticism as having ulterior motives, have kept repeating the same mistakes. Other researchers in remote viewing slavishly followed their example. The tragic result is seven more years of wasted research.

The Nonscientific Case for Psi

The bottom line is that there is no scientifically convincing case for remote viewing. As the preceding quotations indicate, Targ and Harary, while insisting the scientific case for remote viewing is overwhelmingly strong, concede that they have little hope of convincing critics and the scientific establishment with such data. Consequently, the authors employ two other modes of argument to persuade the reader that psi is real. They supply many qualitative and compelling accounts of psychic successes, and they urge their readers to try experiencing psi for themselves.

Many of the qualitative accounts illustrate striking correspondences between portions of a transcript and the actual target during a remote viewing session. In one example, the target was the Palo Alto Airport tower. The verbatim transcript and drawing made by the viewer, Hella Hammid, indeed seem to match the target well beyond any forced matching that one usually can achieve between a scenic description and a reasonably complex geographic site. But this particular session occurred after three preceding unsuccessful sessions. A skeptic might want to study all the transcripts in this series before jumping to conclusions about possible psychic correspondence.

This particular transcript obviously has been selected from hundreds available to the authors. Presumably it is presented in its entirety just because it appears to be a striking match. The authors present a number of other apparently striking matches between description and target, but in most of these cases only selected portions of the transcript are given. Again, the skeptic would want to study the entire transcript as well as all the other transcripts in the series.

Marks and Kammann (1980) employ the phrase "subjective validation" to label the subjectively compelling matches that viewers and judges discovered in their remote viewing experiments. When they initiated their series of experiments in an attempt to replicate the remote viewing experiments, Marks and Kammann first thought remote viewing was, in fact, occurring. Both they and their viewer, after getting the immediate feedback from the visits to the target sites, found amazing correspondences between the viewer's descriptions and the target. When the judging began, the judges also found amazing correspondences between the transcripts and the targets to which they matched them. Unfortunately, the judges' matchings of targets to transcripts did not correspond with the factual pairings in the experiment. Even when told of this, the viewers did not change their belief in the success of their remote viewing.

This tendency to find meaningful and compelling matches between verbal descriptions and arbitrary targets is quite pervasive. It helps account, for example, for the success of character readers and astrologers (Hyman 1977a). Furthermore, once an individual has found such a match, it is difficult to dissuade him or her from believing in the nonaccidental nature of the correspondence (Nisbett and Ross 1980).

For such reasons as these, striking and "meaningful" correspondences between target and descriptions cannot be accepted as scientific evidence. This is why the elaborate blind-judging and complicated statistical methodologies have been devised. The scientific enterprise aims at separating out true correlations from subjectively compelling, but spurious, ones.

Unfortunately, the lay reader as well as the uncritical scientist will more likely be swayed by the colorful and vivid qualitative illustrations than they will by the abstract and quantitative scientific arguments. Nisbett and Ross (1980) cite abundant evidence to this effect. So we can anticipate that Targ and Harary will succeed in their tactic of bypassing their scientific case in favor of nonscientific arguments. They will succeed, that is, if their goal is to gain the adherence of their readers to their claims rather than to arrive at the truth.

Targ and Harary also describe successful applications of psi. An interesting example is the successful use of remote viewing by Elisabeth Targ to predict the winner of the sixth race at Bay Meadows. She picked a horse named Shamgo, and students from all over her college dormitory contributed to a betting pool. Shamgo won and paid six to one. As in other such accounts in this book, we are not told if this was Elisabeth's first attempt at predicting races or if she ever tried it again. Targ and Harary also retell the story of their venture into psychically predicting the silver-futures market. They claim to have correctly predicted both the magnitude and the direction of the change in all nine forecasts they made in the fall of 1982. Again they fail to tell us about any preceding or future forecasts (although in the "Nova" program on ESP, the narrator casually mentioned that Targ and Harary's later attempt to repeat this feat failed).

Developing Psychic Abilities

Psychologists also will not be surprised if the readers who follow the authors' recipes for developing their own psychic powers become believers in the reality of psi. The authors write that readers can test the reality of psi for themselves. They supply general guidelines to follow to develop latent psychic abilities. The basic idea makes some sense in terms of general learning principles. If we accept their argument, then at any point in time our conscious experience consists of sensory impressions, memories, and inferences. In addition, some of this content may be impressions that have arrived psychically. If the viewer attempts to describe the psychic impression, the description is often contaminated and transformed by the viewer's expectations, memories, and current sensory impressions. The authors refer to this contamination as "mental noise." Developing one's psychic abilities involves learning to discriminate true psychic signals from "mental noise." This can be achieved, according to the authors' optimistic projections, by indulging in exercises in which immediate feedback supplies us clues as to which of our impressions were truly psychic and which were mental noise.

One exercise involves finding a parking place. Readers are urged to visualize a certain area of the city in which they want to find a parking place. When they get some sort of impression of a possibility, they drive to that spot. If the spot is occupied, they try again. They are to keep this up until they either find a parking spot or run out of gas. By repeatedly trying this exercise the learner, allegedly, can gradually improve the ability to discriminate between those impressions that work and those that do not. Exercises in playing blackjack, doing remote viewing, anticipating traffic jams, and so on, are similar.

Targ and Harary confidently put forth such exercises as a way for the readers to find the truth for themselves. But we do not have to postulate psi to predict many of those who try such exercises will end up believing they are experiencing psi. For a sampling of just some of the enormous amount of psychological evidence for this expectation see Nisbett and Ross (1980). The authors do not bother to warn their readers of the traps that await them. Instead of forearming the readers, they *disarm* them. Consequently, instead of a path to the truth, they supply a recipe for self-deception.

Several things are wrong with such exercises. For one thing, one of them can succeed for reasons unrelated to psi. Indeed, the authors talk about developing intuition as if it is the same thing as psychic functioning. Some learners might actually improve their ability to find parking places. In some shopping areas the southern boundary, for example, might tend to have more unoccupied spaces than the other sections (because of prevailing traffic patterns). As learners practice trying to home in psychically on a parking space, they may gradually learn to follow impressions that lead them to the southern boundary. Such learning could take place without any conscious awareness on the learner's part. Very likely, the learner will attribute this increasing success to developing psychic powers. Other unconscious cues, such as hearing a motor start up as an auto vacates a parking place, could also become part of what the learner comes to rely upon as psychic abilities.

But even without any actual learning taking place, several psychological mechanisms can easily contribute to the illusion that psychic abilities are gradually leading to more and more successful outcomes. These are well-known distortions of memory, thinking, and other cognitive processes. And it is dismaying, especially when one of the authors claims to be an experimental psychologist, that Targ and Harary do nothing to protect the reader from such powerful pitfalls.

Furthermore, Targ and Harary provide no evidence that learning to discriminate psychic signals from "mental noise" according to their directions can actually occur. They refer vaguely to their experience with remote viewing sessions. But they fail to hint at even one scientific experiment that suggests that such learning can take place.

Additional Problems

So far I have noted some serious weaknesses in the arguments for the propositions being asserted in *Mind Race*. My notes suggest a variety of other difficulties, but it would only make a long article much longer to try to list them all. In this section I just want to point to a few inconsistencies in the arguments of the book.

The key to developing psychic abilities, according to the authors, is learning to discriminate "mental noise" from true psi impressions. The authors repeatedly assert that their viewers become better and better at this with practice. Harary gives examples from his own experience as a viewer where he was actually able to indicate to the judge which of his statements were "mental noise."

Such a claim would seem simple to test, but the authors supply nothing but a few qualitative observations to back up their assertion. As a standard procedure, for example, each viewer, immediately after each trial, could review the transcript and indicate which statements are "mental noise" and which are true impressions. The experimenter could easily quantify such data and see whether the proportion of correctly identified statements increases with practice.

Furthermore, even if their claim is only partially true, it allows for an excellent control for the judging procedure. Each transcript could be divided into two transcripts—one part containing all the items identified by the viewer as "mental noise" and one part containing the items identified as true impressions. The judges should show high accuracy in matching the second transcripts and should be at chance in matching the first.

Nor do the authors face up to another inconsistency raised by their claim. It is the practice in remote viewing experiments of employing independent judges to gauge the correspondence between target and description. The researchers who use this paradigm claim that they cannot get adequate results if they employ the viewers as judges because of "mental noise" that interferes with their seeing the correspondences. One inconsistency is that in the ganzfeld experiments, which started at the same time as the remote viewing paradigm, the reverse seems to be the case. In those experiments, the percipients are used to judge the correspondence of their own descriptions against the targets. This is done because apparently the results from independent judges do not work as well. Despite this odd reversal, the claims for success in the ganzfeld experiments equal those for the remote viewing experiments.

A second inconsistency is that, if in fact the viewer is learning to discriminate true psi signals from "mental noise," then the viewer should be a better judge than an outsider. The independent judge, after all, has to deal with the entire transcript and has no way of gauging which statements should be ignored in trying to match transcript with target.

The claims for gambling successes employing psi also hint at a variety of inconsistencies. Millions of gamblers over the years have presumably employed hunches and intuition in making their bets. They have gained enormous amounts of immediate feedback that should have taught them, according to the theory advanced in this book, which of their impressions should be trustworthy and which should be ignored. Even if such learning is only partial and even if it occurs in only some of the gamblers, it should raise the odds in favor of the players by some percentage. Yet the gambling industry rests on the assumption that odds that are only slightly (one or two percentage points) in their favor along with other restrictions upon the betting will ensure them against serious losses. If Targ and Harary are correct, the casinos in Las Vegas, Reno, Monte Carlo, Atlantic City, and elsewhere should have long ago gone bankrupt.

A third inconsistency arises from evolutionary theory. Targ and Harary assert not only that we all have latent pyschic abilities that can easily be developed but that we *must* develop them if we are to realize our human potential and escape becoming robots. This first of all raises the question of the evolutionary forces that allowed such a capacity to develop and yet remain unused. Presumably, it must have had some survival value to have developed in the first place. But, then, we have to ask why it is now latent and needs special exercises to develop.

I can imagine possible answers to these inconsistencies, but it is strange that the authors have felt no obligation to deal with them.

Going Beyond the Data

In his review of Targ's earlier book *Mind-Reach,* Robert Ornstein (1977) wrote:

> Throughout the book the authors state their hope that the study of para-psychology will become primarily a scientific one in which speculations are firmly grounded in the evidence. In their own writing, however, Targ and Puthoff almost always go beyond evidence and claim they have proven their case when they have done nothing of the sort. In writing this book, the authors have done more harm, perhaps, to their own position and to their field of study than they have helped.

These words apply with equal force to the current book. Targ and Harary's most conspicuous faults are hasty generalizations and overstated claims. On almost every page they make assertions based on inadequate or nonexistent evidence. I have already given samples in the preceding sections. But to back up my own assertion, I will list a sample of some of the more blatant cases:

1. As already documented, the authors overstate greatly the strength of the scientific support for remote viewing. They strongly imply that 15 of 28 "formal published experiments" from laboratories all over the world were successful. But, if we deal with papers actually published under accepted standards, only 9 "successes" can be counted. Of these, 7 were conducted by Targ and Puthoff and only 2 come from other laboratories. All but one of these "successful" experiments suffer a fatal flaw that I pointed out in 1977, as did Kennedy in 1979.

2. On the basis of just two remote viewing trials conducted with the viewers in a submarine, Targ and Harary conclude that ocean water provides no barrier to the psi signal and that remote viewing is unaffected by seasickness. There is just no way such a conclusion can be drawn on the basis of just two data points. Even if the authors want to claim that remote viewing took place under these circumstances, they would need many more data points collected

under the underwater conditions before they could say that no difference existed between this and land conditions.

3. Targ and Harary admit that they do not know if evil psychics can implant harmful thoughts in other people, but they do not hesitate to suggest steps that the readers can employ for "psychic self-defense." If we do not know if the disease exists, how in the world can we know if the cure will work or even if it may cause harmful side-effects?

4. As already indicated, the authors provide elaborate instructions for developing psi but cite not one piece of scientific evidence that suggests that such instruction works.

5. Targ and Harary freely accuse critics of fraud on the basis of undocumented or unsubstantiated allegations. They try to smear Martin Gardner by writing that he

criticized the NASA-supported ESP-teaching-machine study carried out at SRI in 1974. He falsely alleged that the subjects in this experiment tore up their unsuccessful data tapes, and only handed in the successful ones. He said in his article, "I am not guessing when I say that the paper tape records from Phase I were handed in to Targ in bits and pieces." We now know the reason he could say that he "wasn't guessing." This is because he recently confided to a fellow reporter that he had just made it up, "because that's the way it must have happened." The reporter was so shocked at this disclosure, that even though he is not particularly sympathetic to our work, he felt compelled to call up the SRI researchers to pass on this remarkable piece of news (p. 157).

On its face this vicious slander does not stand up. First, it is based entirely on an undocumented statement by an unnamed reporter. Second, it just does not make sense for a journalist whose profession is based on the integrity of its members to make such an obviously damaging admission. When I read it, I could tell it was completely false, not only because I know Martin Gardner but also because I am familiar with the circumstances of his having made the claim about the tapes. He felt he could make this statement with confidence because he was given the information by an informant whom he has every reason to trust. To further compound the damage of this slanderous accusation, it was published in *Fate* magazine as the "Quote-of-the-Month." The "fellow reporter" to whom Martin Gardner supposedly confided that he had deliberately lied about the ESP-teaching-machine experiment turns out to be Ron McRae, the author of the recently published book *Mind Wars*. McRae has written to *Fate* magazine that he never made such a statement to Targ or anyone else. Instead, he did happen to mention to Hal Puthoff, who was then Targ's colleague at SRI, that he had overheard another individual make such a claim but did not consider it reliable. As a result of McRae's letter to *Fate,* that magazine published an apology and retraction in its October issue.

Targ and Harary continue this reckless abandon by asserting that CSICOP "was recently caught conspiring to deceive the public about some research results that did not fit their expectations." They go on to say that Randi and the rest of the CSICOP members "were exposed when a member of their group defected and offered documented proof of the deception. . . . It is clear that the goal of the psi-cops is to *control your ability to access and interpret information* and to walk a beat in your mind" (pp. 157–58). The "documented proof" presumably refers to the charges made by Dennis Rawlins in his long attack upon three members of CSICOP published in *Fate* magazine. The incident refers to a controversy over the interpretation of data from a study by Michel Gauquelin. In co-operation with Gauquelin, three skeptics reanalyzed the original data and published an interpretation that was challenged not only by Gauquelin, but also, on certain obscure technical grounds, by Rawlins. All this was initiated before CSICOP was founded, and the project was never sponsored by the Committee. Randi, whom the authors obviously want to paint black, had nothing to do with the Gauquelin study. In addition, the debate involved complicated and subtle matters of how to interpret trends in the data, and no conspiracy to deceive or any other evils that Targ and Harary so carelessly invent were ever implicated.

6. The authors freely question the motives of those critics who disagree with them. "Some of these critics have ulterior motives for not wanting the public or the academic community to take normal psychic functioning seriously. In that, they are like anyone else who hopes to profit by misleading the public about psychic abilities. Critics, like cultists, can sometimes live off the controversy they generate. For example, one critic, now famous, was a minor entertainer until he began a nationwide crusade against psi research" (p. 156).

The "critic" they are talking about in the last sentence of the quotation is Randi, the magician. Randi was an established and well-known entertainer long before his attacks on Uri Geller. He is probably the best-known escape artist since Harry Houdini. It would be difficult to measure whether he profited or lost either professionally or financially from the publicity emerging from his critiques of psychical research. I know that he often gives up profitable engagements to attend conferences and give talks on his views of contemporary paranormal claims. From my personal acquaintance with Randi, I have little doubt that his motivations involve a love of his craft and a desire to prevent conjuring from being used to exploit scientists and the public. Motivations are of course complicated and elusive. I have been a critic of paranormal claims for at least 35 years. I am sure that my motivations have changed drastically over that period of time. And they are complex. Even today I would have a difficult time trying to give a full account of why I put so much time into it. But the complexities and multidimensionality of motivations do not deter Targ and Harary. Unencumbered by facts or proof, they freely and confidently assert which motivations guide the behavior of their critics.

If the critics were fair and honest, Targ and Harary believe, they would carefully scrutinize the parapsychological data and conclude that psi has been proved. But the critics, without having seriously examined the data, freely criticize the claims. This means, according to the authors, that they have ulterior motives for not wanting psi to be true and for keeping the public from believing. In the same breath, Targ and Harary acknowledge that some critics, both within and outside the field of psychical research, have examined the data and still debate the claims for psi. No matter. They say that these critics, too, have religious and philosophical motives and deliberately distort the facts so as to mislead the public.

These seem to be the kinds of rationalizations that enable the authors to cope with the fact that many critics deny that the case for psi has been proved. This rationalization seems to provide a protective shell. It keeps Targ and Harary from facing the reality that the case for psi is much shakier than they would like to believe.

In many ways their book does a disservice to the attempts of other parapsychologists to make their field into a respectable and serious branch of science. The authors boldly assert that the accumulated data are sound, consistent, and scientifically impeccable. Only prejudice and ignorance prevent the scientific establishment from recognizing this fact. They fail to realize that the parapsychologists have much work to do in order to get their house in order before they are ready to withstand the scrutiny of serious scientists.

Some major parapsychologists, fortunately, do recognize this problem. John Beloff (1976), a past president of the Parapsychological Association, told his colleagues: "I think that one thing we have got to recognize is that our field is so much more erratic, anarchic and badly subversive than we like to admit when we are engaged in our public-relations exercises." And Martin Johnson (1976), who holds the Chair of Parapsychology at the University of Utrecht, wrote:

> I must confess that I have some difficulties in understanding the logic of some parapsychologists when they proclaim the standpoint that findings within our field have wide-ranging consequences for science in general, and especially for our world picture. It is often implied that the research findings within our field constitute a death blow to materialism. I am puzzled by this claim, since I thought that few people were really so unsophisticated as to mistake our concepts for reality. . . . I believe that we should not make extravagant and, as I see it, unwarranted claims about the wide-ranging consequences of our scattered, undigested, indeed rather 'soft' facts, if we can speak at all about facts within our field. I firmly believe that wide-ranging interpretations based on such scanty data tend to give us, and with some justification, a bad reputation among our colleagues within the more established fields of science.

Without a doubt, Targ and Harary's careless scholarship will contribute to the "bad reputation" that parapsychology still has among many established scientists. Perhaps it is equally unfortunate that this book may very well achieve the opposite of what the authors intend. They hope to demystify psychic functioning, put their readers in touch with themselves and the world, and to free them from false beliefs. Instead they have set the stage for new mystifications and self-deception.

References

Beloff, J. 1976. The study of the paranormal as an educative epxerience. In B. Shapiro and L. Colby (Eds.)., *Education in Parapsychology,* 16–29. New York: Parapsychology Foundation.

Hyman, R. 1977a. "Cold reading": How to convince strangers that you know all about them. *Zetetic (Skeptical Inquirer),* (Spring/Summer): 18–37.

———. 1977b. Psychics and scientists: A review of Targ, R., and Puthoff, H., *Mind-Reach. The Humanist,* 37 (May/June): 16–20.

Johnson, M. 1976. Parapsychology and education. In B. Shapiro and L. Colby (Eds.), *Education in Parapsychology,* 130–151. New York: Parapsychology Foundation.

Kennedy, J. E. 1979a. Methodological problems in free-response ESP experiments. *Journal of the American Society for Psychical Research,* 73: 1–15.

———. 1979b. More on methodological issues in free-response Psi experiments. *Journal of the American Society for Psychical Research,* 73: 395–401.

Marks, D. 1981. Sensory cues and data selection invalidate remote viewing experiments. *Nature,* 292: 177.

Marks, D., and Kammann, R. 1978. Information transmission in remote viewing experiments. *Nature,* 274: 680–681.

———. 1980. *The Psychology of the Psychic.* Buffalo, N.Y.: Prometheus Books.

Nisbett, R., and Ross, L. 1980. *Human Inference: Strategies and Shortcomings of Social Judgment.* Englewood Cliffs, N.J.: Prentice-Hall.

Ornstein, R. 1977. A case for parapsychology. (Review of *Mind-Reach*). *New York Times Book Review*, March 13.

Puthoff, H., and Targ, R. 1976. A perceptual channel for information transfer over kilometer distances: historical perspectives and recent research. *Proceedings of the IEEE*, 64: 329-354.

————. 1981. Rebuttal of criticisms of remote viewing experiments. *Nature*, 292: 388.

Schlitz, M., and Gruber, E. 1980. Transcontinental remote viewing. *Journal of Parapsychology* 44: 305-317.

Targ, R., and Harary, K. 1984. *The Mind Race: Understanding and Using Psychic Abilities*. New York: Villard Books.

Targ, R., and Puthoff, H. E. 1977. *Mind-Reach: Scientists Look at Psychic Ability*. New York: Delacorte.

Tart, C., Puthoff, E. H., and Targ, R. 1980. Information transmission in remote viewing experiments. *Nature*, 284: 191.

Part Four

The Psychology of Belief

Introduction

Two questions motivate the papers included in this book: (1) Does the evidence offered by proponents justify concluding that something paranormal exists? (2) Why do proponents believe that certain events and experiences are paranormal? The preceding papers provide my reasons for believing that the evidence accumulated so far does not support claims for the paranormal. Some of the reasons are based on technical matters involving statistics, experimental controls, and scientific methodology.

The second question relates to the first in important ways. Even if the proponents' arguments for the adequacy of their evidence has merit, the question of why people believe in the paranormal still matters. Psi could turn out to be real, after all. Another evaluation of the best parapsychological evidence might lead to the conclusion that the evidence does, in fact, justify concluding that something paranormal exists. But whatever the scientific status of psi may be, just about every believer has come to his or her conviction on the basis of nonscientific evidence. Belief in the paranormal comes from personal experience, the testimonies of friends, and the social inputs of peers. A majority of experimental parapsychologists—as one poll of the members of the Parapsychological Association revealed—entered the field because they already believed in the paranormal because of personal experiences.

Psychologists have documented, again and again, the powerful cognitive biases and illusions that create false but compelling beliefs when personal experience, testimony, and anecdotes provide the major basis for believing. Indeed, one can argue that the scientific method is basically a procedure to protect us from our human biases when evaluating evidence.

The two papers in this section on the psychic reading, "Cold Reading" and "The Psychic Reading," have been the most popular of all the papers

I have written on the paranormal. I regard them as very important because the psychic reading serves as a prototype of how compelling, but false, beliefs come about.

If you follow the guidelines in my two papers, you will find it easy to convince complete strangers that you know all about them. Even inept and bungling psychic readers can convince clients that the reading is accurate and full of import for their lives. The psychic reading is a miniature social-communication situation.

Humans are social animals par excellence. We are primed for picking up meaning in both the gestures and words of our fellow animals. We are so good at this, in fact, that we pick up meaning even where none was intended. The psychic reader capitalizes on this tendency. The client receives a meaningful reading without realizing that he or she put all the meaning into the reading.

The psychic reading contains most, if not all, the factors that result in compelling and false beliefs in other domains of the paranormal. Some of these principles are discussed in the two papers.

The paper on "Proper Criticism" has received surprisingly wide circulation among skeptics. It has been reprinted in many of the newsletters published by local skeptical groups. I was motivated to write this by the problems created by fellow skeptics who allow their passion to outrun their reason. I am embarrassed or upset when skeptics behave in ways that I feel are unjustified. I also can point to incidents in which skeptics have behaved in admirable ways.

But what makes the difference between "good" and "bad" skepticism? When is criticism "responsible" and when is it "irresponsible?" Asking such questions reveals that we do not have handbooks for skeptics. Nor do we have explicit standards or guidelines to tell us what is and what is not good critical behavior.

Software for creating expert systems is becoming increasingly available. A few years ago, I entertained the idea of trying to create an expert system that would act as a "good" skeptic. Once the system was created, we would be able to feed it details about a paranormal claim and see how it reacted. I never got very far with this fanciful idea. But just thinking about the types of rules I would need to embed in this system provided me with the basis for writing "Proper Criticism."

We would have to provide our expert critic with more detailed rules for handling specific situations than I have listed in the article. In addition, we would want our expert critic to communicate effectively with a wide range of audiences. At the 1988 Chicago conference of the Committee for the Scientific Investigation of Claims of the Paranormal, Jerry Andrus, Jeff Mayhew, and Paul MacCready collaborated with me in a program called "Enhancing the Skeptics's Message." With this program we wanted to make skeptics aware of the importance of packaging their message to reach a wider audience.

Many different audiences exist. The most frustrating ones for skeptics are those made up of committed believers and "psychics." Many skeptics believe these audiences cannot be reached by any rational, or even irrational, arguments. However, skeptics and believers find themselves confronting each other with increasing frequency in various forums. When they do, they find themselves talking past one another.

As Jeff Mayhew has argued, *if we do try to argue with such committed believers,* we should realize that they have a different agenda than we do. The typical skeptic focuses on the validity of the claims: What is the evidence? How sound is it scientifically? The typical believer, however, could not care less about questions of validity. The believer wants to have experiences of a certain type and is looking for ways to transform the self. When challenged about the validity of a claim, the believer sees this as indicating that the skeptic has missed the point.

Indeed, it might very well be that the believer is not just uninterested in questions of validity. Instead, the believer might feel threatened by issues of validity. Many New Age beliefs seem to be specially formulated to be immune from testing. Those individuals who "channel" entities from another dimension or from 35,000 years ago present a claim that is beyond testing and falsification.

Science education among the adult population in this country is notorious for being almost nonexistent. Yet, most adults have had just enough exposure to science to have a lurking suspicion that their cherished paranormal beliefs might be foolish illusions after all. Because this suspicion is always present just below the surface, the believers have fortified their beliefs by phrasing them in such a way that they become immune from falsification.

"Cold Reading": How to Convince Strangers That You Know All About Them*

Over twenty years ago I taught a course at Harvard University called "Applications of Social Psychology." The sort of applications that I covered were the various ways in which people were manipulated. I invited various manipulators to demonstrate their techniques—pitchmen, sellers of encyclopedias, hypnotists, advertising experts, evangelists, confidence men, and a variety of individuals who dealt with personal problems. The techniques we discussed, especially those concerned with helping people with their personal problems, seem to involve the client's tendency to find more meaning in any situation than is actually there. Students readily accepted this explanation when it was pointed out to them. But I did not feel that they fully realized just how pervasive and powerful this human tendency to make sense out of nonsense really is.

Consequently, in 1955 I wrote a paper entitled "The Psychological Reading: An Infallible Technique for Winning Admiration and Popularity." Over the years I have distributed copies of this paper to my students. The paper begins as follows:

> So you want to be admired? You want people to seek your company, to talk about you, to praise your talents? This manuscript tells you how to satisfy that want. Herein you will find a "sure-fire" gimmick for the achievement of fame and popularity. Just follow the advice that I give you, and, even if you are the most incompetent social bungler, you cannot fail to become the life of the party. What is the secret that underlies this

*The Zetetic 1 (Spring–Summer 1977), 18–37.

infallible system? The secret, my friend, is a simple and obvious one. It has been tried and proven by practitioners since the beginnings of mankind. Here is the gist of the secret: To be popular with your fellow man, tell him what he wants to hear. He wants to hear about himself. So tell him about himself. But not what you know to be true about him. Oh, no! Never tell him the truth. Rather, tell him *what he would like to be true about himself!* And there you have it. Simple and obvious, but yet so powerful. This manuscript details the way in which you can exploit this golden rule by assuming the role of a character reader.

I will include essentially the same recipe for character reading in this paper that I give to my students. In addition I will bring the material up to date, describe some relevant research, and indicate some theoretical reasons why the technique "works." My purpose is not to enable you to enhance your personal magnetism, nor is it to increase the number of character readers. I give you these rules for reading character because I want you to experience how the method works. I want you to see what a powerful technique the psychological reading is, how convincing it is to the psychologist and layman alike.

When you see how easy it is to convince a person that you can read his character on sight, you will better appreciate why fortune tellers and psychologists are frequently lulled into placing credence in techniques which have not been validated by acceptable scientific methods. The recent controversy in *The Humanist* magazine and *The Zetetic* over the scientific status of astrology probably is irrelevant to the reasons that individuals believe in astrology. Almost without exception the defenders of astrology with whom I have contact do not refer to the evidence relating to the underlying theory. They are convinced of astrology's value because it "works." By this they mean that it supplies them with feedback that "feels right"—that convinces them that the horoscope provides a basis for understanding themselves and ordering their lives. It has personal meaning for them.

Some philosophers distinguish between "persuasion" and "conviction." The distinction is subtle. But for our purposes we can think of subjective experiences that persuade us that something is so and of logical and scientific procedures that convince, or ought to convince, us that something is or is not so. Quite frequently a scientist commits time and resources toward generating scientific evidence for a proposition because he has already been persuaded, on nonscientific grounds, that the proposition is true. Such intuitive persuasion plays an important motivational role in science as well as in the arts. Pathological science and false beliefs come about when such intuitive persuasion overrides or colors the evidence from objective procedures for establishing conviction.

The field of personality assessment has always been plagued by this confusion between persuasion and conviction. In contrast to intelligence and aptitude tests, the scientific validation of personality tests, even under ideal conditions, rarely results in unequivocal or satisfactory results. In fact some of the most widely used personality inventories have repeatedly failed to pass validity checks. One of the reasons for this messy state of affairs is the lack of reliable and objective criteria against which to check the results of an assessment.

But the lack of adequate validation has not prevented the use of, and reliance on, such instruments. Assessment psychologists have always placed more reliance on their instruments than is warranted by the scientific evidence. Both psychologist and client are invariably persuaded by the results that the assessment "works."

This state of affairs, of course, is even more true when we consider divination systems beyond those of the academic and professional psychologist. Every system—be it based on the position of the stars, the pattern of lines in the hand, the shape of the face or skull, the fall of the cards or the dice, the accidents of nature, or the intuitions of a "psychic"—claims its quota of satisfied customers. The clients invariably feel satisfied with the results. They are convinced that the reader and the system have penetrated to the core of their "true" self. Such satisfaction on the part of clients also feeds back upon the reader. Even if the reader began his or her career with little belief in the method, the inevitable reinforcement of persuaded clients increases the reader's confidence in him or herself and the system. In this way a "vicious circle" is established. The reader and the clients become more and more persuaded that they have hold of a direct pipeline to the "truth."

The state of affairs in which the evaluation of an assessment instrument depends upon the satisfaction of the client is known as *personal validation.* Personal validation is, for all practical purposes, the major reason for the persistence of divinatory and assessment procedures. If the client is not persuaded, then the system will not survive. Personal validation, of course, is the basis for the acceptance of more than just assessment instruments. The widespread acceptance of myths about Bigfoot, the Bermuda Triangle, ancient astronauts, ghosts, the validity of meditation and consciousness-raising schemes, and a host of other beliefs is based on persuasion through personal validation rather than scientific conviction.

Cold Reading

Cold reading is a procedure by which a "reader" is able to persuade a client whom he or she has never before met that the reader knows all about the client's personality and problems. At one extreme this can be accomplished by delivering a stock spiel, or *psychological reading,* that consists of highly general statements that can fit any individual. A reader who relies on psychological readings will usually have memorized a set of stock spiels. He or she then can select a reading to deliver that is relatively more appropriate to the general category that the client fits—a young unmarried girl, a senior citizen, and so on. Such an attempt to fit the reading to the client makes the psychological reading a closer approximation to the true cold reading.

The cold reading, at its best, provides the client with a character assessment that is uniquely tailored to fit him or her. The reader begins with the same assumptions that guide the psychological reader who relies on the stock spiel. These assumptions are (1) that we all are basically more alike than different; (2) that our problems are generated by the same major transitions of birth, puberty, work, marriage, children, old age, and death; (3) that, with the exception of curiosity seekers and troublemakers, people come to a character reader because they need someone to listen to their conflicts involving love, money, and health. The cold reader goes beyond these common denominators by gathering as much additional information about the client as possible. Sometimes such information is obtained in advance of the reading. If the reading is through appointment, the reader can use directories and other sources to gather information. When the client enters the consulting room, an assistant can examine the coat left behind (and often the purse as well) for papers, notes, labels, and other such cues about socioeconomic status, and so on. Most cold readers, however, do not need such advance information.

The cold reader basically relies on a good memory and acute observation. The client is carefully studied. The clothing—for example, style, neatness, cost, age—provides a host of cues for helping the reader make shrewd guesses about socioeconomic level, conservatism or extroversion, and other characteristics. The client's physical features—weight, posture, looks, eyes, and hands—provide further cues. The hands are especially revealing to the good reader. The manner of speech, use of grammar, gestures, and eye contact are also good sources. To the good reader the huge amount of information coming from an initial sizing up of the client greatly narrows the possible categories into which he or she classifies clients. Knowledge of actuarial and statistical data about various subcultures in the population already provides the basis for making an uncanny and strikingly accurate assessment of the client.

But the skilled reader can go much further in particularizing the reading. He or she wants to zero in as quickly as possible on the precise problem that is bothering the client. On the basis of an initial assessment the reader makes some tentative hypotheses. He or she tests these out by beginning

the assessment in general terms, touching upon general categories of problems and watching the reaction of the client. If the reader is on the wrong
track the client's reactions—eye movements, pupillary dilation, other bodily
mannerisms—will serve as a warning. When the reader is on the right track
other reactions will confirm this. By watching the client's reactions as he
or she tests out different hypotheses during the spiel, the good reader quickly
hits upon what is bothering the customer and begins to adjust the reading
to the situation. By this time, the client has usually been persuaded that
the reader, by some uncanny means, has gained insights into the client's
innermost thoughts. The client's guard is now down. Often the client opens
up and actually tells the reader, who is also a good listener, the details
of his or her situation. The reader, after a suitable interval, will usually
feed back the information that the client has given in such a way that
the client will be further amazed at how much the reader "knows" about
him or her. Invariably the client leaves the reader without realizing that
everything he or she has been told is simply what the client has unwittingly
revealed to the reader.

The Stock Spiel

The preceding paragraphs indicate that the cold reader is a highly skilled
and talented individual. And this is true. But what is amazing about this
area of human assessment is how successfully even an unskilled and incompetent reader can persuade a client that he has fathomed the client's
true nature. It is probably a tribute to the creativity of the human mind
that a client can, under the right circumstances, make sense out of almost
any reading and manage to fit it to his or her own unique situation. All
that is necessary is that the reader make out a plausible case for why the
reading ought to fit. The client will do the rest.

You can achieve a surprisingly high degree of success as a character
reader even if you merely use a stock spiel which you give to every client.
Sundberg (1955), for example, found that if you deliver the following
character sketch to a college male, he will usually accept it as a reasonably
accurate description of himself: "You are a person who is very normal
in his attitudes, behavior and relationships with people. You get along well
without effort. People naturally like you and you are not overly critical
of them or yourself. You are neither overly conventional nor overly individualistic. Your prevailing mood is one of optimism and constructive effort,
and you are not troubled by periods of depression, psychosomatic illness
or nervous symptoms."

Sundberg found that the college female will respond with even more
pleasure to the following sketch: "You appear to be a cheerful, well-balanced

person. You may have some alternation of happy and unhappy moods, but they are not extreme now. You have few or no problems with your health. You are sociable and mix well with others. You are adaptable to social situations. You tend to be adventurous. Your interests are wide. You are fairly self-confident and usually think clearly."

Sundberg conducted his study more than 20 years ago. But the sketches still work well today. Either will tend to work well with both sexes. More recently, several laboratory studies have had excellent success with the following stock spiel (Snyder and Shenkel 1975):

> Some of your aspirations tend to be pretty unrealistic. At times you are extroverted, affable, sociable, while at other times you are introverted, wary and reserved. You have found it unwise to be too frank in revealing yourself to others. You pride yourself on being an independent thinker and do not accept others' opinions without satisfactory proof. You prefer a certain amount of change and variety, and become dissatisfied when hemmed in by restrictions and limitations. At times you have serious doubts as to whether you have made the right decision or done the right thing. Disciplined and controlled on the outside, you tend to be worrisome and insecure on the inside.
>
> Your sexual adjustment has presented some problems for you. While you have some personality weaknesses, you are generally able to compensate for them. You have a great deal of unused capacity which you have not turned to your advantage. You have a tendency to be critical of yourself. You have a strong need for other people to like you and for them to admire you.

Interestingly enough the statements in this stock spiel were first used in 1948 by Bertram Forer (1949) in a classroom demonstration of personal validation. He obtained most of them from a newsstand astrology book. Forer's students, who thought the sketch was uniquely intended for them as a result of a personality test, gave the sketch an average rating of 4.26 on a scale of 0 (poor) to 5 (perfect). As many as 16 out of his 39 students (41 percent) rated it as a perfect fit to their personality. Only five gave it a rating below 4 (the worst being a rating of 2, meaning "average"). Almost 30 years later students give the same sketch an almost identical rating as a unique description of themselves.

The Technique in Action

The acceptability of the stock spiel depends upon the method and circumstances of its delivery. As we shall later see, laboratory studies have isolated many of the factors that contribute to persuading clients that the sketch is a unique description of themselves. A great deal of the success of the spiel depends upon "setting the stage." The reader tries to persuade the client that the sketch is tailored especially for him or her. The reader also creates the impression that it is based on a reliable and proven assessment procedure. The way the sketch is delivered and dramatized also helps. And many of the rules that I give for the cold reading also apply to the delivery of the stock spiel.

The stock spiel, when properly delivered, can be quite effective. In fact, with the right combination of circumstances the stock spiel is often accepted as a perfect and unique description by the client. But, in general, one can achieve even greater success as a character analyst if one uses the more flexible technique of the cold reader. In this method one plays a sort of detective role in which one takes on the role of a Sherlock Holmes. (See the "Case of the Cardboard Box" for an excellent example of cold reading.) One observes the jewelry, prices the clothing, evaluates the speech mannerisms, and studies the reactions of the subject. Then whatever information these observations provide is pieced together into a character reading that is aimed more specifically at the particular client.

A good illustration of the cold reader in action occurs in a story told by the well-known magician John Mulholland. The incident took place in the 1930s. A young lady in her late twenties or early thirties visited a character reader. She was wearing expensive jewelry, a wedding band, and a black dress of cheap material. The observant reader noted that she was wearing shoes that were currently being advertised for people with foot trouble. (Pause at this point and imagine that you are the reader; see what you would make of these clues.)

By means of just these observations the reader proceeded to amaze his client with his insights. He assumed that this client came to see him, as did most of his female customers, because of a love or financial problem. The black dress and the wedding band led him to reason that her husband had died recently. The expensive jewelry suggested that she had been financially comfortable during marriage, but the cheap dress indicated that her husband's death had left her penniless. The therapeutic shoes signified that she was working to support herself since her husband's death.

The reader's shrewdness led him to the following conclusion—which turned out to be correct: The lady had met a man who had proposed to her. She wanted to marry the man to end her economic hardship. But she felt guilty about marrying so soon after her husband's death. The reader told her what she had come to hear—that it was all right to marry without further delay.

The Rules of the Game

Whether you prefer to use the formula reading or to emply the more flexible technique of the cold reader, the following bits of advice will help to contribute to your success as a character reader.

1. *Remember that the key ingredient of a successful character reading is confidence.* If you *look* and *act* as if you believe in what you are doing, you will be able to sell even a bad reading to most of your subjects.

    The laboratory studies support this rule. Many readings are accepted as accurate because the statements do fit most people. But even readings that would ordinarily be rejected as inaccurate will be accepted if the reader is viewed as a person with prestige or as someone who knows what he is doing.

    One danger of playing the role of reader is that you will persuade yourself that you really are divining true character. This happened to me. I started reading palms when I was in my teens as a way to supplement my income from doing magic and mental shows. When I began I did not believe in palmistry. But I knew that to "sell" it I had to act as if I did. After a few years I became a firm believer in palmistry. One day the late Dr. Stanley Jaks, who was a professional mentalist and a man I respected, tactfully suggested that it would make an interesting experiment if I deliberately gave readings opposite to what the lines indicated. I tried this out with a few clients. To my surprise and horror my readings were just as successful. Ever since then I have been interested in the powerful forces that convince us, reader and client alike, that something is so when it really isn't.

2. *Make creative use of the latest statistical abstracts, polls, and surveys.* This can provide you with a wealth of material about what various subclasses of our society believe, do, want, worry about, and so on. For example if you can ascertain about a client such things as the part of the country he comes from, the size of the city he was brought up in, his parents' religion and vocations, his educational level and age, you already are in possession of information that should enable you to predict with high probability his voting preferences, his beliefs on many issues, and other traits.

3. *Set the stage for your reading.* Profess a modesty about your talents. Make no excessive claims. This catches your subject off guard. You are not challenging her to a battle of wits. You can read her character; whether she cares to believe you or not is her concern.

4. *Gain the client's cooperation in advance.* Emphasize that the success of the reading depends as much upon his sincere cooperation as upon your efforts. (After all, you imply, you already have a successful career at reading characters. You are not on trial—he is.) State that due to difficulties of language and communication, *you may not always convey the exact meaning you intend.* In these cases he is to strive to reinterpret the message in terms of his own vocabulary and life.

You accomplish two invaluable ends with this dodge. You have an alibi in case the reading doesn't click; it's his fault, not yours! And your subject will strive to fit your generalities to his specific life occurences. Later, when he recalls the reading he will recall it in terms of specifics; thus you gain credit for much more than you actually said.

Of all the pieces of advice this is the most crucial. To the extent that the client is made an active participant in the reading, the reading will succeed. The good reader, deliberately or unwittingly, is the one who forces the client to actively search his memory to make sense of the reader's statements.

5. *Use a gimmick such as a crystal ball, tarot cards, or palm reading.* The use of palmistry, say, serves two useful purposes. It lends an air of novelty to the reading, but, more important, it serves as a cover for you to stall and to formulate your next statement. While you are trying to think of something to say next, you are apparently carefully studying a new wrinkle or line in the hand. Holding hands, in addition to any emotional thrills you may give or receive thereby, is another good way of detecting the reactions of the subject to what you are saying (the principle is the same as "muscle reading").

It helps, in the case of palmistry or other gimmicks, to study some manuals so that you know roughly what the various diagnostic signs are supposed to mean. A clever way of using such gimmicks to pin down a client's problem is to use a variant of "Twenty Questions," somewhat like this: Tell the client you have only a limited amount of time for the reading. You could focus on the heart line, which deals with emotional entanglements; on the fate line, which deals with vocational pursuits and money matters; the head line, which deals with personal problems; the health line, and so on. Ask her which one to focus on first. This quickly pins down the major category of problem on the client's mind.

6. *Have a list of stock phrases at the tip of your tongue.* Even if you are doing a cold reading, the liberal sprinkling of stock phrases

amidst your regular reading will add body to the reading and will fill in time as you try to formulate more precise characterizations. You can use the statements in the preceding stock spiels as a start. Memorize a few of them before undertaking your initial ventures into character reading. Palmistry, tarot, and other fortune telling manuals also are rich sources for good phrases.

7. *Keep your eyes open.* Also use your other senses. We have seen how to size up the client on the basis of clothing, jewelry, mannerisms, and speech. Even a crude classification on such a basis can provide sufficient information for a good reading. Watch the impact of your statements upon the subject. Very quickly you will learn when you are "hitting home" and when you are "missing the boat."

8. *Use the technique of "fishing."* This is simply a device for getting the subject to tell you about himself. Then you rephrase what he has told you into a coherent sketch and feed it back to him. One version of fishing is to phrase each statement in the form of a question. Then wait for the subject to reply (or react). If the reaction is positive, then the reader turns the statement into a positive assertion. Often the subject will respond by answering the implied question and then some. Later he will tend to forget that he was the source of your information. By making your statements into questions you also force the subject to search through his memory to retrieve specific instances to fit your general statement.

9. *Learn to be a good listener.* During the course of a reading your client will be bursting to talk about incidents that are brought up. The good reader allows the client to talk at will. On one occasion I observed a tea-leaf reader. The client actually spent 75 percent of the total time talking. Afterward when I questioned the client about the reading she vehemently insisted that she had not uttered a single word during the course of the reading. The client praised the reader for having so astutely told her what in fact she herself had spoken.

Another value of listening is that most clients who seek the services of a reader actually want someone to listen to their problems. In addition many clients have already made up their minds about what choices they are going to make. They merely want support to carry out their decision.

10. *Dramatize your reading.* Give back what little information you do have or pick up a little bit at a time. Make it seem more than it is. Build word pictures around each divulgence. Don't be afraid of hamming it up.

11. *Always give the impression that you know more than you are saying.* The successful reader, like the family doctor, always acts as if he or she knows much more. Once you persuade the client that you know one item of information about him that you could not possibly have obtained through normal channels, the client will automatically assume you know all. At this point he will typically open up and confide in you.

12. *Don't be afraid to flatter your subject every chance you get.* An occasional subject will protest such flattery, but will still cherish it. In such cases you can further flatter her by saying, "You are always suspicious of people who flatter you. You just can't believe that someone will say good of you unles he is trying to achieve some ulterior goal."

13. Finally, remember the golden rule: *Tell the client what he wants to hear.*

Sigmund Freud once made an astute observation. He had a client who had been to a fortune-teller many years previously. The fortune-teller had predicted that she would have twins. Actually she never had children. Yet, despite the fact that the reader had been wrong, the client still spoke of her in glowing terms. Freud tried to figure out why this was so. He finally concluded that at the time of the original reading the client wanted desperately to have children. The fortune-teller sensed this and told her what she wanted to hear. From this Freud inferred that the successful fortune-teller is one who predicts what the client secretly wishes to happen rather than what actually will happen (Freud 1933).

The Fallacy of Personal Validation

As we have seen, clients will readily accept stock spiels, such as those I have presented, as unique descriptions of themselves. Many laboratory experiments have demonstrated this effect. Forer (1949) called the tendency to accept as valid a personality sketch on the basis of the client's willingness to accept it the *fallacy of personal validation.*

The early studies on personal validation were simply demonstrations to show that students, personnel directors, and others can readily be persuaded to accept a fake sketch as a valid description of themselves. A few studies tried to go beyond the demonstration and tease out factors that influence the acceptability of the fake sketch. Sundberg (1955), for example, gave the Minnesota Multiphasic Personality Inventory (known as the MMPI) to 44 students. The MMPI is the most carefully standardized personality inventory in the psychologist's tool kit. Two psychologists, highly experienced in interpreting the outcome of the MMPI, wrote a personality sketch for each student on the basis of his or her test results. Each student then received two personality sketches—the one actually written for him or her and a fake sketch. When asked to pick which sketch described him or her better, 26 of the 44 students (59 percent) picked the fake sketch!

Sundberg's study highlights one of the difficulties in this area. A fake, universal sketch can be seen as a better description of oneself than can a uniquely tailored description by trained psychologists based upon one of the best assessment devices we have. This makes personal validation a completely useless procedure. But it makes the life of the character reader and the pseudopsychologist all the easier. His or her general and universal statements have more persuasive appeal than do the best and most appropriate descriptions that the trained psychologist can come up with.

Some experiments that my students and I conducted during the 1950s also supplied some more information about the acceptability of such sketches. In one experiment we gave some students a fake sketch (the third stock spiel previously discussed) and told half of them that it was the result of an astrological reading and the other half that it was the result of a new test, the Harvard Basic Personality Profile. In those days, unlike today, students had a low opinion of astrology. All the students rated each of the individual statements as generally true of themselves. The groups did not differ in their ratings of the acceptability of the individual statements. But when asked to rate the sketch as a whole, the group that thought it came from an accepted personality test rated the acceptability significantly higher than did the group that thought it came from an astrologer. From talking to individual students it was clear that those who were in the personality-test group believed that they had received a highly accurate and unique characterization of themselves. Those in the astrology group admitted that the individual statements were appplicable to themselves but dismissed the apparent success of the astrologer as due to the fact that the statements were so general that they would fit anyone. In other words, by changing the context in which they received the statements we were able to manipulate the subjects' perceptions as to whether the statements were generalities that applied to everyone or were specific characterizations of themselves.

In a further experiment we obtained a pool of items that 80 percent or more of Harvard students endorsed as true of themselves. We then had another group of Harvard students rate these items as "desirable" or "undesirable" and as "general" or "particular" (true of only a few students). Thus we had a set of items that we knew almost all our subjects would endorse as true of themselves, but which varied on desirability and on perceived generality. We were then able to compose fake sketches that varied in their proportion of desirable and specific items. We found that the best recipe for creating stock spiels was to include about 75 percent desirable items, but ones that were seen as specific, and about 25 percent undesirable items, but ones that were seen as general. The undesirable items had the apparent effect of making the spiel plausible. The fact that the items were seen as being generally true of other students made them more acceptable.

The most extensive program of research to study the factors making for acceptability of fake sketches is that by C. R. Snyder and his associates at the University of Kansas. A brief summary of many of his findings was given in an article in *Psychology Today* (Snyder and Shenkel 1975). In most of his studies Snyder uses a control condition in which the subject is given the fake sketch and told that this sketch is generally true for all people. On a rating scale from 1 to 5 (1, very poor; 2, poor; 3, average; 4, good; 5, excellent) the subject rates how well the interpretation fits his or her personality. A typical result for this control condition is a rating of around 3 to 4, or between average and good. But when the sketch is presented to the subject as one which was written "for you, personally," the acceptability tends to go up to around 4.5, or between good and excellent.

In a related experiment the subjects were given the fake sketch under the pretense that it was based on an astrological reading. The control group, given the sketch as "generally true of all people," rated it about 3.2, or just about average. A second group was asked to supply the astrologer with information on the year and month of their birth. When they received their sketches they rated them on the average at 3.76, or just below good. A third group supplied the mythical astrologer with information on year, month, and day of birth. These subjects gave a mean rating of 4.38.

From experiments such as these we have learned the following. The acceptability of a general sketch is enhanced when (1) the reader or source is believed to know what he is doing, (2) the instrument or assessment device is plausible, (3) a lot of mumbo jumbo is associated with the procedure (such as giving month, day, hour, and minute of birth along with a lot of complicated calculations), and (4) the client is led to believe that the sketch has been tailored to his or her personality. When these conditions are met, the client, and possibly the reader as well, have a strong "illusion of uniqueness"—that is, the client is persuaded that the sketch describes himself or herself and no one else.

Why Does It Work?

But why does the reading work? And why does it work so well? It does not help to say that people are gullible or suggestible. Nor can we dismiss the findings by implying that some individuals are just not sufficiently discriminating or lack sufficient intelligence to see through the reading. Indeed one can argue that it requires a certain degree of intelligence on the part of a client for the reading to work well. Once the client is actively engaged in trying to make sense of the series of sometimes contradictory statements issuing from the reader, the client becomes a creative problem-solver trying to find coherence and meaning in the total set of statements. The task is not unlike that of trying to make sense of a work of art, a poem, or, for that matter, a sentence. The work of art, the poem, or the sentence serve as a blueprint or plan from which we can construct a meaningful experience by bringing to bear our own past experiences and memories.

In other words the reading succeeds just because it calls upon the normal processes of comprehension that we ordinarily bring to bear in making sense out of any form of communication. The raw information in a communication is rarely, if ever, sufficient in itself for comprehension. A shared context and background are assumed. Much has to be filled in by inference. The good reader, like anyone who manipulates our perceptions, is merely exploiting the normal processes by which we make sense out of the disorderly array of inputs that constantly bombard us.

A variety of examples and experiments could be drawn upon to illustrate this point. Let us look at a couple of instructive cases. Dr. Joseph Weizenbaum, of M.I.T., developed a computer program that would enable a human apparently to carry on a conversation with a computer. One version of his program is called "Doctor." The program is designed to "talk" like a Rogerian psychotherapist. Such a therapist is relatively easy to imitate because the basis of Rogers' technique is simply to feed the patient's statements back to him in a paraphrased form. The human, playing the role of the patient, types in questions and answers on a teletype machine. The computer, under control of the program, types replies and questions on the same teletype paper. A typical example (Weizenbaum 1976) of a conversation between a young woman and "Doctor" follows. (The woman speaks first. The computer's responses are printed in italics.)

Men are all alike.
In what way?
They're always bugging us about something or other.
Can you think of a specific example?
Well, my boyfriend made me come here.
Your boyfriend made you come here?
He says I'm depressed much of the time.
I am sorry to hear you are depressed.
It's true. I am unhappy.

Do you think coming here will help you not to be unhappy?
I need some help, that much seems certain.
What would it mean to you if you got some help?
Perhaps I could learn to get along with my mother.
Tell me more about your family.
My mother takes care of me.
Who else in your family takes care of you?
My father.
Your father?
You are like my father in some ways.
What resemblance do you see?
You are not very aggressive, but I think you don't want me to notice that.
What makes you think I am not very aggressive?
You don't argue with me.
Why do you think I don't argue with you?
You are afraid of me.
Does it please you to believe I am afraid of you?
My father is afraid of everybody.
What else comes to mind when you think of your father?
Bullies.
Does that have anything to do with the fact that your boyfriend made you come here?

"Doctor" is a quite primitive program as natural-language programs go. It employs a lot of tricks and stock phrases. It has no mechanisms for actually understanding sentences. Instead it seeks out key words that are typed and does some simple syntactical transformations. For example, if the program sees a sentence of the form "Do you X" it automatically prints out the response *"What makes you think I X?"* When "Doctor" cannot match the syntax of a given sentence it can cover up in two ways. It can say something noncommittal, such as *"Please go on"* or *"What does that suggest to you?"* Or it can recall an earlier match and refer back to it, as for example, *"How does this relate to your depression?"* where depression was an earlier topic of conversation.

In essence "Doctor" is a primitive cold reader. It uses stock phrases to cover up when it cannot deal with a given question or input. And it uses the patient's own input to feed back information and create the illusion that it understands and even sympathizes with the patient. This illusion is so powerful that patients, even when told they are dealing with a relatively simple-minded program, become emotionally involved in the interaction. Many refuse to believe that they are dealing with a program and insist that a sympathetic human must be at the controls at the other end of the teletype.

Sociologist Harold Garfinkel has supplied another instructive example (1967). He conducted the following experiment. The subjects were told that the Department of Psychiatry was exploring alternative means to therapy "as a way of giving persons advice about their personal problems." Each subject was then asked to discuss the background of some serious problem on which he or she would like advice. After having done this the subject was to address some questions that could be answered "yes" or "no" to the "counselor" (actually an experimenter). The experimenter-counselor heard the questions from an adjoining room and supplied a "yes" or "no" answer to each question after a suitable pause. Unknown to the subject, the series of yes-no answers had been preprogrammed according to a table of random numbers and was not related to the questions. Yet the typical subject was sure that the counselor fully understood the subject's problem and was giving sound and helpful advice.

Let me emphasize again that statements as such have no meaning. They convey meaning only in context and only when the listeners or readers can bring to bear their large store of worldly knowledge. Clients are not necessarily acting irrationally when they find meaning in the stock spiels or cold readings. Meaning is an interaction of expectations, context, memory, and given statements. An experiment by the Gestalt psychologist Solomon Asch (1948) will help make this point. Subjects were given the following passage and asked to think about it: "I hold it that a little rebellion, now and then, is a good thing, and as necessary in the political world as storms are in the physical." One group of subjects was told that the author of the passage was Thomas Jefferson (which happens to be true). The subjects were asked if they agreed with the passage and what it meant to them. These subjects generally approved of it and interpreted the word *rebellion* to mean minor agitation. But when subjects were given the same passage and told that its author was Lenin, they disagreed with it and interpreted *rebellion* to mean a violent revolution.

According to some social psychologists the different reactions show the irrationality of prejudice. But Asch points out that the subjects could be acting quite rationally. Given what they know about Thomas Jefferson and Lenin, or what they believe about them, it makes sense to attribute different meanings to the same word spoken by each of them. If one thinks that Jefferson believed in orderly government and peaceful processes, then it would not make sense to interpret his statement to actually mean a bloody revolution. If one thinks that Lenin favored war and bloodshed, then it makes sense, when the statement is attributed to him, to interpret *rebellion* in the more extreme form.

Some recent research that my colleagues and I conducted might also be relevant here. Our subjects were given the task of forming an impression of a hypothetical individual on the basis of a brief personality sketch. In one condition the subjects were given a sketch that generally led to an impression of a nice, personable, friendly sort of fellow. In a second condition the subjects were given a sketch that created an impression of a withdrawn, niggardly individual. Both groups of subjects were then given a new sketch that supposedly contained more information about the hypothetical individual. In both cases the subjects were given an identical sketch. This sketch contained some descriptors that were consistent with the friendly image and some that were consistent with the niggardly image. The subjects were later tested to see how well they recognized the actual adjectives that were used in the second sketch. One of the adjectives, for example, was *charitable.* The test contained foils for each adjective. For example, the word *generous* also appeared on the test but did not appear in the sketch. Yet subjects who had been given the friendly impression checked *generous* just as frequently as they checked *charitable.* But subjects in the other condition did not confuse *charitable* with *generous.* Why? Because, we theorize, two different contexts into which *charitable* had to be integrated produced quite different meanings. When subjects who have already built up an impression of a "friendly" individual encounter the additional descriptor *charitable,* it is treated as merely further confirmation of their general impression. In that context *charitable* is simply further confirmation of the nice-guy image. Consequently when these subjects are asked to remember what was actually said, they can remember only that the individual was further described in some way to enhance the good-guy image, and *generous* is just as good a candidate for the description as is *charitable* in that context.

But when the subjects who have an image of the person as a withdrawn, niggardly individual encounter *charitable,* the last thing that comes to mind is generosity. Instead, they probably interpret *charitable* as implying that he donates money to charities as a way of gaining tax deductions. In this latter condition the subjects have no subsequent tendency to confuse *charitable* with *generous.*

The cold reading works so well, then, because it taps a fundamental and necessary human process. We have to bring our knowledge and expectations to bear in order to comprehend anything in our world. In most ordinary situations this use of context and memory enables us to interpret statements correctly and supply the necessary inferences to do this. But this powerful mechanism can go astray in situations where there is no actual message being conveyed. Instead of picking up random noise we still manage to find meaning in the situation. So the same system that enables us creatively to find meanings and make new discoveries also makes us extremely vulnerable to exploitation by all sorts of manipulators. In the case of the cold reading the manipulator may be conscious of this deception; but often the reader, too, is a victim of personal validation.

References

Asch, S. E. 1948. "The Doctrine of Suggestion, Prestige, and Imitations in Social Psychology." *Psychological Review* 55: 250–76.

Forer, B. R. 1949. "The Fallacy of Personal Validation: A Classroom Demonstration of Gullibility." *Journal of Abnormal and Social Psychology* 44: 118–23.

Freud, S. 1933. *New Introductory Lectures on Psychoanalysis*. New York: W. W. Norton.

Garfinkel, H. 1967. *Studies in Ethnomethodology*. Englewood Cliffs, N.J.: Prentice-Hall.

Snyder, C. R., and R. J. Shenkel. 1975. "The P. T. Barnum Effect." *Psychology Today* 8: 52–54.

Sundberg, N. D. 1955. "The Acceptability of 'Fake' versus 'Bona Fide' Personality Test Interpretations." *Journal of Abnormal and Social Psychology* 50: 145–57.

Weizenbaum, J. 1976. *Computer Power and Human Reason*. San Francisco, Calif.: Freeman.

Type III Errors*

Dave listened with patience and understanding as I told him why I was skeptical about his beliefs in auras, astrology, out-of-body experiences and reincarnation. "I understand where you are coming from, Ray," he said. "I've been there myself. Up until ten years ago I lived in the same materialistic, scientific world that you occupy. But now I've gone beyond that—far beyond. I've dared to let my mind soar. And I've been to places you have no conception of. Until you also have dared to let your spirit soar, to experience what I have experienced, you are in no position to evaluate or criticize my current beliefs. Your current way of thinking is fine for evaluating the safety of a new bridge. But it is entirely irrelevant when trying to judge the value of my beliefs about the spiritual world. There are other ways of knowing and experiencing. And these require new viewpoints and conscious states beyond those that you and your fellow critics acknowledge or allow yourselves to encounter."

Dave is a professor at a large midwestern university. Quite a stir was created when he told the campus newspaper how he can diagnose moods and illnesses of students by the shape and colors of their auras. It also turned out that he teaches a little astrology along with aura-reading in his regular classes. Matters came to a head when he decided to offer a special course in reincarnation. Many townspeople were opposed to his teaching "far-out religious nonsense" in a publicly supported school. Some of his scientific colleagues were upset because he was teaching pseudoscientific nonsense. What is worse, he steadfastly refused to defend his beliefs by standard scientific arguments.

It was because of this furor over Dave's teachings that I was invited

*_Spirals_ 14 (1979), 11-14. Reprinted by permission.

by a group of professors to visit the campus to give a talk on the psychology behind current beliefs in astrology, reincarnation, psychic phenomena, and other occult matters. I am a member of the Committee for the Scientific Investigation of Claims of the Paranormal, and the professors, I am sure, were hoping that I could expose all such claims as nonsense. They also had hoped that Dave and I would confront each other on a public platform and debate the merits of his claims. But Dave refused. He felt that such a confrontation would serve no useful purpose, especially since skeptics such as myself were in no position to evaluate the sorts of experiences he was dealing with.

However, at my request, Dave did grant me a private interview. During this, he made it plain why he felt I was in no position to analyze him or his beliefs. His opening remarks removed any possibility of my debating or even communicating sensibly with him. He quickly established that he fully understood my viewpoint and arguments. His own viewpoint included mine, but also went beyond. He also encompassed a view that included things I was as yet incapable of seeing or experiencing. Therefore I was in command of neither the necessary experiences nor conceptual framework for dealing with his enlarged world. Dave "knew" things that I could not possibly "know"; and he "knew" them in a way that I was unaware of.

I made a fruitless attempt to reach him. I pointed out the many people in the past and present who also were sure that they "knew" something was so, but turned out to be sadly wrong. Just think of the number of people in institutions who are absolutely certain they are Jesus Christ. Surely, all of them cannot be right? I also pointed out the number of psychological studies demonstrating that the "illusion of certainty" is invariably unconnected with reality. But all this was to no avail. Dave understood what I was talking about. But only if I had been in his place could I grasp the sense in which he "knows" he is right and knows it in such a way that he could not be fooling himself.

My encounter with Dave suggests that an unbridgeable communication gap may exist between believers and skeptics. Indeed, some contemporary philosophers argue that it may be impossible *rationally* to settle differences between individuals who adhere to different theoretical or cultural viewpoints. Even with the best of intentions, the individuals arguing for their own system can do so only within a framework of standards, concepts, and meaningful relationships that is "rational" only in terms of that framework. Within the same framework, however, an individual cannot argue that a set of beliefs and claims from another system is right or wrong. Such beliefs can only be adequately evaluated in terms of standards and rules appropriate to their own framework. Not all philosophers, of course, accept this relativistic or incommensurability viewpoint. But regardless of whether the gulf is actually unbridgeable or just extremely difficult to bridge, I have yet to sense that skeptics and believers have even come close to communicating with one another.

One reason for this communication gap is that we confuse differences of value with differences of fact. Dave and I focused our conversation upon an alleged difference in facts. He was claiming that he had adequate evidence for a new realm of experience and phenomena—auras, reincarnation, cosmic interconnections, and so forth. I was claiming that his evidence was suspect. The same sort of evidence supports a variety of self-deceptive and delusional systems. But, in retrospect, I think a more serious difference between us was in values—values about the risks each of us was willing to take. In a way, Dave was telling me that he had been willing to risk academic reputation in a way that I was too cowardly to do. He had let his mind soar and did so by leaving behind the safeguards and protections of scientific method.

Statisticians talk about two types of error. *Type I error* is that involved in saying that an effect is really so when, in fact, only chance was operating. When statistics was developed as a tool to help researchers decide if they were observing something real or accidental, this was the sort of error that was of most concern. The statisticians wanted to protect the researcher and the public from the all-too-human tendency to see patterns where only chance exists. Scientists knew, often from very embarrassing incidents, how easy it is to find what you are looking for, even when it isn't there. Irving Langmuir, the late Nobel Prize winner, named this phenomenon "pathological science" or "the science of things that are not."

Statistical procedures, then, are employed by scientists to help protect us against Type I errors or pathological science. After the development of tools to protect us against Type I errors, some scientists and statisticians realized that we also should be concerned about another kind of error. *Type II errors,* they pointed out, were those involved in *not* finding something that is really there. We can become so concerned about avoiding Type I errors that we continually fail to discover new phenomena and see only randomness where real patterns actually exist.

Today, scientists realize that both sorts of errors can be costly. If we are overly cautious before deciding that a new treatment may actually work, lives that could have been saved might be lost. On the other hand, if we are too eager to certify the new treatment as successful, we may needlessly expose people to unknown side-effects.

Obviously it would be nice to avoid both errors. But there's the rub. The errors work against each other. With a fixed amount of resources any attempt to lower the risk of Type II errors increases the risk of Type I errors, and vice versa. The rational approach is to weigh the costs of each type of error and try to reduce that error which has the higher costs attached to it. In most realistic cases, however, such costs are highly subjective and debatable. All things considered, scientists tend to place more emphasis upon reducing Type I errors. It is considered a much more serious mishap to falsely say something is so than to overlook a real phenomenon. This is what people usually mean when they say that science is basically conservative.

Now what does this lecture on Type I and Type II errors tell us about the differences between Dave and myself? Or between skeptics and believers in general? You probably have already guessed. Dave sees Type II errors as much more serious than Type I errors. For me, the skeptic, it is just the opposite. And this is not a matter of rational judgment as such. But it is more a matter of how we weigh the costs of each type of mistake. Dave, like all believers in the paranormal, believes that the phenomena of reincarnation, psychic communication, mystical experiences, and the like are just too important and meaningful to overlook because of excessive demands of scientific rigor. Scientists and skeptics are so afraid of making a Type I error that they set up impossibly high standards for claims of the paranormal to meet.

The skeptics, however, have other concerns. They are familiar with cases such as N-rays, Martian canals, mitogenetic radiation, and many others in which scientists made false claims about things that were not so. They want to make sure Type I errors are not being committed again. So when Dave and his fellow believers argue for the reality of new sorts of phenomena on grounds that do not meet rigorous scientific standards, the skeptics run the risk of Type II errors. They *may* be missing out on very important new phenomena. But that is the risk *they* are willing to take.

We can talk about *Type III errors* in connection with this communication gap. We could designate this error as that involved in wrongly believing you understand the basis for the opposition to your position. For the skeptic to think wrongly that the believer's position is understood or for the believer to think that the skeptic's reasons are obvious would be examples of this sort of error. Obviously Type III errors characterize the current situation.

I hope in putting forth one possible difference between skeptics and believers I have not committed a *Type IV error*. This would be the error of oversimplifying what is an enormously complicated situation. I could just as well have focused upon other differences between skeptics and believers. For example, it is obvious that believers place overwhelming importance in the value of direct, personal experience. Whereas the skeptics distrust just this type of subjectivity and place more trust in indirect, objective assessments. At any rate, I hope I have made a start, however small, towards beginning to understand ways in which we differ from each other.

The Psychic Reading*

Mike, a freelance writer, visited a number of psychic readers to gather material for an article. He obtained a reading from each one. He also interviewed me to see how a psychologist would react to his experiences. Only one of the psychics, a palm-reader called Barbara, impressed Mike. In this article he wrote that "this woman was studying lines of my hands and telling me, with devastating accuracy, about my strengths and weaknesses, my obsessions and my yearnings, my talents and my needs. As I drove away . . . I felt ready to chuck skepticism forever."

Mike discussed with me his experience with Barbara shortly after his visit with her and before he wrote his article. He had some difficulty in articulating just what it was about the reading that had so impressed him. He told me that during the first part of the session, Barbara made the usual assortment of general and ambiguous statements. His mind began to wander and he found himself thinking about a problem he was having with his girlfriend. Suddenly his attention was brought back to what Barbara was saying. He heard her say, "I feel you are worried about a relationship."

This conjunction in time between her statement about a relationship and his conscious concern about his relationship with a girlfriend hit Mike with an emotional wallop. He had no doubt that the relationship Barbara was talking about was *the* relationship he was worried about. This emotional release converted an otherwise typical reading into something special. And Mike was now convinced that Barbara had some special powers.

From the skeptical viewpoint, Mike's account does not justify attributing special knowledge or insight to Barbara. Mike was impressed by her. To account for this impression he pointed to her accuracy in telling him he

---

*In T. A. Sebeok and R. Rosenthal (eds.), *The Clever Hans Phenomenon* (New York: New York Academy of Sciences, 1981), 169-81. Reprinted by permission.

was worried about a relationship. We do not need to assume any powers to account for this sort of accuracy. We can safely assume that any individual who comes to a psychic has some sort of a problem with a relationship. Mike, of course, is sufficiently sophisticated to realize this. Yet he could not shake the conviction that Barbara's accuracy was more than just the use of statements that could apply to anyone. He was sure that Barbara had somehow tapped into his innermost secrets. And he had experienced, as a result, a compelling and rewarding emotional experience.

We can raise a number of questions about Mike's encounter with the psychic reader. The question that naturally occurs to the psychologist involves validity. Did the psychic's statements actually correspond to the facts of Mike's personality and situation? Did they do so in a way that would differentiate him from other clients? Notice that this same focus on the accuracy of the reading was the basis that Mike employed to justify his positive evaluation of Barbara. Another question asks what it is that the reading actually does for the client. Why do clients such as Mike experience the reading as both revealing and helpful? Notice that a reading need not be accurate to be helpful. We can ask, also, how much the client gets out of the reading in relation to how much he or she puts into it.

This last question relates the psychic reading to the topic of this conference—The Clever Hans Phenomenon. When the horse, Clever Hans, was asked a question, he would often give the correct answer by tapping an appropriate number with his hoof.[1] This would occur under circumstances that seemingly precluded the horse's actions being under the control of signals from the owner. Because the questioner knew he was not cueing the horse, he assumed that Hans's answer was a response to the verbal question and that the answer, by being correct, revealed the conscious understanding of the question and the requisite knowledge to supply the answer. In fact, Hans was responding to a simple, involuntary postural adjustment by the questioner, which was his cue to start tapping, and an unconscious, almost imperceptible head movement, which was his cue to stop. The horse was simply a channel through which the information the questioner unwittingly put into the situation was fed back to the questioner. The fallacy involved treating the horse as the source of the message rather than as a channel through which the questioner's own message is reflected back.

The psychic reading shares this fallacy with the Clever Hans situation. In most such readings the psychic is simply a channel through which information unwittingly emitted by the client is fed back to the client. The client typically asumes that the message originates from some secret or occult source to which the psychic has access.

But the psychic reading is richer and more complicated than the Clever Hans situation. Both situations deal with an individual who is unknowingly both the source and the destination of the message. In both cases, the assumption is made that actual communication is taking place because the information being received is "accurate." Hans answers the questions accurately. The psychic apparently tells the client things that he or she accepts as accurate. And this is just how it should be if actual communication were taking place. But it is just at this point in determining the accuracy of the communication that we notice an added feature that contributes to the success of the reading.

The questioner has no difficulties in deciding whether Hans has answered correctly or not. Either Hans has tapped the appropriate number of times or he has not. But the output from a psychic reading is both complex and highly ambiguous. The referent is the life history, personality, concerns, and problems of the client. And the language of personality description is notoriously difficult to interpret and apply.[2] This gives rise to what has become known as the *Barnum effect*—the phenomenon whereby people willingly accept personality interpretations composed of vague statements with a high base rate occurrence in the general population.[3]

Beginning with the 1949 publication by Forer on "the fallacy of personal validation,"[4] an area of research has emerged that follows more or less the same paradigm: (1) the subject completes a personality test or supplies information relevant to an assessment procedure; (2) the subject waits while the assessment information is processed; (3) the subject then receives a personality sketch allegedly derived from the assessment information; and (4) the subject rates the sketch for its "accuracy." In actual fact, all the subjects receive the same stock spiel composed of "Barnum" statements. The results are quite consistent and robust. When the subjects believe that the sketch was specifically meant for them they tend to rate it as a highly accurate and unique description of themselves.[3]

The appeal of these Barnum-type statements is so strong that it even overrides personality sketches especially written for the subjects. Sundberg, for example, administered the Minnesota Multiphasic Personality Inventory to 44 students.[5] Subsequently each student was presented with two personality sketches. One was written by a trained psychologist especially for the student on the basis of the student's answers to the inventory. The other was a fake sketch. Each student was asked to choose "which interpretation describes you better." Of the 44 students, 26, or almost 60%, chose the fake sketch over the one written especially for them. Since Sundberg's study, several other investigators have demonstrated the same result.[3]

In a way this outcome should not be surprising. The fake sketches are composed of items that are true of almost everyone. The personalized sketches are composed of statements that discriminate the subject from others. When Barbara told Mike that he was worried about a relationship, we should not be surprised that Mike accepted the statement as accurate because such a statement applies with high probability to just about every young, single male. But Mike accepted the statement not because he recognized its universal applicability, but rather because he understood it to apply to his unique circumstances. And subjects in the experiments on the Barnum effect accept the sketch as not only accurate, but as uniquely descriptive of themselves as distinct from others.

Much of the research on the fallacy of personal validation tries to isolate the conditions under which the fake sketch will be read and accepted as a unique description. Subjects *can,* under appropriate circumstances, recognize that the items in the sketch apply to them just because they are universally true for everyone. If the subject is handed the fake sketch and simply told it is a general description rather than one made especially for the subject, then he or she is less likely to accept it as a unique self-description. But the subject will not only accept as accurate the very same sketch, if presented under the belief that it was prepared especially for him or her, but will fail to realize that it is just as accurate for the general population. In addition, as a result of this acceptance, the subjects also increase their faith in the assessment procedure and the skill of the assessor.[3]

Almost certainly the situations in which subjects accept the fake sketch as unique and those in which they recognize its general applicability are experienced quite differently. The meaning of the sketch, like the meaning of any literary product, cannot be separated from the reader or listener. As the semioticians and structuralists keep emphasizing, there is no unique relationship between signifier and signified—nor is there a unique referent or reading for any given message.[6] The reader of the sketch that is not allegedly prepared especially for him or her is doing something different from the reader of the sketch that is allegedly prepared especially for him or her. Each reader is actually reading a different sketch.

All cognition and all sign-interpretation (the two are almost synonymous) involve a heavy contribution by the recipient in addition to that of the sign and the sender. In both the psychic reading and the Clever Hans situation, the contributions of the receiver almost totally determine the message and its interpretation. The fallacy in these situations is due to the fact that the receivers do not realize how much of the message and its meaning is their own contribution.

The Barnum effect is sufficient to account for the apparent accuracy in certain kinds of psychic readings. In some types of readings, the client is presented with a complete sketch. In such situations the psychic or "sender" need not even be physically present (getting an astrological write-up through the mail or receiving a printout of personality decriptions selected by a computer). No opportunity is afforded for the client to ask questions, clarify

428	PART FOUR: THE PSYCHOLOGY OF BELIEF

statements, or to agree or disagree while the message is being delivered. Nor does the psychic have the opportunity to alter or modify statements as a result of the client's reactions.

In contrast to such a static reading, most psychic readings are "dynamic" in the sense that the message is delivered to the client sequentially with the opportunity for the client to interact with the psychic during the process. It is in these dynamic readings that the Clever Hans effect combines with the Barnum effect to yield very effective results. In the typical reading, both the psychic and the client are equally victims of these two effects. Both believe that the client's conviction of having been helped stems from the psychic's access to hidden knowledge and to skills in diagnosing and advising.

But there is a class of psychic readers who are quite conscious of how they are managing the reading and the client to create the illusion that the psychic is the source of both the information and successful solutions to problems. These readers have sometimes written manuals to guide other readers. (Examples of such manuals, which I consulted, are listed in the bibliography.[7-13]) The manuals divide readings into two types: the *psychological reading* and the *cold reading*. The psychological reading, which corresponds to the static reading, involves delivering a stock spiel to the client. Because the sketch is usually memorized and delivered to several different clients, the studies of the Barnum effect apply directly. The cold reading is so called because the client is encountered without any prior knowledge. The cold reading employs the dynamics of the dyadic relationship between psychic and client to develop a sketch that is tailored to the client. The reader employs shrewd observation, nonverbal and verbal feedback from the client, and the client's active cooperation to create a description that the client is sure penetrates to the core of his or her psyche. The cold reader achieves this goal by feeding back to the client information the client has unwittingly revealed during the course of the reading. (Elsewhere I have written another version of how this is done and why it apparently works.[14])

The manuals for both the psychological reading and the cold reading essentially provide guidelines for creating just those conditions that convince the client that the reading is accurate and that the accuracy is a function of the special knowledge of the psychic. These guidelines, while sometimes vague, clearly indicate that the writers operate under assumptions and theories very much in accord with modern cognitive science, literary structuralism, semiotics, and social cognition. None of these writers, of course, are familiar with such disciplines. And their assumptions and theories antedate the development of these fields of inquiry.

But before I indicate some of the ways the manuals anticipate current academic disciplines that deal with communication and signs, it is worth considering again the issue of accuracy. The success of the psychic reading depends entirely upon acceptance by the clients—upon personal validation. And, on the surface, such acceptance seems to be related to how accurate the sketch appears to the client. But why should the client care or be concerned about such accuracy? The client accepts what the psychic says about him or her only if it agrees with what the client already knows. Why should the client pay for being told what he or she already knows?

Several answers come to mind. One is that many of the things that the client is being told are recognized or accepted as "true" but were not consciously considered previously. In this sense, the client is learning new things about himself or herself—but things that are acceptable because they "ring" true.

But probably the most important reason is that to the extent the psychic can tell the client things that are true, but which the client believes could not be known to the psychic through normal means, the psychic validates the belief that he or she does, indeed, have special powers. Like the shaman, the psychic reader is most successful if the client attributes to him or her mysterious powers and occult sources of knowledge.

The client does not patronize the psychic to discover things that the client already knows. The client is typically a person with a problem who seeks help. If the helper clearly has access to hidden knowledge and magical forces, this increases the chances that he or she can work wonders for the client. If the psychic can convince the client that he or she knows things that could only come from mysterious sources, then the psychic's powers are validated. So the client has a big stake in the accuracy of the psychic. And part of the success of the reading stems from the client's need to see the psychic as omniscient.

The manuals, then, can be seen as guidelines for creating in the client the illusion of the reader's omniscience. As such, they embody a theory or a set of presuppositions about how to manage the dyadic interaction so that the client "reads" the results in the desired manner. And these presuppositions, as previously indicated, seem to anticipate the ideas emerging from the variety of overlapping contemporary disciplines that study humans as sign-using systems. To illustrate this point, I will consider the types of advice provided by the manuals under four categories: (1) setting the stage; (2) preliminary observations and categorization; (3) constructing the preliminary script; (4) delivering the message and revising the script.

Setting the Stage

The psychological and cold readers attribute much of their success to how the client is prepared prior to the reading. Such preparation consists of advertising, word-of-mouth accounts by previous clients, the preliminary introduction and statements to the client, the dress and mannerisms of the psychic, the furnishings and arrangement of the consultation room, and other ways that help to "define the situation" for the client and that specify what role the client is to play in this interaction.

Such preparations accomplish a number of important goals. The manuals specify that the psychic should make it clear from the outset that the psychic is the one who is in control of the situation. The psychic is not only experienced and an authority in this sort of interaction, but he or she has already proven that the psychic can do his or her part successfully. But, as the psychic will indicate to the client, the reading is a cooperative venture that requires the active participation of the client. This puts much of the burden for success on the client. It also emphasizes that the client has to collaborate with the reader to produce a satisfactory outcome.

It also reinforces the idea that the reader is omniscient and knows what he or she is saying and doing. If something that the reader later says does not tally with the client's beliefs or does not make sense, the client has been prepared to treat the apparent confusion as due to the client's own failure to understand adequately rather than to the psychic's lack of knowledge.

Some manuals further suggest ways to encourage this attitude in the client by having the reader state, as part of the preparation, something like, "During the course of the reading, impressions and images will come to me that will make no sense to me, but are very meaningful for your current or future situation. It will be up to you to make sense of these thoughts."

This setting of the stage recognizes what is now taken for granted in cognitive science—that the listener/reader reacts not to a message or test as such, but to the message as encoded. And this encoding must always be in terms of frameworks, concepts, expectations, and attitudes that the listener/reader brings to the situation. The role of the listener/reader in constructing the context and meaning of stories and literature is also recognized in semiotics and structuralism.[6] The concept of genre, for example, is considered to be a guide to the reader on how to interpret the text. The same set of words, when set out in the form of a poem, is "read" differently than when set out in the form of a brief note. And it is recognized that no matter how concrete and specific a message appears to be, it still can bear a variety of "readings."

The client who is actively processing the message from the psychic as a meaningful account of the client's current situation and the client who is skeptically processing the same message as a set of Barnum propositions are experiencing two qualitatively different types of communication.

Another very important part of the preparation of the client is not directly under the control of the reader. This is the client's objective in participating in the reading. Most clients have problems, concerns, worries, and feelings of inadequacy. They seek solace, advice, support, or simply a good listener. For some the problems are chronic and of long standing. For others, the difficulty is a current and acute crisis. Such clients obviously have a vested interest in extracting the greatest benefit possible from their exchange with the reader. They are going to encode and react to what the reader says much differently than the casual curiosity seeker might. Even in the latter case, such as happened with Mike, the client who is merely curious or even skeptical is often surprised and impressed by what takes place.

But, given the highly involved client and the proper setting of the stage, even the crudest psychological reading—as evidenced by the work on the Barnum effect—is almost sure to meet with "success." But the readers have further items in their bag of tricks.

Preliminary Observations and Categorization

Even the manuals that supply the user with stock spiels to memorize and deliver suggest that some accommodations be made to take into consideration characteristics of the clients such as age, sex, socioeconomic status, and obvious signs of health. Sometimes such adjustments require minor alterations in statements indicating whether a problem was in the past, present, or future, or adapting sexual and age-related references. In other cases, the manuals actually supply different stock spiels for different categories of clients: the young, unmarried female; the young, married female; the young, unmarried, male; the elderly woman; and so forth. Such adjustments based on preliminary observations and categorization of the client move the psychological reading towards the flexibility of the cold reading. The cold reader goes beyond this preliminary categorization and keeps refining and revising the reading to reach what is eventually a customized description.

All the manuals emphasize the surprising amount of specific information that one can pick up from a careful study of dress, physical characteristics, gestures and mannerisms, posture and attitudes, speech, jewelry, name, address, coat labels, and the like. The shrewd reader employs this information not only to make preliminary categorizations, but also to surprise the client with statements that the client believes could only have come from some occult source.

Constructing the Preliminary Script

The psychological reader, having set the stage and made some preliminary categorizations of the client, is ready to deliver the final version of the reading. This final version is a combination of facts based on the preliminary observations and a generalized or schematic script, which serves as a framework for ordering these facts. The psychological reading is based on the explicit assumption that there are universal features to all human lives as well as common characteristics and problems that face individuals in similar times and environments. Many manuals offer stock spiels for delivering a cradle-to-grave reading—with provisos for adjustments based upon sex, age, and other obvious characteristics of the client. Such a reading is based on the assumption that most of us live through the same major milestones: birth, childhood, school, work, marriage, children, and death. And during that life span we face more or less the same general problems such as career choice, love, sex, health, financial matters, and family.

The success of a book such as Gail Sheehy's *Passages* confirms what the psychological readers already know—that we share, despite our various lifestyles and unique histories, common problems and "predictable crises" at various ages such as the 20s, 30s, 40s, 50s, and beyond. The paperback edition says on its cover, "At last this is your story. You'll recognize yourself, your friends, and your lovers." It is just such recognition that the reader counts upon in his clients to make the reading succeed. Indeed, contemporary manuals strongly urge the psychic readers to study such books as *Passages* to make their script more realistic and convincing.

The use of a generalized, universal script around which to construct the reading contributes in many ways to its acceptability. Many of the ideas in structuralism and contemporary cognitive science testify to the value of such an underlying schema. Both the psychological and the cold reading are constructed on the basis that there are universal themes shared by all human lives. And this idea that diverse lives and unique histories are constructed from a limited set of constituent components motivates structuralist and semiotic approaches to literature, myths, and cultures.[6] In psychology, the idea that we both encode and remember our experiences in terms of underlying schemata was emphasized by Bartlett in his classic *Remembering*.[16] However, it is only recently that psychologists and cognitive scientists have begun seriously applying Bartlett's insights into how we encode, understand, and remember prose.[17-19]

The reader's generalized script, among other things, acts both as a memory probe and an organizational framework for the client. To encode and make sense of what the reader is saying, the client has to supply the flesh to the skeleton. He or she retrieves from memory incidents and examples to instantiate the more general things being described. Mike did not simply hear Barbara say something about a relationship; he heard her talking about his particular problem with his girlfriend. Furthermore, this particular prob-

THE PYSCHIC READING   433

lem was now placed within an organized setting created by the underlying script and other relevant incidents that it brought to mind. Anything that Barbara said that did not make sense in terms of this script or anything that Mike thought about that was inconsistent or contradictory to the over-all unfolding story would later be forgotten or difficult to retrieve. The script not only provides organization and meaning to the client's experiences, but it also guides how and what he or she will recall from the reading. Both laboratory research and what we know about actual psychic readings predict that the client will remember mainly those things the psychic said that were consistent with the overall script and will also remember them in terms of those concrete memories that the client brought to bear in order to make sense of the reading.

Delivering the Message and Revising the Script

The cold reader does not stop with the preliminary script. He or she delivers the message in the presence of the client and modifies it as it unfolds on the basis of reactions and inputs from the client. This is where the Clever Hans phenomenon works to supplement the Barnum effect. The cold reader uses Barnum-type statements organized around the preliminary script as trial probes. These statements are modified, withdrawn, revised, or elaborated in terms of the reactions of the client. These reactions are typically nonver-bal, such as pupillary enlargement, eye movements, postural adjustments, facial changes, and the like. The reader employs these cues to quickly pin down those topics of most interest to the client and to gauge when he or she is or is not on the right track.

Often the client emits verbal responses as well. These vary from exclamations to questions and comments. The manuals encourage the reader to promote such verbal feedback. One technique for doing this, for example, is "fishing"—the psychic seemingly makes statements but phrases them as subtle questions. "I see two dark and tall men in your life—do you recognize them?" "I'm getting a vague image concerning a deed or some such financial document—does that make sense to you?" Once the client does begin responding with questions and comments, the reader takes pains to reward such behavior with careful and attentive listening. By listening to whatever the client says, the reader accomplishes many goals simultaneously. The client is convinced that the reader is sincerely interested. He or she probably has a strong desire for someone simply to listen. The attention encourages further such responses by the client. And, finally, the psychic is carefully storing this information in memory for later use in the reading.

When the client is not talking, the reader overwhelms him or her with a steady stream of patter. Part of the reason for this fluent overflow is to monitor continually the client's reactions and pick out topics and items that create the most reaction. Another reason is to prevent the client from realizing how much the client has already said. The successful reading, as the manuals make clear, is one in which the client ultimately is given what he or she considers a devastatingly accurate and penetrating personality analysis. The information for this analysis has come from both the verbal and nonverbal behavior of the client. The reader has merely fed back to the client information the client has unwittingly supplied to the reader. The reading succeeds because the client is completely unaware that he or she has been the source of the description.

In effect the reader is like a ghost-writer who helps the client construct a coherent autobiography on the basis of information supplied by the client. In the typical psychic reading, both the psychic and the client falsely attribute the accuracy of the final reading to the occult sources to which the reader has access. In the cold reading, the reader is fully conscious that the client is the source of all the information and takes steps to maximize the client's contributions.

The impact and success of the psychic reading go beyond the illusion of accuracy. The client's acceptance is ultimately based on an emotional experience rather than a dispassionate assessment of the accuracy. Indeed, as the case of Mike and Barbara suggests, the attribution of uncanny accuracy to the reader probably stems from the emotional impact achieved during the reading. The attribution of accuracy is based upon information that the client has supplied to the reader. In a sense, the reading the psychic later gives back to the client contains nothing "new." In another sense, however, the repacking of this material and putting it into a coherent order provides new insights to the client. In addition, the client is now looking at his or her memories and experiences from a new vantage point. This provides something similar to what Shklovsky attributes to the function of literary devices. They serve not to represent familiar events, but rather to make them strange—to defamiliarize them.[6] In a way, the reading does for the client's self-concept what Poincaré claims that mathematical discoveries do for already familiar concepts—"they reveal to us unsuspected kinship between other facts, long known, but wrongly believed to be strangers to one another."[20]

It is thus conceivable, then, that despite the false attribution of secret knowledge to the reader, the client emerges from the reading with a new and more adaptive model of his situation. He or she may have a new insight into the conflicts and problems that precipitated the consultation. And new alternatives for coping with the situation may have been opened up. Whether or not the new perspective and vision of the client's life and situation is ultimately beneficial, it is easy to understand how the client might experience the reading as revealing and rewarding.

Much more can be said about the psychic reading. But I hope I have said enough to convince you that it is a rich and challenging opportunity for studying the ways signs, witting and unwitting, combine to create illusions of communication in dyadic settings. Both the Barnum effect and the Clever Hans phenomenon combine to induce the overwhelming conviction that the psychic is the source rather than a mirror of an accurate appraisal of the client and his or her circumstances. In some cases it might be revealing to look upon the reader as a catalyst that aids the client in the construction of a coherent and helpful self-description. In general, however, the psychic reading, like the Clever Hans case, is but one of many illustrations of the human propensity to project meaning into situations even when the situations, themselves, have no meaning.

References

1. Pfungst, O. 1965. Clever Hans. Holt, Rinehart & Winston, New York, N.Y.
2. Bromley, D. B. 1977. Personality Description in Ordinary Language. Wiley & Sons, New York, N.Y.
3. Snyder, C. R., R. J. Shenkel & C. R. Lowery. 1977. Acceptance of Personality; Interpretations: The "Barnum Effect" and Beyond. J. Consult. Clin. Psychol. 45: 104–114.
4. Forer, B. R. 1949. The Fallacy of Personal Validation: A Classroom Demonstration of Gullibility. J. Abnormal Soc. Psychol. 44: 118–123.
5. Sundberg, N. D. 1955. The Acceptability of "Fake" Versus "Bona Fide" Personality Test Interpretations. J. Abnormal Soc. Psychol. 50: 145–147.
6. Hawkes, T. 1977. Structuralism and Semiotics. University of California Press, Berkeley, Calif.
7. Anonymous. 1971. Pages from a Medium's Notebook. Micky Hades, Calgary, Alberta, Canada.
8. Boarde, C. L. 1947. Mainly Mental: Volume I: Billet Reading. Globe Service, New York, N.Y.
9. Corinda, 1968. Thirteen Steps to Mentalism. Louis Tannen, New York, N.Y.
10. Hester, R. & W. Hudson. 1977. Psychic Character Analysis: The Technique of Cold Reading Updated. Magic Media Ltd., Baltimore, Md.
11. Magnuson, W. G. 1935. The Twentieth Century Mindreading Act or the Modern Spiritualist Medium's Act. Albino, Chicago, Ill.
12. Nelson, R. A. 1951. The Art of Cold Reading. Nelson Enterprises, Columbus, Ohio.
13. Ruthchild, M. 1978. Cashing in on the Psychic. Lee Jacobs Productions, Pomeroy, Ohio.
14. Hyman, R. 1977. "Cold Reading": How to Convince Strangers That You Know All About Them. In The Zetetic I (Spring/Summer): 18–37.
15. Sheehy, G. 1977. Passages: Predictable Crises of Adult Life. Bantam Books, New York, N.Y.
16. Bartlett, F. C. 1932. Remembering. Cambridge Univ. Press, London, England.
17. Black, J. B. & G. H. Bower. 1980. Story Understanding as Problem-Solving. Poetics. In press.

18. Bower, G. H. 1976. Experiments on Story Understanding and Recall. Q. J. Exp. Psychol. 28: 511–534.
19. Bower, G. H. 1978. Experiments on Story Comprehension and Recall. Discourse Proc. 1: 211–231.
20. Poincaré, H. 1955. Mathematical Creation. *In* The Creative Process—A Symposium. B. Ghiselin, Ed. pp. 33–42. Mentor, New York, N.Y.

Proper Criticism*

Since the founding of The Committee for the Scientific Investigation of Claims of the Paranormal in 1976, and with the growing numbers of localized skeptical groups, the skeptic finds more ways to state his or her case. The broadcast and print media, along with other forums, provide more opportunities for us to be heard. For some of these occasions, we have the luxury of carefully planning and crafting our reponse. Most of the time we have to formulate our response on the spot. But, regardless of the circumstance, the critic's task, if it is to be carried out properly, is both challenging and loaded with unanticipated hazards.

Many well-intentioned critics have jumped into the fray without carefully thinking through the various implications of their statements. They have sometimes displayed more emotion than logic, made sweeping charges beyond what they reasonably support, failed adequately to document their assertions, and, in general, have failed to do the homework necessary to make their challenges credible.

Such ill-considered criticism can be counterproductive for the cause of serious skepticism. The author of such criticism may fail to achieve the desired effect, may lose credibility, and may even become vulnerable to lawsuits. But the unfavorable effects have consequences beyond the individual critic, and the entire cause of skepticism suffers as a result. Even when the individual critic takes pains to assert that he or she is expressing his or her own personal opinion, the public associates the assertions with all critics.

During CSICOP's first decade of existence, members of the Executive Council often found themselves devoting most of their available time to

---

*Skeptical Briefs 3 (May 1987), 4–5.

damage control—precipitated by the careless remarks of a fellow skeptic—instead of toward the common cause of explaining the skeptical agenda.

Unfortunately, at this time, there are no courses on the proper way to criticize paranormal claims. So far as I know, no manuals or books of rules are currently available to guide us. Until such courses and guide books come into being, what can we do to ensure that our criticisms are both effective and responsible?

I would be irresponsible if I told you that I had an easy solution. The problem is complicated and there are no quick fixes. But I do believe we all could improve our contributions to responsible criticism by keeping a few principles always in mind.

We can make enormous improvements in our collective and individual efforts by simply trying to adhere to those standards that we profess to admire and that we believe that many peddlers of the paranormal violate. If we envision ourselves as the champions of rationality, science, and objectivity, then we ought to display these very same qualities in our criticism. Just by trying to speak and write in the spirit of precision, science, logic, and rationality—those attributes we supposedly admire—we would raise the quality of our critiques by at least one order of magnitude.

The failure to consistently live up to these standards exposes us to a number of hazards. We can find ourselves going beyond the facts at hand. We may fail to communicate exactly what we intended. We can confuse the public as to what skeptics are trying to achieve. We can unwittingly put the paranormal proponents in the position of the underdogs and create sympathy for them. And, as I already mentioned, we can make the task much more difficult for the other skeptics.

What, then, can skeptics do to upgrade the quality of their criticism? What follows are just a few suggestions. Hopefully, they will stimulate further thought and discussion.

1. *Be prepared.* Good criticism is a skill that requires practice, work, and level-headedness. Your response to a sudden challenge is much more likely to be appropriate if you have already anticipated similar challenges. Try to prepare in advance effective and short answers to those questions you are most likely to be asked. Be ready to answer why skeptical activity is important, why people should listen to your views, why false beliefs can be harmful, and the many similar questions that invariably are raised. A useful project would be to compile a list of the most frequently occurring questions along with possible answers.

   Whenever possible, try your ideas out on friends and "enemies" before offering them in the public arena. An effective exercise is to rehearse your arguments with fellow skeptics. Some of you can take the role of the psychic claimants while others play the role of critics. And, for more general preparation, read books on critical thinking, effective writing, and argumentation.

2. *Clarify your objectives.* Before you try to cope with a paranormal claim, ask yourself what you are trying to accomplish. Are you trying to release pent-up resentment? Are you trying to belittle your opponent? Are you trying to gain publicity for your viewpoint? Do you want to demonstrate that the claim lacks reasonable justification? Do you hope to educate the public about what constitutes adequate evidence? Often our objectives, upon examination, turn out to be mixed. And, especially when we act impulsively, some of our objectives conflict with one another.

The difference between short-term and long-term objectives can be especially important. Most skeptics, I believe, would agree that our long-term goal is to educate the public so that it can more effectively cope with various claims. Sometimes this long-range goal is sacrificed because of the desire to expose or debunk a current claim.

Part of clarifying our objectives is to decide who our audience is. Hard-nosed, strident attacks on paranormal claims rarely change opinions, but they do stroke the egos of those who are already skeptics. Arguments that may persuade the readers of the *National Enquirer* may offend academics and important opinion-makers.

Try to make it clear that you are attacking the claim and not the claimant. Avoid, at all costs, creating the impression that you are trying to interfere with someone's civil liberties. Do not try to get someone fired from his or her job. Do not try to have courses dropped or otherwise be put in the position of advocating censorship. Being for rationality and reason should not force us into the position of seeming to be against academic freedom and civil liberties.

3. *Do your homework.* Again, this goes hand in hand with the advice about being prepared. Whenever possible, you should not try to counter a specific paranormal claim without getting as many of the relevant facts as possible. Along the way, you should carefully document your sources. Do not depend upon a report in the media either for what is being claimed or for facts relevant to that claim. Try to get the specifics of the claim directly from the claimant.

4. *Do not go beyond your level of competence.* No one, especially in our times, can credibly claim to be an expert on all subjects. Whenever possible, you should consult appropriate experts. We, understandably, are highly critical of paranormal claimants who

make assertions that are obviously beyond their competence. We should be just as demanding on ourselves. A critic's worst sin is to go beyond the facts and the available evidence.

In this regard, always ask yourself if you really have something to say. Sometimes it is better to remain silent than to jump into an argument that involves aspects that are beyond your present competence. When it is appropriate, do not be afraid to say, "I don't know."

5. *Let the facts speak for themselves.* If you have done your homework and have collected an adequate supply of facts, the audience rarely will need your help in reaching an appropriate conclusion. Indeed, your case is made much stronger if the audience is allowed to draw its own conclusions from the facts. Say that Madame X claims to have psychically located Mrs. A's missing daughter and you have obtained a statement from the police to the effect that her contributions did not help. Under these circumstances it can be counterproductive to assert that Madame X lied about her contribution or that her claim was "fraudulent." For one thing, Madame X may sincerely, if mistakenly, believe that her contributions did in fact help. In addition, some listeners may be offended by the tone of the criticism and become sympathetic to Madame X. However, if you simply report what Madame X claimed along with the response of the police, not only are you sticking to the facts, but your listeners will more likely come to the appropriate conclusion.

6. *Be precise.* Good criticism requires precision and care in the use of language. Because, in challenging psychic claims, we are appealing to objectivity and fairness, we have a special obligation to be as honest and accurate in our own statements as possible. We should take special pains to avoid making assertions about paranormal claims that cannot be backed up with hard evidence. We should be especially careful, in this regard, when being interviewed by the media. Every effort should be made to ensure that the media understand precisely what we are and are not saying.

7. *Use the principle of charity.* I know that many of my fellow critics will find this principle to be unpalatable. To some, the paranormalists are the "enemy," and it seems inconsistent to lean over backward to give them the benefit of the doubt. But being charitable to paranormal claims is simply the other side of being honest and fair. The principle of charity implies that, whenever there is doubt or ambiguity about a paranormal claim, we should try to resolve the ambiguity in favor of the claimant until we acquire strong reasons

for not doing so. In this respect, we should carefully distinguish between being wrong and being dishonest. We often can challenge the accuracy or the validity of a given paranormal claim. But rarely are we in a position to know if the claimant is deliberately lying or is self-deceived. Furthermore, we often have a choice in how to interpret or represent an opponent's arguments. The principle tells us to convey the opponent's position in a fair, objective, and nonemotional manner.

8. *Avoid loaded words and sensationalism.* All these principles are interrelated. The ones previously stated imply that we should avoid using loaded and prejudicial words in our criticisms. We should also try to avoid sensationalism. If the proponents happen to resort to emotionally laden terms and sensationalism, we should avoid stooping to their level. We should not respond in kind.

This is not a matter of simply turning the other cheek. We want to gain credibility for our cause. In the short run, emotional charges and sensationalistic challenges might garner quick publicity. But, most of us see our mission as a long-run effort. We would like to persuade the media and the public that we have a serious and important message to get across. And we would like to earn their trust as a credible and reliable resource. Such a task requires always keeping in mind the scientific principles and standards of rationality and integrity that we would like to make universal.

Epilogue

Perhaps the best way to conclude this collection of articles is to list the various questions I was trying to address in them. For each question, I will provide a short answer in terms of my present perspective.

1. Do Psi and Paranormal Phenomena Exist?

My short answer to this is that I do not have the faintest idea. Psychical researchers and parapsychologists have been trying for approximately 140 years to build a scientific case for psi. At best, the situation is still equivocal. In my opinion, the parapsychologists must first put their own house in order before they invite the rest of the scientific community to come in to inspect their wares.

Even if we grant the parapsychologists their claim that they have at least established the existence of an anomaly of some sort, they still have a long way to go before they can tame this anomaly and specify at least some conditions under which we have a reasonable chance of observing it. If what they say is correct, then they are dealing with a very erratic and elusive phenomenon. Indeed, we do not know if they are dealing with a single phenomenon or several possibly unrelated phenomena.

I suspect that the question of psi's existence is not going to be resolved one way or another in our lifetime. The earliest paper in this collection is the review of Soal and Bateman's *Modern Experiments in Telepathy,* which I wrote more than thirty years ago, in 1957. My concluding paragraph to that review is just as appropriate today as it was then:

> Is the phenomenon of extra-sensory perception a fact that we should be concerned about? The answer to this question must wait upon this amassing of "so much experience of the new kind." For, as Boring has put it,

"Of its importance in the developing scientific skein, posterity will be able to judge, and you cannot hurry history."

I urge patience and more patience. No one has yet put us into a position where we have to decide one way or another. Much of the bitterness of current and past controversies, I believe, is because rash partisans on both sides of the issue have acted as if they had to decide the question *now*. Such a sense of urgency, along with the desire to settle matters once and for all, makes for very bad science.

Another observation might help to keep the issue in perspective. Even some major parapsychologists, such as John Palmer, admit that, at best, the parapsychologists have demonstrated an anomaly. If they are correct, Palmer concedes, such an anomaly might, when further understood, have nothing to do with the paranormal.

In other words, even if the parapsychologists turn out to have "something" by the tail, we have no idea what this something might be. We do not even have a basis for guessing whether this "something" will be trivial and uninteresting or important and informative in some way.

2. Do the Parapsychological Claims Have Adequate Justification?

We should sharply differentiate this question from the preceding one. Psi might or might not exist. But its existence is not the issue in my critiques of the field. My quarrel with the parapsychologists has to do with whether their evidence is of sufficient quality to justify their claims.

Up until 1981, as some of the readers may have detected in previous chapters, I was not sure. I consistently took the position that the better parapsychological experiments displayed more sophisticated statistical and methodological procedures than most critics realized. Since 1981, as a result of my systematic evaluation of the ganzfeld experiments, I have had to amend my position to argue that the best parapsychological experiments are less methodologically adequate than most parapsychologists have previously believed. This opinion was strongly reinforced by Charles Akers's independent survey of the best contemporary research in parapsychology.

3. What Would It Take to Justify the Claims Adequately?

The joint communiqué by Honorton and myself is one attempt to specify some criteria that would be required for a given area of parapsychological research. To his credit, Honorton and his colleagues have been working to produce experimental work that meets these criteria. I have seen no formal publications of any of this work, but Honorton has indicated that he is encouraged by his efforts so far.

If Honorton does succeed in producing successful results under sound methodological conditions, then we would want to see if other parapsychologists can replicate the pattern of successful results using similarly stringent conditions. If such independent replications were successful, this would be unprecedented. In such a case, I would urge that nonparapsychologists also try to replicate the results. If they, too, were successful, then we would have to admit that the parapsychologists were "onto" something. Presumably, it would take more patient work and scientific ingenuity to decide what that "something" was.

Meanwhile, of course, we are nowhere near such an eventuality. Again, all we can do at this point is sit back and wait.

4. What Would It Take to Make Believers Out of Skeptics?

I am often asked to say what it would take to make me a believer. Once I agreed to test a psychic's claim. Everything was arranged, protocols had been agreed to, and I was all set to start. Suddenly the sponsor insisted that I must make a written promise before we went any further. The written statement asserted that, if the experimental results came out in favor of the psychic, I would announce to the world that I had become a believer in psi.

I refused to sign the statement, and the sponsor indignantly called off the experiment. I could not sign such a statement because I have no way of controlling or predicting what my subjective beliefs would be as a result of the outcome. I could promise that however the results came out, I would report them truthfully. But I could not promise that I would suddenly become a believer.

One of the most frequent questions from the audience after one of my talks on the paranormal is, what would it take to convince me that a phenomenon was paranormal? Again, I have to answer that I do not know. I have been investigating psychic claims for more than thirty years. I have yet to encounter any alleged psychic or paranormal event that I could not explain in terms of ordinary causes, self-deception, or just plain trickery.

Yet, I think it is entirely possible that I could encounter a phenomenon for which I had no explanation. Would this convert me into a believer? I cannot say. I used to earn my living doing magic, and I still attend meetings of magicians. At such meetings, magicians sometimes succeed in fooling their colleagues. I myself have managed, on occasion, to fool magicians in such a way that they had no clue whatsoever as to how I could have done the trick.

I mention the fact that magicians can fool one another because it explains why I might not believe that I had witnessed a paranormal event if, in my presence, an alleged psychic bent a spoon or "levitated" his shoe in such a way that I could not think of a normal explanation. The "psychic" might be a clever trickster who had hit upon a new way to trick people.

The best I can offer is to say that if someday I do encounter a "psychic" who produces phenomena that I find inexplicable, I will be honest enough to admit my bafflement. In such a case, I would make every effort to continue observing and conducting research with that "psychic." If the "psychic" were a clever trickster, such as Uri Geller, then he or she would avoid continuing further experiments with me. If the "psychic" was truly psychic, then I would expect that he or she would be more than willing to undergo further testing. Under such conditions, I assume that I would reach whatever the correct conclusion should be.

5. What Would It Take to Make Skeptics of Believers?

Although the phenomenon is apparently quite rare, I do know of some cases in which believers have become skeptics. In most cases, however, the believer has created a self-sealing belief system. Almost every attempt that seems to puncture the system becomes transformed into further proof.

One serious problem with parapsychology is that the phenomena are characterized by whatever attributes are observed with significant results. Thus, the *decline effect* was widely heralded as an important indicator of psi. Several experiments in the past were examined, and some were found to exhibit a decline effect. Unfortunately, many experiments do not show a decline effect. But that does not bother the parapsychologists. They still declare "psi" if the results are significant. The same pattern holds for many other indicators of psi. If they can be found in the data, they provide support for the reality of psi. If they cannot be found in the data, then the investigator can find other reasons to argue for the presence of psi in the data.

I have called this approach the *patchwork quilt fallacy*. This approach makes it impossible to specify any conditions for the *absence* of psi. Consequently, there is no possible way to falsify the existence of psi in a given set of data. Another peculiarity sets psi research apart from other areas of scientific inquiry. Some time ago, some Russian scientists announced the discovery of what they called *mitogenetic radiation*. A few scientists in the West also reported successful experiments with this new form of radiation. But gradually more and more scientists failed to find such radiation. Finally, even the Russians no longer could detect it. No one knows what caused the initial reports. But, because no one can any longer obtain successful results in this area, scientists do not believe in the existence of mitogenetic radiation.

Parapsychology takes a different approach to subsequent failures to detect phenomena. If, for some unknown reason, every parapsychologist could no longer obtain significant results, this would not be sufficient, as I understand it, for them to abandon their belief in psi. This is because, according to their logic, the present failures to find psi in no way diminish the case for psi in the older data.

6. Why Do People Believe in the Paranormal?

As I have already written in Part IV, regardless of the scientific case for psi, most believers come to their conviction through personal experience, social pressure, or on the basis of anecdotal data. Very few, if any, of the believers have been persuaded by the scientific data. Part IV of this book represents a beginning attempt to answer this very important question.

From what the psychological evidence tells us, people will believe in the occult and the paranormal whether or not there is a scientific case to justify such beliefs.

A related issue concerns how responsible critics should react to paranormal claims. A beginning attempt to deal with this question was also made in Part IV.

7. Why Should We Care?

This question, in various guises, inevitably comes up in press conferences and in talks by skeptics. I vividly recall a press conference in the early days of CSICOP. A reporter asked why the group was so concerned about the growing belief in the paranormal. What harm does it do if someone believes that Uri Geller can bend a spoon with his mind? Besides, aren't there more important problems to worry about, such as the population explosion, famine, the homeless, drugs, acid rain, nuclear proliferation, and so on?

Some of my colleagues immediately jumped in to defend the importance of their mission. One referred to the Jim Jones tragedy in Guyana. Another pointed out that belief in the paranormal made Hitler and Nazism possible. One skeptic stood up and dramatically announced that he had in his briefcase several suicide letters by young students who believed they would come back in better incarnations after their deaths.

To me such reflex reactions are no better than the pathetic arguments that believers make for the existence of poltergeists, prophetic dreams, ghosts, and the like. In no case could any of those skeptics' assertions be backed up with anything resembling scientific evidence.

I believe that we should be careful about how we justify our concerns. We should not make rash claims or feel the necessity to sensationalize the possibilities.

My own inclination is to admit that I do not know how to measure the amount of harm that comes from belief in the paranormal. The issue is complicated. But I am concerned because if even some of the claims that are being made today about crystal power, channeled entities, healing effects of imagery, prophetic dreams, psychic metal bending, and the rest are true they represent a very serious challenge to well-established scientific findings and theories about the world.

What is most disturbing is that these claims are based on intuition and other nonscientific methods. Such methods are well known to induce compelling, but illusory, beliefs. If members of our society—including generals, business executives, and political leaders—develop their beliefs about the paranormal on such an illusory foundation, what does this tell us about how they are making decisions that affect the state of the world?

My major interest in this issue lies in the possibility that if we can come to grips with it, we can learn important things about the human mind and how it operates. Such lessons, I believe, can be useful in helping us create a better educational system and a society that is somewhat more rational than the present one.

DATE DUE